Young Flesh Required

Growing Up With The Sex Pistols

Written by Alan G. Parker
With Mick O'Shea

soundcheck books
the stories behind the sounds

First published in Great Britain in 2011 by Soundcheck Books LLP, 88 Northchurch Road, London, N1 3NY, under licence from Helter Skelter Publishing Limited of PO Box 50497, London, W8 9FA

ISBN: 978-0-9566420-1-1

Cover image: © Mirrorpix

Book design: Benn Linfield (www.bennlinfield.com)

Printed by: MPG Biddles, King's Lynn, Norfolk, UK

www.soundcheckbooks.co.uk

Contents

Probably the nearest you'll ever get to a copy signed by the band!

This book is dedicated to Alexa Morris for understanding me better than I do ... (AGP)

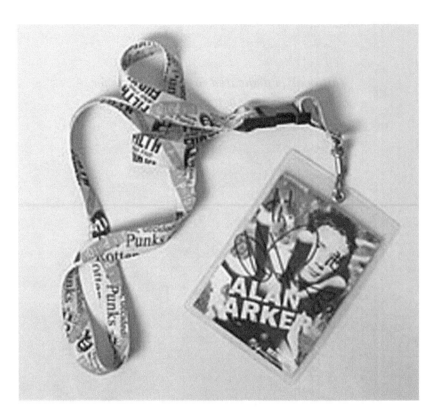

Alan's VIP pass to the Sex Pistols exhibition he opened in Japan

Burning Bridges

'Full credit to Parker, he got to everyone who matters'
Richard Taylor (The Times *Who Killed Nancy* Review)

I'm inside the Glasgow Odeon cinema at around 8 p.m. on a cold night in February 2009, the lights are about to go down and I'm stood near the back of the room sipping on a glass of red wine, when Paul McAvoy from the *Frightfest* team touches me on the shoulder. 'This is it buddy,' he whispers. On the big screen ahead of me they are about to premiere my film *Who Killed Nancy* as part of the 2009 Glasgow Film Festival. Before that they are expecting a few words of wisdom from the director, and in this case that would be yours truly! I start to stroll down the right hand side of the stalls, one hand un-buttoning my jacket.

As I move forward, out pops a guy holding a copy of my book *Vicious: Too Fast To Live*; he stands almost in front of me. 'Can you sign this please Alan?' he says as I pass. I hear myself say 'Afterwards, sure no trouble, mate,' as I start to climb the steps to the stage. 'Would you give a big Glasgow welcome to Alan G. Parker,' says the guy on stage; the place erupts. 'Good evening,' I say nervously through the microphone, 'You know my English teacher said I would amount to nothing!' Much laughter. 'Still, to the best of my knowledge he never made any films!'

Later that night a car drove me to Glasgow Central station, where I boarded a train to London Euston and awaiting me was a guy with a sign; 'Mr Parker' it stated boldly. By 1.20 a.m. I was in bed, knackered. The next day was wall to wall radio interviews and on the Monday we had a DVD launch party for *Who Killed Nancy* at Leicester Square, in the very same venue where Sid first played bass for the Sex Pistols.

The following morning (a Tuesday) I was heading for Los Angeles with a film crew to continue work on the movie *Monty Python: Almost the Truth,* which would pretty much occupy the next five months of my life. On the flight out I had to pinch myself; how did I get here? What put a working class kid from Blackburn in Lancashire at the eye of this particular storm? Well, in order to answer that question correctly, I need to take you back in time to a book launch. It's 12th September 1999 at around 3 p.m. For my part I'm doing pretty near the same thing that I was doing yesterday – painting walls white! Yeah, you heard me right the first time. I'm inside this building called The Tabernacle, just a stone's throw from Notting Hill Gate tube station, and although I don't actually know it yet, a mere short walk from the place I will eventually call home in London W9.

A matter of only weeks before this, Edward Christie of Abstract Sounds phoned me: 'We've got somewhere for a launch party for *Satellite*, the only drawback is that they haven't got the time to get the place ready following the last event there before we need it!'. I remember thinking 'That's cool, we can do it ourselves.' Of course, while I was having that thought I didn't actually know how much work would be involved! I'm willing to get my hands dirty, but painting bloody walls?

Thanks to the incredible forward planning of my mate Dave Henderson we decided to arrive in London a few days earlier than needed. So, along with myself, *Satellite* book co-author Paul Burgess and a bunch of pals roped in from all corners of the UK, we entered the building three days before the launch party. A good job we did too, because the place needed painting, straightening out, and generally re-organising before you could have done anything in there. Finally, after three days of painting, sawing, banging and hammering, the place looked like it meant business; it looked like a book on the Sex Pistols was about to be launched there. What it couldn't tell me, with its *Never Mind the Bollocks* posters or its huge 'Ronnie Biggs says Crime Pays – it's a HIT' blow ups, was just how fascinating the next ten years of my life were going to be, and just how close a moth needs to get to the flame before it burns!

I was a Sex Pistols fan at school; from the minute the needle hit the groove on 'God Save The Queen' they had me, I was hooked and my line and sinker would very quickly follow. But at fifteen years of age you can have no actual clue as to your destiny. So how could I have known what was coming next? I'd been a rock fan since the age of eight, when my father started buying singles for me and my brother. We were committed Glam kids with a good collection of records and a bedroom covered in posters to back up our claim. Four lads from Wolverhampton collectively named Slade were the closest thing we had to heroes. By my mid-teens I was punk obsessed but the thing is, I've always had a hugely eclectic taste, so I was still very much full-on with the Glam thing, and Metal was making a fast impact on my world too. In fact, within a year of my last spiky hair do, my long hair was getting longer, and Iron Maiden, Mötley Crüe & Metallica meant everything to me. But I digress: Sex Pistols, ah yes ... Those four lovable spiky tops from Shepherd's Bush, or so their very first press release would have us believe. The singer was actually from Finsbury Park, but we only knew that much later. The bassist, who taught them how to play and actually be a band, never troubled Shepherd's Bush with his presence much either!

If my fading memory serves me at all well, the first thing I ever did with regard to the aforementioned group that could remotely be considered a 'career opportunity' by anyone, was an article for a fanzine, entitled *Who Killed the Sex Pistols?* I later found out that both Anne Beverley (Sid's mum) and Malcolm McLaren had read that article. My working relationship with Anne Beverley has been written about to the absolute *nth* degree, so if you're new to this, or recently arrived to this planet from Venus, here's the potted version:

Boy meets punk star's mother; mother asks boy to write son's biography; following a number of weeks watching Gary Oldman actually playing the part of late son on a movie set, book is finally written. Punk kids cheer rather loudly; they say they love it; boy and punk star's mother continue to do many deals. More CDs, records, T-shirts and posters are released of legendary son as a result. Mother takes her own life. Boy decides to carry on flying the flag following conversation with family, two more books follow, lots of bits for radio and some television, a place in the 100 year anniversary Converse footwear advertising campaign, and a movie that we like to call *Who Killed Nancy*, of which original Rolling Stones manager Andrew Loog Oldman said; 'The greatest rock 'n' roll movie I've seen in ten years!' Thanks mate.

Bingo! Job done, you'd be thinking. But there was already a bad taste in my mouth. I hadn't actually listened to a single record by the Sex Pistols in over five years. It was already way past the point of having any meaning for me. I was finishing off a biography of Vince Neil of Mötley Crüe in Las Vegas, and was about to direct the 40th Anniversary documentary on Monty Python. This meant pretty near living in The Standard Hotel in LA for six weeks (hard life eh?), while later being nominated for an Emmy award: you just couldn't make it up! I could see plenty of sunlight in what had previously been a fairly dark tunnel. The Sex Pistols aspect of my career was over, and I'd personally nailed the coffin shut by hand.

In which case, how does *Young Flesh Required* come about, I hear you ask? Well, it's a funny story. Sean Body (Head Honcho of Helter Skelter Books) and I were having a coffee in the cafe at Foyle's book store on London's busy Charing Cross Road. Now that's a mere cough and a spit from St Martins School of Art and the Pistol's Denmark Street rehearsal rooms, so you'll not be surprised to learn that it's not long before the conversation turns to the group. I'd better add another important factor: the year is 2005. We were actually present to discuss Steve Grantley and me writing a book on the Who or maybe the Clash or something. However, I guess the surroundings pretty near dictated what we'd finish up chatting about at the end of the meeting!

'You must pretty well know everybody in that set-up by now?' said Sean. It was quite a fair point. I'd been drinking with Steve 'Roadent' Connolly only the night before, pulled Steve English down to The Phoenix bar less than a week earlier, ran into Alan 'Leather & Bones' Jones on the tube (a fairly regular place for us to bump into each other, if I'm honest!), been collared by John 'Boogie' Tiberi for coffee on Portobello Road just the previous afternoon, and seen Glen Matlock in the local coffee bar that very morning. Well, we do live in the same area so that one is hardly rocket science!

Sean was very interested in the few tales I reeled off from an excellent evening's conversation with the Roadent. Indeed he recalled the story in Mick O'Shea's still fairly new book *Only Anarchists Are Pretty* (Helter Skelter, 2004), that told of how Mick and I had decided one Friday night to nip into one of Maida Vale's many watering holes for a quick one, prior to meeting friends in the West End, but having bumped into Glen we were still in Maida Vale at last orders! Sean smiled 'You know you could do a great book on the Pistols, Alan. Tell the story from your point of view and drop in a few of these incredible tales, it would give the whole story a new twist.'

Fate, of course, can be strange. Sean never lived to see the final draft of this book, eventually losing his battle with leukaemia. So

I hope he'd be proud of what has been achieved with it via the involvement of Phil and Sue at Soundcheck Books, who were old pals of his. If you're looking down on things, mate, we did it – that initial dream in Charing Cross Road is now a reality. To me, it's a fitting end to my own personal Sex Pistols odyssey, a bit like passing on the baton near the middle of the race. If I had a pound for every lie that's been spoken or written regarding myself and that group I'd be a millionaire on an annual basis. If somebody else has an opinion, then fine, do something with it: write your own book; start a band; make a difference – wasn't that after all a part of the Pistols' original war cry? I think I've done my bit already. As far as I'm concerned, my voice has been heard. As the bulk of my Sex Pistols memorabilia is packed away, awaiting heaven knows what or where as a final fate, I know a few die-hard fans have already reserved things from one particular record dealer, because they knew I had once owned them. I write this introduction with my mobile phone flashing a text that Public Image Limited are going to record an album on the back of a £400 book by John called *Mr Rotten's Scrapbook:* we live in strange times.

While listening to Metallica, with the new Manic Street Preachers album and a pile of John Lennon 70th Anniversary re-issues lined up to follow it, life in St John's Wood is still good and another chapter of my own personal book is complete. Fate can decide the next step ...

Alan G. Parker – ohnonothimagain!

'Think you know what you think you want?
You just want to be God all the way
Her stone-washed face and your violent persuasion
Aren't you sick of eating cornflakes all bloody day?
Hey! It's alright, you've got your anarchy head screwed on tight
And she said; 'We're burning alive, crack and divide!'
(Ricky Warwick)

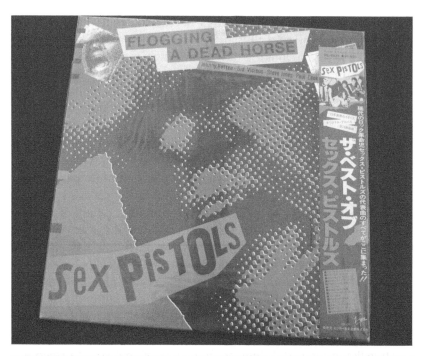

Top: Japanese Flogging a Dead Horse
Bottom: Japanese Filth and the Fury *DVD box set*

MICk's Intro

Now before we start I know there are those who will question our right to pen books on the Sex Pistols as neither Alan nor I were on the scene back in the hallowed day. But there are scores of books about the fall of ancient Rome available on Amazon and yet no one criticises those authors for not being around to witness Caesar's crossing of the Rubicon.

My own baptism to the Sex Pistols came on Sunday 4th September 1977, and seeing them performing 'Anarchy In The UK' on a repeat showing of *So It Goes*, the late-night music show hosted by the late Tony Wilson. Yes, I'd heard something about their antics on the *Today* show, and listened to the nation's indignation at their supposedly calling Queen Elizabeth II a "moron" in what was her Silver Jubilee year. But as I'd no real interest in music other than occasionally watching *Top Of The Pops* on a Thursday evening, I simply assumed that the Sex Pistols were like every other long-haired, denim-flared rock group of the era, even if they did have bizarre names like Johnny Rotten and Sid Vicious. (Such was my ignorance that I was blissfully unaware that the bassist I was seeing on the *So It Goes* stage was actually Glen Matlock – sorry, mate).

I'd heard the more 'radio-friendly' 'Pretty Vacant' on the Radio One chart rundown, so I knew what the Pistols sounded like on vinyl. But seeing them live and unleashed was a kaleidoscopic assault on my senses, and John's guttural 'get off your arse' was the clarion call I'd been waiting for. Within those five minutes my life was changed forever, my rite of passage had begun. It is perhaps worth mentioning that my record collection up to that point in time consisted of a naff Elvis LP and a 7" single from Subbuteo containing three minutes of crowd noise to replicate the atmosphere of a real football match, as well as inane ditties such as 'She'll Be Coming Round The Mountain (When She Comes)'. So my arriving home with a copy of *Never Mind The Bollocks Here's the Sex Pistols* came as something of an eye-opener to my bemused parents.

Of course, there have been times when I've wished that I'd have been conceived several years earlier than I was as I would have undoubtedly latched onto the Sex Pistols that much sooner and followed them along every mile on their path to infamy, and who knows where that adventure might have led? But sometimes not seeing history unfolding makes it all the more alluring, especially to an impressionable 15-year-old from the provinces. And had I been a regular at the 100 Club, sailed on the Queen Elizabeth on Jubilee Day, and enjoyed a slice of Christmas cake at Ivanhoe's, would my fascination with the Sex Pistols have endured over the prevailing decades?

Mick O'Shea
April 2011

CHAPTER one

My Belief In Ruins

'Who is Malcolm McLaren? The white English eccentric who formed the Sex Pistols? The art-school anarchist who lost his virginity to fashion designer Vivienne Westwood, married her, and opened a punk boutique in London where "nothing was for sale"? The cultural alchemist who was asked to "re-brand Poland"? The egomaniacal marketing Svengali who claims he swindled the record industry?'
Swindle *magazine – issue 5, 2005*

Are you familiar with the old saying 'If 'ifs' and 'ands' were pots and pans there'd be no work for tinkers' hands'? It's the sort of phrase your mum would trot out with monotonous regularity when you, as a kid, found yourself wishing frantically that things could be different to the way they actually were. She'd then tell you to stop mithering and get on with it; whatever 'it' happened to be.

Perhaps John Lennon said it best when he said life was what happened when you stop making other plans. One could spend eternity arguing about the old adage of 'ifs' and 'ands', but even if fate, chance, providence, luck – call it what you will – is nothing more than a convenient term to explain or excuse events, there can be no doubt that such seemingly random acts have changed the course of history.

Without wishing to sound too philosophical, a prime example of this came in London during the summer of 1971. An American, called Bradley Mendelson, was funding his stay in the capital by working at a retro fashion boutique called Paradise Garage located at 430 King's Road in Chelsea's then unfashionable World's End (too far away from the tube station, too near the football yobs). He was standing in the shop's doorway, watching the world go by, when his eyes were drawn to a red-headed individual wearing a Teddy Boy drape jacket and a pair of striking lurex drainpipe trousers.

The wearer of the drainpipes was a recent college dropout called Malcolm McLaren, who'd been on his way to the nearby Beaufort Street Market looking to rent a stall from which he could sell his collection of rock 'n' roll records. He readily accepted the affable American's generous and unsolicited offer to sub-let the back quarter of the shop. So, harking back to the adage of 'ifs' and 'ands' threatening an honest tinker's livelihood; *if* Mendelson had been otherwise occupied that afternoon, or *if* McLaren had taken an alternative route to market, or even *if* he had elected to wear another pair of trousers, then it is fair to say 430 King's Road wouldn't have become a meeting place for malcontents and miscreants. Nor, by this logic, would it have spawned the Sex Pistols, who in turn spearheaded the late '70s counter-culture revolution known as Punk Rock.

But Malcolm *did* end up taking over the shop, and the Sex Pistols *did* evolve as a bastard by-product of his endeavours ...and here – for the first time from so many insiders – is the real story behind the band and its four/five self-assured members who positively thrived on being the right collaboration of young flesh required to fill this working class musical void. As Shakespeare might have said: 'The rest is violence'.

#

Malcolm McLaren, along with his 30-year-old girlfriend Vivienne Westwood, set up shop within the extended ground floor confines of 430 King's Road; a narrow four storey late Victorian building located in Chelsea's run-down World's End which, over the course of the century, had served the local Bohemians and down-at-heel clientele as a pawnbrokers and then later a café.

By the 1960s, however, with London in full swing, the upper end of the King's Road – along with the capital's other fashionable walkways Carnaby Street and Portobello Market – was being hailed as a culture and couture epicentre where the Chelsea dandies strolled about in narrow-cut, double breasted velvet suits, hand-painted ties and satin scarves to emulate their pop star heroes; the Beatles, the Who and the Rolling Stones.

The World's End – although a mere stone's throw from the trendy tree-lined King's Road with its fashion boutiques, such as Granny Takes A Trip and Alkasura, and the accompanying coffee bars which had sprung up to cater for their well-to-do clientele – was regarded as something of a poor relation; a home to petty criminals, drug addicts and other ne'er-do-wells. Economic expansion, however, cares little for demographics or for post codes, so slowly but surely those money-minded entrepreneurs, forever looking for means to turn a profit, began taking over the leases of the rundown edifices situated further along the street. In turn, number 430 ceased serving as a local community commodity outlet, and for a time it briefly served as home to a yachting agent and then a scooter dealership, before beginning its long tenure as a clothing emporium, when Michael Rainey (who was one of London's leading stylists at the time) moved his Hung On You menswear boutique from nearby Cale Street.

The *Evening Standard* once, rather uncharitably, described Hung On You as a 'dipsomaniac's nightmare', and Rainey would himself begin hitting the bottle with increasing alacrity upon realising the World's End wasn't quite ready for frilly shirts or pastel-shaded double-breasted suits. He vainly struggled on for a year or so before closing the doors on his Day-Glo emporium in January 1969. The lease was snapped up by chirpy Cockney entrepreneur Tommy Roberts who, together with his 22-year-old business partner Trevor Miles, had owned another boutique called Kleptomania on Carnaby Street. The pair, having renamed the new store 'Mr Freedom', in homage of film maker/photographer William Klein's political cartoon of the same name, began selling garish '50s-style clothing and ephemera, ranging from Superman jackets, Mickey Mouse T-shirts, knee-length ladies T-shirts which could also be worn as dresses, to jitterbug skirts and fake leopard-skin jackets and trousers. Bemused customers would cross 430's new Art Deco-style threshold to be greeted by a giant eight foot tall stuffed gorilla with its fur dyed a fluorescent blue.

Although business was brisk, there was little need – nor indeed room, given Roberts' portly stature – for two kings in such a compact castle, and Roberts dissolved the partnership, opening another larger boutique of the same name on Kensington Church Street, which still trades to this day.

Miles, having decided to continue with the shop, embarked on a New York shopping spree where he spent £5,000 on hundreds of pairs of second-hand Levi jeans, Oshkosh dungarees, bowling jackets and Hawaiian shirts. To complement the new line of clothing, Miles, having decided upon the name 'Paradise Garage', evicted the blue ape and every other vestige of the '50s kitsch emporium. Instead, he erected a green painted corrugated iron facade upon which the shop's new name was spelled out in foot-high Hawaiian-style bamboo lettering. An antique American petrol-pump, the kind James Dean might have stopped to use on his final fateful car ride, stood next to the entrance. The interior was also awash with bamboo, including bamboo cages holding exotic love birds which softly cooed to each other while customers rifled through the various piles of clothing.

Paradise Garage was an instant success, but instead of sitting back and watching the money roll in, Miles naively believed he was the King Midas of the fashion world and sought to pour more gold into them there tills. In early 1971, having tossed out the bamboo and rush-matting, he painted the shop's walls, floor and ceiling disco black, installed a mobile dance floor, as well as an authentic '50s style jukebox; the same jukebox in front of which some five years later John Lydon would audition for the role of singer with the Sex Pistols.

He then filled the racks with black clothing: black trousers, black jackets, black shirts, black skirts and black pantyhose; everything had to be black. Although the idea would eventually find a home at the tail-end of the decade with punk peripherals the Stranglers and, later still, the Goth movement, London's fashion-conscious cognoscenti wanted colour to brighten up their otherwise drab existence and began shopping elsewhere for their clothes.

Instead of trying to salvage his business, Midas Miles married his Danish girlfriend and headed off on a three week Caribbean honeymoon, leaving his friend Bradley Mendelson to mind the store. Little could Mendelson (who today is a successful commercial real estate broker in Manhattan) have realised that, as he and Malcolm talked trousers that balmy summer afternoon, he had inadvertently set into motion a chain reaction: one that would wrench rock 'n' roll away from the bloated '60s rock dinosaurs who were content to live a tax-exile existence, and return it briefly to the streets where it undeniably belonged; as well as bringing about seismic changes in both aptitude and attitude amongst the nation's disenfranchised youth which reverberate to this very day.

Malcolm, who'd dropped out of Goldsmiths College without bothering to complete either his degree or his final-year project – a psycho-geographical film about London's famed shopping thoroughfare Oxford Street – had been drifting aimlessly without any real sense of purpose in his life. Even though he'd quickly got the measure of Mendelson, and knew business at the Paradise Garage was far from brisk, he recognised an opportunity when it presented itself. He struck up a deal with the American whereby he, Vivienne and their art student friend Patrick Casey – who had a flair for finding unique and, more importantly as far as Malcolm was concerned, cheap second-hand clothing such as leather jackets and '50s-style zoot suits – would take over the shop's back quarter and a proportionate share of the rent.

Vivienne abandoned her teaching job in favour of a Singer sewing machine. Malcolm, meanwhile, became enamoured with '50s rock 'n' roll music, particularly Billy Fury, and had amassed a sizable collection of 7" singles, which he intended to sell alongside Casey's eclectic retro clothes. He selected his favourite tunes and installed them on the jukebox.

#

Malcolm Robert Andrew McLaren was born on 22nd January 1946, in the McLaren family home consisting of two adjoining terraced houses at 47-49 Carysfort Road, Stoke Newington, London. At the time this was a respectable solid Jewish neighbourhood just a short walk from Clissold Park, which, years later, would serve as home to one Simon John Ritchie, a.k.a. John Simon Beverley, a.k.a. Spiky John, a.k.a. Sid Vicious. Malcolm's father, Peter James Philip McLaren, had served as a sapper with the Royal Engineers during World War II, before entering 'Civvy Street' as an engine fitter. Malcolm's mother, Emily Isaacs, came from a family of well-to-do Jewish diamond cutters. It was not to be a match made in heaven as far as McLaren senior was concerned, as he couldn't possibly hope to keep Emily in the life to which she was no doubt accustomed. Not only did he struggle in his day job, but he proved equally ill at ease with husbandry and fatherhood; eventually leaving Emily to raise 18-month-old Malcolm and his 4-year-old brother Stuart alone.

Somewhat surprisingly, Emily, or 'Emmy' as she was known, was unwilling to be consigned to a life of drudgery at the kitchen sink, instead embarking on a relationship with Selfridge's supremo Sir Charles Clore! She would often disappear with the self-made retail millionaire for illicit weekends in Monte Carlo, leaving the boys in the care of her mother Rose Corré Isaacs. Their mother's frequent and lengthy disappearances would have a devastating effect on both Malcolm and Stuart, who told Jon Savage for *England's Dreaming* (Faber and Faber) that although she did eventually settle down again by marrying Martin Levi (who was Jewish and therefore infinitely more worthy of attention from the Isaacs than a Scottish motor mechanic), Emily was still found wanting in the maternal stakes.

Levi, who worked in the rag trade, changed his name to the more English sounding Edwards, and together with Emily – who changed her forename to Eve – opened up a *shmatte* [clothing] factory in London's East End called Eve Edwards London Ltd. The business soon became successful, but rather than stay at home with her boys, Eve elected to further her career and was spending most of her week traversing the country on business trips.

The absence of a father figure, other than seeing him develop an effete 'Little Lord Fauntleroy' persona, appeared to have no adverse effects on Malcolm. Indeed, each evening upon returning home from school, the red-headed horror would head next door, where the Isaacs were still living, for tea and jam sandwiches with Rose. Then, after a night's sleep in his own home, he would scurry into his uniform and hop back over the small cement wall, which served to separate the two enclosed rear yards, for breakfast before setting off back to school.

According to Malcolm, in Craig Bromberg's unofficial biography *The Wicked Ways of Malcolm McLaren* (Harper & Row), everyone who came into contact with his grandma Rose, a skilled raconteuse who'd been denied an acting career by her strict Sephardic Jewish parents, fell in love with the old woman and believed her to be someone special. Although both boys were being ignored by their mother, it was Malcolm who enjoyed the greater share of Grandma Rose's affections. He hated school with a passion, and rather than be sent to the nearby William Patton Primary School in Stoke Newington, he somehow persuaded Rose to teach him from her cosy front parlour; an arrangement which went on for some considerable time. 'You have to understand that she positively hated school,' he said of the incorrigible Rose Corré. 'And besides, no amount of schooling could ever compare to her fantastical stories.' Especially those of the Dickensian London her own grandmother had been born into. Malcolm knew his *Oliver Twist* before he took his 11-plus examination.

Emmy, as she was still known, may have been lax in the parental guidance department, but within a year of marrying Levi/Edwards

– during which time she legally changed her sons' surnames to Edwards – she sought to re-establish her authority over her unruly offspring. Her first priority was that both boys should learn the concept of discipline, as well as gain a proper education, so she enrolled them at the nearby Jewish-run Avigdor School in Lordship Road.

The old adage about leading a horse to water sums up Malcolm's schooling, for although his parents had wrestled him from Grandma Corré's clutches – at least for part of the day – and delivered him to a 'proper' place of learning, they were powerless when it came to his taking an interest in the school's curriculum. In a last desperate attempt to get him through his 11-plus exam, which in those days was the only way to advance to grammar school, his parents hired a private tutor. The thought of taking on double helpings of something he already despised was alien to a firebrand like Malcolm, and he purposely frustrated all attempts to further his learning. In September 1957, as a consequence of failing the 11-plus exam, the 11-year-old Malcolm was admitted to the tough, no-nonsense Whitechapel Foundation Secondary School, where he would remain for the next twelve months. He might well have been forced to endure the requisite five year tenure had not his step-father who, thanks to his new-found affluence, decided to uproot the family (including Rose Corré and her long-suffering husband Mick, who was a tailor by trade) and move out to the suburbs.

The Edwards and Corré clan set up home in a three storey house in Cheyne Walk, Hendon, which saw Malcolm enrolled at the nearby Burnt Oak Secondary School in Orange Hill. However, instead of bringing the family closer together, these new living arrangements – which saw Malcolm share the upper floor bedrooms with Mick and Rose, while Martin, Emmy and Stuart occupied the floor below – served to drive an irrevocable wedge between the Edwards' and their youngest son. Malcolm's dislike for his parents, especially his step-father whom he snobbishly despised for his working-class roots and his self-serving veneration of hard work, was surpassed only by his vitriol towards secondary education, and he left school in the summer of 1961 with just two 'O' level passes to his name.

Although he was now free of his scholastic shackles, Malcolm had no game plan as to what to do with his life. However, a visit to the local careers office, with a concerned Emmy Edwards in tow, led to a position with Sandeman's Port & Sherry wine merchants in Orange Street, Piccadilly. He soon handed in his notice upon learning that his employers would require him to spend a significant part of the year in Jerez, in South West Spain, overseeing the company's vineyards. His second, and last, brief stint in gainful employment came as a retail clerk at a West End haberdashery in the Burlington Arcade. However, schemers and dreamers are ill-suited for the mundane existence that accompanies a regular 9-5 life, and one evening during the spring of 1963, he walked past St Martins School of Art on Charing Cross Road. Malcolm was fascinated by the trendy brightly-coloured cut of the students' collective jibs, so he wandered inside and enrolled as a part-time student in life drawing.

His mother, although pleased that her eldest boy was finally taking an interest in something, was somewhat less enamoured with his choice of study. No son of hers was going to sit around drawing nudes and, regardless of Malcolm's heartfelt pleas, she telephoned the school the very next day to have him dropped from the class. Malcolm was beside himself with rage but, as he was still several months shy of seventeen, there was nothing he could do about it. Determined not to be bested by his overbearing mother, Malcolm transferred to a course in 3D Graphic Design. Learning about shape, form and colour content wasn't anywhere near as enjoyable as drawing naked bodies, of course, but the creative spark, which had lain dormant until this time, was well and truly lit.

Within a matter of weeks he was staying behind after class, bombarding his teachers with questions to satiate his new-found thirst for knowledge. He might well have gone on to full-time studies at the college, but the prerequisite for any would-be St Martins student, or indeed a student of any other art college, was four 'O' level passes, which meant Malcolm would have to swallow his pride and go back to school. He enrolled on a 'booster' course at a school in Edgware, and duly gained the extra qualifications. Geography, though, was clearly not one of his chosen subjects, as Cheyne Walk sat within the wrong borough for a place at St Martins. He had to settle instead for a place at nearby Harrow Art School, where he undertook a Diploma in Art and Design; but even this was only achievable thanks to his parents agreeing to pay his full tuition fees.

However, the times they were a-changin' as Bob Dylan observed and, in 1964, Labour was again elected to power after thirteen

Bootleg sleeve in the style of The Beatles. Issue 5

years of Tory rule, following the Profumo sex scandal of twelve months earlier. This had involved the then Secretary of State for War, John 'Jack' Profumo, 21-year-old showgirl Christine Keeler and the Soviet naval attaché Eugene Ivanov; though not as a menage a trois! Profumo had tried to save his skin – as well as his political career – by first denying any impropriety in his relationship with Keeler, and once that wasn't going to wash, he tried denying that said impropriety had been a breach of security. Another massive change came on the musical front as the Beatles, who'd already seized control of the UK charts, conquered America, where teenagers – seemingly en masse – waved goodbye to the quiffs and quivering legs of their rock 'n' roll heroes of yesteryear in favour of the four 'Moptops' from Merseyside.

As far as Malcolm was concerned, however, there had been no revolution. He continued to worship at the altar of Eddie Cochran, who'd died on Easter Sunday, 17th April 1960, as a result of the injuries he sustained when the taxi ferrying him, his girlfriend Sharon Sheeley, and fellow rocker Gene Vincent to the airport, after the final show of his debut UK tour at the Bristol Hippodrome, smashed into a lamppost on the A4 in Chippenham, Wiltshire. Another hero whose life had also been tragically cut short was Buddy Holly, whom Malcolm and his brother Stuart had seen performing live at the Finsbury Park Astoria [later renamed The Rainbow] in 1957. The Beatles may have cut their teeth playing in the strip clubs along Hamburg's Reeperbahn, but they were still too clean cut; Malcolm much preferred the brooding charisma of Mick Jagger, Keith Richards and the rest of the Rolling Stones, who'd caused consternation at the Montreux Festival in Geneva that April for having taken to the stage in 'dishevelled and bizarre' dress.

It was whilst he was enrolled at Harrow that Malcolm first encountered – and befriended – Fred Vermorel, the well-read intellectual and politically astute son of a French chemist who'd swapped pills and prescriptions for bombs and bullets by joining the resistance to thwart the Nazis occupying his country during the war. Another Harrow incumbent was his future King's Road collaborator Patrick Casey. Perhaps, though, the most important person he met within Harrow's labyrinthine white-stoned edifice (and the man who would soon displace Fred Vermorel as his best friend) was the unassuming baby-faced 20-year-old Gordon Swire, whose striking elder sister, Vivienne, was to later play such a significant role in his life.

#

Vivienne Isabelle Swire was born on the 16th April 1941. Like her brother Gordon and the rest of the Swires, she hailed from Hollingworth, a tiny Derbyshire village nestled between the Yorkshire Dales and the Pennines close to the Tintwistle Snake Pass. Gordon Swire Senior was a fruiterer by trade, but had served as a storekeeper during the war at the aircraft manufacturers A.V. Roe – who constructed the famous Lancaster bombers – in Trafford Park, Greater Manchester [now home to a massive retail park]. His wife, and ballroom dancing partner, Dora, toiled as a loom operator at the local mill. When the war ended, Gordon took a job at the local Wall's ice-cream factory and supplemented the family's income by taking odd jobs around the village.

Unlike Malcolm, Vivienne passed her 11-plus and attended Glossop Grammar School, where, although suffering from protruding teeth –which were later straightened – and worse still, a flat chest, she was not considered unattractive by her male peers and later boasted of having had a different boyfriend every week. Like her mother, who made her own ballroom dresses, Vivienne came to recognise the power and beauty of clothes, and would often arrive home from school on a Friday afternoon clutching a piece of brightly-coloured material from which she would cut out a dress pattern to sew up and wear to a dance that same evening.

Upon leaving school in the summer of 1957, by which time the family had moved to nearby Tintwistle on account of her mother Dora taking up the post of village postmistress, Vivienne, with little or no idea of what to do with her life, took a six week holiday job at the nearby Pickerings cannery. She, along with all the other female employees, was dubbed a 'pea pixie', on account of the green overalls and caps they were forced to wear during their ten hour shifts.

The seemingly carefree Vivienne may well have gone on to endure a mediocre life of menial jobs brightened up only by the weekly dances, before getting married and settling down to raise her own family, had fate not stepped in to lend a hand. Later that same year her mother, on account of Gordon senior now being out of work and struggling to find a job, uprooted the family to the more affluent south to take over another post office-cum-grocery store in Harrow in North West London. While their parents occupied themselves providing stamps and spuds to the local community, Gordon Jr enrolled at the London School of Film Technique (LSFT), younger sister Olga went off to do a university degree in sociology, and Vivienne attended a silversmithing and jewellery-making class at Harrow Art School. Her tenure at Harrow, however, would prove even more fleeting than Malcolm's, as she left after one solitary term to take up a secretarial course.

Like her parents, Vivienne lived for dancing, and it was whilst she was cutting her stylish rug at a local dance hall that she came across, and was instantly smitten by, a local Hoover factory toolshop apprentice called Derek John Westwood. Derek, who was two years her senior, shared her passion for dancing and rock 'n' roll, and was supplementing his meagre income by working evenings at bingo halls and hotels. His dream, however, was to become an airline pilot and, within weeks of meeting Vivienne, he secured a position as a steward with British European Airways, which only served to fuel the budding aviator's ambitions. Buoyed by this upturn in his prospects, Derek got down on bended knee and asked Vivienne, who'd recently abandoned her secretarial job to take up a post as a primary school teacher in north Willesden, to marry him. Although Vivienne would later confess that she hadn't wanted to wed her handsome suitor, she couldn't find it in her heart to refuse. So, on 21st July 1962, her father led her down the aisle at St John the Baptist church in nearby Greenhill to become Mrs Derek Westwood. Following a honeymoon in Devon, the newly-weds set up home close to the Swire's post office in Harrow, and on 3rd September 1963 Vivienne gave birth to their son Benjamin Arthur Westwood.

As a means of augmenting her husband's airline pay, Vivienne took a job at the local Kodak factory. Unsurprisingly, menial work bored her witless and, despite Derek's unfaltering love and admiration, she was equally bored with marriage and domesticity. She was also jealous of her siblings, especially Gordon, who was excelling at the LFST and moving within an exciting social circle which, of course, by this time included a certain Malcolm Edwards. Vivienne first encountered Malcolm one evening in late 1965, when she was helping Derek out by serving as a cloakroom attendant at the Railway Hotel, Harrow and Wealdstone, where he was acting manager. Derek's latest income enhancement came courtesy of a management company called Commercial Entertainments. The company was small potatoes compared to Larry Parnes' Tin Pan Alley conglomerate, but it boasted several up-and-coming acts on its roster including the Detours, who would soon be renamed the High Numbers, before then going on to achieve world-wide fame as the Who.

One of the perks of working in entertainment management was that Derek and Vivienne (as well as brother Gordon who, more often than not, was accompanied by Malcolm and Fred Vermorel) were able to gain easy and free access to London's burgeoning rhythm and blues circuit. They saw shows by Alexis Korner, the Yardbirds and the Rolling Stones at trendy venues such as The Marquee, Ealing Jazz Club, The Flamingo, Club 11, and The 100 Club. The latter, of course, would become something of a home from home for Malcolm a little more than a decade hence.

By this time, Gordon Jr had moved out of his parents' post office to occupy one of the rooms in a squalid Victorian house at 31

King's Avenue in Clapham North, and he invited Malcolm to join him. The house was small and cramped, but Malcolm didn't care as the majority of the monthly rent was being picked up by two American friends of Gordon's who were also enrolled at the LSFT. Within months of their arrival, however, one of the Americans, Chuck Coryn, foolishly elected to drop out from school and traffic drugs instead. Chuck's midnight runs came to an abrupt end when customs officers at Heathrow stopped him for a routine search and found the hapless American's suitcase crammed full of illicit substances. Whilst Chuck settled into his new room within the 'house of many doors' at Her Majesty's Pleasure, his old room at King's Avenue was taken over by Vivienne, who'd finally tired of Derek's affections and moved in, bringing 3-year-old Ben with her.

#

At the time of her moving into the house on King's Avenue, Vivienne, by her own admission, looked upon Malcolm as nothing other than a close friend of her brother's and, by default therefore, part of her own social circle. She certainly didn't find the reed-thin redhead sexually attractive. He had a fiery-red complexion that he unsuccessfully tried to disguise with talcum powder, thus earning himself the enduring nick-name 'Talcy Malcy'. The house's second (and more law-abiding) American resident, John Broderick, who eventually went on to become a Hollywood production manager and director, likened residing there to living out a Harold Pinter play. Apparently, each and every evening, the four adult incumbents would gather in the kitchen for an evening meal, which usually consisted of beans on toast washed down with endless cups of tea, before settling down in front of the small electric fire armed with whisky and Woodbines to discuss art, music and current affairs until the small hours.

It was perhaps inevitable, given such closeted environs, that Malcolm developed a crush on his best friend's sister. But, instead of asking Vivienne out on a date and wooing her in the time-honoured fashion, he lured her into his lair, appealing to her maternal instincts by feigning a severe stomach ache which he knew, from watching her around Ben, she wouldn't be able to ignore. This beguilement worked! Vivienne, finding Malcolm curled up in the foetal position on an old mattress on the floor, in supposed agony, invited him to get into her bed while she went out for something to soothe his pain. She then spent the rest of the day nursing her pale-faced patient, and when the time came for her to go to bed – with Malcolm showing no sign of retreating to his own room – she had little option but to get in beside him. Although she could have resisted his amorous advances, she chose not to. Nature took its course and two months later, by which time she was beginning to fall for Malcolm anyway, the local doctor informed her to expect the imminent patter of tiny feet. For his part, although less than thrilled about the prospect of fatherhood (he believed Vivienne, who was still a married woman and well-versed in womanly ways, would have known about contraception), Malcolm was thrilled to finally have a girl he could call his own. His beloved grandma Rose, however, having already formed a steadfast dislike for Vivienne, whom she saw as a scheming older woman saddled with another man's child, strongly advocated a termination.

Although the Abortion Act, legalising abortions by registered practitioners, wouldn't come into force until April 1968, terminations could still be obtained for an exorbitant price at one of the many clinics on London's Harley Street. The old woman was even willing to meet the cost of one of these if it meant keeping her grandson out of Vivienne's conniving clutches. Malcolm went so far as to broach the possibility of a termination with Vivienne, and although she was loath to accept charity from Rose Corré, the only other alternative open to her would be to subject herself to a backstreet abortionist armed with a knitting needle and a quart of gin. The deliberations went on for several weeks, but time was of the essence, of course, and Vivienne finally acquiesced and agreed to the termination. According to Malcolm, they even got as far as the doorstep of the Harley Street physician willing to perform the procedure, but Vivienne couldn't bring herself to cross the threshold. Instead, with Rose Corré's cash burning a hole in her pocket, she scurried off to Bond Street to buy herself a new coat!

On 30th November 1967, Vivienne was rushed to hospital where, after a short but intense labour, she gave birth to her second son whom they christened Joseph Ferdinand Corré; the somewhat bizarre middle name was in homage to Malcolm's favourite Velazquez portrait, *Archbishop Fernando de Valdés y Llanos,* which hung in the National Gallery. However, his decision to bestow Grandma Rose's surname upon the newborn did little to appease the old woman, whose loathing for Vivienne extended to her dissuading Malcolm from attending the delivery.

That autumn, whilst the nation's Young Turks were tuning in to Radio One, the trendy new station which the BBC had launched to counter Radio Caroline and her piratical ilk, Vivienne was busy playing mum and reading Thomas Hardy novels in the couple's newly-acquired ground floor flat in Aigburth Mansions, Hackford Road, whilst Malcolm enrolled at the Croydon College of Art and Design to study painting. Vivienne's maternal sojourn would prove short-lived, however, for Malcolm's grant didn't stretch to meeting the rent, so she reluctantly returned to her teaching post leaving 4-year-old Ben with her parents, and baby Joseph at a nearby crèche. Another downside to Malcolm's latest scholastic venture was that, as Croydon College didn't require their students to gain anything as mundane as qualifications, there would be no diploma waiting for him at the end of the course.

It was whilst he was ensconced at Croydon that Malcolm met and befriended Robin Scott, who, in 1979, under the mystifying guise of 'M', achieved chart success with the one-hit wonder 'Pop Music'. Robin, a self-confessed opportunist, who'd graduated from Croydon Technical College with neither ambition nor agenda, told Jon Savage for *England's Dreaming* that he'd enrolled at Croydon College as a means of remaining close to home so that he could keep tabs on what was happening in London. He readily admitted that he and Malcolm spent precious little time within their own studio, and preferred instead to wander through the halls calling in on – and critiquing the work of – their fellow students.

Another contemporary there was Jamie Reid, his future punk collaborator and the man who would achieve national acclaim – or ignominy, depending on one's point of view – for putting a safety pin through the monarch's nose or lip (depending on which bit of artwork you're holding). Jamie Reid, or MacGregor Reid to give him his full title, hailed from a long line of political activists. His father, John MacGregor Reid, was City editor of the *Daily Sketch*, while his grandfather, Dr George Watson MacGregor Reid, had stood for parliament as one of the first Labour Party candidates and was also the head of the Druid Order, in which capacity he had vociferously defended the Order's right to carry out the ancient Druidic ceremonial rite at Stonehenge at the summer solstice. Jamie's brother Bruce worked as a press officer for the Committee of 100; the British anti-war group set up in 1960 by Lord Bertrand Russell. Like the more easy-going Robin, Jamie was a Croydon native, having grown up in the new town's eastern suburb of

Shirley. Like Malcolm, he had proved a reluctant student at both his *alma mater* John Ruskin Grammar School and Wimbledon Art College, where he developed a passion for utopian politics and Jackson Pollock.

But then came the much-vaunted Croydon student sit-in of 5th June, which saw Malcolm, Robin and Jamie, along with three hundred or so of their fellow students, barricade themselves within the college's South Norwood annexe in support of their Parisian counterparts, who were currently taking on the French government, and issuing demands such as an end to examinations, and a loosening of the requirements for admission to the college. It is even rumoured that the more radically-minded protestors set fire to a desk. Sacre bleu!

The May 1968 Paris riots and, to a lesser degree, the Croydon sit-in, served as a wake-up call for Jamie and stirred his dormant political leanings, which transformed him from a self-absorbed creature, solely concerned with what might affect him personally, into a radical firebrand. His rebellious stance at Croydon would cost him his pre-designated place on a post-graduate course at St Martins, but painting had taken a back seat and, upon leaving Croydon in 1970, he co-founded the Suburban Press with Nigel Edwards and Jeremy Brook, dedicated to promoting civil liberties and exposing local government corruption in the Croydon area. This agitprop trio were constantly strapped for cash and Jamie was forced to improvise by using lettering and images from newspapers and magazines, which he would later use for the Sex Pistols' artwork. Aside from flooding London with stickers bearing subversive slogans such as 'save petrol – burn cars', 'keep warm this winter, make trouble', Suburban Press produced five issues from its Sidney Street office in Stepney, East London. Somewhat ironically, the fifth and final issue, which is also the rarest, entitled 'Lo! A Monster Is Born', which railed against Croydon's mid-seventies redevelopment plans, is now a prized item in the Croydon library collection.

The Paris riots began on 22nd March, sweeping through the rest of France and ultimately bringing about the collapse of President Charles De Gaulle's government. The unrest started when a band of prominent Parisian poets and musicians joined forces with 150 or so disenfranchised students invading an administration building at Paris' Nanterre University in protest at the political bureaucracy controlling the university's funding. This in turn

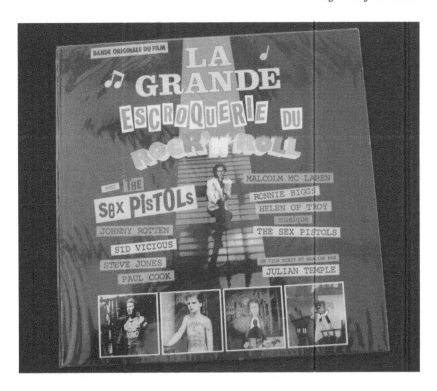

French Rock'n' Roll Swindle *record sleeve*

sparked a series of student protests at various other universities and lycées, including the Sorbonne (where Malcolm's friend Fred Vermorel was studying art). Police mounted baton and tear gas charges against 20,000 students, resulting in many of the students being seriously injured and many more being taken into custody. The government's heavy-handed over-reaction provoked a wave of public sympathy and brought about a general strike involving some ten million French workers (two thirds of the country's workforce), leaving De Gaulle with little option but to step down from office. Malcolm would later claim to have been an active participant in the riots, marching with *les enragés*, and although he did stay with Fred Vermorel in the French capital later that same year, and was taken on a sight-seeing tour of the Latin Quarter battlefields, the truth of the matter is that while the embittered Parisian students were rallying under the '*Sois Jeune et Tais Toi*' (Be Young and Shut Up) banner, Malcolm never left his Croydon confines.

The bemused Croydon faculty, safe in the knowledge that neither baton charge nor tear gas would be required, organised a student-staff meeting in the main college building. Robin Scott, who would shortly abandon his studies altogether to begin a career writing music for television, was one of the six students deputised to negotiate with the college's administration. The meeting went on for six hours and when he and the other weary students returned to the annexe to find themselves locked out, they cried 'foul', claiming the faculty had duped them into attending the meeting. The wonderfully-named Principal, Mr L. Marchbank Salmon, however, responded by claiming the lock-out was unintentional and was more likely to have been the action of an over-conscientious caretaker than a devious scheme to quell the rebellion.

Malcolm, who had adopted the risible nom de guerre 'Malcolm the Rose' during the unrest, was also nominated to participate in the negotiations, but surprised everybody by opting to take a back seat. He led everyone to believe his decision was due to the farcicality of the striking students being locked out of their own sit-in, but the real reason behind his reticence was due to his application to Goldsmiths College, University of London, having already been accepted. Needless to say, the protest, having lost much of its impetus, soon petered out and the students begrudgingly returned to their studies. Malcolm, safe in the knowledge that his immediate future lay elsewhere, headed for Paris to relive *la revolution etudiante* with Fred Vermorel, before then making his way to the south coast where Vivienne, having borrowed the fare from her mother and dumping Ben and Joe in a crèche, joined him for her first venture abroad. Free from parental duties, the couple pitched their tent on Le Trayas beach, where they spent several weeks of bohemian harmony before a strong tide robbed them of their tent and possessions, including their clothes.

In October 1968, by which time the lease on the flat at Aigburth Mansions had expired, and Vivienne had given up her teaching post and moved herself and the two boys in with her now-retired parents at their cottage in Banbury, Oxfordshire, Malcolm arrived at Goldsmiths to study film and photography. It was there that he met a wealthy Jewish South African called Helen Mininberg (later Helen Wellington-Lloyd), who suffered from achondroplasia – a condition which causes dwarfism – and with whom he embarked on an affair. He also met a Jewish Turkish-French woman called

Jocelyn Hakim, whom he married so that she could remain in Britain and continue with her studies. The £50 Hakim paid him to make sure he turned up at Lewisham registry office would be used to fund his Goldsmiths student project: the £2,000 it would take to secure a divorce inevitably fell to Grandma Rose.

Vivienne, however, soon tired of the Oxfordshire cottage's cramped confines, not to mention her parents' disapproval of Malcolm's carefree lifestyle and indifference to parental duties, and took the boys to live in her aunt's caravan on a caravan park just outside Prestatyn in North Wales. Eight months would pass before they were able to return to the capital, renting a flat on Nightingale Lane in South London close to Wandsworth Common, which Malcolm leased for £3.10 a week. Vivienne scraped the rent money together selling homemade jewellery on Portobello Market. It was here the couple would remain together until parting for good in 1980.

It wasn't long before Malcolm began to show his non-conformist colours at Goldsmiths. The college's then student union president, and future Labour district manager for Brent Council, Russell Profitt, told Craig Bromberg for *The Wicked Ways of Malcolm McLaren* that 'Red Malcolm', as he was known both for his flaming red hair and left of centre politics, expressed his feelings at a general meeting by pelting the SEC (Student Executive Committee) members with rotten tomatoes.

Whilst at Goldsmiths, Malcolm's political agitations were more memorable than his paintings, but in the summer of 1969 he ingratiated himself with his fellow students by unveiling plans to stage a massive free festival – akin to the Rolling Stones' recent show in Hyde Park – in the amphitheatre situated to the rear of the college's art annexe. He put together an impressive line-up which boasted the Pretty Things and King Crimson, the Lindsey Kemp mime troupe, renowned writer William Burroughs, who was to give a lecture, cult psychologist R.D. Laing, and pornographic novelist Alexander Trocchi. News of the free Goldsmiths' festival spread across London's college circuit and, come the big day, some 20,000 people – mainly students – descended on the college growing more restless and angry as each and every one of the named acts failed to show. Malcolm, perhaps not surprisingly, also failed to put in an appearance, and whilst Profitt tried desperately to locate him, the festival continued unabated with a steady procession of unbooked, unruly – and largely untalented – bands seizing the opportunity to perform in front of a massive audience. Those in authority tried to maintain order, but with 20,000 freeloaders taking over the college, and helping themselves to whatever wasn't nailed down, the day descended into chaos. 'Some of the students,' Profitt told Bromberg, 'wanted Malcolm's head on a plate, while others wanted him to be glorified as a saint for bringing life to Goldsmiths.'

Having miraculously escaped expulsion over the Free Festival debacle, Malcolm decided to keep a low profile and concentrate on his student project, a conceptual film based on London's Oxford Street, looking at the dehumanising effect of consumer consumption. He borrowed Goldsmiths' one and only camera, a Bolex, and enlisted the recently returned Fred Vermorel to operate the sound, and Helen as assistant director. The intrepid filmmakers descended on London's famous shopping thoroughfare and shot several rolls of film before supposedly losing the camera on the tube. However, if Bromberg and Jane Mulvagh, author of *Vivienne Westwood: An Unfashionable Life*, are to be believed, Malcolm later sold the Bolex to fund his new World's End venture at 430 King's Road.

By May 1970, a film of sorts was beginning to take shape. It opens within the interior of Tommy Roberts' Mr Freedom on Kensington Church Street, where a TV screen blares out the importance of female fashion in society, while the lilting strains of the Rolling Stones' *Satisfaction* drifts in and out of sync. Malcolm was also keen to trace the history of Oxford Street, which follows the route of a Roman road, the via Trinobantina, and runs for approximately a mile and a half from Marble Arch at the north-east corner of Hyde Park, through Oxford Circus to St Giles' Circus at the intersection with Charing Cross Road and Tottenham Court Road. Between the 12th century and 1782 the thoroughfare was known as Tyburn Road, after the river of the same name that ran just to the south of it, and now flows underneath. This became notorious as the route taken by prisoners on their final journey from Newgate Prison, or Horsemonger Lane Gaol, in Southwark to the gallows at Tyburn near the modern-day Marble Arch monument. The film then segues into the Gordon Riots of 1780, named after the religious agitator Lord George Gordon (1751-93) who led the protestant opposition to the Papist's Act of 1778, which relieved the country's Catholic population from certain penalties imposed upon them during the reign of William III.

By the time of the final – and still unfinished – film treatment circa May 1971, however, Malcolm had seemingly lost interest in anarchic history and focused his attention on his rock 'n' roll hero Billy Fury. Interspersed between footage of several dolphins performing tricks alongside scantily-clad 'aquamaids' all within the confines of a tank measuring just 3m deep, 14m long and 5m wide (which was shot at the London Dolphinarium housed within the up-market striptease revue Pleasurama's at 65 Oxford Street), we see the head of the UK Billy Fury fan club gushing about her idol. In the background there are stock photos of Fury and his album covers, as well as footage of Billy's fans queuing up outside theatres waiting to see their hero perform hits such as 'Maybe Tomorrow', 'It's Only Make Believe', 'Jealousy' and 'Halfway To Paradise'.

The ideas may have flowed freely, but Jocelyn Hakim's £50 had long-since been spent. After one last desperate – and fruitless – attempt to raise finance from Fury's frugal manager Larry Parnes, who was known throughout the music industry as 'Parnes, Shillings and Pence', Malcolm shelved the film and drew a final line under his art school wanderings by walking away from Goldsmiths. A lack of funding may have forced Malcolm to put the Oxford Street project on ice, but those close to him fully expected him to reactivate his filmic passions at some point in the future. He just needed to find another way to finance his celluloid dreams.

CHAPTER Two

The Truth Loves To Run Naked

'Distrust any enterprise that requires new clothes.'
Henry David Thoreau (1817–1862)

1971 proved to be a pivotal year in several ways for Malcolm. Not only was it the year in which he bade farewell to academia and embarked on his entrepreneurial path, it was also the year he changed his surname by deed poll back to the one he'd been born with, McLaren.

Vivienne, as a metaphorical means of shedding the last vestiges of her provincial past, had her hair cropped short at a fashionable Mayfair salon and returned to the flat on Nightingale Road, where – razor in hand – she set about layering her considerably shortened tresses into uneven spikes which, with the aid of hair gel, stood erect. She then completed her tonsorial transformation from Jean Brody to Jean Genie by bleaching her spiky mane. She would later boast of being the first person in London to sport the peroxide spiky hairstyle that would become synonymous with the UK punk scene. Indeed, Bromley Contingent perennial and occasional SEX employee, Simon Barker, believes David Bowie, who by 1971 was tired of strumming elfin folk songs and was on the lookout for ideas with which to reinvent himself, copied Vivienne's space-age crop for his androgynous alter ego Ziggy Stardust.

#

Malcolm, Vivienne and Patrick Casey moved their wares into the back quarter of 430 King's Road sometime during November 1971. Having erected a sandwich-board on the pavement, illustrated with guitars and musical notes depicting 'Let It Rock at Paradise Garage', the trio awaited their first customer. They were still waiting by closing time and when they arrived at the shop the following morning, Mendelson, who'd already warned them business had been slow of late, was nowhere to be seen. The American failed to show and, although Malcolm, Vivienne and Patrick were happy to cover for Mendelson as a thank you for giving them their opportunity, when he failed to put in an appearance all that week the trio did what any budding entrepreneurs would do and requisitioned the shop.

There are several versions as to what happened when Miles returned from his honeymoon to find his store filled with old records and retro clothing, but the general consensus was that he wasn't best pleased. Fortunately for Malcolm, however, the downturn in takings meant Miles wasn't in any position to argue and he consented to allow the interlopers to stay providing they coughed up £40 per week for their share of the rent. Malcolm and Patrick agreed to the proposal, but made no attempt to move their stock back to their designated area at the shop's rear. In their minds, at least, the takeover had already begun.

'I didn't disappear, exactly,' Miles recollected for Craig Bromberg's unofficial biography on his erstwhile business partner. 'But because I had no money my wife started going out on her own and she ended up falling for another man. I had no money, and couldn't see any way of getting any out of Malcolm. I was devastated and couldn't see any way out of it.' Miles, realising the shit was about to hit the financial fan in seismic proportions, declared himself bankrupt and walked away leaving Malcolm, Vivienne and Patrick in total control of the shop. He little realised that he'd inadvertently set into motion a counter-culture revolution, which would forever change Britain's musical and cultural landscapes, and earn him a footnote in rock 'n' roll history into the bargain.

Malcolm and Patrick wasted little time in eradicating all traces of the shop's former guise. Having borrowed £50 from Malcolm's former lover Helen Wellington-Lloyd (*née* Mininberg), they tore down the bamboo lettering from the shop's corrugated façade, which they then spray-painted black and daubed 'Let It Rock' in large red lettering. Their entire stock consisted of '50s retro kitsch, including old Bakelite valve radios which had been painstakingly restored, and chrome guitar-shaped mirrors which were bought in. They redesigned the front half of the shop's interior to resemble a Queen Elizabeth II coronation-era 1950s living room complete with authentic period wallpaper, carpeting and furniture, including a teak, glass-panelled sideboard and some Formica cabinets in which to display their wares. To complete the illusion, stacks of period magazines lay scattered about which customers could sit and read whilst taking a cup of tea, without any fear of being pestered into making a purchase by the owners.

#

By the summer of 1972, by which time Patrick had dissolved his partnership with Malcolm, the British music scene – although still some three years away from its darkest nadir – found itself at something of a loose end. The bands left over from the lysergic '60s had either dropped out or were too stoned to tune in to reality. The unholy American triumvirate of Hendrix, Morrison and Joplin were all dead, while the Fab Four, having long since lost their raison d'etre, had sung one last tune for old times' sake from the roof of their ill-fated Apple building in Savile Row, before heading off to pursue their respective solo careers. Let It Rock, therefore, with its cosy kitsch interior, retro clothing and accoutrements, and vintage rock 'n' roll constantly blaring out from the jukebox, acted like a homing beacon attracting like-minded souls who yearned for a return to yesteryear; the time of a pre-G.I Elvis; the time of Eddie and Buddy; the time when rock 'n' roll was king.

Thanks to word of mouth, the shop was finally beginning to take off but, without Patrick to rely on, it wasn't long before Malcolm and Vivienne began to run low on stock. Although rock 'n' roll was enjoying something of a renaissance in the early '70s, original and authentic Teddy Boy apparel was becoming harder and harder to find, and so Vivienne – who'd been making her own clothes since her mid-teens – was co-opted to patch up the stuff that was available. This soon led to her skilfully duplicating the brightly-coloured drape jackets favoured by the Teddy Boys that frequented rock 'n' roll revivalist strongholds like The Black Raven pub in Bishopsgate in the City, which she and Malcolm visited on several occasions. While Malcolm skulked in a corner, Vivienne, provocatively dressed in a canary-yellow mohair sweater, tight black ski-pants and stilettos, quaffed with the pub's quiffed clientele to find out where they bought their gear and, more importantly, how much they were willing to pay for it.

Upon learning the Bishopsgate Teddy Boys were having to buy their drapes made-to-measure, which proved both costly and time-consuming, the couple returned to the World's End safe in the knowledge that if they could lay their hands on the requisite materials then the trousers would be no problem to reproduce en masse, while their contact, an East-End tailor called Sid Green, could undercut any bespoke tailor in London. The shop may have been turning a profit, but sacrifices – including disconnecting the telephone at their Nightingale Lane flat – still had to be made in order to finance the purchase of a sturdy second-hand Singer sewing machine. The lay-out was soon recouped as within a matter of weeks those same Bishopsgate Boppers were forming a queue outside Let It Rock on Saturday mornings waiting for the shop to open.

It wasn't only Teddy Boys that were making a Brylcreemed-beeline to the World's End, however, as stars such as David Bowie, Marc Bolan and Bryan Ferry would pop in on the lookout for an eye-catching item for their latest appearance on *Top Of The Pops*. Costumiers from TV, stage and film companies would also descend upon Let It Rock, and Malcolm and Vivienne's big break came when they were asked to design costumes for Ray Connelly's film *That'll Be The Day* starring David Essex, Ringo Starr and Malcolm's idol, Billy Fury. Encouraged by the interest they were receiving, Malcolm and Vivienne decided to expand the business. In August 1972, they booked a stall at a massive rock 'n' roll festival staged at Wembley Stadium and printed up hundreds of T-shirts of rock 'n' roll's original piano pixie, Little Richard, with the overprinted slogan Vive Le Rock. But although an estimated 50,000 people attended the festival, which boasted a line-up including Bill Haley, Little Richard, Chuck Berry and Billy Fury, little more than a handful of those in attendance were moved to purchase one of Malcolm's T-shirts.

Despite this setback, the shop's first twelve months of trading had been a success. But the year would end on a tragic note, however, when, on 12th December, Malcolm arrived at Grandma Rose's flat and was mortified to find the old woman sitting naked and bolt upright in her bed … having been dead for some considerable time. Her health had been steadily deteriorating to the point where she could no longer look after herself properly; her husband, Mick Isaacs, having passed away earlier in the year. However, her loyalty to Malcolm, which some would say was misguided, meant she wouldn't accept help from Emmy or the rest of the Edwards' and as a result had died from starvation. The flat at Nightingale

Lane was but a five minute walk from Rose's South Clapham flat, so a tacit agreement had been reached between Malcolm and his estranged family, whereby he and Vivienne would take it upon themselves to look after the old woman. However, the demands of running a business were taking up more and more of Malcolm's time, and the weekly visits to look in on Grandma Rose were one of the first casualties. Malcolm was apparently so riddled with guilt at having neglected the one person who had always been there for him that he couldn't even bring himself to attend the funeral service.

#

That'll Be The Day, which was the first major British film to take a look back at the 1950s, was released in April 1973. In that same year Universal Pictures released future *Star Wars* creator George Lucas's *American Graffiti*, starring Richard Dreyfus and Ron Howard, along with a totally unknown Harrison Ford. These two films, in conjunction with the West End opening of the smash Broadway musical *Grease*, brought a wave of nostalgia flooding across the Atlantic.

430 King's Road may have been the place to go for authentic '50s threads, but Malcolm and Vivienne knew they couldn't hope to compete once the rag trade got hold of a style, so they slowly began to diversify towards the biker element of studs and leather. By the spring of 1973, although the odd drape or flecked jacket could still be found at the back of the shop, the couple began exploring other fashion avenues. One of these ideas saw them baking names in glitter, such as Elvis, Eddie Cochran, Buddy Holly, as well as '50s motorcycle brands Triumph and Norton (which were picked out in studs), onto tight sleeveless T-shirts *à la* the ones worn by Gene Vincent and his Bluecaps. Another idea was the 'bike-tyre T-shirt', which involved attaching sections of old bicycle tyres around the armpits of the T-shirts, whilst another – and perhaps the most innovative idea of all – involved the spelling out of motifs such as Rock 'n' Roll or Let It Rock using boiled chicken bones attached to the shirts with tiny chains.

As was to be expected, the shop's clientele shifted away from Teddy Boys to bikers, or 'Ton-up Boys' as the leather-clad rockers preferred to be called. Although Let It Rock certainly had biker connotations, Malcolm and Vivienne began thinking of a change to the shop's name to match its change of direction. The new name

Bootleg sleeve in the style of The Beatles. Issue 1

came courtesy of one of their more creative Saturday helpers, whose latest T-shirt design bore the motto that American biker gangs had adopted in homage to '50s teen idol James Dean (who'd died at the wheel of his Porsche 550 Spyder on 30th September 1955). The red-block Let It Rock lettering on the corrugated hoarding disappeared beneath a fresh coat of matt-black paint, upon which was daubed the shop's new name, Too Fast To Live, Too Young To Die, accompanied by a gleaming white skull and crossbones. The new direction secured another costume commission, this time for Ken Russell's *Mahler*, the flamboyant director's musical biopic on the life of Austrian composer Gustav Mahler, starring Robert Powell. Malcolm and Vivienne received plenty of publicity for their leather-studded S&M ensemble, but according to Shirley Russell, the film's costumier, and the director's ex-wife, the costume in question was actually designed by Lenny Pollock. Let It Rock wasn't entirely eradicated from memory either, as Malcolm and Vivienne retained the title as a brand label for their designs.

In August 1973, Malcolm and Vivienne, along with several other proprietors of the King's Road's more avant-garde emporiums, were invited to exhibit their designs at the National Boutique show, which was being staged in New York City. The venue was the run-down McAlpin Hotel, where each of them was given a room from which to display their wares. To promote themselves, Malcolm and Vivienne had printed a few hundred single-colour flyers bearing the shop's new skull and crossbones logo and, so as not to confuse their potential clientele, they added the legend: 'Clothes by Let It Rock, 430 King's Road, England'. The exhibition was to last three weeks and the couple expected to do well; after all, America was the home of outlaw biker culture. But the studded bike-tyre T-shirts and shirts with chicken-bone motifs were beyond the pale for the bemused New Yorkers, and a chagrined Malcolm later admitted they didn't take a single order during their entire stay. The trip may have been a waste of time in commercial terms, but it would prove the catalyst which first set Malcolm on the road to becoming a pop Svengali.

It was while he was being ignored by New York's supposedly fashion-conscious cognoscenti that he encountered New York Dolls' guitarists Sylvain Sylvain (born Ronald Mizrahi) and Johnny Thunders (born John Anthony Genzale Jr). Aside from being a Doll, Sylvain had a sideline producing hand-knit psychedelic sweaters under his Truth & Soul label, as you do. Both Sylvain and Thunders were aware of Let It Rock, as the Dolls had paid a fleeting visit to 430 King's Road (on a day when Malcolm was away from the shop) during the band's mini UK tour the previous year. They'd put in an appearance at the Empire Pool, Wembley, playing alongside the Pink Fairies and the Faces, in front of 8,000 people.

The five-piece New York Dolls had been together for eighteen months by this time and had built up a small but fanatical following owing to their penchant for taking to the stage dressed like Harlem hookers whilst playing catchy high-energy rock 'n' roll. They had recorded an album's worth of their trademark two-to-three minute vignettes on New York's seedy underbelly. They would often share the billing with the equally unknown KISS, because both groups' drummers ran in the same street gang at one time! Like Malcolm, all five Dolls were aficionados of '50s rock 'n' roll, and their raucous sound was a hybrid of this, plus the Hamburg-era Beatles, and the full-tilt R&B boogie of the Rolling Stones; all served up with a side dish of doo-wop *à la* the Shangri-

Las and other '60s American girl bands such as the Ronettes, the Crystals and the Shirelles.

Unlike New York, however, where the mainstream press dismissed them as faggots and freaks, the British music press couldn't get enough of the Dolls. Before the band had yet to secure a recording contract, both *Melody Maker* and the *NME* took the unprecedented step of placing them on their respective front covers. Prior to their UK jaunt, only Warner Bros and Mercury Records had shown any interest in signing the Dolls, but a bidding war soon broke out. Several major players were competing for their signatures on a contract, including Phonogram, the newly-established Virgin Records, and Atlantic Records, whose CEO, Ahmet Ertegun, wired a telegram to the Dolls' management team, Steve Leber, David Krebs and Marty Thau, offering to sign the band for $50,000 sight unseen. The Rolling Stones were equally keen to secure the Dolls to their own private label, as were the Who's Kit Lambert, and former T.Rex manager Tony Secunda. Indeed, Leber and Thau were sat negotiating terms on a £100,000 deal with the latter, when word reached them that the band's Columbian-born drummer Billy Murcia was dead.

Billy had been staying with the rest of the band at The Whitehouse Hotel in Kensington. The last anyone had seen of him was when he'd stopped off at Thau's room to borrow £5 to buy some more Mandrax, or mandies as they were colloquially known on the street, a powerful – and highly addictive – sedative similar to the American Quaalude, and the current rock 'n' roll drug *de jour*. The drummer had then returned to his own room, where, in a macabre twist of fate, he received an outside call from a stranger wanting to invite someone else to a nearby party, but who clearly had the wrong room number. Instead of hanging up, Billy decided he might as well go to the party where, owing to a combination of Mandrax and alcohol, he passed out. Although Mandrax was available by prescription – and wouldn't be banned until 1977 – the party's other guests were obviously in possession of substances which would have attracted attention from the authorities. So when various attempts at resuscitation failed, they panicked and dragged the stricken drummer into the bathroom, dumped him into a bathtub filled with cold water, before then attempting to revive him by pouring hot coffee down his throat. At some point Billy suffocated. Had he not taken that call he would have inked his name on a six-figure contract along with the rest of the Dolls. Instead of which, he lay on a mortuary slab far from home while his stunned band mates were bundled on the next available flight back to New York.

Although Malcolm didn't see the Dolls play live during his stay in New York, he hung out with the band – which now included Murcia's replacement, Jerry Nolan (whose best friend Peter Criss, of KISS, had also auditioned) – and attended many a party at the McAlpin as well as at the Dolls' rehearsal loft. It was at one of the now-legendary loft parties that Malcolm first heard – and expressed his dislike for – the Dolls' seminal debut album. During the bath scene in *The Great Rock 'n' Roll Swindle,* he would pontificate to Helen of Troy (Helen Wellington-Lloyd) about the advantages of having a band that couldn't play, as opposed to one that could. And it was surely upon hearing the Dolls' album that this inverted aesthetic first took root.

The Dolls may not have been the most musically proficient outfit in town, but they were imbued with a wildness that had been sorely lacking since the '50s. They also oozed style and attitude, traits which Malcolm greatly appreciated. The Dolls returned to London – as part of a European tour – in late November 1973, where they played two shows over consecutive nights at Biba's Rainbow Room, as well as putting in a memorable appearance on *The Old Grey Whistle Test.* Malcolm latched on to the band and their charismatic Jagger-esque frontman David Johansen in particular. Indeed, such was his amour for the Americans that he followed the band to Paris and remained with them through the remainder of the tour. He didn't return to London until the New Year, by which time his pop perception had been irrevocably altered: he was convinced the New York Dolls were the future of rock 'n' roll. His only thought now was how he could muscle in on their action. Malcolm later did so by talking his way into managing the band, his first foray into the line of work which etched his name into the public's consciousness.

His first priority, though, was to wrench 430 King's Road away from its staid retro roots and fast-forward it into the future. As he later told Jon Savage: 'Black seemed to be the best colour; where our ideas were the most exciting. I decided to open a shop that was strictly black and design orientated, which would bring out all the sexual clothes that people normally sold as fetish wear.' Vivienne, although less enthused about the fetish notion, gave her full support and together the pair embarked on a painstaking search of London seeking out specialist suppliers of rubber and leatherwear such as John Sutcliffe at AtomAge on Dryden Street in Covent Garden, and London Leatherman in Battersea. The new direction would of course require a total revamping of both the shop's interior and exterior, but the builder brought in to carry out said renovations proved not only unreliable but also incompetent. Malcolm and Vivienne ended up doing most of the work themselves.

The inept artisan had dismantled Miles' portable dance floor, but it fell to Malcolm and Vivienne to gather up the dust-covered components scattered about the floor. Once they'd cleared away the debris they then set about sanding, varnishing and bevelling the wooden rails which were then reattached to the walls in the form of gymnasium monkey bars. The walls and ceiling were draped with sheets of peach-coloured surgical rubber and sponge-like grey foam purchased from the Pentonville Rubber Company. To complete their masterpiece, Malcolm daubed the womblike interior with spray-painted slogans and quotations lifted from pornographic literature. These would ultimately appear as T-shirt designs, including the SCUM manifesto (Society for Cutting Up Men) by Valerie Solanas (who tried to bump off Andy Warhol in 1968), and Alexander Trocchi's *School for Wives* and *Thongs*. Although the jukebox remained, it was usurped as the shop's focal point by a rusting surgical bed, which was inexplicably placed in the corner and covered with a pink rubber sheet. To accompany the shop's new line of rubber and leather fetish gear, as well as Vivienne's own designs, a salacious array of fetish and sado-masochistic accessories, such as inflatable rubber 'gimp' masks, whips, chains and tit clamps lined the walls; while the upper torsos of several naked headless mannequins were piled on top of each other – orgy-fashion – in the windows.

Once they were satisfied with the interior, Malcolm and Vivienne then set about the shop's public façade by stripping away the corrugated-iron hoarding and replacing it with the shop's new identity 'SEX' spelt out in three-foot high Claes Oldenburg-style provocative pink-padded plastic. On the lintel above the door, Malcolm sprayed a fitting aphorism from 18th century French philosopher Jean Jacques Rousseau: 'craft must have clothes but the truth loves to go naked'.

Needless to say, taking seedy fetish wear from the dog-eared back pages of top-shelf magazines and parading it on the high street attracted a certain clientele: individuals who can only achieve sexual gratification by dressing head-to-toe in rubber

The Cambridge Rapist Hotel, A prop from the Swindle film

and attaching metal implements to their nipples and genitals. Although SEX, which opened its doors in April 1974, offended the moral majority – as it was surely designed to do – it also began to attract a coterie of curious strong-willed individuals, many of whom would at one time or another end up on the shop's payroll. They were all looking for something other than what was available on the King's Road and the rest of London's fashion houses. The most recognisable, of course, being 19-year-old Pamela Rooke, a curvaceous, kohl-eyed fashion freak who'd taken to calling herself Jordan. Indeed, *England's Dreaming* author, Jon Savage, believes Jordan was the first Sex Pistol. This theory certainly holds true, for she was serving as the living embodiment of 430 King's Road long before Steve, Paul, Glen and John took to the small upstairs stage at St Martins School of Art on 6th November 1975.

Indeed, she'd been experimenting with her appearance since her early teens in her home town of Seaford in Sussex, and had developed a sartorial style in the discos of nearby Brighton before gravitating to London's gay club scene. 'I went to the Masquerade Club in Earls Court, which was outrageous even by today's standards,' she told Savage. 'They were very worried about women coming into their clubs and so the only way you got in was by how you looked. If you looked crazy and outrageous you were alright.' Shortly after securing a job at SEX, however, she lost her flat in Drayton Place, which meant she was forced to return to sleepy Seaford and commute up to London each morning. Her provocative dress, fastidious make-up and peroxide hair swept up into a beehive, would cause bowler-hatted businessmen to shuffle nervously in their seats and tactfully adjust their newspapers.

The steadily increasing number of young libertines who were beating a path to the World's End, had little interest in the shop's fetish line, but were queuing up to purchase Malcolm and Vivienne's new range of sexually explicit T-shirts. Indeed, the term 'T-shirt' doesn't actually apply to the crudely constructed garments as Vivienne viewed sleeves as superfluous and simply sewed two patches of cotton cloth together leaving adequate space for the head and arms. The earliest designs, which were painstakingly wood-block printed by hand on Vivienne's kitchen table back at the flat on Nightingale Lane, included images of Mickey and Minnie Mouse fornicating, a pre-pubescent youth suggestively smoking a cigarette, and the 'Rape' shirt which featured text lifted from Trocchi's *School for Wives*. The designs, although risqué for mid-70s England, were relatively harmless, but other designs such as the one depicting the full-face leather mask as worn by Peter Samuel Cook, a.k.a. the notorious 'Cambridge Rapist' were more controversial. Cook was finally found guilty at Norwich Crown Court in 1975 of raping six women and injuring two more and given two life sentences. The design was later amended to include the caption: 'It's Been A Hard Day's Night' which was an oblique reference to the death of the Beatles' manager Brian Epstein who died in August 1967.

Malcolm supposedly got the idea for the shirt following a visit to SEX by detectives from the Metropolitan Police, who were pursuing information that the rapist had actually purchased his grim mask from SEX. Another design which would bring SEX to the attention of the law, resulting in a raid on the shop and the prosecution of Malcolm and Vivienne, was the notorious 'Two Cowboys' shirt. This was drawn in the Tom of Finland style, and depicted two cowboys, both naked from the waist down except for their boots, and with their flaccid penises almost touching. The trouble started in July 1975, when SEX employee Alan 'Leather & Bones' Jones (who today is a successful film reviewer specialising in horror, and the brains behind the annual 'Frightfest' screenings in London) was arrested in Piccadilly for wearing the shirt, and taken to Vine Street police station where he was charged with having 'exposed to public view an indecent exhibition'.

Malcolm was beside himself with rage over what he saw as draconian censorship and promised Jones he would hire the best lawyers to defend him. But of course when the case came before the courts, Malcolm was nowhere to be seen and Jones, finding himself on his own, pleaded guilty. That wasn't the end of the matter, however. On 7th August, following a police raid on the shop, which saw officers remove a range of garments deemed offensive – including all copies of the Two Cowboys shirt – Malcolm and Vivienne were arrested and charged under the same archaic 19th century law as Jones, and they too were duly fined.

\#

The shop may have taken a new direction, but within weeks of the transition Malcolm found himself standing at the crossroads of indecision. His European jaunt with the Dolls had fuelled his desire to get involved with the band and, leaving Vivienne to mind the store, he booked a flight to New York. Another, and infinitely more personal, reason for his trip was to try and locate Addie Isman; the errant daughter of a wealthy New Jersey family, with whom he'd enjoyed a brief dalliance during her equally-brief tenure as an assistant at TFTLTYTD. Little is known about the mysterious Addie, other than she returned to New York to try and emulate her father (who owned a franchise of the Two Guys retail chain) by making a name for herself in the fashion world, and that she died of an accidental barbiturate overdose in 1978.

Several of the miscreants often to be found lurking at the back of the shop had formed a band. Their leader, a nearly illiterate self-confessed kleptomaniac called Steve Jones, had renewed his pestering to get Malcolm to act as the band's manager. Malcolm had been too distracted overseeing the shop's revamping at the time, but had put them in touch with his new Saturday lad, an 18-year-old art student called Glen Matlock, who just happened to be teaching himself bass guitar. Although Malcolm had no interest whatsoever in getting involved with the ad hoc combo, who'd yet to play a single show, and were toying with the name 'Swankers', he'd been captivated by Jones' childlike tenacity. So before setting off for New York in November 1974, he'd paid for a rehearsal room at the Covent Garden Community Centre, as well as instructing his bespectacled business associate Bernard Rhodes to keep an eye on Steve's band.

Bernard Rhodes (or 'Bernie' as he later became known during his tenure as manager of the Pistols' punk contemporaries, the Clash) was, like Malcolm, of Jewish ancestry and had been raised by his mother. She was a Russian emigre to London's East End where, according to Bernie, she was forced to purchase a forged birth certificate on the black market to escape deportation back to the motherland. During the 1950s Bernie's mother worked as a seamstress for several tailors on Savile Row, and it was whilst she was working at Hawes & Curtis that she was apprenticed by John Pearse who, a decade or so later, would found renowned King's Road psychedelic fashion emporium Granny Takes A Trip. By 1963, by which time Bernie was at art school, he and Pearse were sharing a flat at 68 Hamilton Terrace in St John's Wood. Thanks to Mick Jagger apparently having one of his mistresses ensconced in the flat above, the house became a hang-out for a colourful coterie of flower-powering misfits such as Donovan, the soon-to-be-famous 'bopping elf' Marc Bolan, and the Who's Pete Townshend and Roger Daltrey.

It was during this period that Bernie also encountered Malcolm for the first time, as both were regular habitués of the Soho coffee bar scene. They became friends, only to lose touch once Malcolm became involved with Vivienne. By the end of the decade Bernie had also fallen for a maiden's charms and had married his girlfriend Sheila, who worked as a librarian at the London School of Economics. A child followed soon after, and the couple bought a flat on Camden Road located within walking distance of Harry's, the Renault dealership/garage housed within a disused red-bricked two storey railway storage shed on Chalk Farm Road in Camden Town, in which he'd bought a share. Although he'd turned his back on pop culture, Bernie had a stall on Chelsea's Antiquarius antiques market from which he sold second-hand leather jackets. A chance encounter with Malcolm led to an invitation to 430 King's Road, which served to reignite his passion for counter-culture and he readily accepted Malcolm's offer to help with designing T-shirts intended for sale in SEX.

Shortly before he embarked on his quest to conquer New York, Malcolm collaborated with Vivienne and Bernie on a new T-shirt which, over the ensuing twelve months, would become their manifesto. Entitled 'You're Gonna Wake Up One Morning And Know Which Side Of The Bed You've Been Lying On', the polarising design bore a list of 'hates' down the left-hand side and a list of 'loves' down the right. Not surprisingly, the 'hates' column consisted of antiquated ideals, floundering institutions, fascists, and pompous rockers; while the 'loves' championed renegades, outlaws, and other gauche and outré heroes. Listed alongside Bob Marley, Jimi Hendrix and Sam Cooke, was the first printed mention of the band which over the course of the next three years would reshape the musical landscape: Kutie Jones and his Sex Pistols.

CHAPTER THREE

Young Flesh Required

'It's like my Daddy used to say; better to be judged by
twelve men than carried by six!'
From the movie *Streets of Blood*

Okay, so if we are agreed that without Bradley Mendelson, Malcolm wouldn't have taken ownership of 430 King's Road, and there wouldn't have been a Sex Pistols – at least not in the guise the world came to know – then it is equally fair to argue that without Warwick 'Wally' Nightingale there wouldn't have been a band which Malcolm could mould into the Sex Pistols. The much-maligned Wally died from a heart attack in 1996, shortly before the reconstituted Sex Pistols embarked on their aptly-entitled Filthy Lucre world tour, and just after he had finally received a royalty cheque for his part in the song 'Did You No Wrong'. In Julien Temple's 1999 documentary *The Filth And The Fury* Wally is treated with disdain even by Paul Cook and Steve Jones. However, without Wally, Paul would be working a regular 9-5 as an electrician, while Steve – by his own admission – would probably be serving a five-stretch, tucked up in the Scrubs with only porridge for breakfast!

Today, Wally is seen as the Sex Pistols' equivalent to Pete Best. But unlike the Beatles' original drummer, who was supplanted by Ringo Starr shortly before Beatlemania swept the globe, Wally was to be denied both recognition for having planted the seed from which the Sex Pistols would grow, and subsequent royalties – despite having written the tune for 'Scarface', which evolved into 'Did You No Wrong', the B-side to 'God Save The Queen'. Although Malcolm would readily cite Steve as being the band's progenitor, and that there couldn't have been a Sex Pistols without his 'artful dodger', it was in fact Wally, who was already familiar with the workings of a guitar, who cajoled Steve and Paul – as well as fellow

Christopher Wren School reprobates Jimmy Mackin and Stephen Hayes – into forming a band.

Wally, like Steve, was totally disinterested in school, and by the third year he'd abandoned the three 'R's altogether in favour of staying at home at 50 Hemlock Road in Acton, learning rock 'n' roll licks on his Les Paul copy. As Wally's parents were usually out at work all day, it was only natural that the five absconders would while away the afternoons of their final school year availing themselves of Wally's dad's beer and homemade wine whilst listening to music in the back garden. When the time came to bid adieu to secondary school education, the work-shy gang – with the exception of Paul who'd gained an electrician's apprenticeship at Watney's Brewery in Mortlake – had signed on the dole and were spending their weekly giro down the local pub. Steve would later tell Fred Vermorel for *The Sex Pistols* (Universal 1977, written with Judy Vermorel) he'd been too lazy to sign on, which – unless he was accruing enough money from his thieving – seems at odds with his love of easy money.

Stephen Philip Jones was born on 3rd September 1955 in Queen Charlotte's [Hammersmith & Chelsea] Hospital – next door to Wormwood Scrubs HM Prison – on Du Cane Road Shepherd's Bush, London. Shortly after Steve was born, he and his parents moved into a tiny one bedroom basement flat at No. 13 Benbow Road (the family were later to move into the upstairs first floor flat), situated close to Shepherd's Bush common, and – unbeknownst to him at the time – a mere rattle throw from the home of his future best mate, and fellow Sex Pistol, Paul Cook, whose family lived on nearby Carthew Road. Unlike Paul, however, Steve was to be denied a stable upbringing as his father, an aspiring middleweight boxer called Don Jarvis, threw the towel in on fatherhood whilst his son was still in short trousers. Steve would keep Jarvis' name under wraps to all but his closest confidants throughout his time with the Sex Pistols, and only mentioned the boxer's role – or lack thereof – in his turbulent upbringing in *The Filth And The Fury*. His mother Mary, who worked as a hairdresser, remarried when Steve was two years old. And although her new husband was willing to take on 'damaged goods' so to speak, as well as providing respectability by adopting Steve and giving him his surname, the relationship between step-father and son was turbulent from the off.

It is a matter of record that Steve struggled academically, and although domestic discord is no excuse for bunking off school, the lack of firm parental guidance meant that he – like any other kid in his position – was free to choose whether to go in to class or seek other ways of passing his day. Mary, who by her own admission had communication problems with her own parents, readily confessed to Fred and Judy Vermorel that she had little or no control over her wayward son. At the time, London was basking in its 'Swinging' sobriquet, and she was too busy providing local teenagers with Beatles Moptops and Dusty Springfield Beehives to oversee his schooling.

#

Although Steve and Paul lived within spitting distance of each other, they attended separate primary schools and didn't become friends until both – having failed the 11-plus exam – were enrolled at the Christopher Wren Secondary Modern, situated on the nearby council-run Wormholt Estate, close to Queen's Park Rangers' Loftus Road football ground. By this time, Steve was developing into something of a kleptomaniac, and Paul later admitted that one of his earliest memories is of being in the Jones' basement flat, watching on while his friend disassembled and reassembled the motorbikes he'd nefariously acquired.

In the Sex Pistols' *The Knowledge* interview Steve confesses that the flat's outdoor coal bunker was used to stash his ill-gotten gains. As we all know, Malcolm, as part of his woefully inaccurate and fanciful telling of the Sex Pistols' story in *The Great Rock 'n' Roll Swindle*, extolled Steve to be a 'brilliant cat burglar'. And although some of his pre-Pistols thieving exploits are worthy of mention, his teenage forays into crime were somewhat less successful and usually resulted in his collar being tugged by the boys in blue. Indeed, he would later admit to Fred Vermorel that he was caught – and convicted – thirteen times over a three year period, for a variety of crimes ranging from petty burglary and breaking and entering, through to stealing cars and driving under age without a license or insurance. Although several of these convictions resulted in his being incarcerated at Stanford House Juvenile Remand Centre, as well as a more serious three week spell at Ashford Remand Centre in Kent, the guitarist considers himself lucky not to have been sent to Borstal.

In her interview with Fred Vermorel, Mary bemoaned the late-night calls from whichever station happened to be holding Steve. As she couldn't drive, his put-upon stepfather – who started

Bootleg sleeve in the style of The Beatles. Issue 4

work at 6am – would have to give her a lift to collect him. Again, the lack of firm parental guidance is no excuse for thievery, but it does at least go some way to explain why Steve had so little respect for right and wrong. In fact, his own childhood memories are of accompanying his parents on shoplifting forays at the local supermarket suggesting that his views on 'mine' and 'thine' were always likely to be confused.

As already mentioned, Paul, who was born on 20th July 1956, the second of three children, and the only boy, was born into a stable hard-working family. His father, Thomas, was a carpenter and joiner by trade, while his mother, Sylvia, worked as a cleaner. Unlike Steve, who was already the bane of many a teacher's working life, and had been held back a year due to his academic failings, Paul appeared both diligent and conscientious, and one has to wonder why his teachers didn't step in when his end of term report cards started to take a downturn. His 1967-68 final report showed him to be the form captain with a 229/230 attendance record, and saw him achieving consistently good grades (mainly 'A's and 'B+'s); whereas during the 1969-70 term – although still form captain – Paul's grades had begun to slip, as did his attendance record (now 277/294).

His form master, although observant enough to express his concerns at Paul's choice of friends who 'occasionally lead him into trouble', did nothing to separate him from Steve. Paul's final end of term report card, although showing a marked improvement in attendance, 110/112, (which seeing as he himself admits to bunking off most afternoons with Steve and Wally meant he hung around for registration before absconding) showed that some of his grades had slipped alarmingly to 'C's and 'D's. Once again, his form teacher calls into question Paul's choice of friends, and his failure to work independently of these 'unfavourable influences'. The 'unfavourable influences' to which the teacher is referring are of course Steve, Wally and Stephen Hayes. All three were incorrigible truants, and would cajole the 'easily led' Paul into abandoning lessons for the day and heading down to the local shopping centre, where they would make nuisances of themselves by nicking anything that came to hand. Years later, whilst filming in the Brazilian hotspot Rio de Janeiro for the *Swindle* film project, Steve would confess to Great Train Robber Ronnie Biggs that his first thieving job had been nicking pens and pencils from Woolworths (like Don Jarvis, he had an aversion to rubbers!), which – unless he intended selling them to his fellow pupils – seems a strange choice of booty for someone with no academic leanings.

#

By the age of sixteen, Steve had fled the family home, and after a six month stint sleeping on the Hayes' sofa, he moved in with the Cooks on Carthew Road, taking over the bedroom of Paul's elder sister who'd recently got married. Like most teenagers, Steve and Paul were into the latest bands and fashions, and both were also keen concert goers. But as Steve had already developed an aversion to work, and Paul's meagre apprentice wage wouldn't stretch to purchasing tickets, they – accompanied as ever by Wally, Mackin and Hayes – would more often than not gain entry by sneaking through a side door or window. One such freebie came at the Faces' Empire Wembley Pool Arena show in October 1972, which, as we've already mentioned, also included the New York Dolls on the bill. According to Wally, they gained entrance to the venue by ripping a panel from a side door and, having enjoyed the musical fare, scurried backstage and got stuck into the free booze, while Ronnie Wood and Rod Stewart (who would shortly quit the Faces to embark on a solo career) watched on in bemusement. While it's more than likely that this tale could easily have been manufactured for anybody who cared to listen, what is true is that the reputation of this 'Famous Five' was quickly growing.

This, of course, was at the height of the UK Glam scene. Gary Glitter was the self-proclaimed leader of a gang which included 'Cat-suit Queen' Suzi Quatro and 'Bacofoil Bandits' Slade and Sweet, who were both near-perennial fixtures on the UK singles chart, regularly strutting their stack-heeled stuff on *Top Of The Pops*. Noddy and Co. came under fire over the intentional misspellings of some of their song titles such as 'Gudbuy T'Jane', 'Cum On Feel The Noize' and 'Mama Weer All Crazee Now'. However, no one thought to question Sweet's blond-banged frontman Brian Connolly and his hell-raising sidekick Andy Scott who regularly took to the *Top Of The Pops* stage bedecked in Iron Crosses and other Nazi regalia - a luxury which would not be afforded to the Sex Pistols or any other band associated with the nascent UK punk scene.

With the 'let's-start-a-band' seed firmly planted, the five fashion-conscious tearaways began dressing like their heroes. Each Saturday they would descend on the King's Road – usually in a car stolen courtesy of Steve – and hang out at, as well as steal from, shops such as Alkasura, Granny Takes A Trip and City Lights, where Rod Stewart, David Bowie, and the gang's favourite glamsters, Roxy Music, all had their flamboyant stage costumes made. Another King's Road haunt the gang regularly frequented was the newly-opened Too Fast To Live Too Young To Die, which had been on Steve's radar since its Let It Rock incarnation. Although they thought Malcolm something of a weirdo and a pervert, they knew they could while away their day listening to music and watching the world go by, without any fear of their being pressed into making a purchase. Steve, however, wasn't satisfied with simply looking like his musical heroes – he went one better by thieving from them as well. An expensive full-length fur coat came courtesy of a nocturnal visit to The Wick, in Richmond Hill, the 18th century house of cheeky Faces guitarist (and soon-to-be Rolling Stone) Ronnie Wood. Inveterate Stone's guitarist Keith

Richards' home in Chelsea's Cheyne Walk provided more stylish threads, and a state-of-the-art colour TV.

Of course, dressing and acting like rock stars, no matter how romantic, isn't quite the same as actually being one. If the boys were ever going to bring their fanciful dream to reality then they would need to procure the necessary instruments to accompany Wally's humble Les Paul copy and practice amp. There was little point in their perusing for the requisite instruments on London's famous musical thoroughfare Denmark Street – colloquially known as Tin Pan Alley – as the vendors there expected money to change hands before parting with the goods. So a cunning plan was hatched. The gang targeted local clubs which were in possession of a music license and laid in wait. Whilst the act which happened to be playing that night was inside introducing themselves to the owner, the boys simply helped themselves to the contents of their van.

These commando-style raids provided the fledgling band with a near-complete PA (Public Address system), an amplifier and a Fender bass guitar. Another daring raid on a rock star's home – this time Rod Stewart's Windsor mansion – provided two guitars, one of which was a genuine Les Paul. In order to keep the instruments in tune, a strobe stage tuner was acquired by way of a five-fingered discount courtesy of Roxy Music. Several components of a Premier drum kit were 'borrowed' from the BBC studio in Shepherd's Bush, and as Paul had been designated the embryonic outfit's drummer – and the only one with a regular income – he actually saved up for the remainder. Stephen Hayes was 'volunteered' to act as Paul's rhythmic partner in crime, and was handed the Fender bass; while Jimmy Mackin, having bought himself a Farfisa organ, would serve as keyboards player. Wally happily traded in his guitar for Rod Stewart's Les Paul, and Steve, fancying himself as something of a Bryan Ferry, elected to be the band's singer.

Having initially toyed with the idea of calling themselves Swankers, they instead decided upon the name the Strand, in homage to the Roxy Music song 'Do The Strand'; the opening track on the band's second album *For Your Pleasure*. The boys obtained a practice room at the Furniture Cave located at 533 King's Road – just a stone's throw from SEX – where they could begin rehearsing in earnest. With no songs to call their own, they were forced to play numbers they all knew, such as Rod Stewart's

'It's All Over Now', and the Small Faces classic 'All Or Nothing'. Things were finally moving, but within a few weeks Jimmy and Stephen – neither one having shown any real commitment to the band idea – left to seek alternative means of entertainment. Steve, Paul and Wally, however, were determined to carry on, and having decided to dispense with keyboards, brought in Paul's brother-in-law, Del Noone, to take over on bass. The four-piece settled into a routine and knuckled down to master their respective instruments. Although they already had more than enough gear to suit their needs, the thrill of thieving from other bands had taken hold of Steve and Wally, and in July 1973 the duo engineered their greatest – and most daring – feat to date.

David Bowie was currently wowing UK audiences on a sell-out tour. The final night – which was also being filmed by D. A. Pennebaker for future cinematic release – was to be staged at the Hammersmith Odeon. Gaining entrance to the venue proved no problem as the Odeon was practically in their backyard and, having found a suitable hidey-hole, they waited until the hapless security guard had dozed off, before taking to the stage each armed with a pair of pliers. They relieved Bowie of his entire backline PA, which owing to the singer's record company, RCA, having agreed to fund Pennebaker's film, included several Neumann microphones costing around £500 each (and that was at 1973 prices!). The valuable haul was ferried back to their rehearsal room on the King's Road in a minivan which Steve had nicked the previous evening.

Despite having enough musical accessories to restage the Isle of Wight festival, as well as a new Covent Garden rehearsal space courtesy of Malcolm – who naively believed getting Steve to channel his energies into the band would stop him from thieving from his shop – things didn't appear to be progressing on the music front. Steve had even managed to persuade Malcolm to come along and check them out, but Del's lack of commitment had seriously restricted rehearsal time, and the showcase rapidly descended into chaos. Wally could hold down the riffs well enough, but his Rod Stewart feather-cut and National Health jam-jar glasses gave him the look of a postman; while Steve, despite his best efforts to emulate Rod the Mod, was incapable of carrying the tune. Paul was in a constant struggle to find, let alone keep, the beat, and was getting little help from his brother-in-law who would have much preferred to be at home 'plucking' the wife!

Satellite *book launch. Glen Matlock and Kevin Rowland*

There was, however, something about the cacophonic chaos that appealed to Malcolm's non-pop sensibilities, and there was something captivating about Steve's stage presence. He was no Billy Fury, that was for sure, but he possessed that certain something which grabbed your attention. To Malcolm's mind Steve was the key, but not as a singer. He would also have to do something about Wally, but that could wait for a later day as there was the more immediate matter of Paul's totally disinterested brother-in-law. It was then that he remembered that the fresh-faced art student, Glen Matlock, who worked as the Saturday lad at the shop, had mentioned something about learning to play the bass. Glen was already aware of Steve, Paul and Wally, mainly due to Malcolm's instruction for him to keep a watchful eye on Steve – especially his hands! Also, he and Wally had been press-ganged into providing most of the muscle during the shop's revamping. Although Malcolm wasn't sure whether a clean cut introvert like Glen would fit in with the three rowdy Wormholt reprobates, he decided to bring them together. His chance came later that same month when, upon discovering Glen was a fan of Thin Lizzy, he invited him to see the Irish rockers performing at the Marquee, where he was sure they'd bump into Steve, Paul and Wally.

\#

Glen Matlock was born on 27th August 1956 in Kensal Rise, North West London, the only son of a coach builder and a Gas Board accounts clerk. Despite subsequent claims to the contrary from John Lydon, Glen's formative years weren't spent in a cocoon of suburban bliss. Indeed, until he was 14, when Glen's dad was able to purchase the whole house, he and his parents shared the Victorian two-up-two-down (at 18 Ravensworth Road, situated close to Kensal Rise cemetery) with an unruly Irish family. There were incessant territorial disputes over which family held domain over the squalid rear garden, which Glen himself later described as a 15 square-foot litter tray. He attended Princess Frederica Primary School, and unlike Steve, Paul or Wally, passed his 11-plus. This allowed him to go to the all-boys St Clement Danes Grammar School where he proved a solid, if somewhat shy, student. The shyness came from his being an only child, and with most of his grammar school friends living out in Greenford and Ealing – his childhood playmates having ostracised him for having the audacity to pass his 11-plus – he sought solace in music, and began teaching himself to play guitar.

Glen's parents harboured ambitions that their son would go on to university and be the first male member of the Matlock family to earn a living without getting his hands dirty. Although Glen diligently sat both his 'O' and 'A' levels, he had no interest in pursuing an academic life. He also had an equally strong aversion to working a regular 9-5 day job, and a compromise was reached which saw him apply to – and be accepted by – St Martins School of Art. This, however, wasn't due to any particular interest in art, but due to his having read that many a musician –particularly John Lennon, Ray Davies and Keith Richards – had enrolled at art school to while away the day before embarking on their respective musical paths.

It was whilst he was in his final year at St Clement Danes that he first began working at 430 King's Road. Like most boys his age, Glen took a part-time job to supplement his pocket money and provide life's little luxuries. His first brush with casual employment came at Whiteleys department store, the large Victorian white edifice situated on Queensway in Bayswater, where, for a few hours after school on Thursday evening and all day on Saturday, he received the princely sum of 36 shillings or £1.86 following decimalisation in 1971. His tenure at Whiteleys came to an abrupt end one fateful Saturday, when sleep deprivation – owing to his having been at an all-night concert at the Lyceum Ballroom – resulted in a cock-up in the cashier's office. Rather than hang around and wait until the manager figured out who was to blame he abandoned his post and went in search of a less stressful pay packet.

He was also on the lookout for a pair of brothel creepers as worn by the Teddy Boys frequenting the King's Road and Ronnie Lane of the Faces, his current musical hero. Following a fruitless search of the stalls on Beaufort Street Market, Glen followed his nose up the King's Road towards World's End, and the shop which would satisfy both his needs, and irrevocably alter his career path. Upon entering Let It Rock, Glen could have been forgiven for thinking he'd done a Mr Benn and stepped through a time portal back to the golden age of rock 'n' roll. Aside from the brothel creepers on display in the window, he was also captivated by the attention to detail which had gone into recreating an authentic mid-fifties sitting room. He just knew he had to get involved somehow and while the guy behind the counter (most likely Michael Collins who managed the shop from 1972-1982), wrapped up the footwear, Glen enquired as to whether the shop required any extra help. His luck was in that day, as not only did he procure his coveted creepers, he also landed a job which came with a substantial pay rise [£3.50] for working a Saturday only. He even got a lie-in as he wasn't required until 11 a.m.

#

Glen's audition was held in Wally's bedroom the afternoon following the Thin Lizzy gig. Despite having wowed his prospective band mátes by nailing the intricate bass line from the Faces' song 'Three Button Hand Me Down', his postal code and grammar school background proved something of a sticking point as far as the others were concerned; they felt he was too pure to be a 'Swanker'. Steve was also concerned that Glen would baulk at joining a band that had stolen most of its gear and might even skulk off to inform the proper authorities. So they decided to test the mummy's boy's mettle by subjecting him to a surreptitious 'bottle' test. Steve had recently had it away with a bass guitar from Macari's on Shaftesbury Avenue, which he'd stolen simply to impress his latest squeeze and gain access to the girl's knickers. He nonchalantly gave it to Glen with instructions to get a good price for it at one of the music shops on Tin Pan Alley.

Unfortunately for Glen, the wily shopkeeper smelt a rat and kept him waiting long enough for the police to arrive. To add humiliation to his red-faced shame, his arrest came in full view of his fellow St Martins students, who were lined up across the street to wave him off to West End Central police station. Instead of grassing Steve up, however, Glen told the station sergeant that he'd bought the guitar in good faith from a bloke in the Roebuck Pub on the King's Road, even giving the gullible desk sergeant a description of the non-existent spiv. Selling stolen goods, although not as serious as stealing said items, was still a crime in the eyes of the law, but Glen's previous good character saw him get off with a slapped wrist. The band had found its new bassist.

About this time, the three-month lease on their Covent Garden rehearsal space expired, but once again Providence lent a hand. Wally's dad was a self-employed electrician and had recently secured the contract to work on the old BBC Riverside Studios in Crisp Road, Hammersmith (which today is a television studio and was at one time home to Chris Evans' *TFI Friday*). Wally's dad's task was to rip out and replace the old wiring which would take several months. Upon hearing of his son's dilemma, he had an extra set of keys cut and the boys moved their gear into the studio's defunct acoustic room, which happened to be one of the best in Europe.

With free rein, albeit a temporary one, over the facilities, and a makeshift bar courtesy of Paul having raided the Watney's storeroom, the boys began rehearsing in earnest. They were steadily building up a repertoire containing '60s classics such as the Who's 'Call Me Lightning', the Small Faces' 'Understanding', the Rolling Stones' 'It's All Over Now', and the Love Affair's 'A Day Without Love'. Their most bizarre choice of cover though, given their future notoriety, was 'Build Me Up Buttercup' by the Foundations, which they renamed 'Proctor & Gamble' after the pharmaceutical company of the same name who made Buttercup infant cough syrup.

It was whilst the boys were rehearsing at the BBC studio in Hammersmith that they fleetingly became a five-piece, when Malcolm brought in Nick Kent as a second guitarist to bolster the band's sound and credibility. Although Kent's arrival saw the boys stretch their eclectic repertoire to include songs like Ronnie Wood's 'I Can feel The Fire' and 'Slow Death' by the American outfit, Flamin' Groovies, Steve and the others never actually considered him anything other than what he was: a druggie mate of Malcolm's who came along now and again to hang out and jam. Kent may have been a leading light at the *NME*, but he definitely wasn't a Swanker, and neither was he Strand material. He was four years older than the others for a start, had gone to university for heaven's sake, and his conservative middle-class upbringing also set him at odds with their working class ethos. The elegantly wasted journalist's three month association with the band came to an abrupt end and Kent was sent packing back to his *NME* office on Carnaby Street. Little could he have realised, that within three years the seemingly directionless band would have evolved into a musical and cultural phenomenon; or that his name would become intrinsically linked with the Sex Pistols courtesy of an unprovoked assault on him at the band's 100 Club gig on 29th June 1976 by Sid (who as a result of his bike-chain wielding antics would earn his celebrity sobriquet 'Sid Vicious').

The culling of guitarists wouldn't end with Kent's departure, however. Malcolm returned to London in the summer of 1975, following an ill-conceived attempt to resuscitate the New York Dolls' ailing career by dressing the band in red patent-leather outfits and have them play in front of a Hammer & Sickle backdrop. His first undertaking was to persuade Steve to abandon the microphone in favour of taking up the guitar and thus rendering Wally's six-stringed services obsolete. The fact that Steve would have had difficulty spelling the word 'guitar', let alone picking out a tune on the instrument, was irrelevant as far as Malcolm was

Japanese 'Silly Thing' *sleeve*

concerned, however. For he had glimpsed the future of rock 'n' roll within a shit-and-spit Bowery bar called CBGB's, where raw and exciting new bands such as Talking Heads, The Ramones and Television were playing simplistic two-to-three minute songs to ecstatic audiences every night.

By this time the boys had made their 'live' debut by playing three songs for a friend's party at a flat above Tom Salter's Café at 205 King's Road. Today, Glen claims to remember very little about the performance other than they definitely did 'Scarface' and that it was a great party. And isn't it strange, given that this was the equivalent of seeing the Quarrymen or Little Boy Blue and the Blue Boys – the bands that begat the Beatles and the Rolling Stones – at close quarters, yet no one has ever come forward to 'swear they were there'?

#

During Malcolm's latest trip to America, the Dolls had imploded in a Tampa trailer park during their lowbrow tour of the Southern states, when Thunders and Nolan quit the group. Malcolm and Sylvain had been left stranded with nothing to their name other than a few hundred dollars and a battered station wagon. En route back to New York they stopped off at New Orleans taking in the sights and pondering the possibility of recruiting some of the blues musicians, strumming for their supper along Beale Street, for a new Sylvain-fronted band. On returning to New York, Malcolm soon forgot all about bringing the Big Easy to the Big Apple, upon witnessing what was going down on the Bowery: waif-like kids in cheap clothes, playing second-rate instruments, and with little or no obvious musical talent, were tearing the place up. As far as Malcolm was concerned, it was their collective lack of musical proficiency which made the scene all the more exciting.

Attitude had seemingly replaced aptitude. Fleetwood Mac and the Eagles may have been packing them in at Madison Square Garden, but the Bowery bands were living proof that rock 'n' roll was finally being returned to the streets where it truly belonged. And although each Bowery band had their own inimitable style, be it Talking Heads' syncopated beats or the Ramones' cartoonish image, one kid in particular caught Malcolm's sartorial interest: Television's Rimbaud-esque bassist, Richard Meyers. Meyers had arrived in New York several years earlier with aspirations of becoming a poet and had adopted the *nom de plume* Richard Hell. Malcolm saw him taking to CBGBs' postage stamp-sized stage with his dishevelled hair sticking out at all angles and safety pins holding his torn clothes together, looking for all the world like the prototype punk he was.

John Lydon would no doubt caustically contest the notion that he borrowed Hell's look for his own punk persona Johnny Rotten. Although John was certainly cutting a dash on the King's Road circa June/July 1975, Hell can call upon photographs taken some twelve months earlier proving he was strutting his safety pinned stuff, while John was still sporting shoulder length Hawkwind-esque tresses.

Malcolm had returned to London bursting with excitement and safe in the knowledge that he had six months before England got hip to what was happening across the pond. He'd tried to persuade Hell to accompany him back to London to front Steve's band, but when the poet declined in favour of remaining in New

York to fulfil his artistic yearnings, Malcolm then began courting Sylvain. The ex-Doll had initially consented to the proposal, and even gave Malcolm his cherished white Gibson Les Paul as proof of his commitment. But when Sylvain also shied off, Malcolm simply moved on to option C, which saw him undermine Wally's position in the group by giving Sylvain's guitar to Steve, along with the ultimatum that he had three months to familiarise himself with the instrument. Once Wally had been extricated from the line-up, he then truncated the fledgling outfit's name by dropping the risible 'Kutie Jones' prefix, and told everyone to keep their eyes peeled for a suitable candidate to front the Sex Pistols.

CHAPTER FOUR

The Boys Looked At Johnny

'I don't know anything about music.
In my line you don't have to.'
Elvis Presley (1935-1977)

Sex Pistols: Day By Day author Lee Wood believed 23rd August 1975 to be the day Glen approached John Lydon in SEX with a view to the latter trying out as singer with the Sex Pistols. Although there is no documented evidence to either support or oppose Lee's assertion, we believe the actual date was Saturday 16th, this being the opening day of the 1975-76 football season and John's beloved Arsenal were up in Lancashire playing out a goalless draw at Burnley. Otherwise he and his friends – all of whom also happened to be called John – would surely have been tearing it up on Highbury's North Bank cheering on their heroes instead of hanging about the World's End.

Malcolm was already aware of the Richard Hell-esque Lydon and his green spiky hair, thanks to Bernie having spotted John and his chums making a nuisance of themselves on the King's Road several days earlier. Although John's hair would have been sufficient to stop the traffic in mid-seventies London, it was his customised Pink Floyd T-shirt – with the words 'I HATE' scrawled above the Prog Rock outfit's logo – which had caught Bernie's eye. Bernie had been too unnerved to make an approach, but thanks to Vivienne, who'd also recently encountered the lad in question, he now had a name, and Bernie told Steve, Paul and Glen to be on the lookout for a kid called 'Spiky John'.

Once again we are obliged to forage for 'ifs' and 'ands' and threaten another poor tinker's bank balance, because the 'Spiky John' Vivienne was referring to was none other than John

Beverley, who would no doubt have been present in SEX that fateful afternoon if he hadn't been otherwise engaged manning a stall on Portobello Market. *And* although John Beverley, or 'Sid' as he was known within the 'Johns' fraternity, was a striking and charismatic individual who stood out from the crowd, Fate had decreed it wasn't yet his time to step into the spotlight. *And* without Lydon's alter ego 'Johnny Rotten', there wouldn't have been a spotlight for him to step into. *But* if Malcolm had chosen Sid above John, then the Sex Pistols – regardless of Glen's talents as a tunesmith and Malcolm's entrepreneurial skills – probably wouldn't have progressed beyond gigging on London's college circuit, and they certainly wouldn't have secured a contract with EMI. *Which* in turn led to the band's infamous tea-time TV spat with Bill Grundy that set them on the road to infamy. *And* if Jim 'Midge' Ure, whom Malcolm and Bernie encountered in a Glasgow music shop whilst trying to offload some of the band's surplus equipment, hadn't been on the verge of pop success with his band Slik who scored a No. 1 UK hit with 'Forever And Ever' in February 1976 then … well, you get the picture …

John Joseph Lydon was born on 31st January 1956, the first of four sons to John and Eileen Lydon, who, shortly after tying the knot – and accompanied by their own parents – arrived in London in search of work. John Sr was something of a 'Jack of all trades' having tried his hand as a car mechanic, lorry driver, cabbie and crane operator. Shortly after arriving in London from Galway, he got a job working for William Press & Company on the North Sea oil rigs, which meant he spent long periods away from his family. After several years of living a nomadic existence in and around London, as well as in southern seaside towns such as Eastbourne and Hastings – during which time John contracted spinal meningitis which left him with a slight stoop and impaired eyesight – the Lydons returned to London, setting up home on the Holloway Road before eventually moving into a council flat in Pooles Park, Finsbury Park.

John lost a year of lessons whilst at Eden Park primary school because of the meningitis, which almost claimed him. Not surprisingly therefore he failed his 11-plus, and he went to William of York Catholic comprehensive school (which has since amalgamated with Aloysius College). It was here – or so he later told Jon Savage in *England's Dreaming* – that pupils were brainwashed into accepting that when they died they'd spend eternity roasting in hellfire unless they were willing to 'believe in the lightning rod of Jesus Christ Almighty and the sanctity of his virgin mother'.

By his own admission, John was a belligerent pupil and purposely went out of his way to antagonise his teachers by openly questioning their teaching methods. He'd also had enough of being force-fed religious dogma and refused to attend the school's mandatory morning masses. This carefree attitude towards authority no doubt made him popular amongst his peers, but those in control don't like to be made to look foolish, especially by those entrusted into their care, and John was expelled. His parents went to the school and pleaded with the headmaster to reconsider his decision, but it seemed the William of York faculty had long since tired of John's disruptive attitude – not to mention his non-regulation shoulder-length hair and failure to adhere to school uniform – and the expulsion ruling was upheld. He was forced to undertake his fifth and final year of secondary schooling at Stoke Newington College of Further Education, before being begrudgingly allowed back to William of York to sit, and pass, his 'O' level exams.

One might have thought his experiences at William of York would have been enough to put John off academia, but after spending the summer of 1972 drifting from one dead-end job to the next, mostly as a labourer on local building sites, he enrolled at Hackney Technical College to add to the two 'O' levels he'd already accrued. It was at Hackney that he met and befriended Simon John Beverley, who was also known as John. A love of music – mainly Bowie and Roxy Music – brought the two Johns together and the pair soon became inseparable; a bonding which proved both confusing and problematic to their mutual friends. The confusion was thankfully resolved by the Lydon family's toothless pet hamster, named 'Sid' in homage of Pink Floyd's lysergic sugar-lump munching erstwhile frontman Syd Barrett. The little rodent supposedly 'attacked' John Beverley during a visit to the Lydon abode in Finsbury Park, inadvertently bestowing his monosyllabic moniker on his hapless victim.

In September 1974, John, slavishly accompanied by the newly-christened 'Sid', enrolled at Kingsway College, a further education institution in King's Cross catering for day-release apprentices and errant kids belatedly sitting their 'O' levels. It was here that John encountered another future rock 'n' roll confederate, the roguish East Ender John Wardle, who'd been obliged to enrol at

Kingsway following his recent expulsion from the London Nautical School. Wardle was warmly welcomed into the 'Johns' clique and duly rechristened Jah Wobble; the name he still trades under to this day. A name which came about because it was the closest a drunken Sid ever came to pronouncing John Wardle – a fact brought to light by Wobble himself in his 2009 biography. It was also whilst he was at Kingsway that John became ever more fashion conscious and began experimenting with his style of dress. 'We used to go to stores out Ilford way,' Wobble told Jon Savage for *England's Dreaming*. 'John had his long hair, a black tux and baggies, but one day he turned up with dyed, shaved hair and saying that he'd found his new way of life.'

John's new-found 'proto-punk' way of life, which came sometime during the summer of 1975, would result in his being cast out of the family home for having hacked off his hippy hairstyle. So, he set about bleaching and colouring what remained. Unfortunately for him though, the blue dye he'd chosen was actually a clothes dye and its chemicals reacted with the bleach turning his hair a vile green colour. Getting himself expelled from school was one thing, but strutting about like a spring cabbage was a step beyond the pale, as far as his dad was concerned, and John was shown the door. He could, of course, have easily thrown himself at his father's feet and pleaded mercy, but he accepted the patriarchal decision with good grace and went to live with Sid in a Hampstead squat. By this time, the three 'Johns' were taking regular trips to the King's Road, making nuisances of themselves by gobbing at the passers-by, as well as trying out the latest fashions. They would invariably end up at the World's End and SEX.

#

John had no ambitions to join a band, let alone to become its singer and, if asked, would probably have likened his singing voice to an out of tune violin. However, Glen's offer for him to come along and meet up with Malcolm and the rest of the band at the nearby Roebuck pub later that evening was an invite he simply couldn't turn down. With his old school friend John Grey (who by default was co-founder of the 'Johns') acting as moral support, John duly arrived at the Roebuck at the appointed hour. Glen, having arranged the meet, did his utmost to make the new arrivals feel welcome. Steve was less accommodating though, taking an instant dislike to John and mistaking his shyness for attitude. John was understandably nervous, and his curt noncommittal responses to Malcolm's probing did little to assuage Steve's mood. He did, however, agree to Malcolm's proposal to accompany them back to the shop for an impromptu audition. The band's gear was set up at their latest rehearsal space above The Crunchy Frog pub in Rotherhithe, South East London, so Malcolm improvised by getting John to sing along to the jukebox. The song chosen was Alice Cooper's 'I'm Eighteen', from the American shock-rocker's 1971 Platinum-selling album *Love It To Death*. In the absence of a microphone John sang into a plastic showerhead.

His spastic mewlings may have left Steve unimpressed, but Glen and Paul were willing to look beyond John's limited vocal talents and knew they'd found their talismanic frontman. They invited John to a full rehearsal, but it never took place as Steve, having had the chance to work on Glen and Paul away from Malcolm's prying eyes, had convinced them John was a cunt and that he probably wouldn't show up anyway. But John, with John Grey once again in support, did show up, and suffice to say he was not best pleased at having schlepped across London on a fool's errand. 'I felt stupid walking round Bermondsey Wharf,' he later recounted. 'It's dangerous down there, particularly the way I looked at the time.'

It was left to Glen to call and apologise, as well as to bear the brunt of John's homicidal wrath. He managed though to get John to agree to a second rehearsal, this time at a newer and much closer space above The Rose & Crown pub in Wandsworth. Their tenure at the pub proved short-lived, however, as the landlord was simply looking for a means to supplement his bar takings and hadn't bothered with any soundproofing. One guitar stroke was enough to send the pool balls vibrating across the table. The band went to check out several other potential rehearsal spaces above pubs, or in community centres and warehouses, but none of them proved suitable for one reason or another. The band had their singer, but there was nowhere for them to play and John's interest was beginning to wane.

It was then that Malcolm finally made a firm commitment to the band by guaranteeing the £1,000 deposit on a rehearsal space located to the rear of Denmark Street in the heart of Tin Pan Alley. The two storey space was owned by Bill Collins, the father of actor Lewis Collins of *The Professionals* fame. It consisted of an upstairs attic and a soundproofed rehearsal room situated to the rear of

No. 6 Denmark Street, and was only accessible from the street via a narrow, dank Dickensian passageway. The premises also boasted a rat-infested cellar, but while John had once worked as a rat-catcher, he and the rest of the band purposely steered clear of the cellar and its disease-carrying inhabitants.

Collins Sr had been involved in the music business since the mid-60s serving as a roadie for the Beatles. He stepped up into pop management with the Mojos and later Badfinger, whose song 'Without You', from the band's 1970 album *No Dice*, became a massive hit for Harry Nilsson in 1972 and Mariah Carey in 1993. Badfinger had once been hailed as heirs to the Beatles' crown but the band's ill-fated career was blighted by mismanagement and lawsuits, tragically culminating in lead singer Pete Ham hanging himself in his garage studio in April 1975, which was how the rehearsal room came to be available. Incidentally, the Badfinger story had another tragic episode with Ham's songwriting partner Tom Evans also committing suicide in 1983.

The ground-floor room, although fully soundproofed, was both dark and dingy and the stench from the clogged-up outside lavatory had permeated the cork soundproofing. No matter, as the boys were simply happy to have a permanent rehearsal place, especially Steve and Glen who commandeered the attic space as their ad hoc bachelor pad. Sometime later, to alleviate the boredom one afternoon, John set about the upstairs walls with a magic marker pen drawing caricatures of Steve, Sid and Nancy, whom he named Fatty Jones, Ego Sloshus, and Nancy Spunger respectively. There is also a telling one of Malcolm showing him clutching a swag bag full of pound notes! And, as can be seen in the Sex Pistols' *Knowledge of London* DVD extra, the subsequent – and current – tenants have respected this light-hearted historical legacy, and the caricatures have survived to the present day.

Within weeks of their moving into the new HQ, however, Paul dropped a bombshell by announcing he was quitting the band. The drummer cited Steve's rudimentary guitar style as the reason for his decision, but Glen believes Paul was using his mate's supposed lack of talent to stall for time. He was about to sit his City & Guilds electricians exam and wanted to get the qualification under his belt in case the group imploded. With the benefit of hindsight, Glen's claim certainly holds water for he himself thought Steve, thanks to the stimulating aid of uppers commonly known as 'Black Bombers', was actually improving with each rehearsal. Malcolm managed to placate Paul by agreeing to bring in another guitarist to supplement Steve's playing, but their search – with the exception of Steve New, who at only 15 years old was considered too new – ultimately came to nought. Funnily enough, the drummer – having sat and passed his exam – remained at his post.

The ad Malcolm placed in the 'musicians wanted' section of *Melody Maker* on 27th September, requested the services of a 'whizz-kid guitarist no older than 20 and no worse looking than Johnny Thunders'. Despite not hiring anybody from the advert, it wasn't a total waste of time and money, however, as it did at least bring like-minded individuals, such as art student Mick Jones and Brunel University maths graduate Tony James into the band's orbit. Jones and James were both keen New York Dolls aficionados and naively believed they were the only ones in London hip to the American band. The two were trying to put their own outfit together, the now-legendary London SS, and were fruitlessly auditioning vocalists and drummers within their shabby basement rehearsal space beneath the Paddington Kitchen café at 113-115 Praed Street. They couldn't believe their eyes when they spotted the Pistols' ad which name-checked their idol Johnny Thunders. Through their hooking up with Bernie – who by this time had cut his losses and severed all ties with Malcolm over the latter's failure to offer him an equal partnership in the Sex Pistols – they would pay a visit to Denmark Street. Indeed, this so-called meeting of minds led to Mick, who stuck around to jam with Steve, Paul and Glen, being considered for the role as second guitarist in the Sex Pistols. However, nothing came of this as no one was quite sure where Mick lived!

Now that the band finally had a place to call their own, they knuckled down and got on with writing new songs so they could get out and make a name for themselves on the live circuit. 'Scarface', their one and only original song to date, was reworked around John's new lyric entitled 'Did You No Wrong'. Another of John's offerings was 'Only Seventeen' (later truncated to 'Seventeen'). Glen came up with 'Pretty Vacant', which had been inspired in part by a flyer Malcolm had brought back with him from New York advertising a show by the band Television at CBGBs. The flyer featured several of the band's song titles, one of which was Richard Hell's 'I Belong To The Blank Generation'. Another early Glen composition was 'Go Now', but the saccharine-sweet ditty was quickly shelved owing to John's refusal to sing it. The band supplemented their meagre set with suitable covers such as 'Psychotic Reaction' by Count Five, 'Through My Eyes' by the Creation, 'Substitute' by the Who, 'Steppin' Stone' by the Monkees, 'No Lip' by Dave Berry, and 'Whatcha Gonna Do About It' by the Small Faces, which John twisted to suit his own needs: 'I want you to know that I *hate* you baby/I want you to know I *don't* care'.

It was during these early Denmark Street rehearsals that Steve endeared himself to his band mates by attempting to force-feed Glen a chopped liver and hot water sandwich, which he'd first used as a makeshift vagina (though this story has actually been denied by all the band members). It was during these times as well that the rechristening of their acerbic front man to 'Johnny Rotten' took place, on account of John constantly coughing up mucus and phlegm – a leftover from his childhood bout of meningitis – and his woefully neglected 'dog-end' molars. The name stuck, much to John's chagrin, and little could Steve have imagined that his cutting remark about John's indifference to dental hygiene would give rise to one of rock music's most iconic names. Twelve months on, Fleet Street would also inadvertently owe Steve a debt of gratitude as 'Johnny Lydon: King of the Punks' doesn't have the same ring to it as 'Johnny Rotten'.

Given that his hero was Larry Parnes, it is surprising that Malcolm didn't think to emulate the Tin Pan Alley impresario by conjuring up a more rock 'n' roll name for John Lydon. Parnes' roster, which boasted teen heartthrobs Billy Fury (Ronald Wycherley), Marty Wilde (Reginald Smith), Vince Eager (Roy Taylor), Dickie Pride (Richard Knellar) and Johnny Gentle (John Askew) were all given rock 'n' roll monikers. However, Joe Brown, whom Parnes wanted to rename Elmer Twitch, understandably stood his ground and argued that if 'Joe Brown' was good enough for the man in the street then it was good enough for him. He had a point, after all Elvis Presley, the king of rock 'n' roll, ascended to the throne with the name he'd been born with.

#

The Sex Pistols made their live debut in a tiny nondescript upstairs room at St Martins School of Art on Charing Cross Road on Thursday 6th November 1975. They were supporting a rock 'n' roll revivalist act called Bazooka Joe, who'd taken their name from the eye-patched hero of the Bazooka bubblegum comic strip. Incidentally, on the 6th November 2005 we were both in attendance at St Martins to watch Glen unveil a blue plaque commemorating the 30th anniversary of the event. By this time, Malcolm and Vivienne's relationship had hit a new low and, following a series of heated and seemingly never-ending rows, Malcolm collected his things and moved out of Nightingale Lane to take up residence with Helen Wellington-Lloyd at her one bedroom flat at 93 Bell Street, just off the Edgware Road in Marylebone. This address would now be name-checked on business cards as the home of Glitterbest Management, even though the actual entity of Glitterbest Management didn't yet exist.

Unlike some of the band's later live escapades, such as the El Paradise Strip Club London show of 4th April 1976, the first Manchester Lesser Free Trade Hall show (4th June 1976), the 'Midnight Special' at the Screen On The Green (29th August 1976) or the 100 Club Punk Festival (20/21st September 1976), no one from Joe Public 'swears they were there' to witness the Sex Pistols' shambolic debut; primarily because no one outside the band's immediate circle and the SEX staffers knew the Sex Pistols even existed. One who can definitely lay claim to being in attendance that evening, however, is Stuart Goddard, who was the bassist in the headline band. He would reinvent himself as Adam Ant, of course.

He remembers being struck by the Sex Pistols' 'gang mentality' and their distinctive dress sense, which was certainly unique for late 1975 London. He was also impressed by Rotten's 'don't give a fuck attitude', as well as the band's short three-minute songs being devoid of fancy fills or guitar solos. As we all know, someone within the Bazooka Joe camp brought the show to an uncharitable halt by pulling the plug on the Pistols after just five songs, which led to an altercation of sorts, owing to John calling the headliners a 'bunch of fucking cunts'. Although the rest of Bazooka Joe dismissed the Sex Pistols as half-arsed amateurs, the future Mr Ant was savvy enough to recognise a change was in the air, and quit the group the following day to form his own band.

#

There are those who would have you believe that the Sex Pistols burst onto the mid-seventies staid British music scene like a biblical flash flood and swept away everything before them. This, of course, wasn't the case, as some thirteen months of hard graft would pass between the band's St Martins debut and their prime-time

TV spat with Bill Grundy which propelled them into the national conscience. Each of their early shows – which were predominantly on London's college and university circuit – served to polarise the audience. Whilst the majority of the students present would shake their heads in disgust and either head for the bar or the exit, the more open-minded, who were looking for excitement rather than exactitude, were instantly converted to the cause.

Ever so slowly, the Sex Pistols began to accrue a colourful and eclectic following which became known as the 'Bromley Contingent'. It was either Vivienne, or *Melody Maker's* punk aficionado Caroline Coon, who inadvertently gave rise to the legend by supplying the appellation to the suburban crew consisting of Simon Barker, Susan 'Candy Sue' Ballion (Siouxsie Sioux), Steven Bailey (Steve Severin), Bill Broad (Billy Idol), Debbie 'Juvenile' Wilson, Simone Thomas and Bertie 'Berlin' Marshall. Most of these were habitués of the World's End and SEX by the time they became aware of the Sex Pistols.

It is fair to say that the low-key college dates the band undertook during the winter of 1975-76 would have been bereft of an audience had it not been for Candy Sue Ballion and her *Cabaret*-obsessed posse. *Cabaret,* the 1972 film directed by Bob Fosse, starred Liza Minnelli as Sally Bowles, a female girlie club entertainer in Weimar Republic-era Berlin, who seduced a young Englishman abroad (Michael York) while Hitler's Nazi Party rose to power around them. Indeed, the Bromley Contingent could have been forgiven for thinking of the Sex Pistols as their personal in-house entertainment. But, as the girls who frequented The Cavern Club in Liverpool during the early Sixties will gladly tell you, nothing stays secret for ever …

On 12th February 1976, the Sex Pistols got an unexpected break by opening for current music-media darlings Eddie & the Hot Rods at the Marquee Club on Wardour Street. The support slot was viewed as a means of paving the way to their getting a shot at headlining, but an altercation with the Hot Rods management – this time over John's mistreatment of the Rods' PA – led to their being banned from the prestigious Soho venue; the first of several such expulsions the band would accrue in London during 1976. The 'break' therefore came not from their performance, as electrifying as it was, but rather due to Steve capturing the attention of NME staffer Neil Spencer, with his now-legendary 'We're not into music, we're into chaos' comment. The banner headline to Spencer's subsequent *NME* review, which made no mention whatsoever of the Hot Rods, was the first to give notice that things were never going to be the same again: **DON'T LOOK OVER YOUR SHOULDER BUT THE SEX PISTOLS ARE COMING**.

It was at the Marquee show that the band's road manager Nils Stevenson (unsurprisingly no one ever called him by his actual Christian name, Rolf) was first introduced to the Sex Pistols live experience. He'd already met Steve and Paul at the Roebuck, and although he'd found the roguish pair likeable enough, he couldn't understand why Malcolm was putting so much faith into their band. He was instantly hooked, however, by Rotten's galvanising stage presence.

Nils hailed from Dalston, in East London and, like Malcolm, had turned his back on art school. After a short stint working for *Observer* ballet critic Richard Buckle, Nils was running a stall on Beaufort Street Market. He already knew Malcolm and Vivienne on a social level as the three of them – usually with Nick Kent's ex-girlfriend and future Pretenders star Chrissie Hynde – would go to the parties of sculptor and socialite Andrew Logan in his Shad Thames studio at Butler's Wharf. An additional benefit of bringing Nils on board was that his older brother Ray, a renowned rock photographer who'd served his apprenticeship on the mid-sixties folk scene snapping the likes of David Bowie and Marc Bolan, came out of his self-imposed exile as a mini-cab driver, and was willing to provide his camera services free of charge. Ray's first assignment with the Sex Pistols came five days after the Marquee show at St Albans College of Art & Design on 19th February. Over the course of the next 18 months he took hundreds of photographs of the band, many of which appeared firstly in his self-published *Sex Pistols Scrap Book*, and then later in the *Sex Pistols File* (Omnibus Press).

On 14th February, with Neil Spencer once again in attendance, the Sex Pistols caused another rumpus, this time at Andrew Logan's Valentine's Ball held at his rented studio. Logan, who founded the Alternative Miss World contest in 1972 (an event he is still actively involved in), was well known on London's fashion scene, and earlier that month had encountered Malcolm and Vivienne at the ICA (Institute of Contemporary Arts), which was staging a week-long Fashion Forum for new designers. He naively allowed the conniving pair to convince him that his forthcoming ball wouldn't be complete without a performance by the Sex Pistols. Promoting one's charges is of course part and parcel of a manager's role, but Malcolm had another, less altruistic, agenda. It had been he who'd invited Spencer, along with everyone else he knew in London, and – having ensured that all four band members were decked out in SEX T-shirts – he was determined to give the journalist something to write about.

When the time came for the band to take to the makeshift stage, which comprised of the set from the court scene of director Derek Jarman's debut feature film *Sebastiane*, and a castle Logan had purchased from the children's department of the recently shut down Biba store, John was nowhere to be found. Malcolm had purposely given instructions to keep the singer left outside in the cold until long after Steve, Paul and Glen had taken to the stage as he knew John had done drugs and the results could prove interesting for Jarman, who was on hand to film the proceedings on his hand-held Super 8 camera.

Snippets of the band's performance can be seen in *The Great Rock 'n' Roll Swindle*. John was off his head on a combination of speed and acid, and when Vivienne finally opened the door to allow him in, he smacked her one in the eye before heading in search of another drink. Logan's studio had a corrugated-metal roof like an aircraft hanger, and the sound came bouncing off it, with the reverberations sending many of the sculptor's prized works crashing to the floor. Malcolm pushed Jordan towards the stage and told her to start stripping. Jordan initially refused to go along with the scam, but relented and leapt up on stage beside John who ripped her top off, giving everyone in the room an eyeful of her pendulous breasts. Not surprisingly Spencer reached for his camera, and the resulting photo also found its way into the *NME*. Britain may have been slowly sinking under a mountain of debt with bankruptcies rising by a staggering 110 percent on 1973's figures, but the Sex Pistols were on the rise.

#

Brian Southall, in his informative and highly enjoyable book *Sex Pistols: 90 Days at EMI* (Bobcat Books), freely admits to having missed Neil Spencer's Marquee review of 21st February 1976. This would have come as something of a disappointment to his bosses at EMI, given that scouring the *NME* and the music weeklies for 'interesting music industry titbits' was part and parcel of a press officer's remit. The fact that the Sex Pistols remained unsigned for another eight months only goes to show that Brian wasn't the only music industry insider sleeping on his watch that particular week. The ripples, though, of Spencer's review had spread far and wide; the Sex Pistols were suddenly no longer London's 'best kept secret'.

One young man who'd been galvanised by Spencer's review was 23-year-old Bolton Institute of Technology student Howard Trafford who, along with fellow student and musical collaborator Pete McNeish, would form the nucleus of the Buzzcocks. This was the band that rejuvenated Manchester's mid-seventies music scene, which ultimately begat 'Madchester', and inspired the likes of the Stone Roses, the Charlatans, Oasis and Happy Mondays; as well as providing the name for a long-standing BBC2 music quiz show. Howard, who originally hailed from the Midlands, was suffering a 'mid-course crisis' on his humanities degree and, having already made a hash of his psychology degree, was looking for other less stressful distractions. He had hooked up with Pete, who was three years his junior, through his posting a 'musicians wanted' ad on the college notice board. While Howard was a novice, albeit one with a non-stylised attitude, Pete had five years experience as a guitarist playing in his Leigh Grammar School band, Kogg, and Jets Of Air who supplemented their own compositions with Bowie, Roxy Music and Velvet Underground covers.

'I was already into the Stooges at the time of Neil Spencer's *NME* review, and looking to put together a musical project that would be equally as confrontational,' says Howard today. 'And so reading about a band in London called the Sex Pistols who were into chaos and playing a Stooges song, I thought "hello that sounds interesting", and so me and Pete borrowed a friend's car and we drove down to London the following day'. Howard phoned Neil Spencer at the *NME*, who told him that the Sex Pistols' manager also ran a shop called SEX on the King's Road. So, after a detour via Reading to pick up their mutual friend Richard Boon (who would go on to manage the Buzzcocks during their initial spurt), the three made their way to Sloane Square and headed for 430 King's Road, fully expecting the shop to be an Ann Summers saucy undies outlet.

They purchased a copy of *Time Out*, London's popular 'what's on' guide, and believed their 500 mile round trip to the capital would be in vain, as there was no mention of any forthcoming Sex Pistols shows in the listings. Their luck was in though, as the band were playing another Valentine's dance that very night, this time at

Bucks College of Higher Education in High Wycombe, supporting Screaming Lord Sutch. Better yet, another show was scheduled for the following night in Welwyn Garden City too.

Screaming Lord Sutch, born David Edward Sutch, adopted his 'Screaming' prefix during the mid-sixties in homage to Afro-American blues singer Screamin' Jay Hawkins. If you're wondering where the 'Lord' bit comes from, the truth is that he took advantage of the deed poll laws to declare himself the 3rd Earl of Harrow, despite having absolutely no connection with the peerage. During the early to mid-sixties he released several horror-themed singles, the most popular being 'Jack The Ripper'. He was a suitably macabre act for the Pistols to open for.

By the time of the High Wycombe show the Sex Pistols had ten gigs under their belt, and were fast becoming a tight musical combo; a 'good little war unit' as John Lydon reminisced for *The Filth And The Fury*. Paul and Glen had forged an understanding worthy of Wyman and Watts or Entwistle and Moon, allowing the rapidly-improving Steve and John to run amok; the only criticism being Steve's blatant copying of Pete Townshend's guitar style and Johnny Thunders' poses. Not content with Sylvain's Les Paul, Steve was stealing another Doll's stage act.

Once again the Pistols' high-octane set included a cover of the Stooges 'No Fun', the song that had made Howard's ears prick up initially. There were also two new compositions: 'New York', a put down of the New York music scene generally and the New York Dolls in particular, and 'Submission', a tongue-in-cheek jibe aimed at their seemingly S&M-obsessed manager.

The Valentine's Ball was supposedly an evening for the young bucks of Bucks College to express their feelings for the opposite sex, as well as sow their wild oats. However, a sizable number of the male students were intent on testing the Pistols' boast that they preferred mayhem over music and they stormed the stage during 'No Fun'. Indeed, the show could well have descended into chaos had it not been for Steve and Paul's mate, the formidable Steve English and his gang, who threw the assailants from the stage before forming a line in front of the band to keep the students at bay. Not everybody, however, was antagonistic towards the band and once again another handful were converted to the cause. One of the new converts was Sutch's buddy Ron Watts, the promoter from the 100 Club. He was sufficiently moved to offer the group a slot on 'New Band Night' at his sedate Oxford Street basement jazz club on 31ˢᵗ March, which in turn led to their securing a Tuesday night residency commencing 11ᵗʰ May.

The Wycombe show saw John get embroiled in another fracas with the headliners owing to his getting carried away and smashing a defective –but still expensive – microphone against the stage floor during the band's set. When Sutch confronted John after the Pistols came off stage, he had the audacity to deny responsibility despite everyone present having witnessed his wanton destruction of said mic.

The searing intensity of the band's performance had also justified Howard and Pete's madcap spur of the moment drive from Manchester. Once they'd made the necessary arrangements with Richard to stay over an extra night so they could see the Sex Pistols in Welwyn Garden City, they approached Malcolm with an offer for the Pistols to come up North to play at their college. Malcolm – having delegated Nils as the band's road manager – was naturally keen to broaden the group's horizons, as well as garner national exposure by organising a few gigs up and down the country. So a date was tentatively set for Friday 4ᵗʰ June.

#

On 3ʳᵈ April, the Sex Pistols arrived at The Nashville Rooms at 171 North End Road in West Kensington, to support Pub Rock stalwarts the 101'ers. The 101'ers had taken their name from the squat they all inhabited at 101 Walterton Road, Maida Vale, and featured John 'Woody' Mellor a.k.a. Joe Strummer on lead vocals. They had built up a faithful following in their two year career and were being widely touted to follow Pub Rockers Dr Feelgood into mainstream success. One glimpse, however, of the wild-eyed Rotten, and a verse and chorus of the Pistols' opening number 'Did You No Wrong', was enough for Joe: he underwent a seismic epiphany similar to that experienced by St Paul on his daytrip to Damascus. By the time both bands returned to the Nashville on 23ʳᵈ April, Joe had stunned his fellow 101'ers by announcing he was quitting the band he'd been instrumental in forming, to team up with Bernie, Mick Jones and Paul Simonon – who were all in attendance on the night – to form the Clash. The 101'ers final show came supporting the Sex Pistols at the 100 Club on 15ᵗʰ June.

Legend has it that Mick and Paul, with Glen, who by now was socialising with Mick, happened upon Joe on the Portobello

Market one Saturday afternoon. They stimulated Joe's interest in a musical collaboration by lauding his talents and dissing his band in equal measure. Another enduring punk parable regarding the birth of the Clash is that Mick and Paul approached Joe in the Lisson Grove dole office whilst the three were queuing up to collect their weekly unemployment stipend. So much water has passed under the bridge over the intervening years that none of the protagonists can remember who said what to whom, or where the encounter took place. Suffice to say, Joe was savvy enough to recognise the 101'ers were yesterday's news, and he accepted Bernie's offer to step into the future.

Joe wasn't the only one to recognise the impending sea change either. The Nashville promoters – who must have caught the *Sounds* two page Sex Pistols spread by Jonh Ingham (he just spelt it that way, don't ask) and were keen to catch the cresting wave – elevated the band to headliners, inadvertently driving another nail into the now rudderless 101'ers' coffin in the process. This, of course, was the show which forged the first link of a nine month working relationship with Dave Goodman who became the band's in-house engineer.

Ingham's feature had also raised the expectation levels, but the Sex Pistols remained unfazed and treated their newly raised status with indifference. After exchanging pleasantries with the more familiar faces dotted amongst the seated audience, they launched into their set which included several new songs such as 'Problems', 'No Feelings' and 'Satellite' (the latter being the closest the band would ever get to writing a love song). Legend has it that the song is about St Albans student Shanne Hasler whom John encountered when the band played the city back in February. John supposedly came up with the vitriolic lyric in response to Glen having teased him about his new girlfriend.

The Nashville's house rule of placing several rows of chairs directly in front of the stage, regardless of who was playing, was hardly conducive to a rocking atmosphere. John appeared particularly subdued, even refraining from his customary between-song banter with the audience. Just as the show was in danger of descending into normality, Vivienne – who'd returned from the bar to find her seat taken – ratcheted up the intensity levels by grabbing the female interloper by the hair and dragging her out of the chair. The girl's hapless hippie boyfriend, who was no doubt anxious to avoid a dust-up with the Pistols crowd, vainly tried to pull the two women apart, receiving a glancing blow from Malcolm for his troubles. Sid, who'd been watching on from the wings, took it upon himself to defend Vivienne's honour and came charging across with fists flying. The hippie's friends could hardly sit staring at their shoes while their mate took a pummelling from Sid, but the moment they got to their feet John and the rest of the Pistols took this as their cue to down instruments and extend the melee. Order was quickly restored and the band nonchalantly clambered back onto the stage to continue with their set, but not before the photographers including Joe Stevens and Kate Simon, rushed in to capture the band *in flagrante*.

The story – along with sequential blow-by-blow photos – of a rock band brawling with its audience was deemed highly newsworthy and made all three leading music weeklies. *Melody Maker* even placed one of Simon's photos on the front cover of Caroline Coon's 7th August 'Punk Rock' special issue. The Nashville's promoters, however, were less enthralled by the band's antics, and underwent a rapid rethink about nailing their colours to the Sex Pistols' mast, banning them indefinitely; although the band did return to the venue six days later under the pretext of a 'private function'.

#

Howard and Pete returned to Manchester doubly determined to get a band together in time for the 4th June show, and in keeping with their new found direction the pair decided on a change of name. Howard became Howard Devoto (Devoto is Latin for 'Bewitching') while Pete opted for Shelley, the name his parents had chosen should he have been born a girl. They now also had a name for their band courtesy of *Time Out*, which although it had proved wanting regarding reviewing the two Sex Pistols shows, did contain a review of ITV's BAFTA winning musical drama series Rock Follies (this starred Rula Lenska, Charlotte Cornwell and Judy Covington). The listings magazine giving an appraisal of the fictional all-girl group Little Ladies' latest episodic escapade, ended with the tag-line 'IT'S A BUZZ, COCK!'

According to legend, the Buzzcocks' first gig came supporting the Sex Pistols in Manchester on 20th July 1976, but this is merely an enduring fallacy. The band made a debut of sorts at Bolton Institute of Technology's textile students' social evening on 1st April. Their set comprised mainly of cover versions interspersed with a couple of Pete's early songs 'Get On Our Own' and 'No Reply', both of which later resurfaced on the Buzzcocks' 1978 debut album *Another Music In A Different Kitchen*.

Another little known fact is that their original bassist Garth Bass (Smith), who also later briefly resurfaced following Howard's departure from the band in February 1977, was previously in the group Jets of Air with Pete. So, having already availed themselves of the college's facilities they were stunned when the student union vetoed their application to rehire the hall for 4th June. The rebuttal, however, wasn't due to any reservations the union had about the Sex Pistols per se, but simply because none of them had heard of the band and didn't think anyone from the college – aside from Howard and Pete of course – would have any interest in a band from London. By doing so they unwittingly talked themselves out of a place in rock 'n' roll folklore.

Howard and Pete remained undaunted, however, and an alternative venue was soon found at the Lesser Free Trade Hall, a 400 all-seater capacity room situated above its more illustrious cousin the Free Trade Hall on Manchester's Peter Street. The Free Trade Hall was built during the 1850s to serve as a permanent monument to commemorate the repeal of the Corn Laws, first introduced in 1804. It stands on the site of the Peterloo Massacre of 16th August 1819, when 18 people were killed and hundreds more injured, including 100 women, following a cavalry charge to disperse a public meeting organised by the Manchester Patriotic Union Society, the political group dedicated to repealing the loathed Corn Laws. But the Free Trade Hall was the scene of a more recent – and some would argue a more despicable – charge when a member of the audience dared to accuse Bob Dylan of being a 'Judas' for having the audacity to go electric during his now-legendary 1966 concert.

Despite all their hard work, which included printing the tickets and several late-night sojourns into Manchester's city centre to put up the A3 promotional posters Malcolm had sent, Howard and Pete's ad in the *NMR* (*New Manchester Review*) had failed to unearth like-minded souls to replace their recently departed drummer and bassist in time for the 4th June show. Howard was forced to call upon an ex-work colleague called Geoff Wild and his Bolton-based prog rock outfit Solstice to open for the Sex Pistols. Thanks to David Nolan's excellent read *I Swear I Was There* (Independent Music Press), we know that Solstice were a seven-

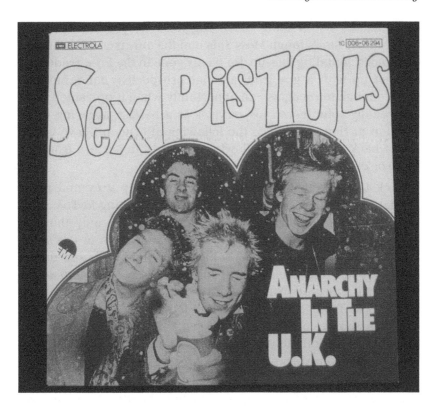

'Anarchy In The UK' – *German sleeve*

piece music collective, complete with their own lighting engineer and soundman. Their set chiefly comprised of typical rock standards of the day including Mountain's 'Nantucket Sleighride', the theme tune for ITV's Sunday lunchtime political magazine programme *Weekend World,* hosted by Brian Walden.

Whilst Malcolm, who was decked from tip to toe in black leather despite the incessant summer heat, remained behind at the venue, Howard and Pete introduced John, Steve, Paul, Glen, Nils and a bemused Jordan to the delights of Tommy Ducks pub. This watering hole on nearby Lower Moseley Street was renowned locally for having its interior festooned with ladies undergarments – not all of which were in pristine condition, if you know what we mean.

Although Howard and Pete were hacked off at not being able to perform at the event they'd helped organise, they were compensated by meeting Steve Diggle, a 20-year-old guitarist from Manchester's tough Moss Side and the only true 'Manc' in the Buzzcocks' founding line-up. He'd only gone to the Free Trade Hall to meet up with a guy from another prospective band, but was savvy enough to recognise an opportunity when it presented itself and readily volunteered his services as a bassist; agreeing to an audition at Howard's place the following afternoon (Steve would revert back to the guitar following Howard's departure from the Buzzcocks in February 1977).

'Back then Manchester was a sea of flat-cap grey and beige flannel,' he told us over a pint or three one evening at The Spice of Life pub in London's Cambridge Circus. 'I was only there to meet some bloke and then we were planning to go to Cox's Bar [a popular pub situated close to the Free Trade Hall] and to this day I can still remember seeing Johnny Rotten, Steve Jones and their road manager [Nils Stevenson] come out of the lift at the Lesser Free Trade Hall. They'd had a few by then, you know, and were dressed like nothing I'd ever seen. I knew straight away that something was definitely gonna happen for them.'

The Pistols and their entourage may have been dressed unlike anything previously seen in Manchester, but it is interesting to note – given that their manager's fashion boutique was making salacious waves on the King's Road – none of the band was actually wearing any items from SEX for the 4th June show. John wore a natty sleeveless yellow top that looked like it had come out second best to a kiddie's scissor class, over a ripped black T-shirt and a pair of tapered bags. Glen chose his customised 'Jackson Pollock' paint-splattered black straight-leg jeans and white T-shirt, while Steve is tipping another subliminal nod to Pete Townshend by taking to the stage in a navy blue boiler suit.

Thanks to Paul Welsh's photographs from the 4th June show, which appear in Nolan's book, we can see just how sartorially challenged the audience were in comparison to the Sex Pistols up on the stage. Flares, denim, cheesecloth shirts, knitted tank-tops, double-breasted jackets and kipper ties were the height of fashion in mid-seventies Manchester, and indeed in every other British city. But those gathered within the cantilevered stalls were at least musically hip to what was happening beyond the city limits and could boast to owning Stooges, MC5 and Velvet Underground albums. The more musically astute amongst them might have even been in possession of an import-only copy of the

Ramones recently released eponymous debut long-player, which Howard had brought along to entertain the troops both before and between bands.

The Lesser Free Trade Hall would need to have been the size of Manchester United's Old Trafford football ground to accommodate everyone who swears they were there the night the Sex Pistols made their Manchester debut. Amazing as it seems, given the importance attached to the show, the actual number of punters – guesstimates range from 40 to 100 – would have struggled to fill United's team bus. Another enduring fallacy is that many of those in attendance went away and formed bands. This is a slight exaggeration given that only future Joy Division/New Order stalwarts Bernard Sumner and Peter Hook, (Joy Division's manic-depressive frontman Ian Curtis would be similarly captivated by the Pistols return to Manchester on 20th July), The Fall's Mark E. Smith, Eddie Garrity, who would go on to front Ed Banger and the Nosebleeds, and the then 15-year-old future Smiths' frontman Steven Morrissey, would actually pick up the gauntlet thrown down by the Sex Pistols.

Another who insisted he was there was Tony Wilson, the late, and much lamented, journalist and Factory Records supremo. Back in 1976 he was working as anchorman on *Granada Reports*, Granada TV's tea-time regional news programme, as well as hosting the station's late-night arts show *So It Goes*. Tony, although having never heard of the Sex Pistols, had had his interest piqued by Howard sending him a cassette tape containing the three tracks ('Problems', 'No Feelings' and 'Pretty Vacant') that Chris Spedding had recently recorded at the RAK-owned Majestic Studios. Meanwhile Stretford teenager Morrissey sent in a battered dog-eared copy of the New York Dolls debut album sleeve along with a note asking Tony why there weren't more bands of their ilk.

Pete Shelley was manning the box office that first night and is of the opinion that Wilson didn't put in an appearance until the second Sex Pistols show, because he doesn't recall the journalist announcing himself on the guest list. Peter Hook and Bernard Sumner, whose post-Joy Division band New Order would become Factory's flagship act, also pour scorn on Wilson's claim to be at 'Gig One' as they can only remember bumping into him at the 20th July show. However, regardless of which Manchester show Tony attended, what is beyond reproof is that he was instrumental in

Original Swindle *cover featuring, and signed by,*
Helen Wellington-Lloyd

providing the Sex Pistols with their first TV exposure by cajoling
his bosses at Granada into letting him have the band on the final
show of the first series of *So It Goes*.

CHAPTER FIVE

Subterranean Circus

'Here's to the crazy ones, the misfits, the rebels,
the troublemakers, the round heads in the square holes;
the ones who see things differently.'
Jack Kerouac (1922 – 69)

The Sex Pistols began their Tuesday night residency at the 100 Club on 11th May 1976. The basement venue's incumbent promoter Ron Watts was constantly on the lookout for new ways to swell the club's coffers and keep it – unlike its décor – out of the red. He believed an exciting and interesting new London band like the Sex Pistols would bring the punters through the doors in their droves.

The band's first incursion into Oxford Street's subterranean future punk rock enclave had come several weeks earlier and had almost derailed their career owing to John disrespectfully taking to the stage pissed out of his brains and forgetting his lyrics. The ensuing on-stage altercation with Glen and Steve saw John abandon the stage mid-set and flee out into the street. The Sex Pistols might have disintegrated there and then had it not been for Malcolm following John out onto Oxford Street and getting him to see the error of his ways. Those amongst the fifty or so punters who weren't au fait with the Sex Pistols thought the singer's tantrums and theatrics were all part of the band's stage act. Watts, of course, knew better and had sensed from the band's small yet dedicated clan of fans that a scene was unfolding and readily offered them a residency.

The band's first few 100 Club dates were distinctly low-key affairs with John, Steve, Paul and Glen treating the shows as no more than live rehearsals. But with each passing week, as the group honed their skills and stage act, their audience, largely down to word of mouth about this wonderful and exciting new band, slowly began to swell in both size and stature. Tuesday 6th July 1976 has gone down in punk folklore as being the night when the London punk flame was truly ignited, as this was the night the Damned made their live debut supporting the Sex Pistols at the 100 Club. The Croydon-based four piece, who would go on to become the 'clown princes of punk', had worked up their repertoire playing the previous four Saturdays at a Lisson Grove gay club in preparation for their debut. Two days earlier, whilst North London was vibrating to the Ramones celebrating America's double-centenary at the Roundhouse, the Clash made their live debut – again supporting the Sex Pistols – at the Black Swan (or the 'Mucky Duck' as it was known to the locals) in Sheffield, South Yorkshire. In the space of three days the UK punk scene's unholy trinity was active; the flame was finally burning.

The Bromley Contingent, by default, were the nascent scene's trendsetters; with 'Candy' Sue Ballion its uncrowned queen. She and her friends had grown up in the late sixties and early seventies and those with older brothers or sisters would have watched on in wide-eyed innocence as their siblings 'turned on', 'tuned in' or 'dropped out' to their respective musical heroes. They had eschewed these same jaded heroes of yesteryear and now it was their turn to strike a pose in the spotlight; their turn to dress up and mess up. In return for being given the keys to their own subterranean playground, the Bromley set introduced the Sex Pistols to Club Louise, an exclusive lesbian club located at 61 Poland Street in nearby Soho, where the band could unwind after their oft-frenetic shows.

Another striking female on the scene was Soo Catwoman (Sue Lucas). Soo also hailed from the suburbs, but even today loathes being associated with the Bromley Contingent. She would spend hour upon hour in front of the mirror sculpting her shorn hair and applying her make-up, until her metamorphism into a feline *femme fatale* was complete. Indeed, it could be said that Soo, whom Malcolm chose to adorn the front cover of the inaugural issue of the Sex Pistols' *Anarchy in the UK* fanzine released later in the year, was the true iconic face of the London punk scene. She would have surely surpassed 'Candy' Sue – or indeed any other of her female contemporaries – had she possessed a singing voice or played an instrument. Sid, of course, was by now the Sex Pistols' über fan, the guy who'd invented the 'pogo', and therefore Soo's natural male suitor. However, Sid had little or no interest in the opposite sex at the time, and often wore a padlock over his crotch to confirm his chastity. He purposely treated 'Candy' Sue and her motley gang of Kent cronies with utter disdain, often using his unique dance technique to deliver a few well-intentioned blows with his elbows whilst leaping about the club's herring-boned dance floor.

#

On Sunday 29th August 1976, Malcolm returned the Buzzcocks' favour by inviting them to London to play alongside the Sex Pistols and the Clash in an 'all-nite special' at the Screen On The Green cinema on Upper Street in Islington, North London. There was, as always, an ulterior motive lurking within the shadows of his seemingly magnanimous gesture, as Malcolm had thus far drawn a blank in trying to secure the Sex Pistols a record deal. He was hoping that by staging a big event he would attract attention from the record companies which had, thus far, remained impervious to his advances. When we interviewed Malcolm in April 2007 for *Never Mind the Sex Pistols: an Alternative History* DVD (Demon Vision), he astounded us by confessing he'd never actually wanted the Pistols to make a record and had only acquiesced following mounting pressure from the band, who to a man wanted a record out, if only to confirm they were more than a passing phase.

The Sex Pistols may have been bringing in converts off the street, but the record companies, or those that were aware of the band (thanks to Jamie Reid's multi-coloured press packs, complete with the ransom-style lettering culled from the *Evening Standard*, courtesy of Helen), were slower to react. Indeed, the only record company executive to show any real interest in the band to date, Polydor's Chris Parry, had long-since cooled his ardour following the Sex Pistols' appearance at The Crypt in Middlesbrough on 21st May, when Steve resorted to form by rifling the pockets of Polydor headliners, the Doctors Of Madness, whilst they were out on stage. This ardour was to be reignited though.

Apart from the three bands, the 'Midnight Special', as it was whimsically billed, also featured two films from American underground avant-garde film-maker, and occasional occultist, Kenneth Anger: *Kustom Kar Kommandos* (1965) and *Scorpio Rising* (1963). Anger happened to be Malcolm's favourite director and although there might have been a few of those nestled within the cinema's stalls who were familiar with Anger's work, it would have surely been more appropriate to run *Cabaret* or the recently released *Rocky Horror Picture Show.* 'Candy' Sue's popcorn-spilling fishnet and fetish ensemble included a risqué peek-a-boo cupless bra from She an' Me (a marital aids shop which was a forerunner to Ann Summers) and a swastika armband. Indeed, she was in danger of taking the spotlight away from the headliners, and probably would have done so had it not been for John inadvertently cracking one of his teeth against the microphone, which made for an angst-ridden performance.

Although Malcolm may have been happy to return the favour by inviting the Buzzcocks – who'd found their drummer John Maher through an ad in *Melody Maker* – to open the show (the band's London debut), his sole interest was to promote the Sex Pistols. The Buzzcocks' eleven song set mysteriously suffered from the sound problems that would also spoil the Clash's set; although the Manchester band was, at least, spared the Clash's humiliation of having to provide the materials for – as well as to erect – the makeshift stage. Joe, Mick and Paul also suffered the indignation of having to fly-post the posters – designed by Jamie Reid – which were woefully biased towards the Sex Pistols and barely gave their own band a mention.

This was also the Clash's first London show – unless, of course, one counts the private showcase at their Camden rehearsal space 'Rehearsal Rehearsals' in front of a select crowd of journalists a couple of weeks earlier on 13th August – and the band was anxious to make a good impression. But by their own admission they weren't very good and blamed their lacklustre performance on their earlier exertions in assembling the stage. *Sounds* journalist Giovanni Dadomo, would unkindly cite the Buzzcocks' set as 'rougher than a bear's ass', but was rather more sympathetic towards the Clash. He'd lauded them as 'the band to scare the Sex Pistols shitless', rightly blaming their blighted performance on the poor sound quality; whereas the *NME*'s Charles Shaar Murray famously suggested the band should be returned to the garage, preferably with the engine left running.

Sabotaging the PA to undermine the competition was a time-honoured trick and although Dave Goodman pleaded ignorance, he must have been in on the subterfuge, for the sound problems magically disappeared the moment the Sex Pistols came on stage. Today, Alan Jones – as did Sid – cites the first Screen On The Green show as one of his three favourite gigs and one of the best performances the Sex Pistols ever gave. Glen and Paul were as solid as ever; Rotten, having inadvertently caught his teeth with the microphone and losing a cap in the process, was utterly electrifying, while Steve was finally beginning to live up to the role of 'Guitar Hero' that he'd mischievously daubed on the meshed front of his Fender amplifier.

Another who was left speechless by the band's performance that night was 27-year-old EMI A&R rep Mike Thorne, who would subsequently work with the Pistols during their 91 day tenure at EMI. 'Because I was younger than the other guys at EMI, and EMI was my first A&R job,' he says today 'I was one of the very few A&R men to actually connect with what they [Sex Pistols] were doing. Everybody now claims they were there but it wasn't true. I was completely alone at many of those gigs.' Indeed, Thorne is something of an unsung hero regarding his role in the Sex Pistols signing to EMI in October 1976, because Nick Mobbs – who received most of the plaudits for getting the band to put pen to paper –had dismissed Chris Spedding's Majestic demos out of hand, commenting that he wouldn't touch the Sex Pistols with a bargepole.

#

On Friday 3rd September, the Sex Pistols flew to Paris to play the opening night at the Club de Chalet du Lac, a trendy new discothèque in the city's upmarket Bois de Vincennes. Malcolm had come up with the idea to compensate for the band having missed out on appearing at the inaugural 'European Punk Rock Festival' on 21st August. Their omission from the event, which was staged in a bullring at Mont de Marsan near Bordeaux in southern France, was due to their fallout with the festival's headliners Eddie And The Hot Rods at the Marquee back in February, and also of being guilty by association following Sid's assault on Nick Kent at the 100 Club at the end of June. The event's promoter, and founder of French indie label Skydog Records, Marc Zermati, would come to rue his decision to veto the Sex Pistols, as the Mont de Marsan bullring could hold an estimated 5000 people, yet a mere 250 or so bemused locals turned out for the entertainment.

The Clash, who'd also been invited onto the bill, had pulled out of the festival in a show of solidarity towards the Pistols. The Damned, however, had felt no such compunction, and stood in bleary-eyed line beside the Hot Rods, the Gorillas, Nick Lowe, Roogalator and the Pink Fairies at Victoria Coach Station, awaiting the bus to ferry them to Dover. It was during this journey that their bassist Ray Burns received his enduring moniker 'Captain Sensible'. 'We was driving down to Dover to catch the ferry to Calais when I started muckin' about pretending to be the pilot. You know, shoutin' things like "it's alright, everything's under control". Just havin' a laugh really,' the Captain told us backstage one night back in December 2006 following the Damned's appearance at a punk fest at Nottingham's Rock City. 'But cos I was wearing some cheap second-hand shirt that had epaulettes some wag shouted out something like "who the fuck do you think you are, Captain Sensible"?'

'Well it kinda stuck as at the time everyone was giving themselves silly punk names weren't they? I thought it was a laugh at the time and maybe, I dunno, cause a bit of confusion down the dole office. But here I am thirty years on and still "The Captain". You'd think I'd have had a promotion by now, though.'

As Paris was the Pistols' first foreign jaunt, 'Candy' Sue Ballion, Steve 'Spunker' Bailey, Simon Barker and Billy Broad followed the band to France in Billy's battered bright-yellow GPO Morris van. Once again Sue caused a sensation in her peep-hole bra and swastika armband. It wasn't so much her pert breasts that caused the continental consternation, but rather her wantonly brandishing a Nazi totem on the anniversary of the day Britain and France declared war on Germany precipitating World War II. They had been making their way to the venue when they were accosted by a gang of knife-wielding young Frenchmen, one of whom punched Sue in the face. Fortunately the club's manager saw what was happening, stepped in and bundled them inside. But even then he had to tuck Sue away in his private office while the Pistols were on stage.

The travelling party had been delayed at Heathrow airport owing to Malcolm having forgotten his passport. He'd also neglected to arrange a carnet – the customs licence required for the temporary transportation of goods across certain borders; namely, the group's equipment. The delays meant the band didn't arrive at the club until late afternoon, and the boys were obliged to carry out their soundcheck while workmen were busy putting the finishing touches to the decorous interior. Oh yeah, and another thing no one had actually mentioned, was that the club was still being built! It was tradition within the French capital that the opening night of any new establishment should be *'entrée libré'* (admission free) so the place was packed to its freshly-painted rafters. Ray Stevenson, Jonh Ingham and Caroline Coon were forced to jockey for position with their French counterparts gathered at the edge of the dance floor.

The jostling became even fiercer when John walked onto the futuristic neon-lit glass stage sporting Malcolm and Vivienne's latest fashion statement, the bondage suit; a shiny sateen ensemble, replete with buckles, D-rings and zips – one of which ran from crotch to coccyx – as well as straps at the knee and across the chest, restricting the wearer's movements. He'd worn the upper garment at Heathrow earlier in the day and had almost brought the airport to a standstill as his bewildered fellow passengers couldn't believe what they were seeing.

As the Sex Pistols were scheduled to play a paying matinée show on the Sunday, the travelling party, which included Nils, Vivienne and Jordan, had a day off. Caroline Coon suggested spending the afternoon hanging out at the *Les Deux Magots* café on the Place Saint Germain des Prés. It was famed for being a rendezvous point for the city's literary and intellectual elite including authors Albert Camus, Simone de Beauvoir and a young Ernest Hemingway, as well as French philosopher Jean-Paul Sartre and Spanish painter Pablo Picasso. Once again John brought traffic to a halt and had the restaurant's clientele choking on their croque monsieurs with his natty ensemble of baby pink sweater ripped up to the armpit, a crucifix dangling from a solitary safety pin, Peter Pan SEX shirt and baggy Oxfam trousers. He was also wearing Steve's beret and the granny glasses he occasionally wore to protect his eyes from the on-stage glare.

It was under the sightless gaze of the two wooden Chinese commercial agents (the Magots which gave the café its name), that Malcolm first muted the idea of possibly staging a punk rock festival at the 100 Club with Zermati, and his aristocratic fashion designer friend Charles le Duc de Castelbarjac.

#

The 100 Club Punk Festival, staged over consecutive nights on 20th and 21st September 1976, wasn't so much a celebration of London punk – or to show France and New York how it could and should be done – but rather the culmination of Malcolm's campaign to secure the Sex Pistols a deal with a major record company. Time

'God Save The Queen' *unique French sleeve signed by Jamie Reid*

was now a factor, for although the Screen On The Green 'Midnight Special' had been a resounding success in terms of keeping the spotlight on the Sex Pistols, it had failed to drum up any significant music industry interest in the band.

The Damned were now signed to Stiff Records, the independent label set up by Pub Rock entrepreneurs Jake Riviera (Andrew Jakeman) and Dave Robinson. Malcolm was determined at all costs to avoid the humiliation of seeing his charges usurped by a band that had only been together for two months.

Stiff had launched that July, courtesy of a £400 loan from Dr Feelgood frontman Lee Brilleaux. Stiff's debut single – the upbeat rocker 'So It Goes' by ex-Brinsley Schwarz bassist Nick Lowe – did exactly what it said on the tin and 'stiffed'. Malcolm, not to mention everyone else with their ear to the ground, must have wondered what could have possessed Riviera and Robinson to launch the label with a song by a bass player. (Looking back – even with the safety net of hindsight – it still seems a strange choice. Nick's a talented singer/songwriter, and has written some very catchy tunes, but he was at this stage no Paul McCartney). The label's follow-up, however, 'Between The Lines' by popular underground psychedelic hippie outfit the Pink Fairies had fared much better and Riviera and Robinson were making noises about issuing a Damned single. If that were to happen then the Damned would supplant the Sex Pistols as the scene's leading exponents and Jake Riviera would reap the rewards while all McLaren's hard work over the past year would count for nothing.

Signing to a low-rent label such as Stiff, which had mockingly taken its name from the music biz idiom for a failed record, was contrary to Malcolm's way of conducting business though. Monkeys were meddlesome to deal with and wasn't it the organ grinders that called the tune? If the band was so determined to have a record out, then he was equally resolved that said record would be released through a recognised major label. Despite backbiting from certain quarters about safeguarding the band's credibility, his fixation with getting the group signed to a major label had nothing to do with selling out. It was about distribution. What was the point of releasing a record if the label couldn't guarantee getting it into the shops on time?

Upon his return from Paris, Malcolm set to work laying the foundations for the proposed festival and, to help him, he enlisted Jamie Reid's girlfriend Sophie Richmond as his personal assistant/ secretary. Sophie, who was living in Aberdeen when she took the call, had worked with Jamie at the Suburban Press after leaving Warwick University in 1972.

The only problem, of course, was that London simply didn't have enough so called 'punk' bands. If he was to have any hope of convincing the record companies – not to mention the mainstream media – that the London scene was worthy of their attention then he would have to look further afield to supplement the festival's running order. Indeed, the original A3 posters, which featured Ray Stevenson's now-legendary photograph of the four Sex Pistols playing sardines inside the public telephone box outside St Giles-in-the-Fields Church (located within a short walk from their Denmark Street HQ), omitted the word 'festival' in favour of 'punk special'(and it also made no mention of Tuesday night's acts).

As the Sex Pistols were already contracted to appear at Cardiff's Top Rank on the Tuesday night, they would headline Monday night's fare. The recently truncated Clash, following Keith Levene's departure, were placed second on the bill. Another of Bernie's acts, the newly formed Subway Sect, along with French punksters Stinky Toys, would support. Tuesday night's bill was to be headlined by the Damned – as loath as Malcolm was to invite them – with the Buzzcocks and the Vibrators (along with Chris Spedding guesting during the latter half of their set) making up the numbers. The Vibrators were regarded as little more than bandwagon jumpers, having cut their hair and tapered their trousers since supporting the Sex Pistols back in August.

Even then, Malcolm felt he needed another band for the Monday night and he found one in the unlikeliest of places. He and Sophie were holding a late-night meeting with Bernie at Club Louise to discuss the latest developments when 'Candy' Sue – who'd been eavesdropping on their conversation – volunteered herself and her non-existent band for the vacant Monday night spot. Malcolm, although sceptical, was also desperate and he ignored Bernie's protestations and pencilled Sue's as yet unnamed outfit onto the bill. The makeshift band's initial line-up was 'Candy' Sue on vocals, Billy Broad, who'd recently assumed the name Billy Idol, on guitar, and a rhythm section consisting of Steve Bailey (who'd also undergone a name change from Steve 'Spunker' to Steve Havoc) on bass, and Sid Vicious on drums; despite neither of them having any grounding whatsoever on their respective instruments.

The four arranged to meet up the following afternoon, but Billy had had a night to reconsider the potential pitfalls of going on stage with three novices and absconded, with Tony James, to join Gene October's newly formed Chelsea. Sue, however, remained undaunted and brought in Soo Catwoman's friend – and SEX *habitué* – Marco Perroni as Billy's replacement. The band opted for the name Suzie and the Banshees after catching the Hammer film *The Cry of the Banshee* starring Vincent Price on television, and booked a rehearsal at the Clash's space in Camden.

However, seeing as their appearance at the festival – which kick-started a thirty year career for Suzie (later renamed Siouxsie) and Steve Havoc (later renamed Severin) – was intended as a one-off, there seemed little point in their learning any kind of real set.

The Clash had also consented to allow the band to use their equipment – including their recently customised fluorescent-pink backline – but Sue's stubborn refusal to remove her swastika armband, coupled with Sid calling Bernie a 'mean old Jew', led to the offer being rescinded. This wasn't due solely to his Jewish heritage, but also an unwillingness to risk the Clash's highly distinctive gear being associated with the National Front or any other right wing political body. Just when it seemed the Banshees would have to forego the pleasure of wailing in front of their peers, Malcolm – who perversely had no problem with Nazi imagery despite his own Jewish ancestry – stepped in to save the day by allowing them to use the Sex Pistols' gear.

The initial idea had been to perform John Barry's 'Goldfinger' from the 1964 James Bond film of the same name. This was abandoned in favour of a meandering twenty minute or so nondescript Velvet Underground-orientated dirge over which Sue intoned lyrics from Bob Dylan's 'Knockin' On Heaven's Door' and the Beatles' 'Twist And Shout', interspersed with snippets from 'Deutschland Uber Alles' and 'The Lord's Prayer'. As the ad hoc elegy had no recognised structure, none of the three 'musicians' (with Sid and Steve being considered musicians in the loosest possible sense) knew how to bring it to a close. Indeed, they might have kept on playing until closing time had Sid not tired of his first Warholian fifteen minute burst of fame and downed tools.

Subway Sect too, who would also be making their live debut at the festival, as well as opening the event, were a little rusty. The Mortlake-based outfit had been content building up their rhythm and blues repertoire until their singer Vic Goddard and guitarist Rob Simmons saw the Sex Pistols at the Marquee back in February. The pair had literally wandered in off the street and although the Pistols music had left them unmoved, they were won over by their image and Rotten's on-stage chair-throwing antics. Bernie had taken them under his wing but couldn't offer them any real rehearsal time, as the Clash were in Rehearsals every God-given hour ironing out their own rough edges. Malcolm had gone along to watch the Sect rehearse in Camden and had thought them awful, but his desperation to accrue enough bands was so great that he booked them a week's rehearsal time at Manos restaurant in Chelsea in order to spruce up their monotone five song repertoire. His willingness to put his hand in his pocket is a telling indication as to the level of Malcolm's desperation.

#

The Clash put in a blinding amphetamine-fuelled set which opened with their new composition 'White Riot', the song Joe had written in response to the trouble between police and black youths at the August Bank Holiday Notting Hill Caribbean Carnival. He, Paul and Bernie had inadvertently got caught up in the disturbance which erupted following the police's attempt to arrest a suspected pickpocket. The three managed to emerge from the ensuing carnage injury-free, but the experience had left them shaken nonetheless. The Clash didn't appear to be suffering any hangover following Levene's departure; if anything, it added a new dynamic as their bassist Paul Simonon had been given the freedom to express himself on stage. Unlike the Sex Pistols or the Damned, the Clash's eleven song set was totally devoid of covers. The band finished with the portentous '1977', with its Orwellian coda and propagandistic declaration of 'no Elvis, Beatles or Rolling Stones' in the coming year when the two sevens clash. Sadly this proved prophetic for Elvis Presley, who would succumb to a heart attack at his Graceland mansion on 16th August 1977.

The festival was the Sex Pistols' tenth appearance at the 100 Club and the days when their eclectic following could saunter about the normally sedate basement venue as though they were at a social gathering had been consigned to sepia-toned memory; the secret was out. In the six months since the band made their Oxford Street debut, the trickle had become a deluge as more and more disenfranchised kids came looking to see if the fuss surrounding the Sex Pistols was justified.

The ceiling was already dripping from the generated steam heat coming off the sweaty massed ranks at the front of the stage, but the temperature gauge cranked up another couple of notches as John, once again sporting Malcolm and Vivienne's bondage ensemble, and the rest of the Sex Pistols emerged from the dressing room and took to the stage. The audience barely had time to catch its collective breath before the band launched into 'Anarchy in the UK', which they'd first unveiled at the second Manchester show in July and was now a searing statement of intent.

Those who had been following the Pistols since the start of the year had already noticed a seismic change in the band, especially John who rarely ventured away from the microphone. Gone were the days when he would trawl the stage captivating the audience with his frenetic jerks and rapacious wit. The disjointed 'robot dance' with which he'd entertained the Lydon clan as a youngster, was also becoming a fast-fading memory. Even his youthful exuberance, although still evident on occasions, was largely buried beneath a haughty veneer. The playful bantering with the audience between songs had given way to an icy stare; his expressionless features and parchment-like skin giving him the look of an angel of death. Steve, Glen and Paul, who had finally quit his job at the brewery to concentrate on the band, also appeared more self-assured. It's as though they too had finally begun to believe in their own destiny and they majestically powered through the remainder of the set which now included 'I Wanna Be Me', John's acerbic rant against 'typewriter gods' such as Nick Kent. There was also an air of professionalism about the Pistols now, which could be construed as a belief in their abilities, though it's more likely due to their having signed their names to Malcolm's managerial contract.

The signing took place that very afternoon in the offices of Malcolm's solicitor Stephen Fisher. Fisher was also a co-director of Glitterbest, the Sex Pistols new management company, which was bought off the shelf for £100 and incorporated on 23rd September. The contract was to last for three years, with options for a further two years. In return for his services, Malcolm, through Glitterbest, was to take 25 per cent of the band's pre-tax earnings and a staggering 50 per cent of all future merchandising. The contract also contained covenants regarding every aspect of the band's professional lives and, tucked away within Fisher's carefully worded legal jargon, was Clause 14, which basically stated that the name 'Sex Pistols' had been created by the Manager and therefore belonged to, and was owned by, the Manager.

Glen, in his autobiography *I Was A Teenage Sex Pistol* (Virgin), says he was the only band member that bothered to peruse – or at least try to understand – the legal mumbo jumbo contained within the contract, while Nils, who witnessed the contract despite his reticence, later claimed he told the band not to sign anything without first seeking independent legal representation. Needless to say, Steve and Paul were blinkered when it came to Malcolm's managerial duties and the pair steadfastly refused to believe Malcolm had anything other than their best interests at heart. John, of course, has had three decades to rue his show of indifference.

#

The second night of the festival was – with the exception of Sid's glass-throwing antics, which would have long-lasting repercussions for anyone associated with punk – a rather more demure affair. The atmosphere was still spirited but the audience was marginally older, longer-haired and more sensibly dressed; leather and lace having been replaced by denim and flares. The first band up was Stinky Toys who'd been held over from the previous night due in part to time restrictions, but mainly because 95% of the audience had made a beeline for the exits the moment the Pistols departed the stage. Elli, their highly-strung singer, was so distraught at the prospect of playing to an empty house that she fled up the stairs and out into busy Oxford Street, where she almost had her pretty features rearranged by a passing bus.

Somewhat bizarrely, given their headline status, the Damned were next up, and the band launched into their opening number – and future Stiff release – 'Neat, Neat, Neat', instantly followed by their soon-to-be released debut 'New Rose'. Their vampire-fixated singer Dave Vanian, who up until signing with Stiff had been digging graves instead of scenes, positively fed off the contempt emanating from the furrowed brows of 'Candy' Sue, Steve Havoc, Billy Idol (who'd been forgiven for going AWOL the previous day) and Sid, who watched on from the bar, a mere stone's throw from the stage. The rest of the crowd, however, appeared to be enjoying the Damned's high camp theatrics. All four band members were total extroverts who were born to perform – even a ten minute unscheduled halt to replace a guitar string failed to diminish their exuberance. Another cheer erupted as the band tore into the Stooges classic '1970', but one disgruntled audience member was somewhat less enthused and expressed his displeasure by hurling an empty beer glass towards the stage.

There has been much debate as to Sid's culpability over the glass-throwing incident which resulted in his being incarcerated in Ashford Remand Centre and punk being expelled indefinitely from its spiritual home. Caroline Coon, who was also arrested for trying to defend Sid (and given an absolute discharge), believes him to be innocent. But shit tends to stick where it's thrown and Steve Severin is as adamant now as he was then that Sid was the culprit and, given that he was standing next to Sid at the time, he should know. Let's not forget either that Malcolm, who'd remained in London rather than accompany the Sex Pistols to Cardiff, disliked the Damned and their new manager Jake Riviera in equal measure. Is it therefore possible that Sid – who'd bought into Malcolm's Machiavellian schemes 'lock, stock and padlock' – might have misconstrued the latter's haranguing of the Damned and taken matters into his own hands?

Had the glass reached its intended target then it's fair to surmise that Sid would have only had to defend his actions to the band, or more likely go toe-to-toe with drummer Chris 'Rat Scabies' Millar (he being an ex-Millwall thug). But unfortunately for Sid, his aim – like his drumming the previous night – was woefully off and the glass struck one of the supporting pillars, sending shards of glass cascading down onto the audience injuring several people, with one girl supposedly losing an eye. Again, one has to question the validity of this perpetuating myth. Why has the girl in question, who would have been well within her rights to bring a lawsuit against the 100 Club's owners, never come forward to tell of what she remembers about that night? Are we really expected to believe that the tabloids wouldn't have moved heaven and earth to find the girl who'd lost an eye to the punk rock fiends, and put her poor disfigured face on the front page?

Despite Sid's antics, the 100 Club Punk Festival, which was brought to its climactic finale by the Buzzcocks, proved a resounding success. Not least for the Vibrators who were signed to Mickey Most's RAK label within a matter of weeks. Whilst Jonh Ingham and Caroline Coon busied themselves with blow-by-blow accounts for their respective papers, the London-only *Evening Standard* set the ball rolling with a two page special feature on the event which heralded a new musical cult – one imbued with a 'harsh dogmatic attitude'. The *Standard* concluded its piece by mentioning that the Sex Pistols, the disturbing new cult's leading exponents, had been 'attracting a great deal of interest from leading record companies'.

CHAPTER SIX

Ridicule Is Nothing To Be Scared Of ...

*'A lie can be half-way around the world
before the truth has got its boots on.'*
James Callaghan (Labour Prime Minister 1976-79)

On 7th October 1976, the Bank of England announced it was raising interest on its minimum lending rate from 13 to 15 per cent, and the country's anxious building societies followed suit the next day by raising mortgage interest rates to an incredible 12.25 per cent. The newspapers of Friday the 8th October made for particularly grim reading, especially for James Callaghan's woefully inept Labour government who seemed incapable of halting Britain's headlong descent into financial meltdown. Polydor Records' 25-year-old A&R manager Chris Parry, although no doubt concerned about the personal implications of the latest hike in interest rates, had a spring in his step after having overcome the objections of his superiors at the company to pip his opposite number at EMI in acquiring the Sex Pistols to the label's roster.

He'd been courting Malcolm since catching the Pistols' show at the Screen on the Green on the 29th August. Although the band had yet to put their names to the £20,000 contract lying on his desk (with an additional £20,000 set aside for recording costs and other sundries), he was so confident he'd clinched the deal that he'd already booked the band into Polydor's DeLane Lea Studios in Soho so they could begin working on their debut single 'Anarchy In The UK'. Indeed, the crestfallen Parry only discovered he'd been gazumped by his EMI counterparts on the Saturday afternoon when he'd called Malcolm at SEX to see how the initial day of recording had gone. This wasn't the first time that Polydor had lost out to EMI. The Dutch-owned label had originally been an independent branch of the German classical music label Deutsche

Grammophon Gesellschaft, which had held the rights to the His Master's Voice trademark, but had been forced to relinquish those rights to EMI as part of Germany's surrender terms at the end of World War II.

It is rumoured in some quarters that Parry actually broke down and cried upon receiving Malcolm's rebuttal. If true, then the A&R man was reaching for the Kleenex again when the Clash knocked him back in favour of signing a £100,000 deal with American label CBS. Parry, however, would remain focused on his objective to sign a leading new wave act to the label. Perhaps it was a case of 'third time lucky' as he secured the Jam's signatures for Polydor in February 1977 for a paltry £6,000. (The deal was eventually renegotiated in the band's favour by Paul Weller's dad, John, who was acting as their manager).

Malcolm's decision to favour EMI over Polydor wasn't a monetary one, as both companies were more or less offering the same deal. But whereas Polydor was Dutch-owned, which might make for unnecessary complications further down the line, EMI was as English as afternoon tea and buttered scones, and had come to be regarded as the cornerstone of the British music industry. It hadn't simply been a case of choosing EMI over Polydor, however, as Malcolm certainly faced a few hurdles during his negotiations with EMI; most notably in persuading the label's A&R chief, Nick Mobbs, that the Sex Pistols were worthy of his attention. Mobbs finally caved in under A&R rep Mike Thorne's enthusiasm and relentless persistence, even cutting short a trip to Venice to see ex-Beatle Paul McCartney's Wings and travelling up to less glamorous Doncaster to watch the Pistols perform at the Outlook Club on the 27th September.

Mobbs was already familiar with most of the songs played that night, as they featured on the cassette tape Malcolm had sent him containing the Dave Goodman demos recorded at the band's Denmark Street HQ in July. He'd already been given approval by his bosses to sign the band, and although he could certainly see what had got Thorne so excited, he remained unconvinced as to whether EMI was the right home for the Sex Pistols.

So the problem facing Malcolm, when he presented his case to Mobbs that cold October morning, wasn't about the £40,000 asking price for the band's signatures, it was more about overcoming the bespectacled A&R man's own personal doubts as to whether the Sex Pistols' rough and ready sound would translate onto vinyl.

Malcolm, however, refused to allow Mobbs' personal tastes to enter the equation and sealed the deal by convincing Mobbs that if he wasn't willing to sign a hot new act like the Sex Pistols that was right here before his very eyes, then EMI was living in the past and the label might as well shut up shop. Having convinced Mobbs, he refused to leave the latter's office until the contract had been drawn up. In that one single day, McLaren spent seven hours in the company's Manchester Square offices! Only then did he grab a cab to Denmark Street to collect the band, as well as his American photographer friend Bob Gruen, who'd called at the band's rehearsal place to take some photos of Malcolm's new group for the folks back home.

The contract was signed, sealed and delivered in a single day, making it the fastest-ever signing in EMI's illustrious history: marry in haste, repent at leisure as the old saying goes. It wasn't a case of everybody smiling for the camera, however, as the penny finally dropped for Nils, who realised that co-management didn't feature in Malcolm's lexicon, and that Malcolm had only ever viewed him as, at best, a roadie or some other level of lowly assistant. Nils therefore tendered his resignation and went off to manage Suzie (now spelt 'Siouxsie') and the Banshees.

The Pistols contract covered the UK, as well as EMI's overseas territories, and was a two album deal over an initial two-year period with two further one-year options (exercisable only by the label). The group, or rather Glitterbest – as per Clause 17 of the managerial contract – received a £40,000 non-returnable advance, £20,000 of which was paid upon signing, with the remaining £20,000 to be paid on the corresponding date twelve months later. EMI would also shoulder reasonable recording costs which could be recouped from future royalties. The band would have record sleeve approval, as well as a say in the choice of producer, which EMI would pay for. The Sex Pistols had already secured a £10,000 publishing deal with EMI's publishing arm and although EMI Records and EMI Publishing carried the same company logo, the two companies were entirely separate entities operating from different offices at either end of Oxford Street.

Aside from its music interests EMI was also involved in broadcasting, notably providing the BBC with its first television transmitter, as well as investing in leisure industries such as restaurants, cinemas and hotels. Not forgetting either its heavy investment in its radical CAT (Computerised Axial Tomography)

Bootleg sleeve in the style of The Beatles. Issue 3

scanner, which would enable doctors to examine the inner workings of the human brain without resorting to surgery. The company could also count on forty years of success with larger-scale electronics such as radar and guided missiles, which were developed at EMI's Laboratories in Hayes, Middlesex, both during and after World War II.

By 1976, the sixth floor of EMI's Manchester Square citadel was the hallowed reserve of its new chairman Sir John Read and his illustrious board of directors, including Sir Joseph Lockwood; former Attorney General, and Britain's chief prosecutor at Nuremberg, Lord Shawcross; and the then Conservative Shadow Chancellor of the Exchequer, Geoffrey Howe. However, there were those further down the company's food chain at EMI Records who were acutely aware that music and missiles didn't make for comfortable bedfellows. They were fearful that EMI having its interconnected digits in so many lucrative pastries would one day end up with one of those pinkies getting burned.

#

The Sex Pistols had just twenty-four hours to celebrate their becoming an EMI act as on the Sunday morning they, along with engineer Dave Goodman and his partner Kim Thraves, headed into Lansdowne Studios in upmarket Holland Park to record 'Anarchy In The UK'. EMI had initially wanted 'Pretty Vacant' to be the band's first single as the song was certainly more radio-friendly, and would therefore generate more immediate sales in their view. The label, however, had acquiesced in the face of the band's steadfast insistence that their debut release would be 'Anarchy'. The band spent seven days holed away inside Lansdowne repeatedly playing the song over and over again without having anything to show for their labours – let alone a hefty slice of EMI's £10,000 recording budget.

With the original 19th November release date pushed back another week, the recording party then moved on to the decidedly more compact Wessex Studios in Highbury, where they again wasted countless reels of expensive two-inch tape as Goodman vainly attempted to capture the Pistols' live energy in the studio. The normal recording process for a single took about three weeks, and the powers-that-be over at EMI were beginning to express doubts. The clock was ticking, and with no sign of Goodman producing the goods, the engineer was summoned to Manchester Square to be told he was off the case. Goodman's version of 'Anarchy In The UK' wouldn't surface until its inclusion on *The Great Rock 'n' Roll Swindle* soundtrack in March 1979, by which time this group called the Sex Pistols would no longer exist!

Goodman's replacement at the Wessex console was the studio's affiliate producer Chris Thomas, who'd cut his teeth on the Beatles' *White Album* before going on to work with Procol Harum and Roxy Music, as well as overseeing the mixing of Pink Floyd's *Dark Side Of The Moon*. Thomas had accompanied his friend Chris Spedding to Malcolm's 'Midnight Special' at the Screen On The Green show at the end of August, but by his own admission the Pistols' live show had left him largely unmoved. He was, however, impressed with the chord changes on the version of 'Anarchy' that Thorne had sent him, so he tentatively agreed to meet with the band at his home in Ealing.

While Thomas' no nonsense approach to recording – and his favouring of overdubbing the guitars – may have bruised a certain spiky ego, no one could argue that Thomas wasn't a master of his craft: within five takes the finished song was in the can. Having won the battle to get John to enunciate his lyrics, as well as eradicating a discrepancy on the timing on Paul's snare drum by splicing two backing tracks together, Thomas opted for a sonic shutdown by cutting the song immediately after John's 'get pissed ... destroy' coda in the hope that the needle would actually leap up out of the groove to escape the invective; whereas Goodman's four minutes and counting version had subsided into wave upon wave of meandering feedback.

'Anarchy In The UK' (EMI 2566) was released in the UK on Friday 26th November 1976, with the first 2000 copies being issued in a plain black bag, accompanied by Jamie Reid's now iconic fold-out poster of a torn Union Jack held together with safety pins and paper clips. Reid had originally submitted an old piece of Suburban Press artwork titled 'Monster on a House Roof' for the cover, which EMI hated; so that was placed back in its box pretty sharpish. Strangely though, it never re-surfaced while a lot of other Suburban Press work did. Mobbs had tried to talk McLaren into a Beatles style photo session over the balcony at Manchester Square, but McLaren was having none of this pop star picture sleeve nonsense. The photo was actually taken, but it would be years before the 'fab four' pictures actually emerged anywhere.

EMI, having already capitulated on two fronts in the choice of song and the Pistols' refusal to be housed with the company's subsidiary label Harvest (established in 1969 to cater for bands in the emerging Prog Rock genre such as Pink Floyd), also had to comply with Malcolm's wishes in avoiding the usual clichéd promotional packaging. When the bemused head of EMI's marketing department had questioned how anybody was supposed to find the single, Malcolm responded by saying he didn't want just 'anybody' to find the record; he only wanted the 'somebodies' to go into their local record store and ask for it by name.

This, of course, was in accordance with the terms of the contract and the label had to comply with Malcolm's wishes. However, the defacing of the national flag had ruffled a few well-heeled feathers within the corporate boardroom. Thirty years passing hadn't totally eradicated the memory of the Luftwaffe's bombing raids, and the red-poppied wreaths to commemorate the countless thousands who'd laid down their lives for King and Country were still on display at the Whitehall Cenotaph. Whilst those involved in promoting the Sex Pistols single avoided a tongue lashing from the board by explaining the poster idea had had nothing to do with them, a version of Reid's poster did feature EMI's circular logo and the record's catalogue number.

Perhaps not surprisingly, most of the leading music weeklies made 'Anarchy' their 'single of the week' with *Melody Maker*'s Caroline Coon going into superlative hyperbole in her gushing praise. *Sounds* gave the task of reviewing it to Alan Lewis, rather than Jonh Ingham, who was equally favourable towards the Sex Pistols. Whereas Ingham would have strived to match or even outdo Coon, Lewis, although happy to point out 'this was where you read about 'em first', was sagacious enough to recognise it was 'the same old rock 'n' roll ... only younger and more intense then we've heard it for a long while.' The *NME*, however, (possibly still looking to settle the score over the attack on Nick Kent at the 100 Club), gave the single to their R&B/soul connoisseur Cliff White. White was clearly no fan of the Sex Pistols or punk rock, and took great pleasure in declaring the record 'lousy'. He then attempted to further belittle the Pistols' efforts with his snide comment about how their having made a record meant they'd already been assimilated into the system.

Due to an oversight at EMI, Chris Thomas had been inadvertently credited as producer on the single's B-side 'I Wanna Be Me', which had in fact been culled from Dave Goodman's Denmark Street demo sessions. Needless to say, Goodman was not best pleased and was still smarting from having been sidelined in favour of Thomas. Three days after the single's release, Goodman's solicitors wrote to EMI's legal department threatening an injunction, whilst also demanding that the label sent out notices to the media and all other interested parties admitting their error and regretting any embarrassment the oversight had caused. Also that after the initial 15,000 pressing with incorrect labels had been sold through, all future records would bear a label correctly crediting their client. Such inconveniences – although tiresome – were part and parcel of a record company's day-to-day remit. And dealing with a band like the Sex Pistols was bound to throw up a few problems. But EMI's headache was about to get worse ... much, much worse.

#

On Wednesday December 1st 1976 the Sex Pistols could be found holed up at the Roxy Theatre in Harlesden, North West London, rehearsing for their nineteen date national tour to promote 'Anarchy In The UK'. Malcolm received a call from EMI's promotions chief Eric 'Monster' Hall to see if he was amenable to having the band appear on that evening's edition of the *Today* show. EMI's plugger had just been informed by Michael Housego, the producer of Thames TV's early evening regional news magazine programme, that the video he'd sent across to Thames for Queen's latest single 'Somebody To Love' hadn't been cleared for broadcast by the Musicians' Union and therefore couldn't be screened.

Apparently it was Housego, upon being told that no other EMI acts were available at such short notice, who enquired about the Sex Pistols. Another version of events is that the Pistols' eleventh hour invitation to appear on the show came about due to their EMI label mates Queen having been forced to cancel their own scheduled appearance owing to singer Freddie Mercury being kept over at the dentist. Although when asked at the Kerrang! Awards in 2004 whether Queen were even supposed to be on the *Today* show, Brian May shook his head: 'Ah, that old wives' tale. I think you'll find it's more a part of Pistols folklore than anything to do with us!' But no matter which version is true, what is indisputable is that yet again fate played its part in determining the Pistols' path.

If Hall had cleared the Queen video with the Musicians' Union, or *if* Freddie's dental appointment been scheduled for another day, *then* the Sex Pistols would have undertaken the tour – no doubt attracting a few more fans at each stop off along the way – and remained an EMI act.

Some would argue that such a scenario would have merely delayed the band's date with ignominy until the release of 'God Save The Queen' in May 1977. Possibly, but one can't help but wonder whether a dyed-in-the-wool English institution such as EMI would have ever agreed to release the highly controversial single in Queen Elizabeth II's Silver Jubilee year.

Malcolm, of course, was up to his neck dotting the 'i's and crossing the 't's for the forthcoming tour, which commenced in two days. In addition to his own wayward charges, the other acts scheduled to appear on the bill were Johnny Thunders' new outfit The Heartbreakers, plus the Clash and (begrudgingly) the Damned. It was due to open at Norwich's University of East Anglia, before taking in 17 other towns and cities across England, Scotland and Wales with a triumphal homecoming finale at The Roxy in Covent Garden on 26th December. That was the theory anyway.

Malcolm proved surprisingly reluctant to interrupt the band's busy rehearsal schedule for what he saw as just another regional television appearance. The Sex Pistols had already made it onto prime-time television when the Mike Mansfield-directed 'Anarchy' promo video was aired on BBC's *Nationwide* on the 12th November as part of the programme's special feature on the new music phenomenon Punk Rock. The band had also appeared on the previous Sunday's edition of LWT's *London Weekend Show* hosted by Janet Street-Porter. Janet and her crew had interviewed the band members at Denmark Street, as well as filming their recent show at the Notre Dame Hall, a Catholic-run basement venue on Leicester Place, just off Leicester Square.

Hall was anxious to avoid getting carpeted by his superiors for failing to dot one of his own 'i's in getting the necessary clearance for the Queen video and played to Malcolm's vanity. He launched into his spiel about the *Today* slot being beneficial to the Sex Pistols seeing as EMI held a 50 per cent share in Thames Television. Malcolm begrudgingly acquiesced, but only on the proviso that EMI provided a limousine to pick the band up in Harlesden and ferry them to the Thames Studio located beneath the Euston Tower on Marylebone Road. That way, the driver could drop the boys off and then head out to Heathrow to pick up the Heartbreakers and their entourage, which consisted of the band's colourful manager Leee Black Childers and their roadie Lee Paul, and deliver them to the Roxy. After all, it couldn't hurt to give New York Johnny and his boys a little five-star pampering, as there would be no limos once the tour got underway.

Malcolm met the band in the foyer from where they were escorted up to the studio's Green Room for complimentary refreshments while awaiting their turn to go before the cameras. Glen later recalled getting his hands on a warm can of lager, as did Paul and John, whereas Steve drew the bonus ball and got a bottle of Blue Nun wine to himself. Before setting off to the studio Malcolm had called Simon Barker at SEX and told him to get himself and some of his friends along to the studio. This, of course, was light years before mobile phones became an everyday accessory, but fortunately occasional SEX employee Simone Thomas was available and Simon also managed to get hold of Siouxsie and Steve at the Banshees' rehearsal place. Siouxsie would later recall how Today's cantankerous host, Bill Grundy, was already in there topping up his liquid lunch from earlier in the day, and spent much of the time eyeing her up over the rim of his whisky glass.

During a subsequent interview, Paul Cook said he and the rest of the band were lined up behind the camera while an unseen voice – aping Rolling Stones' manager Andrew Loog Oldham's memorable line aimed at his own wayward charges – jokingly asked the viewers at home if they would be willing to let their daughters go out with a Sex Pistol. Then the band were escorted through to the action, where a soused Grundy was sat waiting. Hall, to his credit, had warned Housego that EMI's latest acquisitions were looking for publicity to promote their record by any means necessary and that Grundy should be extra careful with the band. Housego, however, believed that a straight-talking old pro like Grundy would know how to handle a rock group. He'd been the first television presenter to interview the Beatles back in October 1962 and, after all, the interview was an inconsequential three minute affair slotted in at the end of the programme. What could possibly go wrong?

Although the band and their small entourage were all aware of *Today*, as the half-hour programme was broadcast in and around the London area five days a week between 6 - 6.30 p.m., there was no way for them to know the show went out live. It might therefore have been prudent for one of the behind-the-scenes assistants to make the band aware of this before putting them in front of the camera. As a result the battle lines between host and band were drawn the moment the autocue sprang into life and Steve and John started reading out Grundy's lines to try and throw him off kilter. Grundy simply ignored them and launched into his pre-prepared dialogue about Punk Rock being the latest craze, as well as informing the viewers that the band were as drunk as he was, before the screen was taken up with thirty seconds or so of Mike Mansfield's 'Anarchy' promo.

With the red light indicating a return to action and little time left for pleasantries, Grundy cut straight to the chase by suggesting a £40,000 advance from a record company (strange that he should choose not to mention EMI by name given that the label owned a 50 per cent share in the company that paid his wages) should be contrary to the band's supposedly anti-materialistic view of life. The question was no doubt aimed at all four band members, but Glen, being the only one showing any interest at this stage, responded with a chirpy 'no, the more the merrier'. The bassist's blasé retort seemed to irritate Grundy and it was while he was pressing Glen for more information about the EMI advance that Steve – loud enough for any Londoner born within the sound of Big Ben to hear – said that they'd 'fuckin' spent it'.

Now this should have been the cue for Housego, or someone else with a clipboard, to get Malcolm to signal his boys to cease fire. Instead the interview continued unabated, and Grundy was even allowed to insist on John repeating the expletive he'd purposely mumbled for the sake of propriety. At this point Grundy actually had the upper hand as John had visibly reddened on camera. But instead of acknowledging his victory with a telling smile and switching the subject onto the forthcoming tour, or making a joke about wanting to see Tony Blackburn's face upon being asked to play a record called 'Anarchy In The UK', he chose to turn his attention to Siouxsie.

Siouxsie, looking like an extra from a Marcel Marceau film, in her face paint and polka-dot cravat and braces ensemble, surprisingly went all coy at finding herself centre stage. With the whole of London awaiting her response, she could think of nothing else to say to Grundy other than how she'd always wanted to meet him. The comment was obviously meant tongue-in-cheek given that Siouxsie was a svelte 21-year-old and Grundy was overweight and the wrong side of 50, but it provided Grundy with another opportunity to come out on top; all he needed to do was turn and make a suggestive face to camera and he'd have been home and dry. But no, and after getting Siouxsie to confirm what she'd said, he suggested they should meet up after the show, without giving any thought as to whether Siouxsie was the girlfriend of one of the band members.

Steve, who was quickly coming to the conclusion that a free bottle of plonk wasn't going to make up for being dragged away from rehearsals only to be ignored by a drunken letch, called Grundy a 'dirty old sod' and a 'dirty old man'. Let's not forget either that Steve was wearing a SEX 'Tits' T-shirt while all this was going down. Jordan's swastika armband may have proved too much for a late-night music programme, but a T-shirt bearing an image of a naked pair of breasts was obviously acceptable for prime time family viewing. Malcolm probably made a mental note to have a couple of thousand shirts printed up on the off-chance.

Grundy, who died in February 1999, probably spent the ensuing three decades pondering what possessed him to utter the ten words that would make the Sex Pistols a household name and set his own career adrift on TV's equivalent of the Mario Celeste: 'Go on. You've got another five seconds. Say something outrageous ... ' Giving a well-oiled 21-year-old an open mic and challenging him to 'say something outrageous' on live tea-time television, whilst kids were sat at home doing their homework, was both irresponsible and reprehensible – not to mention totally unprofessional. Had Grundy made his idiotic offer to John, he might have been spared as the singer's sarcastic riposte would probably have been something along the line of 'not until you say something intelligent, chief,' and with honours even everyone could have gone home happy. But Steve, being both inebriated and inarticulate, responded the only way he knew how and called Grundy a 'dirty bastard'. One has to wonder why Housego didn't step in at this point, but for some reason Grundy was allowed to push the envelope and Steve obliged by licking the stamp not once, but twice; the second time to actually call Grundy a 'fucking rotter'.

The word 'rotter' which is slang for a 'despicable or unpleasant character', had long-since disappeared from the English vernacular, but had resurfaced leading up to the Christmas period in a television commercial for *Cadbury's Schweppes* tonic water. So we can only assume there was a television set in the Thames hospitality room and that Steve caught the advert which carried the tagline – spoken by caddish actor William 'Schhh... You Know Who' Franklyn – 'You can always tell a rotter by his Schweppes.'

Although it was a measure of Grundy's conceited arrogance that he actually turned to the camera to tell the viewers he'd 'be seeing them soon', inwardly he must have known he'd overstepped the mark. If you watch the footage you can see him mouth the words 'oh shit' as he turns away from the camera and Steve leaps out of his chair to gyrate in time to the show's chirpy theme tune 'Windy'. Steve may not have been the first person to say 'fuck' on live television, as that dubious honour went to controversial film and theatre critic Kenneth Tynan. He had dared to utter the dreaded 'F' word back in 1965 during a live debate on the subject of censorship on the late-night weekend satirical show BBC-3, hosted by Robert '*Ask The Family*' Robinson. But his tossing of it into the domain of tea-time TV with such carefree abandon was more than some of the Today viewers could take; with one in particular, a 47-year-old lorry driver called James Holmes, being so outraged that he smashed his television. As John Lydon later chuckled, 'It's ridiculous to hear of people kicking in their TV sets, haven't they heard of the off button?'

The limo driver, of course, would have had no idea as to what had just occurred inside the studio, and was waiting to ferry the Sex Pistols back to Harlesden where they jovially regaled their astounded tour mates with what had happened. Siouxsie, Simon and Steve Severin headed into town to carry on with their merry-making and find that they were now punk *cause célebres*.

Malcolm later boasted to Eddie 'Legs' McNeil for the latter's brilliant book on the New York punk scene *Please Kill Me*, that he believed the Sex Pistols' appearance on *Today* was 'history in the making'. Indeed it was, but this consideration came long after the event, for at the time he was gripped with panic and feared it was the end of the band; he even went so far as to chastise Steve over his behaviour.

Thames issued an immediate on-air apology – as it would do for the remainder of the evening – expressing its regret over the interview and to apologise for the foul language. There were mixed reactions over at Manchester Square, where several of those specifically involved with the Sex Pistols had remained behind to watch the interview. Mark Rye from marketing was apparently in raptures over the number of records he was going to shift on the back of Grundy's ineptitude; though EMI Records Group Repertoire Division's general manager Paul Watts saw things very differently. It is a well-known maxim within the world of rock 'n' roll that 'all publicity is good publicity', and had EMI Records been an independent entity then Watts would have also rubbed his hands with festive glee at Thames' early Christmas gift. But EMI Records was merely a cog, albeit a very important and highly profitable cog, housed within a huge corporate machine. A few thousand extra record sales paled into insignificance against safeguarding the company's reputation.

And what would the morning papers say...?

#

For Fleet Street's newshounds, Christmas had indeed come early. For instead of trying to further highlight Callaghan's ongoing governmental failings, the tabloids – and the broadsheets – launched into a feeding frenzy over the Sex Pistols and the shocking new music craze, Punk Rock. *The Sun* was perhaps the most charitable towards the band in so much that its front page demanded to know '**WERE THE PISTOLS LOADED?**' as well as informing its readers of the two week ban imposed on Grundy over his 'filthy show'. *The Evening News* also pitched their tent on the Pistols' side of the fence with '**GRUNDY GOADED PUNK BOYS SAYS RECORD CHIEF**'. *The Evening Standard*, however, called it as they saw it, and declared the Sex Pistols to be '**FOUL-MOUTHED YOBS**', while the *Daily Express* came in with '**PUNK? CALL IT FILTHY LUCRE**' inadvertently providing Steve and Paul with another *bon mot* for the title song to *The Great Rock 'n' Roll Swindle* film; as well as the title for the reconstituted Sex Pistols' 1996 world tour. *The Daily Mail* threw its hat into the ring with '**FOUR-LETTER PUNK GROUP IN TV STORM**,' and the following day's edition featured a stinging editorial entitled '**NEVER MIND MORALS OR STANDARDS, THE ONLY NOTES THAT MATTER COME IN WADS**'. This was the first article to actually point the finger of blame at EMI by insinuating that the label stood to benefit from the band's verbal spat with Grundy as it would receive a percentage of every record the band sold.

But first prize in the witch-hunt surely went to the *Daily Mirror* for its catchy couplet: '**THE FILTH AND THE FURY**' (a memorable little headline, that would provide the group with a documentary title some 24 years later, and a million T-shirt sales). The paper cleverly accompanied their front page outrage with a photograph taken of the band leaving EMI's Manchester Square offices having just signed to the label on 8th October. All four band members – having celebrated with beer and champagne – are grinning profusely, and John sprays the photographer with a purloined can of lager just at the moment he snaps the shutter, causing flecks of beer foam to spatter the image. The paper's readers, having no idea of where or when the photo was from, would therefore assume it had been taken as the band was leaving Thames' studio, and that their ebullience was due to what had just occurred.

The incident naturally made the headlines on TV, with both ITV and the BBC choosing to lay the blame squarely at the band's door; while the few radio stations that hadn't taken offence to 'Anarchy

In The UK' upon its release, removed the record from their playlist. Only Radio One's late-night DJ John Peel, who regularly aired the single on his two hour show – as well as deeming it worthy of the top slot on his festive playlist for five years running - came out in support of the Pistols. 'I was frankly appalled,' he told Fred Vermorel the following year in *The Sex Pistols*, 'because if you took any four or five lads off the street … made them feel important, filled them with beer, put them on television and said "say something outrageous", they'd say something outrageous. I rather suspect that – as a middle-class individual of 38 – if they did the same to me, I'd do the same. So for those people then to wring their hands in horror and say "this is outrageous" is just bare-faced hypocrisy.' The 'unofficial' ban had extended to other radio stations such as London's Capital Radio, Manchester's Piccadilly Radio, and Birmingham's BRMB. Sheffield's Radio Hallam had also recently decided to pull the single from its playlist, but only after conducting a poll amongst its listeners; while Radio Luxembourg's Tony Prince had received a one night suspension for having had the nerve to send out an on-air invitation to the Sex Pistols to perform live on his show.

Although Thames TV had been quick to broadcast its on-air apologies, as well as severely reprimanding Michael Housego and suspending the hapless Grundy, neither Malcolm nor EMI appeared willing to express similar contrition. Indeed, Malcolm, having woken up to the possibilities the scandal made available to him, was probably wishing the Today *tête-à-tête* had come before he'd invited the Damned onto the tour.

EMI, however, was wishing the whole sorry saga would just disappear, but this seemed unlikely to happen anytime soon with reporters setting up base camps outside its Manchester Square offices. With the storm cloud showing little sign of abating, EMI Records managing director Leslie Hill (who would be unfairly targeted by the press and suffer the indignation of having his neighbours canvassed and see his home address – accompanied by a photograph of his house – printed in *The Daily Mail*) decided to hold a press conference to attempt to clarify the label's position. As he hadn't actually been involved in the Sex Pistols signing to the label due to the relatively small amount of cash involved, he called Malcolm and got him to bring the band down to Manchester Square so that they could field the majority of the questions.

Earlier that day Hill had received a call from Roy Matthews, the manager of the label's Hayes pressing plant, to be informed that the [predominantly female] workforce had gone out on strike and were refusing to handle the Pistols' single. So, as soon as the conference was over, Hill then had to drive down to the plant where he spent the rest of the day overcoming the workers' objections and getting them back to their labours. The women were back at their stations by the following morning, but the damage had already been done as far as the Sex Pistols were concerned, as the knock-on effect from the disruption was a delay in distribution to the smaller retail outlets. As Woolworths, W.H. Smith and Boots had already gone public in their denouncement of the Sex Pistols by refusing to stock the single, these independent record stores were the only remaining outlets available.

Chapter Seven

Not In My Backyard

*'Before I went down for breakfast each morning I'd
pull out my tour poster and cross out the name of
whichever venue had cancelled and write in the
substitute venue. But by lunch I'd have scribbled
that one out and replaced it with another.'*
Steve 'Roadent' Connolly
(whilst serving as Clash roadie on the Anarchy Tour)

Fri 3ʳᵈ December Norwich East Anglia University Cancelled
Sat 4ᵗʰ December Derby King's Hall Cancelled
Sun 5ᵗʰ December Newcastle City Hall Cancelled
Mon 6ᵗʰ December Leeds Polytechnic Played
Tue 7ᵗʰ December Bournemouth Village Bowl Cancelled
Sheffield University Fell Through
Thu 9ᵗʰ December Manchester Electric Circus Played
Fri 10ᵗʰ December Lancaster University Cancelled
Preston Charter Fell Through
Sat 11ᵗʰ December Liverpool Stadium Cancelled
The Cavern Fell Through
Mon 13ᵗʰ December Bristol Colston Hall Cancelled
Bristol University Fell Through
Tue 14ᵗʰ December Cardiff Top Rank Cancelled
Caerphilly Castle Cinema Played
Wed 15ᵗʰ December Glasgow Apollo Cancelled
Wolverhampton Lafayettes Fell Through
Thu 16ᵗʰ December Dundee Caird Hall Cancelled
Fri 17ᵗʰ December Sheffield City Hall Cancelled
Carlisle Market Hall Fell Through
Sat 18ᵗʰ December Southend Kursaal Cancelled
Maidenhead Skindles Fell Through
Sun 19ᵗʰ December Guildford Civic Hall Cancelled
Manchester Electric Circus Played

Mon 20th December Birmingham Town Hall Cancelled
Bingley Hall Fell Through
Cleethorpes Winter Gardens Played
Tue 21st December Plymouth Woods Centre Played
Wed 22nd December Torquay 400 Ballroom Cancelled
Paignton Penelope's Ballroom Fell Through
Plymouth Woods Centre Played
Sun 26th December London Roxy Theatre Cancelled

[The Anarchy Tour's original 19 venues are in normal type, with alternate venues in italics]

The Anarchy tour will surely go down as the greatest rock 'n' roll extravaganza never to be undertaken; it simply fell apart before the eyes of those responsible for actually doing it. Although Malcolm had failed to entice either the Ramones or Talking Heads to come over to London to share headline billing on the Sex Pistols tour, Johnny Thunders and his new band the Heartbreakers – which included ex-New York Doll, Jerry Nolan on drums – were no slouches. Some of the venues, such as the 550 capacity Torquay Ballroom, and the 650 capacity Woods Centre in Plymouth, were only marginally larger than the 100 Club. However, the other venues could hold 2,000, while the 3,000 capacity Glasgow Apollo would be by far the largest audience the Sex Pistols had faced to date. Aside from the Heartbreakers, the Clash were on the bill too. Malcolm had also been forced to invite the Damned onto the tour (a decision that was taken before the Grundy interview and its ensuing publicity), with the sole aim of putting enough bums on seats to make the venture a success.

The Clash and the Heartbreakers were to be taken care of from the proceeds of the EMI advance, and both bands could look forward to travelling on a luxury coach, staying in upmarket hotels, and eating three square meals a day. No such luck for Captain Sensible and his merry men, who were reliant on their own label's budget and would have to make do with bed & breakfast amenities and travel to the venues in a transit van. 'Being signed to Stiff,' the Captain later bemoaned, 'meant that if the latest Elvis Costello record didn't sell, then the next Ian Dury record didn't get made. It was very cramped in the back of that van and constantly smelled of sweat and stale farts. And there was very little in the way of luxuries.'

Not since the days of Larry Parnes' early to mid-sixties roster roustabouts had a tour line-up been bursting with so much emerging British talent. However, the country's knee-jerk reaction following Steve's verbal spat with Bill Grundy put paid to Malcolm's plans to emulate his Tin Pan Alley hero. Prior to the Sex Pistols' appearance on the *Today* show, punk rock had been viewed by the media as little more than an insular London fancy dress fraternity with affiliations in Manchester and Birmingham; now it was a rapidly escalating youth movement. As with the seat-slashing Teddy Boys of the fifties, and the beach-brawling Mods and Rockers of the sixties, punk had its own music, style of dress and attitude. Malcolm, who was poised ready to cash in on the chaos by outfitting the latest teenage craze, would have been creaming himself had just two or three of the tour dates cancelled over the *Today* furore, as the publicity would have brought more kids into the World's End in search of bondage trousers. But with venues cancelling left, right and centre, it was he who ended up out of pocket. For although the Sex Pistols, the Clash, the Heartbreakers and the Damned – as well as the latter band's Manchester stand-ins the Buzzcocks – managed to play seven shows, only three of those gigs had appeared on the original 19 date tour itinerary. The remaining original tour dates, as well as a further nine alternative venues, fell foul of various local councils.

Anyone who owns a copy of Ray Stevenson's *Sex Pistols File* will have seen the photographs he took of John and Steve the morning following the band's appearance on the Today show. Steve, whose literary failings meant he could barely read about the uproar he'd caused, grins while holding up a copy of the *Daily Mirror* to the camera; well, it's not every day you're responsible for shocking a nation at its breakfast. John has obviously just arrived at Malcolm's Dryden Chambers office (where he can be seen lurking in the background) as he's still wearing his overcoat fastened at the collar with a nappy pin. In another photo he poses with a knowing look in his eyes; a folded (and possibly the same) copy of the *Daily Mirror* lies on the desk in front of him. The tabloid headlines and the reporters swarming outside Malcolm's new offices may have given John some indication of the whirlwind awaiting the band, but little could he have imagined that those same journalists would proclaim *him* – a London-Irish shit-kicker from Finsbury Park – the figurehead of the punk rock craze. Some of the journalists were even calling punk rock the latest youth movement, but although the band's fanbase had increased ten-fold since the 100 Club Punk Festival, it could hardly be described as a 'movement'. Not yet, at any rate.

This, of course, was about to change as the subtext behind the tabloid headlines was that the Sex Pistols were playing to the dole queues of Britain. This was just Fleet Street's way of further denigrating the band and their fans as, aside from a few work-shy individuals within their inner circle, their following consisted mainly of art students. Those who were signing on were probably using their weekly government stipend, the princely sum of £9.70, to put a band together and get off the dole and into rock 'n' roll.

As the *Today* show only went out in the London area, the rest of the country didn't get to hear about 'the night the air turned blue' until the following morning's cornflake-choking headlines. While Malcolm and the band were basking in the afterglow of having made the front page of every leading newspaper, those in positions of authority on the councils of the nineteen towns and cities the Sex Pistols would shortly be gracing with their presence began plotting their revenge.

The nightmare, from which very few of the tour participants would emerge unscathed, began the following morning with the University of East Anglia's vice-chancellor, Frank Thistlewaite, announced he was cancelling that night's tour opening show as he wasn't convinced the event would pass without incident. The university's Students' Union social committee was outraged and organised a mass sit-in to protest against Thistlewaite's draconian measures. It seems likely though that their ire probably had more to do with having their liberties so blatantly infringed rather than missing out on the Sex Pistols concert per se. With no time to arrange an alternative venue at such short notice, the tour bus headed up the M1 for Derby, where the bands were due to appear the following evening.

The tour party included Ray Stevenson serving as official photographer, and his brother Nils, whom Malcolm had temporarily lured back to the fold with the promise of £300 back pay for services rendered. When they arrived at the Derby Crest Hotel the lobby was swarming with journalists and the three bands were forced to spend the evening confined to their rooms. That said, however, the musicians were still able to avail themselves of room service and kept the hotel's porters fully occupied in providing a never-ending supply of lager and club sandwiches; while Dave

Goodman was also on hand to provide the ambience with one of his special tour spliffs.

You could argue that it was Goodman who was inadvertently responsible for the unfolding tour disaster. *For* had he not exhausted EMI's patience by attempting to capture the Sex Pistols' live sound onto tape then the 'Anarchy' single would have been released on the 19th November, as the label had originally intended. *Had* it done so, the tour would surely have started a week earlier, with the joyful and triumphant London homecoming show at the Roxy Theatre taking place on Sunday 19th December, before everyone headed off to enjoy Christmas with their nearest or weirdest. *And* this would have entailed the Sex Pistols being in mid-tour on 1st December and so they couldn't have done the *Today* slot as they'd have been enjoying a night off in Manchester – probably at Tommy Ducks – looking forward to playing the Electric Circus the following night. Isn't hindsight grand?

#

It was upon arriving at the Derby Crest that Malcolm discovered the following night's show in Newcastle had been cancelled by Tyneside city council in the interests of protecting its children from the spiky-haired Antichrist. Although Derby's elected officials didn't quite feel their own youth was in peril, the city's Leisure Committee issued a proposal whereby that night's concert could only go ahead on the proviso that the Sex Pistols consented to perform a private matinee show in front of the committee in order to determine whether the band's stage act was suitable. The understanding being that, should the Sex Pistols be deemed too risqué, the other three bands on the bill could still appear.

Whether a truncated three-band bill with the Damned as headliners would have had the same appeal quickly became a moot point as the Clash and the Heartbreakers closed ranks behind the Sex Pistols. The Damned, of course, were holed up in a bed and breakfast on the other side of town and were therefore unable to keep pace with the unfolding developments. The last they'd heard was that Malcolm had consented to the committee's wishes and so their tour manager, Rick Rogers, issued a statement to the press saying there was nothing offensive about their stage act and that they'd be happy to play. Malcolm did indeed appear to be acquiescing to the Leisure Committee's demands, and even instructed Dave Goodman to arrange for the band's gear to be taken down to the King's Hall and set up on stage. This, however, was simply a ruse to throw the baying press hounds off the scent.

Although it was a Saturday, and no one of any significant rank at EMI would be at their desk, Malcolm had managed to get hold of Paul Watts on his home telephone number. The EMI man was initially reluctant to get involved, but must have sensed that Malcolm was at the end of his tether and agreed to cover the hotel bill. And so while Derby's mayor and mayoress (dressed in their civic robes and chains of office), the city's chief constable, and councillors, Edith Wood, Les Shipley and Richard Wayman – who was himself an ex-mayor – sat waiting patiently for the band to make their appearance on stage, the tour party loaded up the bus and headed straight for Leeds.

The ill-fated tour was to be re-enacted for *The Great Rock 'n' Roll Swindle* film, complete with voiceover from a disgruntled Derby dignitary informing the assembled media of the Leisure Committee's decision to deny the Sex Pistols the right to appear at the city's King's Hall. Contrary to legend, or indeed what appears on screen, the destination board of the Anarchy tour bus didn't read 'nowhere', and nor was it intentionally left blank. Malcolm, though, might as well have daubed a blood-red cross on the vehicle's side panels as the councillors within each town and city in turn reacted to the Sex Pistols as though they were carrying the plague. However, whereas Edgar Allan Poe's Prince Prospero staged elegant masquerade balls to keep the disease away from his castle walls, Britain's outraged councillors wanted no pogoing within their cosy realms and closed their doors to the Sex Pistols. Glasgow's Lord Provost – who declared Scotland had enough hooligans of its own without importing them from across the border – went so far as to revoke the Apollo's entertainment license for the night in question.

Malcolm's ruse may have thwarted Derby's local press pack, but Fleet Street couldn't be shaken off that easily and an army of reporters was waiting to greet the arrival of the tour bus at the four star Dragonara Hotel in Leeds. Having stuck two fingers up at Derby Council's attempt at censorship, Malcolm held an impromptu press conference in the hotel's foyer and gleefully informed the gathering that the highlight of the following night's show would be the Sex Pistols' as yet unrecorded song 'No Future' with its opening line 'God bless the Queen and her fascist regime' [sic]. A song which supposedly likened the British Establishment to Hitler's brown shirts on the cusp of Queen Elizabeth entering her Silver Jubilee year was alone worthy of a headline – as indeed, it would be six months later. This wasn't enough though for your man from the muck-raking *Daily Mirror,* who was so desperate to find more filth to feed the nation's fury that he handed the hotel's bemused manager £25 to cover any damages before goading Steve and Paul into throwing a few potted plants around. The pair duly obliged – more out of mischief than malice – the manager was in pocket, the hack had his story and the Mirror's morning edition screamed: '**PUNK ROCK GROUP WRECK HOTEL'.**

Front page headlines about uprooted plants and soiled carpets were the least of Malcolm's worries, however, as Rank Leisure Services, the owners of Bournemouth's Village Bowl – the next stop on the itinerary – had announced they were cancelling the show. A spokesman for Rank told reporters the company was pulling the plug owing to its concerns over safety, before hinting at the underlying factor behind the decision by stating that Rank Leisure Services wasn't particularly keen to be associated with the Sex Pistols at that time.

Later that same Monday afternoon Malcolm surprisingly consented to an interview with Yorkshire Television's Ken Rees, with the band sat looking suitably bored in the background. Before going on air Rees told Malcolm about his interview earlier in the day with Leeds Polytechnic's dean, Dr Nashenter, who'd thought it worthy of mention that the institution was also staging an in-house production of Handel's Messiah, which would be taking place simultaneously within the faculty's main hall. He found it highly amusing that such widely-contrasting musical forms would be simultaneously emanating from the two halls. Although this was meant as an amusing aside to the situation, it called into question the high-handed actions of Nashenter's East Anglian counterpart Frank Thistlewaite, as Nashenter had insisted that he himself didn't have the authority to cancel the Sex Pistols' show; such decisions rested with the 'autonomous' Students Union. Yet Thistlewaite was allowed to ride roughshod over Norwich University's student body.

Once the interview got underway Rees reverted to type and asked a series of equally banal questions about how the band's supposed spitting and vomiting on stage could possibly be a good example to children? Did Malcolm feel the Today interview had had any damaging effect on the band? Had the band's behaviour been premeditated simply to boost ticket sales? What sort of future could the Sex Pistols expect from this point on? Malcolm, having already answered similar – if not identical – questions back in Derby, gave a measured response. It was only when Rees asked him his reaction to the Sex Pistols having the reputation of being the most revolting band in the country that he decided enough was enough and launched into an oratory of how the Sex Pistols were creating a generation gap in the country and that was why people were feeling threatened. And if the kids wanted to buy the record it was in the shops and they could make their own decisions. He ended his rhetoric by calling on the mothers of the kids who wanted to buy the record and see the band play live, to exercise their democratic right and challenge their local councillors, who were currently making his own life a misery.

Perhaps not surprisingly, given all the hype surrounding the Grundy incident, the Leeds show was a rather lacklustre affair, as the majority of the punters gathered inside the polytechnic's draughty sports hall had come along out of morbid curiosity rather than for the musical fare. The Clash finally got the Anarchy tour underway at 8 p.m., but neither they nor the Damned – who were blissfully unaware that they were making their one and only appearance before being thrown off the tour over their supposed collusion with the Derby councillors – made any impression on the punters. Johnny Thunders, of course, was an old hand at dealing with apathetic and difficult audiences from his Dolls days, and after admonishing Leeds for its apparent lack of junkies, he and the Heartbreakers got the crowd rocking with some old fashioned Lower East Side rock 'n' roll.

The Sex Pistols' arrival on stage was greeted with catcalls and a few token missiles, most of which failed to find their intended target. John, dressed in a vermillion-red SEX waistcoat, white shirt and skinny black tie, responded in kind by spraying the audience with a can of lager before dedicating the opening number 'Anarchy In The UK' to 'the Leeds council, Bill Grundy and the Queen'. Tony Parsons, the *NME*'s new hip young gunslinger, who was covering the tour as his first assignment, opened his '**BLANK GENERATION OUT ON THE ROAD**' review with the gambit: 'Kenneth Anger called James Dean a human ashtray. Maybe he should have waited twenty years to see the self-inflicted fag burns on Rotten's forearms'. Many of those in the audience, however, weren't prepared to hang around for the next three minutes to catch sight of John's masochistic markings for, according to Steve Kendall who was covering the show for *Record Mirror*, many of the punters left after one song, while those who did stay remained unmoved and continued expressing their displeasure by chucking beer at the stage. Unlike Parsons, who would heap praise on the Sex Pistols, especially the band's rhythm section of Glen and Paul whom he cited as 'tighter than tomorrow', Kendall was clearly no fan of the Sex Pistols or their music as he vilified their 'predictably loud and crude' efforts as being 'dismally disappointing, relentless and unimaginative'.

In-between songs John attempted a little levity by taunting the audience for not living up to the expectations of the press and wrecking the place. But this wasn't the 100 Club, and the Sex Pistols were a long way from London. The interaction remained woefully one-sided and John finally lost patience and pointed out the exits for those who'd rather be elsewhere. The band brought the largely uneventful evening to an end with the rather apt 'No Fun' before trudging off the beer-sodden stage.

#

Tuesday 7th December was the day of EMI's Annual General Meeting and, with the Sex Pistols sure to feature on the agenda, it wasn't only Fleet Street's financial press that were gathering like hopeful vultures in Manchester Square. It seemed that one of their number, the Daily Express, had gotten a head start on its competitors with an article in that morning's edition which intimated that EMI, on its corporate side at least, was attempting to distance itself from the band. The paper had even secured a quote from Lord Shawcross who, when asked to comment on the band's plant-throwing antics at the Dragonara Hotel, had declared that he believed EMI was 'being taken for a ride'. EMI's corporate arm may have been looking to ditch the Sex Pistols, but its music division was still very much behind the band. Leslie Hill had gone so far as to prepare a brief for the AGM, in which he'd outlined his plans for the Sex Pistols to go into the studio later in the month with EMI's in-house engineer Mike Thorne. They would be recording songs for their follow-up single scheduled for release in either late January or early February 1977, with an album following in March or April.

In an attempt to play down the tour cancellations, he'd singled out the one at Derby which – according to the information gleaned thus far – had been cancelled due to fifty members of a motorcycle club having made a block-booking and who were expected to cause trouble inside the hall. It was also understood that the National Front had been planning to stage a protest outside the venue, and that it had been at Paul Watts' behest that the show be cancelled; not as a result of the Sex Pistols' refusal to perform before the town's Leisure Committee as reported in the press. He'd also attached sales figures for the single (some 9,000 copies sold to date) in the hope they might help sway any decision on the label's future relationship with the band.

Sir John Read, however, although keen to stress he wasn't looking to lead a witch-hunt against the Sex Pistols per se, was equally determined to do what was right by the corporation as a whole. As its chairman he believed it was his job to safeguard EMI's interests as well as protect its share price on the financial markets: in other words, he wasn't about to allow a smutty pop group to besmirch the company's reputation. Despite EMI Records' worldwide music business having reported profits of more than £27million in the financial year 1975-76 (some 42% of the company's total profit), the suits holding sway in the boardroom wouldn't have known a Beatle from a Bay City Roller, and were of the collective opinion that their defence interests were the jewels within EMI's corporate crown. But the AGM was open to investors and shareholders, who would no doubt want to voice their concerns, as well as demand answers as to what EMI intended to do with regard to the Sex Pistols. So for the first time in EMI's proud and distinguished history, its chairman was forced to discuss the merits of a pop group.

Having provided some background information on the band to those board members, investors and shareholders who weren't au fait with the Sex Pistols, as well as how they came to be signed to EMI, Read then turned to the matter in hand. Whilst condemning the band's 'disgraceful' behaviour on the *Today* show, he was careful to point out that the company's own experience of working with the group had been satisfactory. He then attempted to put the situation into context by speaking of the present-day social values against which EMI had to make value judgements about the content of records. Whilst assuring the well-heeled gathering that EMI would be reviewing its general guidelines regarding the content of pop records, he was quick to stress that EMI should not attempt to set itself up as a public censor.

Such moral posturing was of course only to be expected, as no one with a vested interest in EMI wanted a repeat of the previous Wednesday. Although Read made it clear that EMI would do everything within its power to restrain the band's public behaviour, he readily admitted this was an area over which the company had no real control. Whilst he made no mention of terminating the Sex Pistols' two month old contract, neither did he appear willing to confirm the label would be standing by the group. For those who could read between the lines, Read's ambiguous comment as to whether EMI would release any more Sex Pistols records left little doubt... the band's days at EMI were numbered.

The following day's newspaper headlines merely served to confirm this: '**EMI MAY DRUM OUT PISTOLS**' proclaimed *The Guardian*; '**WE'LL TRY TO MUZZLE PISTOLS PLEDGE EMI**' said the *Evening News*, while the *Evening Standard* went with what proved to be a most prescient piece of journalism: '**EMI GIVE GROUP A WEEK TO IMPROVE: SEX PISTOLS – ULTIMATUM**'. If there was anyone within EMI Records who had still been clinging to the belief that the situation could be resolved amicably, then all bets were off with the *Daily Mail*'s banner-headline '**SEX PISTOLS GIVE EMI CHIEF FOUR-LETTER REPLY**'. The chief in question being Sir John Read, and the four-letter reply being John's retort: 'Tell him to go fuck himself!' upon being informed by the paper of EMI's intention to restrain the Sex Pistols' behaviour in public.

#

With the Bournemouth date already cancelled, the tour bus headed down the M1 to Sheffield where a last-minute replacement show had been tentatively booked at the city's university. The question of whether the show would have been given the go ahead, however, was rendered obsolete as the roadies somehow managed to take a wrong turn off the motorway and they, along with the PA, ended up stranded somewhere in darkest Berkshire.

The following day, Wednesday 8th December, had originally been designated a rest day, but with only one date out of five having gone ahead as planned, and Malcolm having failed to secure a second date at Leeds Polytechnic, the tour bus headed back up the M1 to Manchester for the following evening's show. There was more bad news awaiting their arrival at the Midland Hotel in Manchester's Piccadilly.

Despite repeated assurances to the contrary from both Leslie Hill and Paul Watts, EMI had announced – following on from its AGM two days earlier – that it was withdrawing support and finance for the tour. EMI Records may have been willing to stand by the Sex Pistols, but its less-enamoured corporate parent was still seething at having EMI's proud name tarnished by a pop group. From a financial point they regarded it as throwing good money after bad. To all intents and purposes Glitterbest was on its own. Hill, finding his hands tied, advised Malcolm to cut his losses and return to London, but unbeknownst to the EMI Records MD a cheque from EMI Publishing had arrived at Dryden Chambers that very morning. Malcolm's world may indeed have been unravelling around him, but imbued by the unexpected influx of cash, he decided to look the devil in the eye to see who would blink first. To his mind, it was a case of EMI be damned. As long as the tour continued, then so would the publicity. More publicity for the Sex Pistols would generate more record sales and put more money into the Glitterbest coffers.

Once it became apparent in Manchester Square that Malcolm had no intention of quitting, Hill called to inform him he was sending Harvest Records' label manager, Frank Brunger, up to Manchester to act as on-the-road liaison. Malcolm was, of course, already familiar with Brunger's name from EMI having tried to foist the band onto their subsidiary 'hippy' label Harvest. As he was rooming with Dave Goodman, he couldn't help but wonder what the engineer's reaction would be on coming face to face with the man who had – albeit inadvertently – credited Chris Thomas as producer for both tracks on the 'Anarchy' single.

Finding themselves free from the record company's fiscal restraints, the Sex Pistols could have been forgiven for thinking their stay in Manchester would have been as memorable and as pleasurable as their previous visits. Those locals of a romantic disposition might have preferred to see their heroes play another show at the Lesser Free Trade Hall, but the fundamental idea behind the Anarchy Tour – and even more so now – was to promote the Sex Pistols to a wider audience, so Malcolm had booked the 2000 capacity Electric Circus in Collyhurst.

Today, the long-since demolished Electric Circus is revered amongst the punk faithful for being to Manchester what the 100

Club and subsequently The Roxy were to London. It had once been a thriving picture palace bringing the stars of the silver-screen to lighten Collyhurst's gas-lit gloom, and then a bingo hall to tempt the bored housewives from the surrounding high-rise council estates. By December 1976 though – much like its Oxford Street counterpart – Manchester's soon-to-be punk Mecca was serving as a music venue, predominantly catering to the city's heavy metal scene.

The Sex Pistols return to Manchester wasn't entirely without incident, as on the morning of the Electric Circus show the Midland's management informed the tour party that they were no longer welcome. Malcolm was forced to spend most of the morning telephoning every other hotel within the city limits and, just when it seemed the bands and their respective entourages would have to bunk down in the coach, a booking was finally arranged at the Arosa Hotel in nearby Withington. There would be no rest for the fans, however, as they were forced to run the gauntlet of a marauding gang of Manchester United football hooligans who pelted them and the venue with bricks, bottles and anything else that came to hand. These same 'Red Devils' had themselves made the headlines having gone on a season-long rampage following their beloved football club's relegation to the old Division Two in 1974.

Johnny Thunders and Jerry Nolan, having both grown up in New York's tough borough of Queens, were certainly no strangers to street violence. Surely though, even they must have wondered what they'd let themselves in for as they peered through the dressing room's boarded-up windows to watch mounted police charging up and down the street trying to keep the thugs at bay, whilst the venue's beleaguered security staff attempted to get everyone inside. Of course, not everyone attuned to what the Sex Pistols were offering had spiky hair or sported bondage trousers, and so a sizable contingent of the local thugs managed to bluff their way past the bouncers. 'Some loonies were going around the hall asking people whether or not they were punks,' Dave Goodman later recalled. 'And if the answer was yes, they would punch them!'

It wasn't just the fans who were left feeling vulnerable, as the only way for the band to get from the dressing room to the small stage was through the audience. If the crowd turned nasty, then whichever act happened to be on stage at the time would be at their mercy. Pete Silverton, who later assisted Glen to write his autobiography *I Was A Teenage Sex Pistol*, was at the Electric

Circus reviewing the show for *Sounds*. Pete was savvy enough to recognise that the Anarchy tour was not only living up to its name, but was also shaping up to be an all-time rock 'n' roll classic. That said, however, he was less poetic about the musical fare and, although he deemed the Clash – and particularly Joe Strummer – worthy of praise, he dismissed the Buzzcocks, who were filling in for the Damned, as 'a second-rate provincial Pistols copy'. The Heartbreakers he cited as a band in need of 'match practice'. He was equally uncharitable about the Sex Pistols, but was willing to put their sloppy performance down to mental strain caused by the extraordinary happenings of the previous week.

It was at the Manchester show that the inaugural issue of the *Anarchy in the UK* fanzine went on sale. The 20p mag, which featured Soo Catwoman on the cover, was a mixture of Jamie Reid's graphics interspersed with Ray Stevenson's photographs of the Sex Pistols and the other bands at the 100 Punk Festival in September; as well as the Bromley Contingent at play in Linda Ashby's Westminster flat. Although various rough layouts were, by all accounts, completed there would never be an issue 2. Alan remembers giving John his copy of the *Anarchy* fanzine to sign in Ezee Hire Studios in 1992; he took one look at the cover and held it up for the gathered Virgin, PIL and SLF crowd to see. 'Now that,' he said 'is Soo Catwoman, not some silly 15-year-old little girl in Malcolm's movie.' Much laughter followed.

If the Sex Pistols were suffering from fatigue and disorientation then they would now have four days to recuperate as the tour calendar was blank until the following Tuesday. Malcolm had tried to replace the Lancaster show – which had been cancelled due to certain sections of the university's female populace believing the Sex Pistols to be sexist – with one at the Preston Charter, but this had also blown out too. His attempt to restage the Liverpool show at the city's legendary Cavern Club had also fallen foul of the city's council. Despite the club's owner, Roy Adams, having no objections to the Sex Pistols treading the hallowed cellar stage made famous by the Fab Four, Malcolm's efforts were thwarted by local councillor, Doreen Jones, who'd persuaded her council colleagues to place a special banning order on punk rock groups. Although he'd managed to secure a booking at Caerphilly's Castle Cinema to replace the cancelled Cardiff Top Rank date, there seemed little point in running up hotel bills over the coming weekend and so the tour was put on temporary hiatus and the bands returned to London.

Soo Catwoman actress – Unissued poster for Swindle *film*

Despite having endured a gruelling six hour overnight coach ride back to the capital, Malcolm called in at Manchester Square on the Friday morning to find out if anyone at EMI was still fighting the Sex Pistols' corner. However, it seemed that everyone within EMI Records, from Leslie Hill down, was suddenly unavailable. Brian Southall's PR team was no longer allowed to field any calls relating to the band; even the group's supposedly loyal A&R man John Bagnall had dispensed with the safety pins and was back to wearing flares.

Malcolm's next port of call was to the office where even more bad news was waiting. The show at Dundee Caird Hall on the 16th December – which had survived longer than Glasgow – had finally fallen through; while the Glasgow replacement show at Wolverhampton's Lafayette's had also become a casualty of the local council. Sheffield's council had now also joined in the witch-hunt, as had their Cumbrian counterparts who scuppered Malcolm's attempts to book a replacement show at Carlisle's Market Hall. The Southend Kursaal show for Saturday 18th December had been cancelled a few days earlier, but now the replacement at Maidenhead Skindles was also off. An alternative venue would need to be found for the end-of-tour London homecoming show as the manager of the Roxy, Terry Collins, had rescinded his offer. Collins told the *Evening Standard* that he'd pulled the show because of the Sex Pistols' behaviour on *Today*, as well as what they represented ... and for having defaced the walls of the Gents toilets while rehearsing at the cinema.

#

On Tuesday 14ᵗʰ December, with tour losses already running in the region of £9,000, the Anarchy tour rolled into Caerphilly to play the town's 110 all-seater Castle Cinema. Needless to say, Rhymney Valley District Council was not best pleased at having the Sex Pistols invade their land and had even taken its objections to the High Court. Its put-upon Vice-Chairman, Madeline Ryland, told reporters that the people of Caerphilly had been horrified at reports of the Sex Pistols' previous concerts in Wales [Fact: the band had only played two dates in Wales, in Cardiff and Swansea on the 21ˢᵗ and 22ⁿᵈ September 1976, both of which had passed without incident], and that she and her fellow councillors felt the good Christian folk of Rhymney Valley shouldn't have to be subjected to such treatment.

It seemed the council's bid to have the show stopped had failed due to its having been arranged at such short notice after the one in Cardiff had been cancelled. The Castle Cinema's pragmatic proprietor, Pauline Uttley, told those same reporters that she was perfectly willing to offer shelter to the Sex Pistols simply because there had been no reports of trouble when the band had played in Cardiff and Swansea back in September. Hers, however, was to be the sole voice of reason in Rhymney as Caerphilly's shopkeepers and publicans – having held a special meeting to consider their options – decided upon closing their respective establishments until the punk rock battle bus was across the border and back on English soil.

As they couldn't stop the show from taking place, Ryland and several other outraged local dignitaries, including Pastor John Cooper – whose vociferous protestations would be forever immortalised in *The Great Rock 'n' Roll Swindle* – held a carol service in the car park directly opposite the Castle Cinema. The religious zealots were also handing out leaflets to the bemused concert-goers entitled '**IS GOD THE ANSWER???**' which appeared to challenge the reader to decide whether the Sex Pistols' Anarchy tour offered any real solution to the needs of today's 'youth', as well as the meaning of this latest controversial music trend. In reality, this was little more than a promotional missive to swell their congregation.

Several news crews – including the BBC and HTV – were also on hand to provide a social commentary on the new music craze currently sweeping Britain. The news crews were quick to point out that in terms of numbers the night was a victory for the carol singers, but there were enough free-spirited local souls willing to risk eternal damnation by attending the show to make a night of it. One of these was 17-year-old Steven Harrington who – having adopted the pop pseudonym Steve Strange – would later assimilate punk's 'do-it-yourself' attitude into his own band Visage, who would spearhead the early eighties New Romantic movement. Visage would score a Top 10 UK hit in January 1981 with 'Fade To Grey'.

With the tour calendar void until the following Monday (19th December), when Malcolm had managed to replace the scrapped Guildford Civic Hall date with a second show at Manchester's Electric Circus, the party returned to London. As there was no money available to pay the wages that week, the members of all three bands headed down to Dingwalls on Camden Lock, where the *NME* was holding its Christmas shindig, and happily availed themselves of the free food and booze. The Damned were also in attendance, but the season of good will to all men didn't quite extend to supposed quislings and the groups kept their distance.

With the original 20th December show at Birmingham Town Hall – as well as the substitute show at the region's Bingley Hall – having been put asunder by the local council, the tour bus headed for Cleethorpes in North Humberside, where Malcolm had managed to book a second replacement show at the coastal resort's Winter Gardens. This – aside from trousering the £200 fee – would prove to be Malcolm's last involvement with the tour. He had got wind that the overworked and underpaid road crew were plotting their revenge for his and Bernie's high-handed management style, so he slipped off to catch the last train back to London. Bernie wouldn't be so fortunate and the crew extracted their 'roadie rage' revenge by taking a dump in his bed.

By this stage, there were many others aboard the tour bus who would have also gladly bailed out given the opportunity, but with the following night's show at Plymouth Woods Centre still proceeding – the third and last of the original nineteen dates to go ahead as scheduled – the party was obliged to undertake a gruelling overnight twelve hour drive down to Devon in order to honour its West Country commitment. Yet despite having endured another fitful night sleeping in their seats, all three bands rallied to the cause and put in blistering performances, as much to get the £300 fee as to entertain the 150 or so punters that had braved the wintry weather.

In an attempt to end the tour on a high note, a second Plymouth show had been booked for 23rd December, but when the following night's replacement gig at Paignton's Penelope's Ballroom went the same way as its Torquay predecessor, to save on any unnecessary expenditure the local promoter brought the second Plymouth date forward. Unfortunately for all concerned, the lack of adequate promotion meant that all three bands played to a near-empty hall. But this being the final night of the odyssey – coupled with the prospect of the end of tour party back at the hotel – served to reinvigorate the collective spirit; so much so that each band took to the stage in what they happened to be wearing and shared the Pistols' equipment. Those few Woods Centre waifs and strays, which included Sophie, Debbie and Tracey who'd made the trip from London, that were lucky enough to catch the show were treated to blinding sets by both the Clash and the Heartbreakers, but the Sex Pistols' set was blighted by chronic sound problems owing to Dave Goodman having started the party early.

The end of tour late night revelry back at the hotel – including a free-for-all water fight – brought a plethora of complaints from the hotel's disgruntled guests and led to the manager closing the residents' bar in an attempt to curtail the mayhem. However, he and his beleaguered staff had failed to lock the door leading down to the indoor swimming pool and, instead of everyone returning to their respective rooms, the water fight escalated. An array of plastic chairs, sun-loungers and tables were tossed into the pool as the drunken revellers engaged in running, dive-bombing and plenty of heavy petting. The frolics came to a bloody end though when Roadent lost his bearings, dived into the shallow end and gashed his head open. By the morning yet another hotel had added the Sex Pistols to their *persona non grata* shit list.

CHAPTER EIGHT

And Blind Acceptance Is A Sign ...

'The right honourable gentleman's smile
is like the silver fittings on a coffin'
Benjamin Disraeli on Robert Peel

Marcus Garvey, who was declared Jamaica's first national hero and was an inspiration to many reggae bands, had predicted that there would be chaos in 1977, and the apocalyptic year of the double numeral didn't start off too brightly for the Sex Pistols. The band had returned to London following the Anarchy Tour debacle with nothing to show for their exhaustive efforts other than a few on the road war stories – some with accompanying bruises – and a hefty £10,000 deficit on their EMI advance. The record label's gift of a Fortnum & Mason's Christmas hamper did little to raise the festive cheer within Dryden Chambers. To add insult to injury, whilst they'd been fruitlessly traversing Britain's highways and byways in search of a friendly stage, a new punk-friendly venue had opened up in London's West End. The Roxy, a former gay club located on Neal Street in Covent Garden, had opened up on 14th December with Tony James and Billy Idol's post-Chelsea outfit Generation X topping the bill. The Heartbreakers, having found themselves with yet another Anarchy Tour interlude after the Caerphilly show, played the following night, while Siouxsie and the Banshees, with Generation X in support, had played there on 21st December.

Malcolm's one-time associate Andy Czezowski, who was running The Roxy as well as managing Generation X, had approached him with an offer for the Sex Pistols to headline a New Year's Day show to serve as the venue's official opening, as well as to help cement The Roxy's credentials as London's new bonafide punk hangout. Despite having spent the previous month bemoaning the lack of venues within the capital willing to host the Sex Pistols, Malcolm declined Czezowski's offer. By this time he'd not only developed a bunker mentality as far as the Sex Pistols were concerned, but he was also anxious to distance both himself and the band from their new-found New Wave contemporaries. So somewhat prophetically, given that 1977 was the portentous year when the two sevens clashed, it was the Clash, with the Heartbreakers in support, who took to The Roxy Stage on the 1st January 1977 to herald in the coming year.

#

With no one of any importance at EMI available during the Christmas holidays, the music papers had been forced to rely on Malcolm to keep them up-to-date on what was occurring between the Sex Pistols and the label. Needless to say, Malcolm was happy to snipe from every rooftop and sent a warning shot over EMI's Manchester Square palisades by telling the *NME* that the record company couldn't hold the Sex Pistols to their contract indefinitely. Furthermore, should EMI be thinking of terminating the contract then there were several other interested parties. As he later put it: 'If you didn't take from this guy, then you took from that guy. There was always another whore further along the street.' He also told the paper that he was seeking a meeting with EMI Records to get the label to confirm its support to the Sex Pistols by commissioning the band's follow-up single. Indeed, Frank Brunger and his Harvest team had already tentatively lined up 'Pretty Vacant' as the band's second release should the label come out and confirm its support to the group. Within that same *NME* issue, however, the paper's T-zers column hedged its bets by hinting that the dramas between the Sex Pistols and the EMI board were still to come.

On the morning of 4th January 1977, by which time almost a calendar month had elapsed without EMI reaching any decision regarding its future relationship with the Sex Pistols, the boys flew out to Amsterdam to undertake a mini three-date promotional tour (two dates in Amsterdam with the third in Rotterdam); as well as to appear on the Dutch TV show *Disco Circus,* which was staged within a circus tent in a field on the outskirts of the city. Although the Anarchy Tour had proved an unmitigated disaster, no one within EMI Records thought anything of the news that the Sex Pistols would be embarking on a European jaunt, as such undertakings were considered part and parcel of a band's promotional duties.

'Anarchy In The UK' had sold moderately well in the Netherlands, and EMI's International Division had booked the Dutch TV slot in order to further promote the Sex Pistols in northern Europe, so building up further interest in time for the band's follow-up single and subsequent album. To ensure nothing untoward might occur, EMI International sent along its in-house Sex Pistols aficionado Graham Fletcher – who'd been championing the band since accompanying Mike Thorne to the 100 Club Punk Festival – to act as its official liaison. Little could Fletcher have imagined as he stood to the rear of the 100 Club that balmy September evening that he would, albeit for one show only, end up serving as the Pistols' lighting engineer for their 5th January concert at Amsterdam's Club Paradiso.

You can imagine then the EMI board's consternation at seeing the *Evening News'* banner headline: '**THESE REVOLTING VIPs! SEX PISTOLS IN RUMPUS AT AIRPORT**' without any prior warning from Fletcher of what was alleged to have occurred. The newspaper claimed the band had caused uproar at Heathrow airport by 'spitting' and 'vomiting' in the Terminal 2 departure lounge prior to boarding the KLM flight to Amsterdam. There was even a quote from one of the Dutch airline's outraged check-in staff – preferring to hide behind the cloak of anonymity – who said the Sex Pistols were the 'most revolting people she'd ever seen in her life'. Also that, in between insulting the check-in staff and everyone else in sight, one of their number vomited in the corridor leading to the aircraft and again later in a rubbish bin.

Graham Fletcher didn't receive the call to contact EMI's London office at the 'earliest opportunity' until he and the Sex Pistols were back at the band's hotel – if indeed a couple of rooms above one of the city's legendary 'brown cafés' could be described as a hotel – having completed their TV obligations. Had he been babysitting any other band the EMI man may well have waited until the following morning, but as the EMI/Sex Pistols situation was still up in the air he decided to make the call. As he waited to be connected, he would have no doubt been conjuring up amusing anecdotes about how the Dutch TV director must have had one too many slices of 'space cake' for breakfast that morning for having the notorious Sex Pistols perform 'Anarchy In The UK', whilst sharing the stage with a plate-spinning dwarf: with Steve threatening to stave the hapless diminutive's head in with his Gibson.

However, the EMI man could have been forgiven for thinking that his own breakfast had been laced with weed upon being informed of the *Evening News'* headline. He hadn't left the band's side whilst they were at Heathrow and was understandably mystified as to where the story had come from. As far as he was concerned, none of them had come anywhere close to stepping out of line at the airport and he'd personally overseen the ticket and baggage handling at the KLM check-in desk. The closest any of them came to vomiting was when John – playfully parodying his alter ego Johnny Rotten – decided to shock his fellow passengers by pretending to throw up on the aeroplane; even then the 'vomit' in question was only chewed-up orange peel, which he proceeded to disgorge into his sick-bag.

If one stops to consider that the KLM quotes contained within the *Evening News* article, which told of the Sex Pistols spitting and vomiting, were nearly identical to the tabloid headlines following the band's appearance on the *Today* show, then it isn't beyond the bounds of possibility that the *Evening News'* on-the-scene reporter had handed over a few quid to a couple of happy to oblige check-in girls to get his story. Another conveniently unnamed KLM official told the reporter that he'd been keeping an eye on the band as their behaviour was becoming more and more unsavoury and alarming the other passengers, and that he'd seen something which had forced him to take action. Just what this 'something' might have been was never explained, and the *Evening News* reporter further over-egged the punitive pudding by claiming that the incident had been so bad that the KLM official couldn't even bring himself to speak of it to his female co-workers.

Another possibility as to how the *Evening News* got hold of the story is that Malcolm called the newspaper's editor, as the fabricated tale is remarkably similar to the one concerning Johnny Thunders throwing up at Paris airport, which he had witnessed two years earlier. After all, the Sex Pistols were now Public Enemies No. 1 and had a reputation to live up to. Their fellow travellers, having read about these vile punk rockers in the newspapers, would have been watching the band's every move hoping to catch them engaged in some unsavoury activity which they could recount to friends and family; the tales no doubt becoming further embellished with every telling.

Despite Fletcher's insistence that nothing untoward had occurred either on the ground or in the air, there were those in senior positions at EMI that wanted the Sex Pistols off their label and saw this as the perfect opportunity to wield the axe. Whether Sir John Read was aware of what had supposedly occurred at Heathrow or not, he arrived at his office the following morning to find a copy of the *Evening Standard* lying upon his desk. Knowing that no one working in EMI Records ever set foot in the office before 10 a.m. at the earliest normally, he decided to take matters into his own hands by calling a high-ranking acquaintance at KLM.

Read probably sighed with relief when the airline contact confirmed every spurious word written in the *Evening News;* despite Brian Southall having checked with several press contacts all of whom confirmed the *Evening News'* piece had indeed been a total fabrication aimed at discrediting the Sex Pistols.

Bob Mercer and Leslie Hill also conducted their own enquiries and found the Sex Pistols to be innocent on all counts. Hill went so far as to petition Read in person, as he feared EMI's terminating the Sex Pistols contract would have an adverse affect on his staff. In a last-ditch attempt to stave off the inevitable he tried explaining that, although the Sex Pistols' appearance on *Today* had been unseemly, such behaviour was to be expected within the realm of rock 'n' roll.

As far as Read was concerned, however, it was irrelevant as to whether the incident had or hadn't occurred. It was the general public's perception of what was believed to have occurred that mattered now. The confirmation of this public perception came courtesy of a personal letter from the MP for Christchurch and Lymington, Robert Adley, who – no doubt having been petitioned by his constituents – was questioning why an eminent company such as EMI should be 'financing a bunch of ill-mannered louts who seem to cause offence wherever they go'. EMI had already been accused in certain quarters of sticking its corporate head in the sand in the wake of the *Today* fiasco. Although getting rid of the Sex Pistols would lose the company £1million in profit, this paled into insignificance against what might happen to the share price if the honourable member for Christchurch and Lymington decided to share his views with the other honourable members of Parliament regarding the company's continued support for the Sex Pistols.

Hill, knowing that the band's fate had been sealed, booked a flight to Amsterdam before telephoning Malcolm with the glad tidings that they were off the label. He also phoned Fletcher and gave instructions for the EMI man to summon Malcolm to his hotel room at nine o'clock the following morning to work out how best to handle this musical divorce in a civilised manner. He then headed out to Heathrow – the scene of the crime as it were – and boarded a plane bound for Holland. According to Brian Southall, Malcolm appeared totally unfazed upon being informed by Hill that the Sex Pistols' recording contract was being terminated. However, he was obviously concerned enough to call Stephen Fisher in London and told the solicitor to book a seat on the first available flight to Amsterdam for the meeting with Hill to protect Glitterbest's interests if nothing else.

'Looking back I thought it was a bit sneaky the way they did it, waiting till we were out of the country and everything,' says Glen Matlock now. Whilst Fisher and Hill were in mid-air en route to Amsterdam's Schiphol airport, possibly on the same flight, EMI's Group Press Relations officer Rachel Nelson issued the following press release:

EMI AND THE SEX PISTOLS

EMI and the Sex Pistols group have mutually agreed to terminate their recording contract.

EMI feels it is unable to promote this group's records internationally in view of the adverse publicity which has been generated over the last two months, although recent press reports of the behaviour of the Sex Pistols appear to have been exaggerated.

The termination of this contract with the Sex Pistols does not in any way affect EMI's intention to remain active in all areas of the music business.

Funnily enough, it was Radio One DJ Tony Blackburn who was the first to broadcast the news of the Sex Pistols dismissal from EMI during his *Housewives Choice* afternoon show. Somewhat surprisingly – given that it was EMI who issued the press release – this was how many of Hill's team in EMI Records found out about it too. The press release stated the decision to terminate the contract had been one of mutual consent, but over in Amsterdam Malcolm was telling local reporters – no doubt summoned to the chase by their Fleet Street paymasters – that he hadn't signed a single piece of paper relating to the termination, and that as far as he was concerned the Sex Pistols were still an EMI act. But with

Leslie Hill on his way to Amsterdam those same reporters knew Malcolm's spiel was little more than face-saving bravado. As soon as Hill arrived in the city, Fletcher escorted Malcolm, Stephen Fisher, and EMI Holland's resident solicitor to the EMI man's hotel where they spent the rest of the day discussing how best to dress up the contractual corpse for the media.

Although there was little likelihood of an open coffin, the Sex Pistols weren't exactly crying at the graveside as they – or Glitterbest to be more precise – would receive the remaining £20,000 of the contract and the master tapes, as well as £10,000 from EMI Publishing. The label's publishing arm may have had a separate office and a certain amount of autonomy but its head, Terry Slater, still had to dance to the corporate tune, and relinquished ownership of the band's publishing rights. Slater was so incensed at the company's decision to drop the Sex Pistols that he threatened to quit, as did Nick Mobbs. The despondent A&R chief, having warned his bosses back in December that he would resign should the label drop the band, had been on the verge of accepting an offer to take control of the A&R department over at CBS. However, he was sweet-talked into staying on at Manchester Square following EMI's decision to match the American label's attractive salary offer.

There were others within EMI Records making similar threats to walk out, but although Sir John Read had consented to sanction Mobbs' pay increase, he wasn't going to allow EMI to be held to ransom by a few disgruntled employees, regardless of their position. So, on the 17th January – the same day the Sex Pistols were laying down tracks in Gooseberry Studios with Dave Goodman – with the dissention in its ranks quelled, EMI officially severed its links with the Sex Pistols with the following press release:

> *In accordance with the previously stated wishes of both parties and the verbal telephone agreement made on Thursday, 6th January, the documents terminating the contract between EMI and the Sex Pistols have now been signed. EMI Records wish the Sex Pistols every success with their next recording contract.*

EMI's insistence that it would remain active in all musical areas saw them sign Australian punk outfit The Saints and then Wire, along with the rather more successful Tom Robinson Band – who scored UK chart hits with 'Glad To Be Gay' and '2-4-6-8 Motorway'.

However, having had its fingers scorched with the Sex Pistols meant the label kept well away from the more confrontational and controversy-riddled side of punk rock.

Although the label was probably sincere in wishing the Sex Pistols every success in the future, it was surely doing so in the belief that it had seen the last of the band. In one of those odd quirks of fate though, following Thorn EMI's corporate acquisition of Virgin Music Group in 1992, for a reported £560million, the then long-defunct Sex Pistols' back catalogue including, of course, the band's vitriolic anti-record label rant *EMI*, came back under its dominion. The lunatics made a more than successful return to the asylum, and the British press never blinked an eye!

Glen, of course, would return to Manchester Square much sooner owing to EMI's overtures following his official expulsion from the Sex Pistols on the 24th February 1977. These overtures came from Mike Thorne, who no doubt having been tipped off by his buddy Graham Fletcher that the bassist's relationship with John was rapidly deteriorating, contacted Glen following the band's return from Holland. Thorne told Glen that although EMI had gotten rid of the Sex Pistols, he – as well as everyone else within EMI Records Division – hoped he and John could sort out their differences and move forward. He also informed the bemused bassist that everyone at the label had recognised his talents and that, if push came to shove, EMI would be interested in listening to whatever solo or band-related proposals he might have in mind. Glen's first post-Pistols outfit was, of course, the Rich Kids who enjoyed a UK Top 30 hit in February 1978 with their eponymous power-pop debut single.

Looking back on those events over thirty years later, it seems pretty obvious that Glen was indeed making contingency plans for a life beyond the Sex Pistols. The power-pop outfit's founding line-up included whizz-kid guitarist Steve New, who was now old enough to shave, and vocalist Midge Ure; both of whom had almost featured in the pre-John Lydon Sex Pistols.

#

In 1999's *The Filth And The Fury*, by which time the Sex Pistols had already kissed and made up for their money-grabbing Filthy Lucre world tour, John attempted to lay the blame for the breakdown of his relationship with Glen at Malcolm's door. According to John, Malcolm had purposely gone out of his way to set one against the other. Although their now deceased manager must indeed shoulder some responsibility for the schism, which effectively killed the band as a creative unit, John should also afford himself a long hard look in the mirror.

When he agreed to join the band back in August 1975, he would have quickly surmised that when it came to band policy he would gain little headway trying to argue against Steve and Paul, as the guitarist and drummer were quite literally as 'thick as thieves' and any decision they made came as a block vote. Even then Glen was regarded as the band's whipping boy, and had John not been such an inverted snob in attacking Glen over his supposed middle-class upbringing (as well as for having the cheek to acknowledge the Beatles' musical legacy), then it might have been they – as the band's song-writing team – who would have dictated policy. Prior to the Sex Pistols appearance on the *Today* show John enjoyed a certain status amongst the band's small gang of fans. Now, however, 'El Dementoid' (as the pre-Pet Shop Boys Neil Tennant had described John whilst penning a first-hand account of the Nashville brawl back in April 1976 for *Sounds*) was being lauded as Prince of the Punks. Journalists were fighting over his every quote; with his ego swelling to match his elevated status.

So when John began making noises about getting rid of Glen, that's when Steve and Paul – especially Paul, given that he and Glen made up a rhythm section Tony Parsons was moved to describe as 'tighter than tomorrow' – should have stood up to him by backing the bassist; instead of which they fucked off to Tenerife for a lads' holiday.

'That fuckin' Grundy show changed everything, it moved the goal posts and made them pack leaders, and let's be honest we could all have done it, I could do "fuck you" on TV no problem mate.' says Captain Sensible today.

On the 2002 *Never Mind The Bollocks Here's The Sex Pistols* DVD, which is part of the *Classic Albums* series, Steve belatedly acknowledges his mistake in allowing John to undermine Glen's position in the band. It shouldn't have mattered that Glen was always polite, and forever washing his feet, or that he had a preference for 'wanky Beatles chords'. The truth is that Glen was the only one amongst them capable of formulating their ideas into a recognisable tune to accompany John's lyrics. The testimony to this lies in the fact that the Sex Pistols only wrote and recorded two new compositions following the bassist's departure. OK, so 'Holidays In The Sun' and 'Bodies' are passable efforts in their own right, but 'Anarchy In The UK' and 'Pretty Vacant' they ain't. At the time though, Steve was too caught up in his new-found celebrity status, which – although he'd been the one who'd sworn on prime-time TV – came courtesy of the tabloids' fascination with Johnny Rotten. Glen was astute enough to accept that it was the singer who got the glory but he resented John's elevated arrogance, whereas Steve was happy to have his own role on the *Today* show overlooked as long the newspapers kept writing about the Sex Pistols.

The column inches afforded the band in recent weeks meant Steve was now a 'face' on the music scene and could hold his own at the Speakeasy, while nobody appeared overly interested in anything their squeaky-clean bass player had to say. This even applied to Malcolm who, having already chastised Glen in Holland for his lack of on-stage energy, summoned him to a band summit meeting – minus John – at a vegetarian café in Covent Garden. Glen may have known Malcolm longer than any of the others, having worked for him in TFTLTYTD and SEX, but Malcolm knew Johnny Rotten was going to sell a lot more bondage trousers than the band's ex-art student bass player. With that in mind, he more or less gave Glen an ultimatum whereby the bassist should agree to put his increasing dislike of John aside in the best interests of the band. This would have been easy enough to do had Glen been desperate to remain a Sex Pistol, but with EMI's offer simmering away on the back burner he was not without other options. He could have walked away there and then but, although he'd already made up his mind he was leaving the band, he decided to delay his decision until Steve and Paul returned from holiday. After all, his £25 weekly wage could be put to good use in funding his new band and, anyway, Glitterbest also held the lease on his flat.

While Steve and Paul were sunning themselves in the Canaries, Malcolm was in California peddling Dave Goodman's latest demos to A&M Records' founding fathers, Herb Alpert and Jerry Moss. One can only imagine what the bronzed Americans thought at seeing a skinny Limey with pale freckled skin and wiry ginger hair, dressed – despite the soaring temperature – in a bondage suit.

As there were no rehearsals that week, Glen – having little urge to convene with John – kept himself to himself working on melodies and arrangements, which would ultimately appear on the Rich Kids eponymous debut album. But when a second week passed without any word from Denmark Street he began to get suspicious. Glen may have been the perennial outsider within the Sex Pistols camp, but he hadn't totally been ostracised and word soon got back to him that John, Steve and Paul were holed away within Denmark Street rehearsing with Sid.

Upon his return from California, Malcolm attempted to play devil's advocate by informing Glen of the others openly rehearsing with Sid. His scheme backfired, however, as Glen was totally unconcerned with the latest developments and he tendered his resignation by offering to give Sid a number of much needed bass lessons. A second summit meeting, this time just between Malcolm and Glen, was convened at The Blue Posts pub located behind the 100 Club. Malcolm – perhaps having heard Sid's rudimentary style – urged Glen to go to Denmark Street and demand his job back. Yes, he was angry and hurt by the betrayal, but Glen had quite simply had enough.

One Friday night back in May 2002 at the Windsor Castle pub in Maida Vale, London, whilst we were attempting to drain a barrel of Strongbow cider without the aid of a safety net, Glen – nursing a Kaliber non-alcoholic lager – opened up about his final days as a Sex Pistol first time around. He had had, by that juncture, twenty-five years to ruminate on the events which led to his parting company with the Sex Pistols. He told us that he was first and foremost a musician, so what was the point of remaining in a band that couldn't play live? To his mind, the Sex Pistols were fast becoming an anglicised version of the Monkees and he wanted out.

Glen knew the publicity surrounding the band would have record company executives falling over themselves to capture the Sex Pistols' signatures. He was also astute enough to recognise that Malcolm's obsession with having 'No Future' (or 'God Save The Queen' as it had been retitled) as the band's follow-up single to coincide with Queen Elizabeth II's Silver Jubilee celebrations, would only result in more outrage and banning orders. Having made his intentions clear he even shook Malcolm's hand and – like EMI – wished the Sex Pistols good luck for the future.

His easy-going nature would prove his undoing though. Instead of rushing off and informing Caroline Coon or Jonh Ingham of his decision to quit the band, he agreed to keep things quiet; agreeing even to go into the studio with the other Pistols to record the bass parts, as the 'new boy' wasn't up to the task. This was merely Malcolm's way of gaining the upper hand. Three days later he sent a telegram to Derek James at the *NME* ridiculing Glen by claiming that he'd been sacked from the Sex Pistols for liking the Beatles, and that his replacement Sid Vicious's best credential was in giving Nick Kent a good hiding at the 100 Club the previous June.

Glen was forced to swallow this humiliation as he was still collecting his wages, whilst Sophie Richmond collated his share of the cash in the Glitterbest coffers. Admittedly, accountancy was never Malcolm's strong point, but all there was to show from the £50,000 EMI cash, was one and a half pages of scribbled biro relating to five-figure debits for various undisclosed sundries and expenses. Glen's share was... a paltry £2,965. Granted, at the time a cheque for the best part of three grand would have been the equivalent of getting a call from Camelot, but today it seems such a pitiable pay-off for two years' contributions. Especially when you consider that the majority of the songs in the Sex Pistols canon at that point would end up on *Never Mind The Bollocks*. Even today, some fifteen years on from the band's 1996 reconciliation, Glen isn't an equal member of Sex Pistols Residuals and has a separate arrangement to that of John, Steve and Paul. Yet without their tunesmith who knows what they would have become ...

Legend has it that Malcolm and Bernie colluded to exchange bass players between their respective acts, which would have seen Paul Simonon joining the Sex Pistols and Glen heading down to Camden. Even Glen's autobiography *I Was A Teenage Sex Pistol* alludes to the apocryphal tale; although Glen hints that it was Joe and Mick who were the supposed instigators. Whilst researching another possible project, we tackled a very amicable Mick Jones about it one night at The Borderline in Soho during August 2000, where Glen was performing with his own band in support of his second solo album. The former Clash six-stringer, however, denied he and Joe even contemplated replacing Paul with Glen. Glen may have been his best mate, and more musically gifted than Paul, but there was only ever going to be one bassist in the Clash.

#

So with Glen refusing to toe the party line or swallow Malcolm's rhetoric, the path was now truly open for Sid to fulfil his ambition by becoming a Sex Pistol.

Simon John Ritchie, a.k.a. John Simon Beverley, a.k.a. Sid Vicious, was born in the London borough of Lewisham on Friday, 10th May 1957, to John George and Anne Jeanette Ritchie. The handsome, yet doleful, John was coming to the end of his two-year stint of National Service in the Royal Guard at the time of his son's birth and, rather than sign up for further military duties, he was demobbed and took up a job as a publisher's rep in London. Anne, on the other hand, was a vivacious, straight-talking 25-year-old who'd already been married and divorced by the time she hooked up with Ritchie. She was serving in the RAF, but was even less cut out for a career in the military than John. Although reluctant to tie the knot a second time, she was happy to give her first-born the Ritchie surname. They set up home in a semi-basement flat in Lea Green, South East London, and although Anne would later stress that this was a very happy time in her life, she was obviously looking back through rose-tinted spectacles. John's sullen demeanour was ill-suited for his new line of work and the family was often forced to live off hand-outs from relatives.

With the publishing game holding little chance of success, and with their debts mounting, Ritchie suggested they should seek a fresh start abroad. He chose the then tranquil fishing isle of Ibiza, in Spain's Balearic Islands, and even persuaded Anne that she and 3-year-old Simon should go on ahead while he sorted out his affairs. He also promised to send money over to the island before joining them there at a later date. The later date, of course, never materialised as Ritchie proved to be as ill-suited to family life as he was to salesmanship, and neither Anne nor Simon would ever see Ritchie again. But to give Ritchie his due, unlike Freddie Lennon or Tommy Gallagher, who both attempted to cash-in on their respective sons' fame, he never came crawling out of the woodwork once Sid was famous.

With no man and no money, life on the sun-kissed Mediterranean isle was anything but idyllic for Anne and she was forced to live off her wits in order to survive. She took occasional bar work – babysitter permitting – and rolled joints for the local fishermen, while her squint-eyed Simon whiled away his days playing on the sands with his dog 'C.P.' (Cachorro Perro is Spanish for puppy-dog) and learning a few choice Spanish swear-words. Eighteen months would pass before the bohemian Anne came to the decision that her extended holiday couldn't continue indefinitely as Simon was fast approaching school age. Had her relationship with a local fisherman called Marty developed into something more meaningful, then she and Simon might have indeed remained on the island – giving the title of David Dalton's 1997 book *El Sid* even more resonance. With young Simon's education – or lack thereof – uppermost in her thoughts, Anne contacted the British High Commission and answered all of their questions in the affirmative. They granted her two one-way air tickets to London, where she, at the very least, could count upon the support of her mother and elder sister Veronica, or so she believed.

Unfortunately for Anne, the London she returned to was as unfamiliar and unyielding as her mother, who had yet to forgive her youngest daughter for marrying the good-for-nothing John Ritchie, let alone clearing off to Ibiza with her grandchild. With life under her mother's roof becoming increasingly unbearable, Anne found herself a one bedroom flat in Balham, South London, which came with a resident babysitter in the form of her housebound landlady.

Taking advantage of her newly found freedom, Anne took a job at Ronnie Scott's jazz club on Frith Street in Soho. However, instead of enjoying what she had, Anne sought to better her lot by registering herself as a drug addict in order to hoist herself to the top of London's housing list. Anne sat up all night smoking joint after joint while stabbing at her arms with a needle to create trackmarks. The plan backfired, for although mother and son were swiftly given a new home, a one bedroom flat situated above a shop at 178 Drury Lane, her new abode came without the services of a babysitter, forcing Anne to give up her job at Ronnie Scott's. Alas, it wasn't only social workers who were familiar with those areas set aside by the GLC for drug-dependent families. Within weeks of their moving into the Drury Lane flat the drug dealers came a-knocking and by Easter 1962 Anne was fast-tracking her way to heroin dependency.

#

Simon John Ritchie first entered Britain's educational system on Monday 3rd September 1962, at the Soho Parish School situated on Great Windmill Street. Ironically, some sixteen years later, the same street would be chosen by Malcolm as the site for the cinema in *The Great Rock 'n' Roll Swindle,* where Tenpole Tudor would inform Irene Handl that Sid Vicious had been arrested for murder. Young Simon's tenure at the parochial primary school would prove short-lived, as Anne – rather than face having her heroin-soaked misery exposed by her son's concerned teachers – soon moved him to St George's Primary School in Farm Street, London. The school was situated close to Grosvenor Square and the American Embassy where, in December 1977, he and the other Sex Pistols would apply for – and be initially denied – their US visas. Simon's report card from St George's states he was a bright pupil with a flair for music (so what happened?), but that he lacked concentration in the classroom. Once again, however, Anne was too preoccupied to oversee her son's schooling, but this time her attention was taken up by love rather than drugs.

The new man in her life was a middle-class intellectual from Tunbridge Wells called Christopher Beverley. The couple had met shortly before Christmas 1964, and such was their ardour that they were married in February the following year. Anne would later describe meeting Chris Beverley as akin to 'winning the football pools', but her eight score draws had been scrawled with a poisoned quill: within weeks of the ceremony Beverley was diagnosed with cancer and he succumbed to the disease in August 1965. Although Beverley died before he had time to go through the legal process of adopting Simon, Anne ensured that he took her dead husband's surname; Beverley was indeed the genuine love of her life.

Rather than return to the depressing day-to-day drudgery of London, Anne elected to remain in Tunbridge Wells, primarily so that she could be close to Beverley's grave. She and Simon set up home in a tiny nondescript one bedroom flat at 43 Lime Hill Road. This, of course, necessitated a move of schools, but instead of the upmarket private establishment which Chris Beverley had wanted for his stepson, Simon was eventually enrolled at the somewhat less salubrious – yet still fee-paying – Sandrock Road Secondary Modern.

Anne and Simon would remain in Tunbridge Wells for another three years before finally returning to London in the summer of 1971, where they set up home in Ayresome Road in Stoke Newington. Simon was enrolled at the nearby Clissold Park Secondary School, but yet again he proved an unwilling student and in 1972 aged fifteen, and against Anne's wishes, he bid a not so fond farewell to the education system, taking a job as a trainee cutter at Simpson's; a local factory of some repute owing to its production of Daks trousers. Had he paid more attention in his classes then he might not have had so much trouble in calculating the trouser pocket sizings and, after one miscalculation too many, he was handed his P45.

Finding himself at a metaphorical crossroads, Simon took time out to consider his options, which were pretty thin on the ground given his lack of qualifications. Rather than endure another meaningless existence working 9 5 in some factory, he decided to follow his cousin David's lead by enrolling at Hackney Technical College to study art and photography. By this time, Anne had acquired a council flat on Queensbridge Road in Haggerston, East London. She was overjoyed at Simon's decision to return to full-time education, but she was much less enthralled with his second life-changing decision – to adopt his biological father's Christian name. To his mind, 'Simon' belonged in the leafy streets of Tunbridge Wells, whereas 'John' was of the street. Little could she have known as her son headed out the front door one crisp September morning in 1973, that he was about to embark on a path that would bring about a cataclysmic and irrevocable change in his life: for it was at Hackney Tech that he encountered John Lydon.

Despite showing an aptitude for art, especially line drawing and watercolours, John became increasingly restless at the Tech. So, when his friend Lydon moved on to Kingsway College in King's Cross in the summer of 1974, he put aside his brushes and headed along Gray's Inn Road to Kingsway. He wasn't able to enroll at the college, but he wasted little time in latching on to its vibrant social scene. It was whilst hanging about the common room there that he acquired the nick-name 'Spiky John' on account of his radical new 'proto-punk' hairstyle – worn in homage to his hero Bowie. Let's not forget either that at this time Lydon was still sporting shoulder-length tresses.

Spiky John certainly cut an interesting figure, and was especially popular with the college's female students. Lydon would later recall his friend being a hapless fashion victim during his Kingsway phase, but despite a fixation for long-flowing scarves and toe-nail varnish, John simply exuded presence, and the camera totally loved him. Yet despite his being tall, dark and handsome, he shied away from getting romantically linked with girls of his own age. He was almost certainly a virgin at this point and although no one thought him gay, those closest to him believed he was sexually confused. His brief dalliance with male prostitution, offering himself out under the pseudonym 'Hymie', certainly goes a long way in backing up this theory. However, like most events in Sid's brief life, this is a fact that is challenged by many.

Simone Stenfors, who was also attending Kingsway during this period, and would herself become a punk scenester, readily admits to having taken an immediate fancy to him, despite her being married at the time. Another who got close to him prior to his induction into the Sex Pistols was future Slits guitarist, Viv Albertine. Viv never spoke much about her friendship with Sid until the movie *Who Killed Nancy*, but their love was a platonic one as at the time she was romantically linked with Mick Jones.

Although John was devoted to his mother, the claustrophobic atmosphere within the depressingly dingy high-rise Queensbridge Road flat left a lot to be desired. He'd already fled the nest on several occasions, but in the autumn of 1975 he finally left home for good, moving into a squat at New Court, Hampstead. It was here that he supposedly engaged in nefarious acts such as mugging an old lady at knife-point, strangling a kitten and roasting a guinea pig. Yet these were obviously fables designed to perpetuate the Sid Vicious image. New Court resident, the late Lindy Poltock (girlfriend – and later wife – of the Clash's road manager, Johnny Green) recalled how the old dears of New Court adored their spiky neighbour, who always had time to stop for a chat, or carry their shopping up the stairs.

It was at New Court that John's use of amphetamines began spiralling out of control, although the seeds were sown back at the Queensbridge high-rise where he was injecting speed. Most kids were happy to snort or rub the gritty white powder across their gums, so it certainly wasn't peer pressure that caused him to mainline the stuff. It was clearly a habit he'd picked up from watching his mum shooting up her afternoon fix on the sofa; with mother and son often sharing the same needle. Anne wasn't like other mums who were content to while away their afternoon watching *General Hospital*, *Quincy*, or *Doctor Kildare* on TV, for she had her own pharmaceutical release.

It wasn't long before his friend Lydon also took up residence in the foreboding five storey Victorian tenement block. Lydon's autobiography *No Irish, No Blacks, No Dogs* would have us believe New Court was a Dickensian slum bereft of such basic amenities as electricity and hot water, which had been declared unfit for human habitation by the local council. This, however, was little more than poetic licence as New Court wasn't technically a squat, it was under the supervision of a woman called Barbara, who kept the rooms tidy. She more or less adopted Spiky John as her surrogate son. With John 'Jah Wobble' Wardle and John Grey often in attendance, New Court became something of a gang hut. When Lydon joined the Sex Pistols in August 1975, it is inconceivable to think that he wouldn't have returned to New Court after rehearsals to tell his best mate all about what was happening in Denmark Street; not to mention his ever-increasing dislike for Glen. In order to halt the confusion between the two spiky-haired Johns, Lydon re-christened his mate 'Sid' in part homage to Pink Floyd's erstwhile enigmatic frontman Syd Barrett, and the Lydon family's toothless pet hamster.

#

Despite having missed out on the role as singer in the Sex Pistols, Sid, as he was now commonly known amongst his peers, was anxious to catch the wave the Pistols were creating and spent the sweltering summer of 1976 – the hottest on record – recruiting good-looking girls from the scene to form his backing band. Aside from Sid, the embryonic outfit's inaugural line-up consisted of Viv Albertine on guitar, her friend Sarah Hall on bass, and Joe Strummer's Spanish emigrée girlfriend – and future Slits tub thumper – Paloma 'Palmolive' Romera on drums. Having co-opted the name of the Sex Pistols' short-lived caterwauling dirge 'Flowers of Romance' (which Johnny and Co. had come up with to bait those journalists who were claiming they couldn't play live) for the band's name, the four-piece began rehearsals in earnest in the basement at 42 Orsett Terrace, the Shepherd's Bush squat where Joe and Palmolive happened to be living at the time. Although the idea of an all-girl backing band was certainly revolutionary – and light-years before Robert Palmer came up with the idea for his 'Addicted To Love' video – the lack of a recognised musician in the line-up proved something of a hindrance. Another drawback was Sid's low boredom threshold and instead of applying himself he preferred getting stoned and talking about where the band was heading rather than getting off his arse and taking it there himself.

Flowers had only been rehearsing for a few weeks when Sid threw Palmolive out of the band following a disagreement over his racist views and fascination with Nazi imagery. It was while the ad hoc outfit was in temporary hiatus following Palmolive's departure that Sid volunteered himself for the role of drummer for the Banshees' debut performance at the 100 Club Punk Festival.

Following his release from Ashford Remand Centre in late October 1976 (he had been banged up there for throwing a beer glass during the Damned's set, as mentioned earlier), he moved out of New Court and took up temporary lodgings at the Clash's rehearsal place in Camden. During his spell at Ashford he'd had plenty of time to pen lyrics for songs with long-forgotten titles such as 'Brains On Vacation', 'Piece Of Garbage', as well as 'Belsen Was A Gas' (the latter would have also been consigned to the recycle bin had the Sex Pistols not co-opted the song to add a little flavour to their staid late'77 setlist).

With the Sex Pistols signed to EMI and working on their debut single, Sid was doubly desperate to revive Flowers of Romance. But during his enforced absence, Viv had gone off to work with Palmolive and so Sid was forced to abandon his 'all-chick backing band' idea. Despite failing to procure the services of a drummer, he brought in ex-Clash guitarist Keith Levene as well as occasional *Sniffin' Glue* contributor Steve Walsh as an additional guitarist. Once again, however, Sid was happy to get off his head and talk the talk just so long as he didn't have to walk anywhere. His disinterest in actually working his song ideas into a proper structure – not to mention bringing in Levene, a fellow speed freak – meant that Flowers of Romance, like London SS, was destined to remain a band in name only.

The Heartbreakers' colourful manager, Leee Black Childers, who got very close to Sid during this period – and would have happily got much closer had Sid been so inclined – says Flowers of Romance were showing great promise. Their Ramones-esque '1-2-3-4 Hey Ho, Let's Go' style of play was perfectly suited for the rapidly-expanding UK punk scene, and would have gone down a storm at The Roxy. Such speculation was, of course, rendered immaterial when John Lydon came a-calling in February 1977 to offer Sid the gig as bass player in the Sex Pistols.

CHAPTER Nine

And We're So Pretty, Oh So Pretty ... We're Vacant!

'Always keep something back; in this industry you'll soon be swallowed whole if you care to put it all on the front page'
Another Hollywood – William Kovac 1966

Aside from engaging in a brief late-night transatlantic telephone radio interview with legendary Los Angeles DJ Rodney Bingenheimer, Sid's first official duty as a Sex Pistol was to put his moniker to the A&M contract on Wednesday, 9th March 1977, at the London offices of Rondor Music (the American label's subsidiary publishing company). The contract negotiated by Malcolm and Stephen Fisher was a two year, eighteen track deal, which excluded publishing rights. This added another £75,000 to Glitterbest's already groaning coffers, with a further £75,000 to follow in twelve month's time.

A&M's 32-year-old English director, Derek Green, had been so totally captivated by the energy of Dave Goodman's demos that he implored his bosses to outbid their fellow American competitors CBS and Warner Bros to procure the Sex Pistols to A&M's otherwise soft-rock roster. However, he purposely chose to avoid meeting his new charges in person for fear their behaviour might put him off; a decision that would prove very costly for his American paymasters. Green later confessed to Malcolm's biographer Craig Bromberg that, as he tended to avoid the miasmic media and music papers to preclude having his judgement clouded, he'd never actually heard of the Sex Pistols – or their irascible manager – until Malcolm came calling in early 1977 touting the Sex Pistols' wares. Malcolm had gravitated towards American-based labels such as A&M, CBS and Warner Bros, after failing to garner any real interest in the Sex Pistols nearer to home. Indeed, the closest he'd come was with Chris Parry at Polydor who, despite failing to secure the Sex Pistols services first time around, was still interested and willing to represent the band to his immediate supervisor Freddie Haayen. Haayen proved equally enthusiastic, giving Parry the go-ahead to sign the Pistols for the original asking price of £40,000. Surprisingly though, Polydor's corporate owners, Philips, refused to sanction the deal.

Having gained an entrée – solely on the grounds that Green was blissfully ignorant that the Sex Pistols were social pariahs – Malcolm then proceeded to woo Green with the cassette tape containing Goodman's demos. By his own admission, Green was becoming increasing disillusioned with the music scene circa February 1977, but his artistic antenna went into raptures upon hearing the Sex Pistols rough and ready sound. He immediately sensed that the Pistols weren't just another English band trying to sound American. They were quintessentially English, the real deal, and he knew he had to have them at any cost. As soon as the time zones permitted he contacted Jerry Moss in Los Angeles to get the go-ahead to enter negotiations.

Although Green was eventually given the go-ahead to sign the Sex Pistols, the protracted negotiations lasted for almost a month as there were several minor points that the two parties couldn't seem to agree on. Although CBS and Warners had expressed interest in the band, the truth of the matter was that both labels' British subsidiaries had already made it clear to their American bosses that they would reject the band if left to their own devices; with CBS going so far as to have Malcolm forcibly ejected from their offices whilst his bemused charges sat in the park opposite. So it was a case of A&M or be damned.

When Green flew out to Los Angeles to petition the Pistols' case to his immediate superiors, Malcolm followed him out to the West Coast. A&M's American staff were used to dealing with the likes of the Carpenters, Peter Frampton and Supertramp, and the Sex Pistols might have been from another planet as far they were concerned. Many of Green's associates told him he'd bitten off more than he could chew but he, however, remained undaunted. Although he was willing to break a few company rules to overcome the contractual sticking points – one being

Sid Vicious 'Chatterbox' – *bootleg sleeve*

acquiescing to Malcolm's demand that the deal would be for eighteen recorded tracks rather than the standard two album deal – the A&M man wasn't prepared to be held to ransom, giving Malcolm an ultimatum whereby he either accepted A&M's offer or the deal was off. With no other offers on the horizon, Malcolm was forced to take a seat at the table.

Despite his supposedly having had no previous knowledge of the Pistols, Green had done his homework on the band and was willing to accept that their bad-boy behaviour had been grossly exaggerated by the tabloids. But in his enthusiasm, he neglected to make a call to Manchester Square to get a little EMI insider information on the Sex Pistols. If he had then he just might have learnt that Glen – the musical mastermind behind the songs on the tape – had now left the band, being replaced by the decidedly non-musical Sid Vicious. Green's face must have been a picture as he scanned Rondor's office looking for Glen and finding instead a studded leather-jacketed, spiky-haired goofball standing in his place. The decision had already been taken to make 'God Save The Queen' the band's first A&M release.

The Rondor signing had been decidedly low-key, but at 7 a.m. the following morning a black Daimler slowly circled twice around the central island housing the Queen Victoria Memorial, opposite the gates to Buckingham Palace, before pulling up to the kerb. Its unruly passengers spilled out onto the pavement in front of the waiting press pack, one of whom was Peter Kodick, who would inadvertently supply Sid with his final and fateful heroin stash a little under two years later.

In *The Filth And The Fury,* John would try to claim Sid's father had been on duty at Buckingham Palace whilst his son was putting his name to the A&M contract. But this was pure hyperbole for – as John himself would have known – John Ritchie Sr had handed in his Busby and bayonet for a suit and satchel by the time his son was walking, let alone strutting his stuff as a Sex Pistol. Overseen by A&M executive Tony Burfield, Sid and the rest of the band hurriedly scribbled their names to the contract, struck a few suitable poses for the cameras and scurried back into the awaiting Daimler. They sped off into the traffic, thus avoiding harassment – and possible arrest – at the hands of an inquisitive Bobby on the beat.

Following on from their early-bird publicity stunt, the four Sex Pistols were whisked to the now-defunct Regent Palace Hotel in Piccadilly for a 'Meet the Beatles' style press conference. The conference was held within the hotel's Apex Room and the clock had yet to strike eight before Sid – obviously keen to establish his credentials as a Sex Pistol in the eyes of the assembled press – set about the complimentary drinks, particularly the Cossack vodka, which he continued to chug throughout the thirty-or-so minute conference as though it was mineral water.

Green, still mulling over the repercussions of Glen's unannounced departure, got the proceedings under way by introducing the still bleary-eyed band members before fielding questions regarding A&M's decision to sign Britain's most notorious, and most newsworthy, band. He told the gathering that the Sex Pistols becoming available had presented A&M with a unique business opportunity to be linked with a new force in music spearheaded by the Sex Pistols. He also expressed his belief that the Pistols would effect some major changes in rock music and that A&M were excited to have entered into a world-wide recording agreement with the band.

John, Steve and Paul, however, were far less enthused and showed little interest in talking to anyone, let alone the press. They purposely maintained their 'bored with it all' expressions throughout, choosing to leave the new boy to handle the questions. Sid, of course, was in his element – he'd been dreaming of this moment for the past eighteen months. Although in his dreams he had been asked to front the Sex Pistols instead of John, he was perfectly happy to be their bass player. He was equally content to share Malcolm's view that his unfamiliarity with the instrument was a plus rather than a minus!

Some of the assembled reporters had flown halfway round the world to be at the conference and although they were understandably inquisitive about the Sex Pistols' new bassist, they were equally interested in seeing whether the band was suffering any mental scars from the press backlash following their appearance on *Today*, as well as the Anarchy Tour fiasco. After all, four months had now passed since the Pistols had made their last London appearance at the Notre Dame Hall and they were in danger of being usurped by their imitators who were gigging regularly.

Sid, though, wasn't interested in talking about the Anarchy Tour as these events – although relatively recent – had occurred prior to his joining the band and were therefore unworthy of his attention. He had his uniform, a la Dee Dee Ramone but, as yet, it was devoid of stripes; he also had eighteen months of catching up to do. So when a female reporter from the *Daily Express* had the temerity to ask what he considered to be another 'dull' question he belittled her by enquiring whether it was she that he'd recently seen at a party 'stuck on so-and-so's cock'. *Sounds*' reggae-loving Vivien Goldman, who was also an acquaintance of John's, stepped in to spare her fellow journalist's blushes, and immediately found herself in Sid's line of fire – receiving no help whatsoever from her so-called buddy John.

Another reporter decided to change tack by asking Green whether he had any contractual obligations over the band's behaviour. Before Green could respond Sid, with exquisite comic timing, lifted his butt cheek off his seat and farted. This seemed to set the tone from there on in, and when another hack enquired of the other Pistols as to why they'd chosen Sid as Glen's replacement, Sid beat them to the punch, regaling the gathering with the tale of his having beaten up their fellow scribe Nick Kent at the 100 Club; although this could also have been a veiled threat for each of them to stay on his good side by writing favourable reviews.

When it was announced that the Sex Pistols would be playing a benefit show at the King's Road Theatre in April, one wag enquired whether the benefit was for Keith Richards, who'd recently been arrested at the Canadian border in possession of heroin. Once again it was left to Sid, and the bassist happily obliged by nonchalantly declaring that he wouldn't piss on the Rolling Stone guitarist if he happened to be on fire. Somewhat surprisingly, given that this was the Sex Pistols' first public outing since the Anarchy Tour, neither Caroline Coon nor Jonh Ingham were present at the conference. In Caroline's stead, *Melody Maker* sent along Brian Harrigan to interrogate the band. Harrigan's first – and lasting – impression of Sid was less than favourable; his jaundiced review described the Pistols' new bassist as 'tall, thin, spiky-haired, with the complexion of a slab of Polyfilla, and looking like a ten-day-old corpse freshly fished from the river'. However, his observations were of little importance as by the time *Melody Maker*'s next issue hit the newsstands the Sex Pistols and A&M records had already parted company.

Immediately following the press conference the band – loaded up with surplus booze – were whisked off to Wessex Studios in Highbury where Chris Thomas was mixing 'God Save The Queen'. They remained at the studio for an hour or so quaffing their free booty and trading stupid jokes, instead of casting an appreciative ear to Thomas' efforts, before being bundled back into the awaiting car. During the thirty minute journey to A&M's plush offices in New King's Road, South West London – where they were supposed to be choosing the B-side for the new single – Sid decided to improve his status within the Sex Pistols' hierarchy by goading Paul. He was desperate to live up to his 'Vicious' name tag, but with John being his best mate and therefore untouchable, and hesitant of going toe-to-toe with Steve, he set about taunting the drummer calling him a cross between an albino gorilla and Rick Wakeman. The taunting soon escalated into a drunken free-for-all with Paul coming off the worst suffering a black eye, while

John's digital watch – a 21st birthday present from his mother – also got damaged. Steve settled the issue by removing Sid's shoes and tossing them out of the window into the oncoming traffic.

Talking of Wakeman, who was also signed to A&M, he would become an unwilling footnote in the Sex Pistols' history owing to Malcolm falsely accusing the keyboard maestro of industrial blackmail. Following A&M's decision to sack the Pistols, Malcolm told reporters that his band's shock dismissal had been engineered by Wakeman and several other A&M artists who'd all threatened to leave the label unless the Sex Pistols were gotten rid of. Their antipathy to the group followed the Pistols' late night altercation with 'Whispering' Bob Harris, the balding ex-police cadet host of BBC2's late-night 'serious music' show *The Old Grey Whistle Test*.

The basis of the treacherous tale came from Malcolm having espied a telegram from Wakeman lying atop Derek Green's desk, in which the keyboardist had told Green to get rid of the Sex Pistols or else start dishing out safety pins to the label's other acts. Had Malcolm bothered to peruse the date on the telegram then he would have seen that it had been sent to Green several days before the Speakeasy incident (which we'll tell you about in a minute), and that Wakeman's comment was nothing more than a light-hearted joke.

#

Apart from supposedly approving the A-side mix, as well as selecting which song should be the single's B-side, Green had arranged the visit to his HQ so that the Sex Pistols could meet the people who would be working on promoting the record following its release, scheduled for Friday 25th May.

When the *Swindle* film finally came out in 1980, the vast majority of the band's fans – although familiar with the backlash following the release of 'God Save The Queen' – would have only been vaguely aware of A&M's involvement in the tale. They would therefore have simply enjoyed the animation scenes showing the five Sex Pistols running amok at the offices of the fictitious MAMIE Records for enjoyment's sake, rather than having any genuine understanding of what occurred that day at A&M.

Derek Green's patience was about to be sorely tested that day as Paul, following his fracas with Sid, emerged from the back of the Daimler with one eye swollen shut and blood smears across the front of his 'Demand The Impossible' shirt. Sid was following behind when he stumbled and lost his grip on one of his purloined bottles of vodka. The bottle shattered against the pavement but Sid, having already necked a full bottle of Cossack back at the Regent Palace, no longer had any mind and body co-ordination and he cut his right foot on the broken glass (you'll recall that Steve had thrown his shoes out of the Daimler). He was totally oblivious to the blood gushing from his foot as he pushed his way past Green's bemused staff, and hobbled into the label's Promotions Office where he promptly passed out in a chair.

Rotten, although smarting from having had his watch broken, retained enough humour to snatch a daffodil from a nearby vase and toss it into the bassist's lap. Steve was so totally hammered that he mistakenly wandered into the women's toilets. Instead of excusing himself as a gentleman ought, he went into letch mode and made a grab for the two girls in there as they tried to make their escape. Regaining consciousness, Sid staggered into the Gents and attempted to cleanse his wounds by sticking his foot into the toilet bowl, which he somehow managed to smash: not an easy 'feet' being shoeless. A window went west too, before he lurched back out into the secretarial pool where, thrusting his bloodied foot into the face of one of the horrified secretaries, he demanded she fetch him a plaster.

With Steve still missing in action, John and Paul bundled Sid into the lift and headed down to the basement, where the B-side selection was to take place. But the three were so off their faces that they could barely keep their eyes open, let alone be expected to make an executive decision. Green may have been willing to view the band's conference antics of earlier in the day as amusing repartee, but he wasn't prepared to stand idly by while the four drunken Sex Pistols abused his staff and ran amok in his offices. Rather than risk a mass walk-out by his staff, he quickly selected 'No Feeling' (they had yet to add the 's' to the song's title) as the single's B-side, before ushering the band out of the building as quickly as was humanly possible.

Steve would later brag to porn star Mary Millington in *Swindle*'s cinema scene that the band were thrown off A&M because he'd 'raped one of the birds down their offices', but it's doubtful the lothario could have raised so much as a smile in his catatonic state. When the guitarist did finally put in an appearance, he and the rest of the band were left standing as their driver refused to allow them back into the car. The Daimler's rear seating area was smeared with blood and littered with shards of broken glass, and as the driver drove off he delivered a Parthian shot to Malcolm that he would be forwarding him the valeting bill.

As there was an American TV film crew waiting for the band back at Denmark Street Malcolm was forced to order two cabs to ferry them back into the West End. If the NBC crew's director had been hanging on at the band's HQ to capture their memories of the A&M signing for posterity, then he was left sorely wanting as – aside from gleaning a slurred quote from Sid about how great it was to be a Sex Pistol – the drunken miscreants collapsed on Steve's bed and nothing more was heard until the following morning.

#

Although Green had been beside himself in having to deal with the Sex Pistols in their drunken state, it had been his idea to stage the press conference at such an un-rock'n'roll hour, as well as laying on such a copious amount of complimentary booze, so he could hardly admonish the band over their loutish and lewd behaviour. Although he still had reservations about Malcolm's managerial style, or lack thereof, he believed the Sex Pistols would be a sizable asset to A&M Records over the course of the next two years and the following morning he gave the go-ahead for the initial 25,000 pressing of 'God Save The Queen'.

The label's artwork department had worked up a rough cover showing the band posing outside Buckingham Palace, while sentries were seen clutching UB40 signing-on cards. Glitterbest, however, as it had done at EMI, rejected the idea in favour of releasing the single in a plain black company sleeve accompanied by a plethora of promotional, and sure to be confrontational, images. These included handbills, posters and stickers that Jamie Reid had designed using Cecil Beaton's official Silver Jubilee portrait of the Queen as his template. Although the American owned A&M had no problem with Reid sticking a safety pin through the British monarch's mouth, the label baulked at the idea of placing swastikas over her eyes.

That same morning, John was up before the bench at Marlborough Street Magistrates Court to answer the charge of possession of amphetamine sulphate following his arrest on 12th

January. Having been caught in possession, John had little option but to plead guilty as charged. He tried to lighten the inevitable debit to his bank balance though by telling the court he gave £15 of his £25 weekly wage to his mum for board and lodgings. His counsel also attempted to put him in a better light by claiming the incident had been a one-off, and that John preferred to have a few beers with his mates in the pub rather than resort to drug use. Although a custodial sentence was never a consideration, there were those within the band's inner circle who feared the magistrate might use the occasion to settle an Establishment score against the Sex Pistols. Those fears proved unfounded and John spent the rest of the day with Sid and Wobble celebrating signing to A&M, after being given nothing more severe than a slap on the wrist and a £40 fine.

Later that evening the three headed over to the Speakeasy on Margaret Street, where they met up with Steve and Paul, and the celebrations went into overdrive. The night would surely have ended with nothing more than a collective hangover the following morning had it not been for the arrival of Bob Harris and his engineer friend George Nicholson. Harris had apparently been making his way through the bar area to where his friends (the long-forgotten band Bandit, as well as Procol Harum's off-duty road crew) were, when Wobble took exception to *The Old Grey Whistle Test* having thus far ignored the Sex Pistols. When the dulcet-toned presenter politely told Wobble in no uncertain terms that the Sex Pistols would never appear on the show as long as he was in charge, Wobble waded in and had to be restrained by several members of Harris' party. It was at this point that Sid decided to get in on the action by attacking Nicholson with a broken bottle, leaving the hapless engineer with a head wound requiring fourteen stitches. An alternative version of events appeared in *Sounds*' 26th March issue and has John down as the culprit, claiming he 'grabbed up two glasses and started punching wildly into the crowd, slamming one of the glasses into George's [Nicholson] forehead'.

Whilst reviewing *No One Is Innocent* (Orion) for the *Independent* in the broadsheet's 17th June 2007 issue, Wobble goes so far as to deny anything untoward happened at the Speakeasy that night; this despite Harris mentioning the incident in his book *Bob Harris: The Whispering Years* and again when being interviewed as part of the BBC series *Seven Ages Of Rock*. Although Wobble naturally wishes to distance himself from his unsavoury act, are we really expected to believe A&M would have severed its connection with the Sex Pistols – not to mention handing over £75,000 – for an incident which never took place? Well, you do the maths!

Aside from shock and a few bruises, Harris managed to escape the melee unscathed, but the unprovoked attack – not to mention Wobble's death threat should he ever see him again – had left him deeply disturbed. The following morning Harris brought his manager Philip Roberge into action. The American Roberge's first call was to Derek Green's home to inform the A&M man of what had occurred. Green's initial reaction was to deny culpability on the grounds that he was merely the head of the band's record label, and that their unsavoury behaviour didn't come under his jurisdiction: sheer sandbagging, of course. He had known Harris for many years, and he couldn't even contemplate taking sides against his old friend. If EMI had been prepared to make a stand against the Sex Pistols' blatant use of offensive language on live television, then could A&M stand idle while the band wilfully attacked anyone who refused to pander to their whims?

The first Malcolm heard of the incident was on the Monday morning when a letter from Roberge arrived at Dryden Chambers. Unlike Green, however, Malcolm was happy to shrug off any responsibility for his charges' behaviour and ran out his by now already well-worn 'boys will be boys' mantra. Even he must have recognised though that the stakes had just been raised, for Roberge was no ordinary business manager. Aside from looking after the likes of Bob Harris and Rick Wakeman, Roberge was also in partnership with Dee Anthony who oversaw the business affairs of Peter Frampton. Frampton, the former Humble Pie frontman, had gone solo in 1971 and although his early releases had stuttered and stumbled, the singer's most recent album, *Frampton Comes Alive*, released on 14th February 1976, had held the coveted Billboard No. 1 spot for 10 weeks, and was still holding its own on the charts some thirteen months later, making him A&M's most successful artist by far.

Having had his Saturday ruined by Roberge's call, Green spent the rest of the weekend contemplating his options regarding the Sex Pistols. He had signed the band against the wishes of the majority of his London-based staff, and allowed his personal opinion to sway his West Coast bosses; now the chickens were coming home to roost. It wasn't so much his reputation that he was worried about, but rather what might occur next should he choose to bury his head in the sand and ignore the Sex Pistols' predilection for violence. He had also put a call in to Dryden Chambers that same Monday demanding to know what Malcolm intended to do to bring his boys into line. Although Malcolm had promised he would try and carpet them, Green sensed from Malcolm's tone that the admonishing, if indeed carried out at all, would be little more than a token gesture.

Green, however, could no longer hide under his corporate hat regarding the Sex Pistols' behaviour, for Harris was a personal friend. His mind was in utter turmoil, so instead of going into the office the following morning he stopped off to collect a friend before driving down to Brighton, where he spent the afternoon hurling pebbles into the surf, while using his pal as a sounding board. Although there was little point in pretending Malcolm could – or indeed would – exercise any real control over the Sex Pistols, A&M still stood to make a lot of money from the band. Profit margins were all that truly counted in the business world, so he came to the only real solution available to him: later that evening he called Jerry Moss in Los Angeles and tendered his resignation. To his surprise, however, Moss refused to accept it and told him that if the label had to choose between keeping the Sex Pistols or losing their trusted English lieutenant, then the Sex Pistols were history. Later that same evening, the reclusive Herb Alpert, whom Green hadn't had any direct dealings with for several years, called him at home to provide a second vote of confidence.

The following morning, Wednesday 16th March, Green summoned Malcolm and Stephen Fisher to his office in order to 'discuss a most important contractual point'. The Glitterbest twins would have arrived at A&M's New King's Road office assuming they were there to iron out some problem with the single's promotional campaign, and were therefore stunned to find A&M's legal team awaiting their arrival. Green walked in and handed Malcolm the following two sentence handwritten press release: *A&M Records wishes to announce that its recording contract with the Sex Pistols has been terminated with immediate effect.* (Although Green also ordered the 25,000 copies of 'God Save The Queen', AMS7284, already pressed to be destroyed, some copies survived the cull. At the time of writing they fetch upwards of £10,000 on a good day at auction or on eBay, so check your attic).

Malcolm tried to laugh it off thinking Green was playing some corporate prank or maybe attempting to call his bluff over the

Harris assault. But the smile slipped from his pale features as the stern-faced A&M man told him that the press release would be going out on the wires at 3 p.m., and that the only thing left open to discussion was how much it was going to cost the label. An hour or so later a shell-shocked Malcolm left A&M's office with a cheque for £25,000 to cover the initial year's contract. Although he would later try to make light of the saga with a quip about walking in and out of offices and being handed cheques, the Silver Jubilee was now less than three months way; the clock was indeed ticking.

#

Sid, having met the press and caused the A&M mess, made his live debut as a Sex Pistol when the band returned to the Notre Dame Hall for a showcase on Monday, 21st March 1977. The venue's pious owners, despite having profited last time round the Pistols performed at their basement venue, were now keen to distance themselves from the band and tried to cancel the show. When that option was denied them owing to Malcolm threatening legal action, the Catholic priests did the next best thing by restricting admittance to just fifty people. Malcolm again petitioned the priests and got the number increased to one hundred and fifty. As far as the select few who managed to gain entrance that night were concerned, the restriction was worse than a cancellation, as the distinct lack of atmosphere only served to belittle the band's efforts. The bemused audience headed off into the night wondering if they'd ever see their beloved Sex Pistols appear in London again. Many of those 150 or so gathered within the Notre Dame had arrived expecting Sid to make a complete arse of himself on stage but, although he was never going to match Glen's musical dexterity, he managed to get through the set without making too many errors. Then again, this was only due to his using a self-taught Ramones-esque 'one riff fits all' throughout the band's truncated eleven song set.

Many of the band's inner circle were thrilled to see one of their own up on stage as a fully-fledged Sex Pistol, though Sid's elevated status didn't sit well with everyone within the band's entourage. The bassist – dressed in his customary ripped jeans, Converse sneakers and Vive Le Rock T-shirt – had been making his way out of the Notre Dame when a voice challenged him that he'd 'sold out'. Sid naturally wheeled round with eyes burning and fists clenched, but the bassist immediately backed down again at finding his agitator was one of the twins from the East End gang that had been following the band for almost as long as himself. Unlike Ronnie and Reggie, however, Michael and John earned an honest crust selling hot dogs to the tourists in Piccadilly. The duo's all purpose put-down of 'never mind the bollocks' would inadvertently provide the Sex Pistols with the title for their debut album.

The NBC film crew was still following the band around and was therefore on hand to capture Sid's debut. However, they weren't the only Americans with their eye on Sid that night. A pudgy, bottle-blonde New York groupie called Nancy Spungen had recently arrived in London, looking to hook up with her old Bowery drug buddies Jerry Nolan and Johnny Thunders. Having fooled herself into believing she and Jerry were an item she made up her mind to follow the drummer to England, after reading about the Sex Pistols and the nascent English punk rock scene.

The Heartbreakers manager Leee Black Childers accidently happened upon Nancy as she was making her way through Carnaby Street on her very first afternoon in London. He was already au fait with Nancy's 'fuck for drugs' *modus operandi* and, knowing what the consequences might be should she find Nolan, warned her to stay away from the Heartbreakers' drummer. 'A few days later, I heard that she'd hooked up with Sid,' he lamented to Jon Savage in *England's Dreaming*. 'A cold chill ran down my spine when I heard the news, because from that day on Sid was no longer the person I knew.'

Nancy Laura Spungen was born on 27th February 1958 in the Huntingdon Valley area of Lower Moreland Township, Pennsylvania, a suburb of Philadelphia. Being born a month prematurely had led to her developing cyanosis, a bluish-purple discoloration of the skin and mucous membranes caused by a deficiency of oxygen in the blood. Although Nancy was an intelligent child, her early years were plagued with uncontrollable rages and she was just three years old when her frustrated parents Frank and Deborah finally faced up to their daughter's problems and sought outside help by booking her into therapy. However, neither these sessions, nor the prescribed medication, alleviated the problems, and by the age of eleven she was receiving lengthy and intensive psychiatric help. Her formative years proved equally exasperating for her parents, yet despite attempting suicide, running away from school on several occasions, and openly experimenting with drugs, she managed to attain sufficient grades to gain entrance to the University of

Colorado. Like her future lover Sid, Nancy found herself at odds with the educational system, and at seventeen she quit college, heading for New York, where she quickly fell into the sordid Max's Kansas scene and embarked on a short-lived affair with Richard Hell. She took a job as a topless dancer in one of the seedy bars off Times Square, and in order to feed her spiralling drug habit she supplemented her income by turning tricks for her clientele.

#

Whilst Malcolm was preoccupied in finding the Sex Pistols a new record label, Vivienne had been busy laying the foundations for her own future empire by overseeing the latest renovations at 430 King's Road. The couple had decided upon the refurbishment back in December, but rather than carry out the work themselves as they had done previously, they enlisted the help of Ben Kelly – who would later design the interior of the Manchester Hacienda – and his draughtsman associate David Connor to oversee things.

The provocative pink plastic letters and Rousseau's telling aphorism gave way to hi-tech – and highly expensive – opaque white-flashed opal glass, giving it the look of a dental surgery rather than a fashion house. A small brass plaque affixed to one of the plates bore the shop's new name *Seditionaries: clothes for heroes* in elegant script. In opting for a glass-plated front, however, Vivienne and Malcolm inadvertently provided anyone bearing a grudge against the Sex Pistols with the perfect means of exacting revenge. The glass panels also garnered plenty of attention from the Chelsea hooligans who would take great delight in using the shop's windows as target practice, whilst making their way to and from nearby Stamford Bridge. With little point in complaining to the authorities, the couple installed protective wire-mesh screens over the glass plates. Even these security measures were rendered ineffective against anyone with the foresight to bring along a screwdriver or some other elongated weapon though.

The shop's radical new exterior broke all the rules of retail marketing, as the passers-by couldn't see inside the store. This was simply an extension of Malcolm and Vivienne's mantra that they didn't want just 'anybody' coming to check out their wares; as far as they were concerned, the curiosity seeking window-lickers could now hang around outside John Krevine's new punk emporium BOY further down the King's Road.

BOY had opened to a great fanfare during the first week of March, with its 'window of forensic cultures' being the main attraction. This was created by Peter Christopherson, a.k.a. 'Sleazy' of avant-garde performance band Throbbing Gristle (he'd also photographed the Sex Pistols in early 1976). The display consisted of simulated burnt body parts set within a series of Petri dishes. Christopherson's pieces were so detailed that many a passer-by was stopped dead in their tracks believing them to be real. Needless to say, the display, not to mention the crowds of onlookers, attracted the attentions of the police, who considered the idea offensive and ordered its removal.

Seditionaries' new minimalistic interior was equally hi-tech. The floor was covered in rugged industrial grey carpeting, while the walls were decorated with full-blown black and white photographs of the German city of Dresden following the allied blanket-bombing campaign of 14th February 1944. Some 800 RAF Lancaster Bombers and another 400 American B-17 Bombers had deluged the baroque city with tonnes of incendiaries reducing it to a smoking ruin and leaving some 130,000 Germans dead or dying amongst the rubble. In keeping with the bombed theme, holes were smashed into the suspended ceiling through which two searing spotlights protruded. The wall directly behind the counter held a full colour photograph of Piccadilly Circus, hung purposely upside-down; the photo having first been spliced into sections to allow access to the cupboards behind it. The gymnasium wall-bars survived, but were polished and moved into the centre of the shop to serve as clothes racks, whilst tacky sixties-style bucket chairs draped in fluorescent orange nylon provided the seating. Towards the rear of the shop, where the surgical bed had once stood, a television set hung suspended above a kidney-shaped counter. The spartan décor was completed with a table – designed by Connor – within which a live rat paced up and down.

Although some articles from SEX were kept on display, the new designs bore a label depicting the Ⓐ anarchy symbol along with the slogan: 'for soldiers, prostitutes, dykes and punks'. 'We did Seditionaries for £2,000, and that £2,000 changed the world.' Connor would later tell Jane Mulvagh in *Vivienne Westwood: An Unfashionable Life*. 'It was all ideas. Money had almost nothing to do with it. Intimidation, that was it.'

#

To paraphrase Lady Bracknell in *The Importance of Being Earnest*, losing one record label may be considered as unfortunate, but to lose two in as many months might be construed as carelessness. Either way it left the band, particularly John, Steve and Paul, totally deflated. Malcolm decided therefore to send them – with Jamie Reid and John 'Boogie' Tiberi acting as chaperones – on a short getaway holiday to Jersey. At the time of writing, Jersey has been rocked by child-sex allegations involving many of the tax-haven's leading figures. But back in March 1977, with the children's skeletons locked away in cupboards, the predominantly French-speaking island was a respectable holiday destination for both the British and the French jet sets, and the island's 'kiddie-fiddling' dignitaries had no intention of allowing the disgusting Sex Pistols to publicly defile its doorway.

Jersey had been occupied by German forces during WWII, and the Sex Pistols could have been forgiven for thinking Hitler's SS had returned to the island. The boys were prohibited from entering their hotel, suffered the indignity of a cavity search by local police and given twenty-four hours to get off the island. Although Jamie managed to find another hotel willing to take them in for the night, when he and the band went out for breakfast the following morning they were followed every step of the way by those same overzealous officers. The boys, with the exception of Sid, who was no doubt loving every minute of being in the spotlight, returned to London more stressed out than before they left, so Malcolm's new second-in-command, Boogie, suggested another excursion; this time to Berlin.

Tiberi had been a face on the Soho scene since the late sixties and had turned his hand to several honest occupations, including photography, before trying a dishonest path which led to an appearance in the dock for cheque fraud. Upon his release from prison he began working with the 101'ers and received the nickname 'Winston O'Boogie' – one of John Lennon's quirky recording pseudonyms – from Joe Strummer on account of Tiberi's predilection for Capstan Full Strength cigarettes [Winston was a popular brand of smokes in the 1970s]. When Joe decamped from the 101'ers to link up with Bernie and Mick Jones, however, the by-now truncated Boogie had no desire to get caught up in Bernie's political rhetoric and instead gravitated towards the King's Road and SEX. He soon formed friendships with both Malcolm and the Sex Pistols and was perfectly placed to take up the reins following Nils' resignation.

Upon arrival in Berlin, Boogie and the band booked into the Hotel Kapinski and hired a Volkswagen to ferry them around the divided city's sights such as the Reichstag Building, the Brandenburg Gate and the notorious graffiti-laden wall that had been dividing capitalist from communist since 1961. Boogie had brought along his Super 8 camera and shot footage of the band clowning around at Checkpoint Charlie. Indeed they might well have crossed through the most notorious of the wall's eight official border crossing points to peruse East Berlin's 'cheap essential scenery' had Sid not forgotten to bring along his passport that day.

Following on from their German jaunt, the Sex Pistols returned to London to play a free show at the Screen On The Green cinema in Islington on Sunday 3rd April. As with the 'Midnight Special' back in August the band didn't actually take to the stage until the early hours of Monday morning. One of those taking advantage of the free festivities was Jon Savage who reviewed the show for the *NME*. Savage opened his review opining 'In which it must be conceded that Malcolm McLaren has a first class media brain with a perfect instinct for theatre.' And theatre it was, for the 350 or so punters were purposely kept waiting longer than was perhaps necessary, to further crank up the atmosphere, until being treated to the inaugural showing of *Sex Pistols Number One*, a homespun film of TV clips and interviews collating the band's adventures to date. This included their appearances on *So It Goes*, *Today*, and some rather bizarre footage taken from Derek Nimmo's recent visit to Seditionaries, when the plummy character actor, who'd made his name in the 1960s religious sit-coms *All Gas And Gaiters* and *Oh Brother!,* got a punk makeover before wandering up and down outside the shop in a pair of bondage trousers.

Support was provided by the Slits making their London debut, but the novelty of their being an all-girl act was lost on Savage on account of their glaring musical ineptitude; although he was willing to concede the girls themselves were a 'great show'. Somewhat amazingly, Savage believed the Pistols had improved since their first Notre Dame show back in November, even if the material – with the exception of 'God Save The Queen' and 'EMI' – was beginning to sound all too familiar. Sid, who was perhaps making his true live debut, got Savage's seal of approval – if only for looking the part – while Steve and Paul had already been rendered side men in the band they had formed. Savage reserved his real praise for John, whose performance he described as 'totally mesmeric: the lurker in derelict alleys, a spastic pantomime villain, with evil for real.'

#

Malcolm spent the following day, 5th April, doing the rounds at various record companies. Whereas he'd once been allowed the luxury of ignoring phone calls from label chiefs, plenty of water had passed under London's bridges since those carefree days of six months earlier, and he found he couldn't even get an appointment with many of them. He was becoming increasingly desperate to land the Sex Pistols another deal and get 'God Save The Queen' into the shops in time for the Silver Jubilee. Unfortunately for his aching soles though, it wasn't just London's premiere venues that were now closing their doors on the band and he found his advances spurned at every turn. With no other labels showing any real interest Malcolm was forced to take the call from Richard Branson at Virgin. Branson, who would later claim to have contacted Leslie Hill the morning following the Sex Pistols' appearance on *Today* offering to take the band off EMI's hands, had been chomping at the bit to sign the Sex Pistols. Although he'd had to wait a further three months, he finally got his act.

Malcolm and Steven Fisher met with Branson at Virgin's offices on Monday 2nd May to hammer out the contractual negotiations and were somewhat amused to find themselves sat at the table with the same solicitor, Robert Lee, who'd represented A&M. Branson, or 'Mr Pickle' as Malcolm called the Virgin supremo, may have been a hippie, but he was the polar opposite of Sir John Read and positively bent over backwards to cater to Glitterbest's every whim. Today, the Virgin logo is omnipresent: one can book train and flight tickets – and pay for said tickets with a Virgin credit card – as well as buy Virgin cola. Had Branson been successful in his bid to take over the beleaguered building society Northern Rock, then he may well have taken over the world. Back in the seventies though, Virgin started life as a mail order music outlet before becoming Virgin Records in 1973.

The bearded one wasn't afraid of turning a blind eye to the excise laws if it meant turning a profit. He would, however, pay the price for flaunting said laws and received a, then hefty, £28,000 fine for faking exports which could then be sold much cheaper as imports minus the VAT in 1971. Unlike EMI and A&M, Virgin was an independent label with no shareholders nor a board made up of well-heeled MPs and middle-aged curmudgeons with little or no understanding of the music industry. It was also a close-knit 'family run' enterprise in that Branson's trusted lieutenants such as Nik Powell, John Varnom, and his second-in-command Simon Draper – who told his boss that Virgin would 'sign the Sex Pistols over his dead body' – were also close personal friends. Thanks to the runaway success of Mike Oldfield's 1973 debut concept album *Tubular Bells* – which would remain in the charts for over four and a half years – the label was now able to break bread with the big boys.

On 12th May, the Sex Pistols were added to the Virgin roster for a one album deal with an initial payment of £15,000, while a further £50,000 was to be paid one month later to allow Virgin the right to release Sex Pistols' product worldwide [Virgin didn't have direct distribution in North America at this time and were represented by WEA, as will become apparent later in the story]. However, with Glitterbest's coffers already close to bulging Malcolm insisted that the sum be paid in twelve instalments as each album track was delivered. The following day, while Sid was in hospital recovering from hepatitis which he picked up from sharing needles (he wouldn't sign until the 16th), John, Steve and Paul put their names to the third recording contract.

CHAPTER TEN

Never Trust A Hippy

'I'm going to tell you something now that you might laugh at, Tony. But hear me out, kids will still be buying our records in the year 2000!'
Beatles manager Brian Epstein to Tony Barrow in 1964

'God Save The Queen' (VS181) was officially released by Virgin Records on Friday, 27th May 1977. Somewhat ironically, given that the Sex Pistols were spearheading the latest British music craze, the first 200 copies of the single actually went on sale the previous day at the Remember Those Oldies record store in Cambridge. The release date was thrown into jeopardy when the staff at the CBS pressing plant in Aylesbury, which at the time manufactured all Virgin's releases, imitated their counterparts at EMI's Hayes plant by threatening strike action if they were forced to handle the controversial platter.

Malcolm had joked at the time of the A&M contract termination that the Sex Pistols were like some contagious disease, and now the quarantine had stretched to anything connected with the band. Thankfully, however, the dispute was resolved amicably and the workers returned to their posts. The initial pressing of 50,000 copies may have gone out on time, but not everybody was as accommodating as Remember Those Oldies, and the three leading high street behemoths Boots, Woolworths, and W.H. Smith all refused to stock the record. Needless to say, all four major music weeklies made 'God Save The Queen' their 'Single Of The Week' with *Record Mirror* and *Melody Maker* placing the Sex Pistols on their respective front covers; while the *NME* practically dedicated that week's 'overkill' issue to the band.

Both the *NME* and *Sounds* featured full-page adverts for the single on their back pages, but the latter paper's advert was somehow amended without consent whilst at the printers, which forced the paper to offer an apology to the band the following week. Jamie Reid's cross-media campaign also fell foul of the censors with both Thames and LWT rejecting the proposed TV advert, while the commercial radio stations refused to broadcast the radio spots. Not surprisingly, given that the record had been banned, the promotional video footage, shot by Julien Temple at the Marquee on 23rd May, was shelved indefinitely and wouldn't resurface until being included in *The Great Rock 'n' Roll Swindle*.

Although the BBC had banned the single on the grounds that it was in 'gross bad taste', the head honchos at Radio One allowed John Peel to air the song twice on his night-time show during the first week of June. The IBA (Independent Broadcasting Authority) instructed all commercial radio and TV stations not to broadcast the single as it contravened Section 4 (10) (A) of the IBA act. Despite being able to implement such draconian measures, the suits in Whitehall were powerless to stop people going out and buying the record; if only to see what all the fuss was about. In its first week of release 'God Save The Queen' sold upwards of 150,000 copies which saw it slam into the UK singles chart at No. 11 week ending 4th June 1977 (the same week the Jam entered the chart at No. 40 with 'In The City'). The following week – Jubilee Week – it shot to No. 2 only to be denied the coveted top spot by Rod Stewart's double A-side 'I Don't Wanna Talk About It/The First Cut Is The Deepest'. Though you'll find people both inside and outside the music industry willing to argue about the songs' chart placings till Doomsday!

#

Although the Silver Jubilee celebrations – which included a two-day public holiday – weren't scheduled to commence until 7th June, the Queen made her Jubilee Speech on 4th May. In this address to the nation she not only spoke of old empire and her hopes for the Commonwealth, but of how Britain's joining the Common Market had been one of the most significant decisions taken during her twenty-five-year reign. Although she was careful not to directly criticise those of her subjects who were advocating Scottish and Welsh devolution, she used the speech to remind them that she had been crowned Queen of the United Kingdom of Great Britain and Northern Ireland.

No other nation can do pomp and circumstance quite like the British, and on Tuesday, 7th June, while the Royal Guard staged a twenty-five gun salute in Hyde Park in honour of the Queen's quarter of a century on the throne, the country became one enormous street party and buried its troubles beneath a sea of red, white and blue bunting. Her Majesty had got the celebrations underway the previous evening by lighting a giant bonfire in Windsor Great Park which was the signal for a hundred or so other bonfires to be lit from Land's End in Cornwall to Saxa Vord up in the Shetland Islands (the same sites as those used by Queen Elizabeth I in 1588 to warn the nation of the approaching Spanish Armada invasion fleet). Following a horse-drawn procession from Buckingham Palace – cheered on by an estimated one million well-wishers – to St Paul's Cathedral for a thanksgiving service, the Queen and Prince Philip attended a lavish banquet at the Guildhall.

Seeing as the Sex Pistols were banned from every recognised music venue in and around London, and weren't likely to be invited guests of honour at the Guildhall banquet, Malcolm organised a special Jubilee Boat Party. He hired the *Queen Elizabeth* for £500 to take the band and around 175 assorted guests (the boat's official capacity limit) up and down the River Thames. The task of making all the necessary arrangements – which fell to John Varnom – wasn't made any easier by the *Daily Mirror*'s 6th June headline, which falsely declared that the Sex Pistols had dared to call the Queen a 'moron'. But the quick-witted Varnom was able to assuage the ship's captain by telling him that although the Sex Pistols were indeed signed to Virgin, the boat had been hired to promote the label's latest German synthesizer band.

At 6.30 p.m., on a slightly chilly evening, the *Queen Elizabeth* pulled away from its moorings at Charing Cross Pier, and as the boat headed downstream two huge banners were unfurled and hung over the rail; one of which was an advert for the new single, while the other proclaimed 'Queen Elizabeth Welcomes The Sex Pistols'. Judging from Temple's footage in *Swindle*, everyone appears to be in fine fettle, with the possible exception of John who surveys the sycophantic Virgin clique with utter disdain before disappearing below decks, where the by-now inseparable Sid and Nancy are holding court with Boogie and Glitterbest's latest hireling, Steve 'Roadent' Connolly. The latter had recently jumped ship (pardon the nautical pun) from the Clash camp midway through the band's *White Riot* tour after tiring of Mick Jones' pampered ego. 'You need a valet not a roadie!' was to be his Parthian shot.

Roadent, or SCON as he was sometimes known, had arrived in London from his native Coventry the previous October, soon after serving a two week custodial sentence for non-payment of a fine. He'd fallen in with the Clash after catching the band's explosive show at the ICA on 23rd October and, after helping out lugging the band's gear in return for free access into the venue, a conversation with Joe – who would surely have recognised a fellow leopard keen to change his spots and distance himself from his middle-class past – led to his being invited to bed down at the band's rehearsal space. Here – along with his enduring nick-name courtesy of Paul Simonon – he acquired a more permanent position within the band's close-knit infrastructure. Paul and Mick would also take the eager new recruit to their hearts, with Mick going so far as to demand that the penny-pinching Bernie dipped into the petty cash to buy Roadent a new pair of socks. Although those socks came in useful and saw action on the ill-fated Anarchy Tour, Roadent had joined the Clash primarily to hump their gear on and off stage, and not simply to cater to Mick's every whim. And after one extravagance too many, he put in a call to Malcolm offering his services.

These days the divorced father of three – whose ex-wife worked as Malcolm's secretary looking after the interests of Bow Wow Wow – can oft be found nursing a Guinness in the Spice Of Life pub in London's Cambridge Circus. He will feign amnesia whenever an outsider attempts to broach the subject of his past endeavours with the Clash and the Sex Pistols, but on rare occasions he will happily take a stroll down memory lane and share whatever anecdotes he stumbles upon. One only has to engage him in a five minute conversation to know that – like Joe Strummer – his yobbish 'up the Hammers' accent is a mere put-on to mask an eloquence and intelligence acquired courtesy of a public school education. 'I might have spent my formative years at such an establishment,' he begrudgingly confessed the first time we attempted to dig into his past. 'But it was only a scholarship 'cos my father worked in a car factory,' he added, taking a leaf out of Joe's book on acquiring street cred.

Unfortunately for Roadent, however, it wasn't only car panels that Connolly Snr was keen to beat into shape, and he would occasionally do a little overtime on his son. Roadent may not have been an angel, but he certainly didn't merit having the shit kicked out of him whenever the mood suited and he packed his bags, spending several months crashing at friends' houses and bedsits in and around Coventry. Even though punk had yet to encroach on the city, his penchant for ambiguous clothes set him apart from the flare-wearing masses and he and his friends took to frequenting gay pubs simply as a means of escaping ridicule.

Although he was happy to forego the pleasures of the Sex Pistols' 1996 reunion tour – 'I'd seen 'em before,' he'd say if anyone enquired – nor bother with any of the band's later live shows, he's been a regular attendee whenever the Sex Pistols Experience (by far the country's best of many tribute acts) come to town to recreate the legendary Jubilee Boat Party. Their inaugural recreation, aboard a rather dilapidated *Queen Elizabeth,* came in June 2004, with Roadent deigning to put in an appearance looking like some absent-minded professor – complete with waistcoat and Dickie bow – who'd perhaps lost his bearings. The boat had barely left the dock when several latter-day punks in freshly painted leathers started ribbing him about his 'being on the wrong boat'. 'Well, if that were true,' he mused whilst peering over the rim of his gin and tonic, 'then I was on the wrong boat twenty-seven years ago.' If memory serves, he was on free gin for the rest of the evening!

In the absence of a proper stage, the Sex Pistols' equipment was set up at the *Queen Elizabeth's* stern as this was the only covered area aboard the vessel. The band were already in place but held off until the boat reached the Houses of Parliament before launching into 'Anarchy In The UK'. Although a piratical jaunt down the River Thames had looked a jolly proposition on paper, no one seemed to have spared any thought for the acoustics, or blatant lack thereof, and the set was marred by feedback throughout. Steve, Paul and Sid carried on regardless, but John, whose mood was still as dark as the churning Thames water, refused to enter the one-sided contest and stood staring into space instead of singing the opening verse of 'No Feelings'.

With Seditionaries having gone upmarket, the singer had abandoned his safety pinned Oxfam garb in favour of leather pants and a white tuxedo worn over one of Malcolm's latest creations: the 'Destroy' shirt. The long-sleeved muslin shirt bore the word 'Destroy' in crumbling roughly-drawn blood-red block lettering across the top, with a swastika at its centre and an inverted image of the crucified Christ lifted from Grünewald's 1515 *Crucifixion.* And – as if in keeping with the Jubilee theme – the shirt also features a postage stamp image of Queen Elizabeth II severed at the neck.

Midway through 'Pretty Vacant' two police river boats came sniffing around, but with everything appearing to be ship-shape and Bristol fashion they were powerless to intrude and headed off upstream. However, the boys in blue were soon back alongside after responding to the captain's SOS, issued because Wobble allegedly struck a French photographer. Although Sophie Richmond had stepped in to separate the pair, the captain, who was looking for any excuse to get the punk rockers off his boat, cut the power and headed for shore, where more police were already forming in a line. Branson's champagne and salmon paté brigade disappeared into the night, but the Sex Pistols and their entourage were understandably irked at having their fun curtailed and refused to disembark. Scuffles broke out as officers began to manhandle people down the gangplank, and the night air was soon filled with the sound of approaching sirens. Thankfully, Boogie kept his wits about him and, with Roadent's assistance, bundled the group's stuff off the boat, while Sophie handed each of the bemused band members £5 cab fare and smuggled them down the vessel's second – and less conspicuous – stairwell. John, Steve and Paul headed back into the West End with their mates, while Sid and Nancy returned to their Chelsea Cloisters love nest to do heroin. To Nancy's mind, Sid was a rock star, and rock stars did drugs.

Malcolm, Vivienne, Jamie, Ben Kelly, John's younger brother Jimmy Lydon, as well as Sophie herself and half a dozen others were bundled into the back of a Black Maria and taken to Bow Street Police Station. Malcolm, who'd dared to call the arresting officers 'fucking fascist bastards', was duly fined £100. Vivienne was found guilty of obstructing a police officer and fined £15 with £15 costs, while Jimmy Lydon was fined £3 after pleading guilty to using obscene language.

Malcolm happily admitted that 'God Save The Queen' was the apex of his accomplishments with the Sex Pistols; well, it's not every day you get to stick a safety pin through the Queen's schnoz, is it? Malcolm's crowning glory surely came though when Woolworths refused to even acknowledge the song's existence. Their in-store displays didn't mention the song title or the Sex Pistols by name, preferring instead a blank space at the top of the chart. Jamie Reid was of the opinion that the Pistols, as well as everyone connected with the band, should call it a day after reaching a pinnacle they could never hope to surpass. It was easy for him to say, because whilst he and Malcolm could easily pull a disappearing act and venture into other creative fields, the four Sex Pistols would be left to fend for themselves as they'd nothing else in the pipeline. Even Jordan, who, along with Sid, was the living embodiment of Malcolm's punk ideals, and would herself take centre stage as Amyl Nitrate in Derek Jarman's 1977 film *Jubilee*, was filled with a sense of foreboding. For Alan Jones, amongst others, the shock of witnessing the police's heavy-handed brutality towards him and his friends was too much to bear. Although Alan still hung out with the Sex Pistols' crowd, he packed away his punk threads and moved onto musical pastures new.

#

As we've already mentioned, Rod Stewart's double A-Side 'I Don't Wanna Talk About It/The First Cut Is The Deepest' held the coveted No. 1 spot during Jubilee week. There are those, however, who believe to this day that shadowy governmental figures were involved in purposely keeping 'God Save The Queen' off the top spot. Their argument is supported by the fact that CBS, who distributed both records, readily admitted that the Sex Pistols' disc was outselling Rod the Mod by two to one. Richard Branson has always maintained that the powers that be at the BPI (British Phonographic Institute) placed pressure on their opposite numbers at the BRMB (British Market Research Bureau) to nobble the Sex Pistols by dropping all chart-return shops connected with Virgin Records from that particular week's census. His argument is given credence by the fact that the BPI's then head, John Fruin – who was also Managing Director of WEA Records – lost his job in 1981 owing to irregularities over chart placings of several WEA acts.

This, of course, was back in the days when singles were still important and some would argue that any record entering the Top 10 at No. 2 should certainly have held off the competition and kept its place; especially if said disc was outselling the No. 1 by two to one. Instead of which 'God Save The Queen' slipped down to No. 4. Then again, if the suits in Whitehall were indeed responsible for pulling the necessary strings to stymie the Sex Pistols, they were hardly going to pat themselves on the back for a job well done only to allow the controversial record to take No. 1 the following week, leaving the bedevilled BBC in the awkward position of having to finally acknowledge the record's existence.

The Establishment may have won the day, but it was clear the Sex Pistols weren't going to go away any time soon. So, once the Jubilee celebrations had died down, and the bunting stored away for the next royal wedding, the *Sunday Mirror*, whose sister paper the *Daily Mirror* had been the only tabloid to run an article on the Boat Party arrests, decided to launch a moral crusade against the Sex Pistols and their ilk.

The paper's 12th June banner headline called upon the nation to '**PUNISH THE PUNKS**'.

Freedom of speech is supposedly one of the fundamentals of democracy, and yet although each and every one of us has the right to voice our opinion on any given subject, nothing antagonises an Englishman more than having his country or sovereign made a mockery of in public. So while it was okay to bemoan Labour's ailing policies, or scoff at Margaret Thatcher's dress sense when you're down the pub with the lads, anyone daring to call Her Majesty a moron on her Silver Jubilee had best come out with their fighting boots on. John would later claim to have written the lyric to 'No Future', which was more of a poem than an actual song, in late October 1976 and that there had been no conscious decision to write a song about the Queen or her approaching Silver Jubilee celebrations. That may well be true, but the Sex Pistols' decision to release 'God Save The Queen' leading up to the Jubilee was bound to ruffle a few patriotic feathers. Indeed, the band got a foretaste of what was to come when they debuted the song – under its original guise of 'No Future' – at Coventry's Lanchester Polytechnic on 29th November 1976. The student body took offence to the song and refused to pay the band their fee on the grounds that they were 'fascists'. Yet had these so-called 'patriots' bothered to listen to the song's lyrical content instead of believing what they read in the *Daily Mirror*, they would have realised the song was actually calling each of them a moron for allowing politicians and Whitehall bureaucrats to dictate how they should live their lives.

The English have also been brought up to believe that those in authority should never be questioned. Pompous MP Marcus Lipton – again in the *Daily Mirror* – suggested that if pop music was attempting to destroy the country's established institutions then it should be destroyed first. Unfortunately, there were enough thugs walking the streets of London willing to take the *Mirror*'s vitriolic credo to their hearts.

The first to feel the backlash was Jamie Reid, who suffered a broken nose and a fractured right tibia after being set upon by four slap-happy yobbos close to his and Sophie's flat the day following the *Mirror*'s dictum. One might have expected the four band members to view the assault on Jamie as a warning to keep their heads below the parapets until the tabloids found someone else to vilify. But the following Saturday, 18th June, following a day spent laying down tracks at Wessex Studios, John, Chris Thomas, and Wessex's in-house engineer Bill Price, had been enjoying a quiet drink in the nearby Pegasus pub, when John came under fire from several of the pub's already well-oiled patrons. The three quickly downed their drinks and made for the exit, but the thugs – who were obviously out for trouble as they were armed with knives – followed them out into the car park. Although John was the obvious target, Chris and Bill were still deemed guilty by association, and Chris suffered a cut to his face, whilst the bespectacled Bill received a deep cut to his left arm trying to fend off their assailants. John sustained cuts to his face and his left hand, severing two tendons. He somehow managed to scramble into Chris' car, but one of the thugs slashed at him with a machete and he may well have been left with a permanent limp had he not been wearing leather trousers. The irony wouldn't have been lost on him that, as the attack happened in Highbury, their assailants were probably fellow Gooners [Arsenal fans].

The following day, Paul was assaulted on the Goldhawk Road close to Shepherd's Bush tube station. This attack, however, was more sartorial than sectarian as the five Teddy Boys had taken affront at the drummer wearing a pair of beetle crushers. Simply outnumbering their victim five to one wasn't enough for the cowardly Teds, however, and one of their number dealt Paul a vicious blow to the back of the head with a crowbar leaving him with a head wound that required fifteen stitches. The tabloids, who were indirectly responsible for the violence, had the gall to ask if the attacks had indeed occurred or whether they were just another one of Malcolm's publicity stunts.

With Virgin intending to release 'Pretty Vacant' (VS184) on 2nd July, Malcolm was probably delighted at the publicity, especially as he was due to fly out to Los Angeles to meet with eccentric soft porn flick king Russ Meyer to discuss his proposals for a Sex

Pistols film. The band – as well as their inner sanctum – were understandably less enthralled about being left to the mercy of every 'Vigilantes R Us' merchant in London. Following a second attack on John at Dingwalls on 23ʳᵈ June, Sid called Malcolm in the middle of the night and threatened to do him some real damage unless he pulled his finger out of his arse and got the band out of the country. So, the following morning – with Sid's threats still ringing in his delicate ears – Malcolm rang John Jackson at the Cowbell Agency and had him arrange a two week 13 date tour of Scandinavia, due to commence on 13ᵗʰ July at Daddy's Dance Hall in the Danish capital of Copenhagen.

#

Virgin Records released 'Pretty Vacant' on Saturday, 2ⁿᵈ July 1977 and two weeks later, with 'God Save The Queen' still making a nuisance of itself at No. 27, the Pistols' follow-up disc slammed into the UK singles chart at No. 7, giving the band their second Top 10 hit in as many months. The expletive-free song was given clearance by the all powerful IBA and the BBC, but Tony Blackburn, Noel Edmonds, Dave Lee Travis and the rest of Radio 1's play-it-safe brigade still refused to include the record on their daytime playlists; although the song was begrudgingly aired once a week on the station's weekly chart rundown. The Sex Pistols would have the last laugh though as dear old Auntie Beeb, who'd got her corporate knickers in a twist over the lyrical content of 'Anarchy In The UK' and 'God Save The Queen', failed to pick up on John's blatant emphasis on the second syllable of 'Va-Cunt'.

The band had surprisingly agreed to make another promo video for 'Pretty Vacant', and, while Malcolm was in Los Angeles courting Russ Meyer at the director's Hollywood home, Virgin sought to get their own film out into the public realm by having the promo aired on *Top Of The Pops*. The promo video – once again directed by Mike Mansfield, and shot within an enclosed studio environment – was filmed at some ridiculous hour, and all three frontmen appear in desperate need of an adrenaline boost. John, once again dressed in his fave chaos-combo of 'Destroy' muslin shirt and leather trousers, is also sporting granny glasses to protect his eyes from the harsh studio glare. He looks as though he's been forcibly dragged from his pit. Sid is again wearing his 'Vive Le Rock' second skin and looks suitably moody for the camera. He remains motionless throughout; his lethargy due to either the early hour or the lasting effect of his heroin withdrawal.

Again, the irony would not have gone unnoticed that the Pistols – a band that prided itself on its non-hard-drug policy – should add a heroin user to the line-up. Prior to the Heartbreakers arrival on the London punk scene the previous December, heroin had been the reserve of rock's elite old guard such as Keith Richards and Eric Clapton. Although the drug wasn't prevalent in London during the mid-to-late seventies, it was available if you had the contacts and an abundance of cash. New York, however, had been awash with the drug and anyone with $30 to their name could score. Thunders and Nolan had been addicts for years by this stage and the duo must have brought their own stash over with them, because they didn't receive much in the way of remuneration from the Anarchy Tour, as their squalid post-tour hand-to-mouth Earls Court existence testified. Nancy wouldn't have risked smuggling junk through Heathrow's stringent customs, which is why she made a beeline to her old Bowery buddies' London lair. Had Sid not been so au fait with the workings of a syringe then he might not have so easily succumbed to either the charms of Nancy or junk.

Under normal circumstances the band might have rejected the promo video proposal out of hand. These, of course, were far from normal circumstances though, and Virgin's promotions team – spearheaded by John Varnom – set to work on the band's collective frailties and got them to consent. When Malcolm heard the news, however, he was beside himself with rage. There he was, trying to sell the Sex Pistols film based on the notion that the band was being denied the right to play in the UK, and yet here they were appearing, albeit via video, on Britain's flagship music show *Top Of The Pops*. He voiced his displeasure to both John and Branson, but he was powerless to intervene as he was stranded some six thousand miles away from the action.

So on 14th July, whilst a still seething Malcolm was courting Russ Meyer at the director's Hollywood Hills home, and the Sex Pistols were playing a second show at Daddy's Dance Hall, the promo video to 'Pretty Vacant' received its first public airing on *Top Of The Pops*. The Sex Pistols were awarded the penultimate slot prior to the week's No. 1 record, Hot Chocolate's 'So You Win Again'. That week's show, hosted by Canadian born DJ David 'Kid' Jensen, was given extra punk cred as it featured a studio performance from

Aussie punksters The Saints, miming along to their third single 'This Perfect Day'. It obviously had the desired effect though, as their song entered the chart the following week at No. 34. The rest of the show, however, was typical *TOTP* fare: Rita Coolidge performed 'We're All Alone'; The Commodores were at No. 21 with 'Easy', but we were at least spared the actual presence of Lionel Ritchie & Co. as the song was set aside for the show's infinitely more appealing dance troupe Legs & Co. (men of a certain age will no doubt agree with us here!). Dave Edmunds, with his latest band Rockpile, was returning to the charts after a four-year absence with 'I Knew The Bride', while the lesser-known Jigsaw performed 'If I Have To Go Away'; a feat they managed to achieve without any difficulty. The Pistols' brief A&M label mates Supertramp were stalled at No. 29 with 'Give A Little Bit'.

#

Aside from Sid emulating Malcolm's amnesia from the previous September by arriving at Heathrow *sans* passport, the two week Scandinavian tour provided the Sex Pistols with a much-needed fillip away from (mis)managerial restraint and vigilante attacks. Apart from Boogie and Roadent, John's photographer friend Dennis Morris, who'd also been present at the 'God Save The Queen' video shoot, was brought along to capture the highlights; many of the snaps would appear in his book *Rebel Rock* (Omnibus Press). Several music press journalists – including Giovanni Dadomo who was covering the tour for his new paymasters at *Sounds* – also accompanied the band on their frolics amongst the fjords, but unlike Morris they had been obliged to pay their own way. The invites had come at Virgin's behest, but inviting journalists onto the road had never featured too highly on Malcolm's agenda and he found a surprising ally in John, who was equally insistent that the music papers pick up the tabs rather than the record company. This would prove a master stroke as the editors – anxious to get maximum return on the unexpected outlay – devoted double-page spreads to the tour.

Following the two Danish Daddy's Dance Hall dates, the Sex Pistols crossed over into Sweden for the first of four Swedish shows at Halmstad's Beach Disco on 15th July. 'When we left the hotel in Sweden,' says Roadent 'the hotel manager turned to me and said, "well, at least you're not as bad as the Bay City Rollers!" So what they'd been like during their stay God knows!!' Then it was onto Norway, where Paul celebrated his 21st birthday and the band attended a press conference followed by a show at the city's Pingvinen Restaurant.

After a show at Trondheim's Student Ssamfundet Club – which was released in 1992 as part of the 2 disc CD box set release *Kiss This* – the band headed back across the Swedish border for two shows over consecutive nights at Barbarella's in Vaxjo; the first show being reserved for 15-to-20-year-olds, with the second night strictly for 21s and over. The normally reserved Swedes took the Sex Pistols to their hearts, especially Sid, who, having already acquired celebrity status in Britain, quickly set about making a name – as well as new friends – in a foreign land. His own childlike innocence and naivety made him especially popular amongst the kids, with two Swedish youngsters in particular latching on to the bassist and showering him with sweets.

On 25th July, however, Sid was forced to turn his attentions to a more serious matter. He returned to London to face the music over his being caught in possession of a flick-knife at the second night of the 100 Club Punk Festival the previous September. His mother Anne came along on her brand new 250cc motorbike to offer moral support. Jonh Ingham, Mick Jones and Paul Simonon, along with Paul's new squeeze Caroline Coon, were all there as witnesses. The fact that the trial date at Wells Street Magistrates' Court had been postponed for ten months owing to a lack of solid evidence against him was a giveaway that the prosecution's case was as thin as a tramp's vest at best. But Sid was desperate to get back to Sweden as soon as possible and was taking no chances. He arrived at the court dressed in a black suit, shirt and tie, with only his choice of footwear – a pair of natty brothel creepers – giving any clue as to his identity.

Sid's solicitor made an impassioned speech about how a custodial sentence might jeopardise his client's future career with the Sex Pistols and, with only one policeman on hand to counter the evidence provided by Mick, Paul, Caroline and Jonh, the judge brought the proceedings to a swift conclusion by issuing a stern reprimand and fining Sid £125. Instead of celebrating with Mick and Paul, or taking tea with his mum, Sid jumped in a taxi and headed straight to Heathrow and boarded a flight bound for the Swedish capital Stockholm, where the band were due to perform two shows over consecutive nights at the Student Karen Happy House commencing 27th July.

With 'God Save The Queen' riding high in the Swedish chart, both shows were complete sell-outs and hundreds of ticketless punters were left stranded outside the venue when the Pistols kicked off their set around 9.15 p.m. The absence of a stage saw the band and audience separated only by a line of rope, but aside from engaging Sid in a gobbing contest, the audience remained in good order and kept to their side of the divide. The opening show had passed without incident, but the second night was marred by the arrival of a local Hells Angels-type gang known as 'The Ragarre', who attacked fans as they made their way out of the venue. The 'Rags' were also intent on getting at the Sex Pistols themselves and the local police were forced to provide the boys and their entourage with an escort back to their hotel. The fanatical Rags followed on behind and laid siege to the hotel where the bemused staff were forced to barricade the doors to prevent the gang from gaining entry.

#

On Friday 19th August 1977, while the rest of the civilised world was still mourning the death of Elvis Presley, the Sex Pistols arrived at Wolverhampton's Club Lafayette. Billed as 'The Spots' this was the first of several incognito shows that were known as the SPOTS (Sex Pistols On Tour Secretly) Tour. Needless to say, the boys had little sympathy upon hearing of the King's passing. 'He [Elvis] forgot what he was about and people had to tell him. He was too stupid to know any better,' were Sid's wise words; while John's 'Good riddance to bad fuckin' rubbish,' rebuke was never going to make the *Memphis Tribune*'s book of condolence. John also chose to castigate the portly singer's life of excess which led to his untimely demise: 'Elvis was dead long before he died,' he opined. 'His gut was so big that it cast a shadow over rock 'n' roll. But our music's what's important now.' Slade bass player Jim Lea's brother Frank was in attendance at the Lafayette and told us some years later 'I was at that club most nights, because me and our James knew the bouncers, and that was one of the craziest gigs I ever saw there! It was more like an event than a gig!!

Contrary to popular belief, the Sex Pistols weren't 'banned on the land' as Malcolm would eloquently state atop Tower Bridge, whilst enunciating his lesson of 'Never Trust A Hippy' to Helen Wellington-Lloyd in *Swindle*. Indeed, many venues were desperate to have the band play, and it was usually only when the local authorities learnt of a prospective show that they dredged up some long-forgotten antiquated law to prevent them from appearing. So Malcolm came up with the idea of thwarting the high-handed authorities by booking the band into venues up and down the country under a variety of throwaway names such as 'Tax Exiles' (Doncaster Outlook Club, 24th August), 'Special Guest' (Scarborough), 'Acne Rabble' (Middlesbrough Rock Garden, 26th August), 'The Hampsters' (Plymouth Woods Hole, 31st August), 'A Mystery Band Of International Repute' (Penzance Winter Gardens, 1st September). Malcolm then relied on word of mouth to ensure each venue was packed to the rafters by the time the band went on stage and revealed their true identity. Club Lafayette's owners, realising the money-making potential, charged a £1.50 entrance fee despite having already stated £1 admission on their hurriedly put up posters.

'They really were great fun, those five or six shows,' Roadent says about the SPOTS Tour today. 'I'm not even sure which I enjoyed the most, the shows themselves, or the thrill of trying to keep each date under wraps as we descended on places like Middlesbrough, Scarborough ... and Blackburn.' he chuckles, tipping a wink to our northern roots. A little known secret is that a SPOTS show almost took place at Blackburn's civic-owned auditorium King George's Hall (the gig was originally booked by local promoter Andy Grimshaw who had been involved in the group's 1976 Blackburn appearance at his mother's club The Loadstar), but fell through at the eleventh hour owing to pressure from the local council.

'Never mind German film star,' Roadent said, punctuating the air with his finger for emphasis, whilst referencing the Passions' 1981 song 'I'm In Love With A German Film Star' which was written in his honour. 'I felt like a Nazi spy, or an agent provocateur, sneaking around making coded telephone calls to venue owners to see if we were still on, or whether the local council had got wind of the evil coming to their town. It was like playing hide and seek, and if we got rumbled, which happened on occasion, especially once the bloody music press picked up on what we were doing, I'd have to call Malcolm and get him to try and book an alternative show somewhere in the vicinity. Otherwise poor old Barbara [Harwood], the band's homeopathic medicine student driver, would have to drive us back to London as we couldn't risk booking into a hotel for the night in case the manager alerted the police. I think the band really enjoyed those shows as well, especially Sid.' he chuckles with a mischievous glint in his eye as a long-forgotten tour incident pervades his memory bank.

'What people seem to forget is that Sid had a terrific sense of humour, and he really was a joy to be around. The band had just done the Scandinavian tour, and although this was before he started mutilating himself and trying to live up to his own myth, he was beginning to develop a relationship with the fans. And I think those secret shows served as a watershed in that they signalled the end of John's holding the spotlight.'

Above: *'We're in the money'. Flashing the cash courtesy of A&M. (Mirrorpix)*

Below: *John keeps his distance from the other three in Holland –
a sign of things to come. (Mirrorpix)*

Above: *John, with Malcolm and solicitor Stephen Fisher, after being up before the Beak for possessing speed. (Mirrorpix)*

Left: *Jon Savage believed Jordan to be the first Sex Pistol – Here she is on a German cigarette card. (Alan G. Parker's collection)*

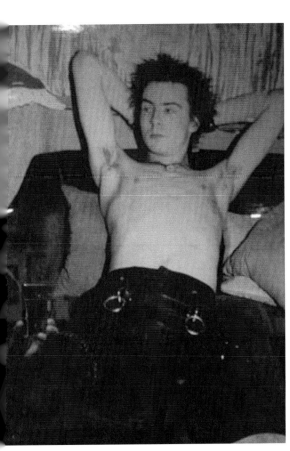

Left: *Sid relaxing (family photo).*

Below: *The band in Sweden (Roadent's collection)*

Overleaf: *A meal at trendy Langan's Brasserie. Michael Caine, who co-owned it at the time, is on the next table - not a lot of people know that. (Mirrorpix).*

Overleaf facing page: *The Jubilee Boat Party ends badly with Vivienne West-wood pictured on the floor. (Mirrorpix)*

Above: The rhythm section Tony Parsons described as 'tighter than tomorrow' in 1976, still rocks in 2007.

Left: Engineer Bill Price reckoned Steve Jones was the tightest rhythm guitarist he had ever worked with. (Both photos Brixton Academy by Brian Jackson)

Facing page: John giving his all at the Brixton Academy (top). After all these years the stare still scares! Hammersmith Apollo 2008 (Brian Jackson both pictures)

Overleaf: 'Goodnight Hammermith' 2008 (Brian Jackson)

CHAPTER eleven

God Save
The Sex Pistols

'You criticise us and you say we're shit,
but we're up here and we're doing it,
so don't criticise the things we do,
cause no fucker pays to go and see you!'
From 'We're The League' by the Anti-Nowhere League

On Friday 28th October, the same day the West Yorkshire police finally accepted they had a serial killer on their patch and appealed for help from the public and New Scotland Yard to track down the man they dubbed the 'Yorkshire Ripper', *Never Mind The Bollocks Here's the Sex Pistols* (V2086) was released. The initial 200,000 copies featured the eleven track album, plus 'Submission' as a one-sided single along with a full-colour poster designed by Jamie Reid. As a taster – if one was indeed needed – Virgin had released 'Holidays In The Sun' (VS 191) as the Sex Pistols' fourth single thirteen days earlier on 15th October.

The song had initially been conceived during the band's trip to the Berlin Wall back in March, and then – with help from Chris Thomas – knocked into shape at Wessex Studios during the *Bollocks* recording sessions. Despite it being a relatively new song, it came in for a rough ride at the hands of the music press. The *NME*, which had been championing the Sex Pistols since the previous February, ran with the headline: 'No Chewn, My Babe, No Chewn'. Although *Melody Maker* and *Sounds* made it their 'Single of the Week', both papers couldn't help having a plagiaristic dig at the Pistols by hinting at the similarities between the song's chugging riff and that of The Jam's 'In The City'. Despite grapevine rumours that Holidays was to be included on the soon-to-be-released album, the single reached No. 8 in the chart.

It also brought further controversy when the Belgian Travel Service issued Glitterbest with an Infringement of Copyright notice on their summer holiday brochure, from which Jamie Reid had lifted the artwork for the single's sleeve. Virgin, anxious to avoid a hefty fine, immediately withdrew the sleeve from circulation and repackaged it with a plain white bag. However, some 50,000 singles had already crossed the counter by this stage and the offending sleeve would provide Pistols fans with another collectable item. With 'Holidays In The Sun' containing a reference to the notorious Bergen-Belsen Nazi concentration camp, there was no way the record was going to receive any radio airplay. We're both of the opinion that the Pistols should have gone straight for pop's jaded jugular by releasing 'Bodies' and 'EMI' as a double A-side single: 'I'm Not An Animal, Mummy! Goodbye A&M'.

#

The hype surrounding the Sex Pistols ensured *Never Mind The Bollocks* was always going to be a massive hit. Advance orders of 125,000 were enough to send the album straight to No. 1 in the UK chart, the first time this had happened since the Beatles; the icing on the cake being that it dislodged EMI's Cliff Richard in the process. It is, however, somewhat ironic that Cliff's latest long-player happened to be a *Greatest Hits* package because, although no one knew it at the time, the album replacing it at the top of the charts was also a *Best Of* containing all four Sex Pistols singles to date, despite repeated assurances to the contrary from both the band and Virgin. Indeed, Virgin's press adverts for 'God Save the Queen' had proclaimed that the song wouldn't feature on the new album. However, in retrospect what else could the Sex Pistols have done? With Glen gone, John had lost his sole songwriting partner. Steve and Paul – although powerhouses in the studio – were found wanting in the creativity department, while Sid was fast becoming neither use nor ornament. With the bassist's self-penned ditty 'Belsen Was A Gas' yet to be given a makeover and added to the Pistols set, the band had just fifteen original songs from which to create an album. Three of which; 'I Wanna Be Me', 'Did You No Wrong' and 'Satellite', had already appeared as B-sides.

Sex Pistols albums are like buses though: you wait ages for one then three come along at once. The first one was actually a bootleg entitled *Spunk* (Sex Pistols UNKnown), consisting of the Denmark

Street and Gooseberry Studio demos recorded by Dave Goodman between July 1976 and January 1977. Was the producer finally getting his revenge on McLaren? This was a point for much debate and argument from both sides of the fence, but Dave, who sadly died in 2005, always denied this. The shock discovery of *Spunk's* existence came courtesy of *Sounds,* which broke the story in its issue of the 22ⁿᵈ October. To Branson's horror, the paper's on-the-spot reporter Chas De Whalley – who'd purchased his copy at the Rough Trade shop in Ladbroke Grove – upped the ante by citing *Spunk* as an album that 'no self-respecting rock fan would turn his nose up at'. The journalist ended his article with the admission that said album had been hogging his turntable for the past week, with no sign of wearing out its welcome. Indeed, many fans have come to share De Whalley's enthusiasm for the alternate – and illegal – album with its rough-and-ready production harking back to the Sex Pistols' sound circa summer of '76 and the 100 Club Punk Festival.

However, during a Radio One interview with John and Sid conducted by John Tobler, John dismissed the *Spunk* recordings as 'dreadful' and 'substandard', and said they should have remained unreleased. Yet conversely, the singer complained to Jon Savage that the official *Bollocks* album was 'over-produced', and that its note-perfect sound reminded him of some American West Coast band. Having said that, if we're being honest, it's still Chris Thomas' chugging multi-guitared 'Wall of Sound' official *Bollocks* album that sets our neck hairs tingling. In one of life's little ironies, Virgin re-released *Spunk* as part of a *Bollocks* double CD in 1996.

The release date of the official UK version of *Bollocks* had been set for Thursday 10ᵗʰ November, but Virgin was forced to bring the date forward to the 28ᵗʰ October when it was discovered that the French version, from Barclay Records, was available in the UK on import and contained twelve tracks. Virgin's initial intention had been to release an eleven track version of the album with 'Submission' as a free one-sided single but, as revenge is a dish best served cold, Malcolm had plenty of time to savour his dessert. As a means of further delaying the UK album, he insisted that Virgin add 'Submission' to the eleven tracks already pressed. This would have proved disastrous for Virgin as Branson knew the band's fans would simply go out and purchase the imported Barclay version of the album, which was already beginning to appear in London's music retail outlets. In a last-ditch attempt to counteract the flood of French imports, the furious Virgin boss ordered the album to be rush-released – with or without 'Submission'.

Malcolm – who would also subsequently admit to preferring *Spunk* over the official album – was rather pleased that a French import version of *Bollocks* might scupper sales of the UK version. This was his way of getting his own back on 'Mr Pickle' for his having allowed the 'Pretty Vacant' promo video to be aired on *Top Of The Pops*. Malcolm took great delight in telling us, in April 2007, that when Branson demanded that he retrieve the master tapes from his French counterpart Eddie Barclay, who was in breach of contract, he'd responded by telling Branson that 'he didn't desire to get them back'. To his mind, Branson was a one-trick hippy who'd capitalised on the situation to land the Sex Pistols, while the suave Eddie Barclay was cut from a similar cloth to his own. The Barclay supremo had invited Malcolm and Stephen Fisher over to his Louis XIV-style penthouse offices on the Avenue Foch in Paris on 6th May to seal the deal to release Sex Pistols product in France, Switzerland, Zanzibar and Algeria. He'd wined and dined them on caviar and lobster washed down with champagne, which was certainly a cut above the sub-standard cheese sandwich/cheap plonk fare Virgin had laid on.

#

The Sex Pistols had headed into Wessex Studios in late April/early May 1977 to begin work on their long-awaited long player. As Chris Thomas was otherwise engaged, in-house engineer Bill Price acted as the sole technical overseer during these initial sessions. Thomas recalls today that he was on hand for the four singles, as well as 'Bodies' and 'EMI', while Bill Price was responsible for the remaining six tracks: 'New York', 'Seventeen', 'No Feelings', 'Liar', 'Problems' and 'Submission'. The producer's enforced absences didn't hinder the recordings, as Steve and Paul had developed a near-telepathic understanding of each other's capabilities and were able to lay down their parts with mundane proficiency. It could be argued that nothing less should have been expected from them as the majority of the songs on the finished album were over twelve months old and perennial mainstays in the band's live repertoire.

For the *Classic Albums* series, Price would pay the ultimate tribute to Steve by citing him as the tightest rhythm guitarist he'd ever worked with. John could also be counted on to lay down his biting vocals in one or two takes. The singer purposely over-articulated the lyrics to avoid sounding American as was the wont of many of his British contemporaries. It soon became apparent to the production team, however, that replicating Glen's rhythmic bass lines was way beyond Sid's capabilities. While Steve compensated for Sid's deficiencies by playing the root note to each chord on the guitar, Sid was left to amuse himself as he saw fit, just as long as he kept away from the grown-ups.

During the aforementioned Radio One interview Sid had also bemoaned the existence of the *Spunk* album. It was patently obvious that he'd been left out of the loop regarding the bootleg recordings, as he told the bemused Tobler that his objection was that 'some stupid fool with a tape-recorder was making a million pounds out of some concert where we sweated our guts out'. Not wishing to appear as ignorant as his guest, Tobler felt obliged to point out that the *Spunk* album consisted entirely of studio recordings. He could have belittled Sid even further, had he chosen, by pointing out that said recordings had been made prior to his joining the band.

If truth be told, Sid's contribution to *Never Mind The Bollocks* was barely worth a mention either. Steve and Paul may have been able to kid themselves that replacing 'goody-two-shoes' Glen with 'mean and moody' Sid had given the line-up an added visual dynamic. However, the absurdity of allowing John to force Glen out of the band hit home when the time came to start recording the album. John too had had time to reconsider his actions, for when he, Steve, Paul and Glen presented a reunited front at their 100 Club press conference on 18th March 1996 to unveil plans for a world tour, John dismissed Sid as having been little more than a 'coat hanger on stage'.

Yet his unkind analogy, which could also be construed as a back-handed compliment to Glen – and the closest the bassist was likely to come to receiving a public apology from John – would have had far more effect if it had been used in reference to Sid's off-stage contributions. For the stage was Sid's personal playground, and it was only in the recording studio that the 'fashion accessory' was truly found wanting. According to Chris Thomas, Sid played bass on 'God Save the Queen' and 'Bodies', but the producer was quick to point out that said efforts were so far down in the mix that only a keen-eared Border Collie would be able to hear them.

The original intention had been to have the album wrapped up by the end of June, and a record of sorts was in the can with an approved sequence featuring a version of The Stooges' 'No Fun'; the only non-original song being mooted for inclusion on the album. Somewhat surprisingly, a preview of the yet-to-be-released LP appeared in the *48 Thrills* fanzine. The article, although undated, must have been compiled prior to 2nd July as it references 'No Fun' as an unreleased song. The review also provided the following eleven track listing: side 1: 'Seventeen', 'New York', 'Pretty Vacant', 'Holidays In The Sun', 'Liar', 'Problems'; while side 2 opened with 'Anarchy In The UK' followed by 'Submission', 'No Feelings', 'Satellite' and 'EMI'. The unnamed reviewer also alluded to the 'Problems' mantra which serves as a coda to side one as being replicated at the end of side two.

With advance orders in excess of 125,000 it didn't really matter what the critics thought of *Never Mind The Bollocks*. Not surprisingly, given the wave of euphoria surrounding the Sex Pistols' long-awaited debut long-player, all the music weeklies were cheering in unison. Kris Needs at *Zigzag* opined: 'The title says it all really. Ignore the press hysteria, dopey articles in *Rolling Stone* and cross-country panic/fear/loathing over 'these foul-mouthed Sex Pistols'. This album transcends it all ... and also puts paid to the ignorant bastards who still say they can't play or are morons.' Kris also pays tribute to Chris Thomas and Bill Price for producing a 'no bullshit album' with a 'killer sound' that incorporates Steve's 'Berlin Wall of gut-wrenching power chords, Cook's simple and just right powerhouse drumming, the metronomic roar of Sid's bass (such erroneous praise could only be due to Sid having recently rescued Needs from a beating at the hands of a group of Teddy Boys), topped off with Rotten's phenomenal voice, which can slide from spine-chilling no-feelings coldness to frenzied manic wailing.'

Over at the *NME*, Julie Burchill was equally favourable in her own unique way. Although she too couldn't resist having a dig at the sonic similarities between 'Holidays in the Sun' and 'In The City' – even going so far as to segue the lyrics – as well criticising the inclusion of all four singles to date, she hailed *Never Mind The Bollocks* as the supreme punk long-player.

Melody Maker's Chris Brazier, despite laying into the album's day-glo sleeve as being one of the most tackily unattractive covers ever (the paper even went so far as to censor the word 'Bollocks' when running Virgin's full-page advert) cited *Never Mind The Bollocks* as one of the most brilliant and important sets of lethal rock 'n' roll ever trapped on vinyl. Although Brazier couldn't help but question the decision to include the singles – three of which were still widely available at the time of the album's release – he was of the opinion that their inclusion made the album more of a masterwork than if the singles had been omitted.

Jon Savage reviewed the album for *Sounds*, and aside from mistakenly listing 'EMI' as a Vicious co-composition, the journalist followed the trend by citing *Bollocks* as a powerful rock 'n' roll album, as well as criticising the K-Tel style inclusion of all four previously-released singles. His having followed the band's career since the previous summer led to him expressing doubts as to whether the Sex Pistols had enough impetus to produce material as good as their 1976 offerings, and felt that some of the newer songs smacked of creeping contrivance.

Across the pond at *Rolling Stone*, Cook Nelson opened his review (which didn't appear until March 1978 – two months after the Sex Pistols had imploded) by lauding the Sex Pistols as the most incendiary rock 'n' roll band since the Rolling Stones and the Who, and likened the album to an atom bomb which had been dropped on both the socio-political aridity of their native England, and most of the music from which they were artistically and philosophically formed. A decade later, as part of the magazine's 20th anniversary celebrations, *Rolling Stone* would proclaim *Never Mind The Bollocks* to be the second-most influential album of the previous twenty years, behind only the Beatles' *Sgt Pepper's Lonely Hearts Club Band*.

#

On 17th November, the Sex Pistols embarked on a nationwide promotional tour of radio stations, both BBC and independent, as well as making personal appearances at the Virgin store in each respective city. This was following on from a promo visit to Radio Luxembourg's offices, accompanied by photographer Bob Gruen. Steve's 'Fuck Your Mother' T-shirt caused consternation amongst the station's female staff and dropping his leather trousers in the car park for a Gruen shot nearly led to the interview being pulled.

For their part, Virgin set aside £40,000 for marketing *Bollocks*, but although the IBA had given provisional clearance for the proposed campaign, the adverts themselves were banned by the ITCA (Independent Television Companies Association) on the grounds that the album's sleeve would cause offence. A spokesman for the ITCA revealed that it wasn't the wording of the adverts that caused offence, but rather the actual product itself. However, the spokesman was quick to point out that the ban wasn't indefinite, and that any future Sex Pistols albums would be judged entirely on their merits.

With the normal commercial channels therefore closed, Virgin was forced to seek alternate means of advertising the album, which included stocking their Notting Hill Gate store with nothing but *Never Mind The Bollocks*. The ITCA may have been powerless to prevent Branson from decking out his own window fronts with the distinctive yellow and pink sleeves, but the authorities were only too happy to respond to complaints from the public. The Metropolitan Police sent plain-clothes officers to visit Virgin's London stores, as well as other retail outlets such as Small Wonder, to warn each manager in turn that they risked being charged under the 1889 Indecent Advertisements Act unless they removed the poster size window displays – or at least agreed to cover up the 'offending' word.

On Saturday, 5th November – the same day that Glen Matlock's Rich Kids signed to EMI – WPC Julie Storey wandered into Virgin's Nottingham store to warn the bemused manager Christopher Searle that by having the album sleeve on open display in his shop he was risking prosecution under the Indecent Advertising Act of 1899 (yes, there really were two such Acts passed within 10 years of each other – those prudish Victorians, eh?). Searle dismissed her ramblings, but the dedicated Julie was keen to show him she meant business. She returned to the shop later in the week to find the album sleeve still on display, and promptly arrested Searle. He was charged under the archaic act for having blatantly refused, on four separate occasions, to adhere to the police's instruction to remove the poster displays from his store window. Many suspect Searle was acting at Branson's behest as the Virgin chief was quick to declare he would provide every penny of his employee's legal costs. Either way, Searle quickly replaced the promotional album sleeves after each police visit, which shows a certain amount of bottle.

A court date was set for the 24th November at Nottingham Magistrates Court. Branson, having been previously charged, and acquitted, under the same Act in 1970 for having produced an inflammatory leaflet during his student days, again called upon the services of John Mortimer QC (he of *Rumpole of the Bailey* fame) to defend Virgin's interests. Needless to say, Virgin attempted to capitalise on the impending court case by placing montage-style advertisements in the following week's music papers bearing the slogan: **'THE ALBUM WILL LAST – THE SLEEVE MAY NOT'.**

The prosecution's case rested largely on its being able to categorise the word 'bollocks' as being as offensive as the more obvious four-letter expletives such as 'fuck' and 'cunt'; something even the most puritanical members of the indignant moral majority would have trouble upholding. To do so would impinge on the reputations of such literary luminaries as William Shakespeare, Dylan Thomas and James Joyce, who had all deemed 'bollocks' an acceptable word in their respective writings. The prosecuting counsel then attempted to switch tack in bringing the court's attention to the album's inflammatory content rather than its lurid sleeve; yet bizarrely failed to name the song ['Bodies'] in question.

In retrospect, Glitterbest's cause might have been better served had the album sleeve been deemed offensive, as the ensuing removal of the offending albums from stores up and down the country would have left Eddie Barclay free to make a killing. Branson, however, had foreseen such an eventuality and hired Mortimer's services to ensure his product remained on sale, and the renowned QC didn't disappoint.

The *coup de grace* was delivered by calling on Mortimer's star witness, Professor James Kingsley. Kingsley was head of English Literature at Nottingham University, but was also an Anglican vicar and took the stand dressed in his ecclesiastical robe and dog-collar. He informed the court that the word 'bollocks' had appeared in records dating back to the Middle Ages, when it was first used as a nick-name for clergymen of the day. He then went on to add that although it was – and still is – colloquial slang for men's testicles, it was also used in everyday vernacular to signify when someone was talking nonsense. In his opinion, he therefore took the album's title to mean: *Never Mind the 'Nonsense', Here's the Sex Pistols.*

\#

On Monday, 5th December 1977, the band flew out to Rotterdam for the first show of a nine date Dutch tour at the city's Eksit club. Finding themselves free from retribution and restraint the Pistols put in a blinding set, which featured every song in the band's canon – including a first outing for 'Belsen Was A Gas'.

Sid, who was still smarting over a botched attempt by Malcolm to kidnap Nancy and bundle her on a plane back to the US on a one-way ticket, told reporters that in his opinion the Eksit show was the best the Pistols had ever played. The bungled kidnapping attempt had taken place four days earlier, the same day that Sid and Nancy had appeared on the front page of *The Sun* following their arrest after being found in possession of illegal substances. With no live dates since the SPOTS tour, and no pressing need for him to attend the *Bollocks* recording sessions at Wessex, Sid had been left to while away his days shooting up smack with Nancy at their Pindock Mews love nest, where the couple had been living since August.

Had Nancy been content to play the dutiful girlfriend and keep her mouth shut, except when pleasuring her lover, the rest of the band might have made some effort to accept her into the fold. Although it was only natural for her to put Sid on a pedestal, her incessant whining about how he was the true star of the show, as well as attempting to dictate band policy, was becoming increasingly difficult for the others to bear. John, of course, having spurned Nancy's advances before mischievously passing her onto Sid, has never minced his words where Nancy is concerned. In *The Filth And The Fury* Steve, who – according to Paul – was the first Sex Pistol to avail himself of Miss Spungen's delights, also makes his opinion abundantly clear. While Malcolm regarded Sid as the ultimate Sex Pistol, and cared little for the bassist's musical shortcomings, he needed to keep the band together as a working unit if his film aspirations were ever going to come to fruition. He certainly wasn't about to allow a brash American junkie hooker to jeopardise his cinematic ambitions.

The Dutch dates made up the first leg of an ambitious world tour that would also include a few UK dates leading up to Christmas, before taking in America (where *Never Mind The Bollocks* had been released on 11th November), Finland, Sweden, Germany, France and Spain, before a triumphant return to the UK in time for a nationwide March tour. The last thing Malcolm wanted was a rift in the band during such a marathon stint and came to the decision that 'Nauseating Nancy' would have to go. So, having bundled the unsuspecting Sid off to the dentist for a routine check-up, Malcolm arranged for his sidekick Sophie to lure Nancy out from the couple's Maida Vale lair under the guise of a shopping trip in

German 'Pretty Vacant' *sleeve*

nearby Paddington, so Nancy could buy items for the flat. Sophie even managed to keep up the pretence long enough for Nancy to make a couple of purchases, but when the latter discovered the next stop on their girlie shopping trip was the duty-free at Heathrow she became hysterical and Sophie was forced to call the Glitterbest office for reinforcements.

Malcolm, accompanied by Roadent and Boogie who looked every inch the hired henchmen dressed in identical Seditionaries double-breasted light-blue raincoats, arrived at the scene. After realising there was no way of getting the still hysterical Nancy into the awaiting car, Malcolm lost his composure and began screaming at her that she was not only ruining Sid's life, but also threatening the band's very existence.

'I honestly had no idea what Malcolm was planning,' says Roadent today. Confirmation of this comes from the fact that he remained on good terms with both Sid and Nancy despite having participated in the failed abduction. 'Me and Boogie were at the office on Shaftesbury Avenue (Glitterbest had moved offices from Dryden Chambers in July) going over the itinerary for the up-and-coming Holland tour, when Sophie called demanding to speak with Malcolm. One minute Malcolm's sitting by the window perusing the music press' speculative reports on the film project, and the next thing I knew we were hurtling along Oxford Street in Boogie's car heading for Paddington. I stayed with the car as I could see it was all going to end in tears – and not necessarily only Nancy's.' he adds with a knowing smile.

Nancy, whilst telling her side of the story to *Record Mirror*'s Rosalind Russell, which appeared in the paper's 8th April 1978 issue (by which time the Sex Pistols had long-since split), said that she had offered to return to New York for a couple of weeks so that the Sex Pistols could sort out their differences in time for the proposed world tour. She also bemoaned Malcolm's vindictiveness in not having the decency to allow her to return to the flat to get her prescribed methadone.

Needless to say, when Sid returned from the dentist and learned of his manager's plot to separate him from his soul-mate he was not best pleased, threatening to kill those involved in the kidnapping if they should attempt any other stunts that interfered with his private life. 'What Malcolm failed to understand,' says Roadent with a sigh, 'is that Nancy – for all her faults – was Sid's first love. I know it sounds slushy and non-punk, but you only had to spend ten minutes in their company to see that they really did love each other.' One also has to question Malcolm's motives here, for if he believed Sid's salvation lay in getting rid of his heroine [sic], then why did he book the Sex Pistols a series of dates in Holland – the drug capital of Europe? 'And another thing people fail to realise,' says Roadent, 'is that when the Sex Pistols played at the Notre Dame Hall and the Screen On The Green earlier in the year, Sid was still John Simon Beverley at heart. But by the time of the SPOTS Tour, Sid Vicious had fully emerged from his shell and was vying with John for centre stage. After all, Sid had known John from their Hackney Tech days, and knew Johnny Rotten was merely the public face his mate presented as a Sex Pistol, and that he could get his share of the headlines by living up to his own punk persona.'

With just one day's rest following their return from Holland, the Sex Pistols kick-started their Never Mind The Bans UK seven date mini-tour with a show at Brunel University in Uxbridge on Friday, 16th December. The show, which took place in the cavernous gymnasium, was the Sex Pistols' first London outing for over eight months, and should have been a triumphal return. However, the ever-frugal Malcolm hired a woefully inadequate PA, which forced John into screeching his lungs out simply to make himself heard beyond the first few rows. Indeed, the singer was so disgruntled at Malcolm's penny-pinching antics that before kicking into the opening number 'God Save The Queen' he apologised to the audience, promising to exact retribution on 'the cunt responsible'. The gym was packed to the rafters, yet the show was memorable only for the violence instigated by a gang of local Teddy Boys who were still intent on waging total war on the punks. Also of note is that although Malcolm had forbidden Nancy from accompanying the band to Holland, there was nothing he could do to prevent her from travelling to Uxbridge to be at her lover's side.

Having lost its battle with the Brunel PA, John's voice was little more than a whisper for the following night's show at Mr George's nightclub in Coventry, and the band were forced to reschedule Sunday night's show at Wolverhampton's Club Lafayette until the following Wednesday. However, John's voice was up to the task for Monday night's show at the Nikkers Club in Keighley, West Yorkshire. Following on from the rescheduled Wolverhampton show, the band put in appearances at the Stowaway Club in Newport, Shropshire on 23rd December, and spent Christmas Eve night in Norfolk playing a sold-out show at Cromer's 600 capacity Links Pavilion.

There was some doubt as to whether the Cromer show would take place owing to protests and threats of legal action from local residents who were objecting to having the 'Antichrist' descending on their town on the eve of the Christ Child's birth. The police initially backed the residents and revoked the Links' music license, but bizarrely rescinded the order on the day of the show after the band supposedly gave a written assurance to Chief Supt Ronald Spalding that they would refrain from using bad language on stage. Once again, John risked ridicule from his fellow Pistols, particularly Sid, by taking to the stage wearing the old army pith helmet he'd worn at Brunel University, while Sid himself swapped his T-shirt for a fan's tie bearing the image of a naked girl.

#

The news that the supposedly vile and nasty Sex Pistols had willingly given up their Christmas to play a benefit matinee show at Ivanhoe's in Huddersfield for 250 local under-14s was equally bewildering to the British public. The benefit, which had been organised by Barbara Harwood, wasn't only open to the kids belonging to local firemen involved in the ongoing national strike, but also those of laid-off workers at David Brown Gears in nearby Lockwood, and those from one parent families. Aside from providing funds for a banquet, which included a giant cream-filled cake, turkey sandwiches, a mountain of sweets and 1,000 bottles of pop, Glitterbest also supplied a variety of Sex Pistols-related sundries such as Anarchy In The UK handkerchiefs and see-through Never Mind The Bollocks T-shirts for the kids, as well as laying on three special coaches to ferry the youngsters to and from the venue.

The four Sex Pistols – who would be bringing their haphazard 1977 touring schedule to a festive finale with a normal show later that evening – were mindful of offending such innocent ears and amended the lyrics of certain songs, while 'Bodies' was understandably omitted from the matinee set list altogether. Malcolm must have received a bump on the head or a visit from the Ghost of Christmas Past, as not only was he happy to dip into the Glitterbest coffers to fund the benefit show, he also allowed Nancy to travel up to Huddersfield to be with her beloved Sid.

With the Establishment's baleful glare otherwise occupied, all four Sex Pistols were in a relaxed mood, especially John, who interrupted proceedings to throw himself off stage into the giant cake and engaged the gleeful audience in a free-for-all food fight, before returning to the stage covered in cream and sponge cake. Christmas may have been the time to bestow good will to all men, but although John was happy to shed his 'Rotten' persona for a few hours, his munificent mood didn't extend to his former songwriting partner Glen Matlock (who'd passed through town with the Rich Kids five days earlier), as he wore a T-shirt bearing the baiting slogan 'Never Mind the Rich Kids we're the Sex Pistols'.

In the absence of a recognised support act, Sid was allowed to take temporary charge centre stage, aided and abetted by Steve and Paul, and he ran through the Heartbreakers' 'Chinese Rocks' and 'Born To Lose'. Letting him loose at the microphone – not to mention his choice of songs – was a strange decision given that it was supposed to be a children's party. For unlike John, who'd grown up sharing Christmas Day with three younger brothers and was therefore able to deal with the demands of excitable youngsters, Sid, who could enjoy the company of kids away from the stage, appeared incapable of shedding his own Sex Pistol persona.

The bassist was equally incapable of shedding his drug habit, and after the show he and Nancy approached the bemused Boogie offering him the chance to film the couple having sex atop a *Never Mind The Bollocks* poster in return for cash. Boogie, perhaps sensing an opportunity to start a pension plan, agreed to the proposal. Heroin withdrawal though played havoc on Sid's libido, and his dick remained as limp as his bass playing. Julien Temple was also on hand with his camera and filmed the proceedings, some of which eventually appeared in *The Filth And The Fury*, for punk posterity. Yet to the continuing dismay of Sex Pistols fans the world over – given that Ivanhoe's was the band's last ever UK show with Sid in the line-up – the director has stubbornly refused to release the footage in its entirety.

CHAPTER Twelve

Anarchy In The USA

' Once the American's get involved the game is up,
they think they invented everything you see,
so they'll happily give you all the advice on
any subject that you don't need!'
Rock' n' Roll Babylon

On January 3rd 1978 the Sex Pistols flew from Heathrow to New York's JFK airport en route to Atlanta, Georgia, where they were due to commence their ill-fated seven date US tour on the 5th January. Once again, according to the 4th January edition of the *Daily Mail*, the band earned the enmity of their fellow Pan Am passengers by spitting and swearing, as well as threatening photographers as they made their way through Heathrow's departure lounge. Sid, whom the *Daily Mail* reporter erroneously cited as the band's guitarist, supposedly yelled at the press hounds: 'You can fuck off. We don't need the press. We don't need anybody!'

One of the offended Americans returning home after spending the Christmas break in little ol' London, had likened the band's behaviour to that of a pack of wild animals, but a spokesman for Pan Am told the same *Daily Mail* reporter that the four band members had 'quietened down considerably' once they'd boarded the aeroplane. The abrupt change in their demeanour could have been due to the recent air disaster when an Air India Boeing 747 had exploded in mid-air over Bombay on New Year's Day killing all 213 passengers. By the time the band boarded their connecting flight from New York to Atlanta, however, Sid had shaken off his lethargy and attempted to 'get the party started' by groping a stewardess while she was leaning across him to hand John his in-flight meal.

It was only natural that the Sex Pistols would set their sights on America, but seven dates wasn't going to make much of a wave

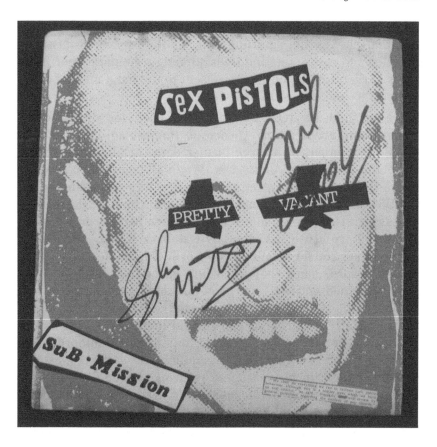

US 'Pretty Vacant' *sleeve*

across the pond. Disco was the current flavour of the month in the US and although *Never Mind The Bollocks* was hailed as a masterpiece by certain quarters within the US music press, the album failed to make any impact on the Billboard chart. Ploughing a lone furrow through the Deep South wasn't going to change that; even if every single one of the 10-12,000 people that attended the shows had gone out and purchased the album. The tried and tested – and most profitable – way to conquer America was to lay siege to its seaboards. Although Malcolm (who didn't fly out until 6th January, missing the Atlanta show) reluctantly agreed to a date in San Francisco at the hippy capital's 5000 capacity Winterland Ballroom, he refused to take the band to the West Coast's musical epicentre, Los Angeles. He was equally loathe for the Pistols to play New York and told anyone who would listen that this was to keep an air of mystery around the band. The truth of the matter was that he was still smarting over the Big Apple's dismissal of his efforts to resuscitate the Dolls' already terminal career three years earlier. He did, however, consent to the band making a live appearance on *Saturday Night Live*.

The original US tour itinerary had been for eleven dates commencing at the Leona Theatre in Homestead, Pennsylvania, on 28th December, with three further dates in Chicago (Illinois), Cleveland (Ohio), and Alexandria (Virginia), before then heading to the Deep South. However, the tour had to be truncated when the US Embassy in London refused to grant the Sex Pistols the necessary visas owing to each band member's criminal past. Paul's solitary brush with the law was back in May 1974 when he was fined £60 for stealing £900 worth of undisclosed property. Steve's record, somewhat amazingly given his sticky-fingered past, contained only one charge of 'breaking and entering' from October 1971, with a further twelve charges ranging from 'drunk and disorderly', 'vagrancy', and several motoring offences. Sid's record was of particular interest to the American authorities, as the bassist had two charges of assaulting police officers, as well as being caught in possession of an illegal weapon (flick-knife). Perhaps most serious of all, John had a drug conviction blotting his otherwise spotless copybook.

At one point it seemed the tour would have to be postponed indefinitely, but Warner Bros were anxious to recoup some of their $700,000 outlay on the band, so sent their top legal brain Ted Jaffe – who'd performed a similar miracle for the Rolling Stones – into battle. On 30th December, the State Department finally relented and issued the Sex Pistols with the visas, but only on the proviso that Warner Bros agreed to put up a $1million surety to guarantee the band's good behaviour whilst on American soil. The eleventh-hour reprieve, however, came too late to save the four original dates. It also came too late to save the highly-coveted *Saturday Night Live* TV slot, which went instead to Elvis Costello and the Attractions who were also currently undertaking a US tour. This unexpected boon saw the band's bassist, Bruce Thomas, take to the TV stage sporting a T-shirt saying 'Thanks Malc'.

Warner Bros vice-president, Bob Regehr, the man who'd been responsible for signing the Sex Pistols to the American label, might have been anxious to break the band in America, but he was equally anxious to protect the label's $1million surety. Up to this point he'd only dealt with the Pistols' US representative Rory Johnston, an ex-pat based in Los Angeles, who'd known Malcolm since the two were at art school together. With little or no faith in either Malcolm's leadership qualities or Boogie's road-managerial skills, the Warner Bros second-in-command enlisted the help of renowned no-nonsense tour manager Noel Monk to oversee proceedings. Monk had cut his rock teeth working as the stage-manager at the Fillmore East in New York and was also an old hand at tour management. He'd spent ten years overseeing tours by the likes of Johnny Cash, the Moody Blues, and the original British rock 'n' roll bad-boys, the Rolling Stones. But if the moustachioed Monk believed he'd seen all there was to see in terms of rock 'n' roll excess after spending time out on the road with Ron and Keef, then he was in for an extremely rude awakening.

In order to keep the band – especially Sid – out of trouble during their brief visit to President Jimmy Carter's home state, they were booked into the nearby Squire Motor Inn where Monk and his crew were also staying. The rectangular venue was woefully ill-suited for a headline grabbing act like the Sex Pistols, and the band's four jet-lagged members were ill-equipped to deal with the intense media scrutiny which followed their every move. Indeed, there were so many cameras and spotlights aimed at the stage that it seemed as though the majority of the tickets had been snapped up by local reporters and media crews.

One of the film crews was in the employ of Thomas King Forcade, the 33-year-old publisher of *High Times* magazine, which took its name from the MC5 song of the same name, and was dedicated to recreational drugs (specifically marijuana) and America's drug culture. Forcade, a former member of the Youth International Party, or 'Yippies' as the theatrical anti-authoritarian youth movement founded in 1967 by Abbot 'Abbie' Hoffman was known, believed he and the Sex Pistols were kindred spirits. He'd invited himself onto the tour after meeting up with small time New York-based director Lech Kowalski who was equally interested in seeing what the Sex Pistols were about. Kowalski had little trouble in persuading Forcade to provide funding for his proposed film about the Pistols US tour. However, the band's collective distrust of Forcade, who was believed to have links with both the FBI and the CIA, meant that Kowalski was denied any access to the group. So, the director had to be content with filming incognito from the rear of each venue. The resulting film/rockumentary *D.O.A* (Dead

On Arrival), released in 1981, certainly captured the Sex Pistols in their self-destructive tailspin. But the film would have been better served had Kowalski concentrated solely on the band and the tour, instead of segueing into inconsequential filler footage of Generation X, X-Ray Spex, the Dead Boys and Sham 69. And the less said about Terry and the Idiots the better!

Forcade also invited *Punk* magazine's John Holmstrom along for the ride (the magazine's co-creator Legs McNeil was hanging out with the Ramones in Los Angeles when the call came through, but Legs was keen to see what all the fuss was about and made the trip up the Pacific Highway to join up with his partner in San Francisco for the Winterland show). Forcade, who reportedly lapsed into depression following the Pistols demise and later put a gun to his head at his Manhattan apartment on 16th November 1978, had moved to New York in 1967 after attending the University of Utah. Within weeks of arriving in the Big Apple he'd helped form the UPS (Underground Press Syndicate), an umbrella group of 150 or so alternative newspapers. By January 1978, by which time *Punk* magazine had been incorporated under the UPS banner, *High Times* had a circulation of over 500,000, and annual advertising revenues in excess of $1.5million. The December 1977 issue – which proved to be one of *High Times'* biggest ever sellers – featured Johnny Rotten on its front cover.

Apart from his involvement in publishing with UPS, Forcade also dabbled in writing. His one and only published work, *Caravan of Love and Money,* had initially been picked up by the movie division of Warner Bros as a possible film option, before the studio's bosses came to their senses and kept the *High Times* owner at arm's length.

Aside from Atlanta's finest, vice-squad officers from Memphis, where the Pistols were due to appear the following night, were also lined up against the rear wall. 'We've heard a lot about these boys,' Memphis PD's Lieutenant Ronald Howell told local reporters in response to the far-fetched tales about the supposed lewd onstage behaviour of the band. 'And if they behave themselves we'll be sure to give them a right friendly welcome'. 'But,' he added narrowing his eyes for measured effect 'Memphis is a clean city and we aim to keep it that way.' And Howell's superior, the Director of Memphis PD, E. Winslow Chapman, who had obviously been taken in by the fanciful newspaper tales about the band, told those same reporters: 'I don't allow no masturbation on stage. Those boys can spit and vomit as much as they like, but no masturbation.'

Bootleg sleeve in the style of The Beatles. Issue 2

Atlanta's 500 capacity Great Southeast Music Hall, where Country & Western loving locals usually viewed the stage sat on comfy cushion-topped wooden risers, was situated above a bowling alley in the city's Broadview Plaza shopping mall (the plaza was later demolished to make way for a Home Depot DIY store and a Starbucks – well, they're everywhere around the world, right Steve?). [For the uninitiated Alan and Mick are referring to Steve Diggle and his song 'Starbucks Around The World']

The hype and hysteria surrounding the Sex Pistols' arrival in America might have been justified had the band put in a brilliant performance. But with John's voice as out of tune as Steve's guitar, they never got out of first gear and died on their collective arse; with the band later admitting to having been found wanting on the night. *Billboard Magazine*'s on-the-spot reporter was sufficiently 'underwhelmed' by the Pistols' debut US outing to opine: '**SEX PISTOLS SHOOT BLANK ON FIRST ATLANTA US GIG**'. Barry Cain was in Atlanta covering the US tour for *Record Mirror* and, while he was a fully paid-up member of the Pistols' Fleet Street fan club, he wasn't prepared to save the band's blushes and rightly condemned the show as one of the worst they'd ever played. The timing was as equally erratic as the tuning, and the band brought their shambolic 12 song set to a conclusion with the topically amended 'Anarchy In The USA' before fleeing the stage. Their embarrassment was so great that they remained in the dressing room instead of returning for an encore; and there would be no aftershow interviews – much to the chagrin of the assembled hacks.

To make matters worse, Sid managed to slope off into the night in search of drugs and didn't return until the following morning. Monk, however, wasn't willing to allow Sid's disappearing act to mess with the schedule, and ordered the rest of the band to get ready for the short bus ride to the airport for the flight to Memphis. New security recruit, Glen Allison, an old friend of Monk's who lived in Atlanta and ran the Great Southeast Music Hall, was sent out in search of the elusive spiky fugitive. As an Atlanta native, Allison knew each and every one of the city's hidey-holes, and he eventually located the errant Sex Pistol at a shooting gallery, where he'd spent the night satiating his narcotic needs.

Allison was assigned to keep an eye on Sid, and the bassist would later attempt to ingratiate himself with the 6' 5" 280lb man-mountain by challenging him to a fight. The bemused Vietnam vet, fearing he'd be risking a murder charge by punching Sid, instead grabbed the bassist by the throat and slammed his head into the tour bus roof several times to ensure his 'don't mess' message got through Sid's Vaseline-matted coif and into his addled brain. Bob Gruen, who'd flown down to Atlanta intending to snap a few shots of the band to add to his already sizable Sex Pistols photo collection before heading back to New York, was checking out of the Squire Motor Inn when he bumped into the returning Sid and Allison. The photographer agreed to split a cab fare to the airport, and whilst en route to Hartsfield-Jackson Atlanta International Airport he decided to take in another show for the folks back home and booked a flight to Memphis.

#

Another 'friendly' New York-based photographer to show up in Memphis was Joe Stevens. Stevens was known to the Sex Pistols owing to his affiliation with the *NME*, and the photographer ended up rooming with Malcolm for the remainder of the tour. With Sid having gone AWOL in Atlanta, and Warner Bros' $1million surety hanging in the balance, one might have expected Monk to pay extra-special attention to the bassist. However, within minutes of the band returning to their motel (a Holiday Inn specifically chosen for its out-of-town location) after conducting a sound-check at the 1200 capacity Taliesyn Ballroom, Sid somehow managed to give Allison the slip and disappeared in search of something to alleviate the returning agonies of heroin withdrawal. A search party was sent out along Route 55 and into the surrounding neighbourhood, but to no avail. Later that afternoon, Tom Forcade attempted to blackmail Monk into allowing Kowalski's film crew access to the Sex Pistols in return for information as to the bassist's whereabouts. It was perhaps fortunate for Sid that he managed to procure some pharmaceutical balm, for when he resurfaced at the motel soon afterwards stoned out of his head – and with the plea 'Gimme A Fix' carved across his chest – he was subjected to the first of several 'non-disabilitating' beatings by Monk's team. Monk may have reunited the band with its bass player, but his pleas to Regehr and the rest of the Warner Bros hierarchy – who up to this point had all feigned ignorance of Sid's drug problems – to provide the bassist with methadone went unheeded.

Memphis, of course, was home to the legendary Sun Studios at 706 Union Avenue (situated just a few blocks away from the Taliesyn Ballroom) where, in 1956, a mild-mannered 18-year-old truck driver called Elvis Aaron Presley had called in to record a song for his mother Gladys and ended up changing the face of music forever. Memphis rejoiced in its being considered as the 'cradle of rock 'n' roll', and the following day, 7th January, would see the city celebrate Elvis' first posthumous birthday, with a line of pilgrims already forming outside Graceland. However, there were enough young impressionable locals who were sick and tired of listening to their parents harping on about 'The King', and were desperate for some new rock 'n' roll rebels to call their own.

Such was their enthusiasm, that local promoter Bob Kelly, who owned Mid-South Productions, had little trouble shifting all 1200 tickets. Kelly, however, had overlooked one small problem. The

Taliesyn Ballroom – which later became a Taco Bell – may have had a capacity of 1200, but the local Fire Marshals (in a forerunner to the problems that would beset the Clash at Bond's Casino in New York, June 1981) had restricted the limit to just 725, which, needless to say, left 475 aggrieved ticket holders left out in the cold. The angry mob began venting their spleen by laying siege to the doors in an attempt to smash their way inside. When the combined efforts of the Fire Marshals and the local police failed to disperse the rioters, the aforementioned Memphis PD Director E. Winslow Chapman called for SWAT reinforcements, whose mere presence proved enough to send the agitators running for cover. As for the show itself, after local heroes Quo Jr had entertained their fellow Memphians, the Pistols inexplicably kept the crowd waiting for ninety minutes before taking to the stage.

Although the band still weren't firing on all cylinders, they put in a far better performance than in Atlanta, with John particularly intent on making reparations for the band's shoddy inaugural American outing the previous night. In between songs, the singer, sporting a new blue/red tartan ensemble courtesy of Vivienne, goaded the crowd with disparaging remarks against Elvis and Dolly Parton, but the kids were in agreement and cheered each and every putdown. In his front page review of the show the following day, Walter Dawson, the music writer at the leading local newspaper the *Commercial Appeal* opined: 'What the Sex Pistols proved was that they are indeed first-rate rock 'n' rollers, soaked heavily in that tradition and possessing a frenzied rage that has been lacking from rock for too long.'

With the show over, Bob Gruen was again intent on returning to New York. However, even as the photographer was saying his goodbyes to the band Malcolm offered him the spare bunk on the twelve-berth bus. With New York gripped in the midst of a harsh winter, and the next stop on the tour being the much milder climate of southern Texas, in his own words he 'climbed aboard the bus for a wild trip across America.'

#

Immediately after the show the four weary Sex Pistols clambered back aboard the battle bus for the gruelling overnight drive from Memphis to Texas. According to Monk, in his and Jimmy Guterman's entertaining – if somewhat over-egged – account of the tour *12 Days On The Road: the Sex Pistols and America* (Quill), he and Rory Johnston had both been alerted by Warner Bros about possible death threats to the band emanating from San Antonio. So instead of going straight to the city, Monk decided to hole up in Austin, the Lone Star State's state capital, which lay eighty miles north of San Antonio. The logic being that Austin was close enough to make a run into 'San Antone' on the afternoon of the show, yet far enough away to allow the tour party 24 hours to unwind and take in Austin's many sights and delights. One of these delights is the University of Texas' 231 foot clock tower where, on 1st August 1966, an ex-Marine sharpshooter called Charles Whitman had taken pot shots at students, police officers and anyone else unfortunate to stray into his line of fire, killing 16 people and wounding 32 others. You can still see the bullet holes to this day.

Monk obviously saw no need to inform those outside of his jurisdiction regarding the change of plan, which left Forcade and Holmstrom – both dressed in identical western outfits purchased on Forcade's *High Times* business credit card – prowling San Antonio in a forlorn search of the supposedly wanted Sex Pistols. It's anyone's guess as to whether the death threats were real, or just one of Monk's embellishments, but Forcade's reasons for wanting to get to the band were purely financial, as he was running up huge bills on his business credit card funding his ever-expanding entourage; while Holmstrom simply wanted to pin the four Sex Pistols down long enough to secure an interview for *Punk*.

Forcade's travelling circus was further expanded following the arrival of yet another New York photographer, Roberta Bayley. Roberta had risen to punk prominence having shot the Ramones' debut album cover, as well as snapping 'da bruddas' and the other up-and-coming bands at CBGBs. Forcade's little blackmail stunt back in Memphis meant he was still firmly pride of place on Monk's and Malcolm's shit-lists. Fortunately for Holmstrom though, Roberta was well-acquainted with Malcolm from his brief tenure managing the New York Dolls and he was therefore able to join her and Malcolm for a pre-show dinner.

Although Malcolm may have had little time for Forcade, Holmstrom, between chowing down and peppering Malcolm with questions about the tour, was struck by the similarities between the two wannabe agents of chaos. Indeed, Roberta is of the opinion that Forcade was intent on wrestling the Sex Pistols away from Malcolm so that he could use them for his own agenda.

Forcade, of course, is no longer around to explain the reason for his fascination with the Sex Pistols, but his obsession didn't end with their demise, for – with Holmstrom again in tow – he followed John to Jamaica that April whilst the singer was scouting for new reggae talent for Virgin. Just what he hoped to achieve is anyone's guess, but the *High Times* publisher could have saved himself the time and trouble, not to mention the expense; for despite John's on-going hatred for Malcolm the singer has long since proved he is his own man.

If disconcerted eyebrows had been raised back in England over the Sex Pistols playing remote off-the-rock 'n' roll radar outposts such as Atlanta and Memphis, then the decision to book the band into Randy's 'Redneck' Rodeo in the southern Tex Mex town of San Antonio – famous for being the site of the legendary thirteen-day Alamo siege of 1836 – was surely stretching the bounds of credibility. For while it could be argued that the Sex Pistols were well-versed in playing to hostile crowds, booking them into a blood and guts Texan saloon bar, where an insult might well be met with a bullet or Bowie knife, was putting the band's lives in serious jeopardy. The 2,200 capacity Randy's Rodeo, named after its owner Randy Sherwood and located at 1534 Bandera Road (State Highway 16), had once served the local community as a bowling alley known as 'Bandera Bowl'. When the alley was renovated into a western dance hall sometime during the late-sixties, the stage was built across where the lanes had ended, and that night – for one night only – the town's predominantly Hispanic populace would have four animated skittles to batter into submission.

The locals had probably never even heard of the Sex Pistols before the local San Antonio Express-News set about informing them of the lewd Limey punk rockers due to descend on their town. The paper's exaggerated stories about the band's behaviour ensured that the tickets – retailing at $3.50 – were sold out well in advance of their arrival. If the Pistols weren't already aware that they were in for a rough ride at the rodeo, then the realisation came shortly after 11 p.m. when they walked out on stage to be greeted with a barrage of beer cans – not all of them empty – and hot-dogs, one of which struck John squarely in the kisser. The band would have been well within their rights to abandon the stage, but had they done so they would have stood little or no chance of getting the hell out of Dodge alive, with 2200 short-changed Rednecks and Hispanics baying for their blood.

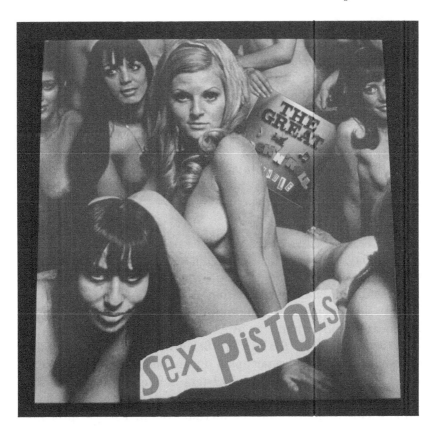

Japanese bootleg based on Electric Ladyland

Just like Colonel William B. Travis at the Alamo Mission 142 years earlier, surrender wasn't an option and they ploughed straight into 'God Save The Queen'. The audience, however, was humming the 'Deguello', the mournful tune which General Santa Anna had ordered played before his army laid siege to the Alamo, signifying that no quarter would be given nor expected during the coming onslaught. The threat of violence hung in the air like cannon smoke, but just in case there were any sections of the already highly charged audience that hadn't quite grasped the connotations of John's Cowboys T-shirt, Sid, sporting a pair of black wraparound shades 'borrowed' from the guitarist of the opening local act The Vamps, stepped up to the microphone and called them 'a bunch of faggots.' When one of said 'faggots' tried to clamber up onto the stage to prove his macho masculinity by challenging the band to a fight, Sid leapt forward and whacked him over the head with his bass. The following day, the San Antonio Express-News carried the headline 'Sex Pistols Win San Antonio Shootout'. Well, it was indeed a victory of sorts, as nobody died and the Sex Pistols had stood tall in the face of the gun-toting Texans.

Kowalski's *DOA* film is a worthwhile purchase if only for the Zapruder-esque Randy's Rodeo footage of Sid's nose exploding (like JFK's head after the fatal Dealy Plaza head-shot), upon his being struck in the mush by a full metal beer can.

#

On Monday 9th January, the Sex Pistols played their fourth US show, this time at the Kingfish Club – named after Louisiana's most successful politician, Senator Huey Pierce 'Kingfish' Long – in the Pelican State's capital Baton Rouge. As with the show in Memphis, the local promoter had way oversold the venue's official capacity, but fortunately for the surfeit ticket-holders the town's Fire Marshal was otherwise occupied on the night. With local sidecar band Rockin' Dopsie and the Twisters having fired the locals up with some washboard wizardry, the Pistols took to the stage to enthusiastic applause, but the fervour wouldn't be reciprocated. The band were clearly jaded following their Mexican stand-off in San Antonio the previous night, and the after-effects of a gruelling 500 mile bus ride, and put in another below-par performance. One of the most bizarre images from the US tour came courtesy of the *NME,* which printed a photograph of John knelt down at the front of the stage spitting into the audience's raised upturned palms: instead of receiving the body of Christ, they clamoured to receive the pent-up phlegm of the self-proclaimed Antichrist. What were they planning to do with their unpalatable prize? Take it home to show mom?

It was here at the Kingfish Club that John first held his hand out to the crowd. The Sex Pistols were four shows in and he was fed up of being pelted with wadded paper cups and beer cans and asked the gullible Americans to throw something more acceptable. The audience, which was predominantly made up of local college kids, responded by pelting the stage with dimes and quarters. And when John asked for larger – less spherical – denominations they showered him with dollar bills. By the end of the show he

Japanese advert

and Sid had pocketed $30 between them, which was a tidy sum considering that he and the rest of the band only received $25 each per day.

Of the seven US tour dates, the Baton Rouge show is probably the least well-documented. That isn't simply down to the Pistols putting in a lacklustre show, as several others on the tour fell into that category. Atlanta could boast being the opening date on the tour; Memphis had the Elvis connotations; San Antonio and Dallas were both memorable for the rough receptions the band received at the hands of their Texan hosts; Tulsa's indignant residents mounted a religious protest; Winterland staged the last ever Sex Pistols show with Sid in the line-up. Baton Rouge's sole claim to fame seems to be Sid picking up a diminutive overweight spandex-clad American groupie. Sound familiar?

Baton Rouge may not have seen much in the way of conflict or confrontation, but it did, however, provide Malcolm – not to mention Sylvain's Les Paul guitar – a second opportunity to sample the Pelican State's charms. The owners were obviously delighted to welcome the Sex Pistols to their humble venue as they had T-shirts printed up to commemorate the band's visit. The grey/black T-shirts, which bore the Sex Pistols logo along with a screen-printed image of one of Dennis Morris' photographs from the 'God Save The Queen' video shoot, were only given to the band members and crew. If one were to come up on eBay today it would command a far higher price than any Westwood/McLaren creation. George X, the lovable Cockney rogue, friend of the group and face-about-London-Town, is in possession of – and occasionally wears – John's Kingfish Club T-shirt, and will happily listen to offers all day long. Though don't ever expect to be wearing it yourself one day! O.K, that's the *Antiques Roadshow* bit over with.

Following on from Baton Rouge, the tour bus headed back across the border into Texas, for a second Lone Star State date at Dallas' Longhorn Ballroom. Dallas, the oil-rich city that lent its name to a phenomenally successful TV series, wasn't quite as hostile to the Sex Pistols as San Antonio. Although no one took a pot shot at this particular 'JR', the band was still given a rough reception by their Country & Western-loving hosts who were far more appreciative of opening act Merle Haggard.

In the days leading up to the Sex Pistols' arrival in Dallas the local radio station, KZMP, set about cranking up the anticipation levels: *'They said no one could be more bizarre than Alice Cooper, or more destructive than Kiss... they have not seen the Sex Pistols. Tuesday night, Stone City Attractions presents live, the Sex Pistols. Banned in their own home country, England's Sex Pistols, denied admittance to the United States, bring the new wave to the Metroplex this Tuesday night, in the Longhorn Ballroom. They said it couldn't happen, but it happens Tuesday night: the Sex Pistols live.'*

The Longhorn Ballroom was perhaps the perfect setting within which to stage a Sex Pistols show as it too was steeped in infamy. Fifteen years earlier the 'L'-shaped venue had been a topless bar known as the Carousel Club, and on Sunday 24th November 1963 the then owner Jack Ruby shot Lee Harvey Oswald on live television. Oswald, of course, was the chief suspect in the assassination of President John F. Kennedy who'd been slain in Dallas two days earlier.

The Longhorn show was recorded and released on video (and later DVD) as *Live At Longhorns* and, despite the cameraman having gone inexplicably AWOL during the opening four numbers, the footage makes for compelling viewing. For it was here at the Longhorn that Sid finally usurped John to become the band's focal point. For the past two years John had held centre stage, but now the 'living circus' had truly come to town – and the ringmaster was dressed in black. Instead of crowding at the front of the stage as was the norm, the Americans jostled with each other for pole position stage right where Sid was holding court.

One such fan was a diminutive blonde called Helen 'Killer' Keller, who was so intent on getting 'up close and personal' with her spiky-maned hero that she couldn't wait until the Pistols arrived in her native California and – with several equally determined friends for company – drove all the way down to Dallas. Having already met with Sid earlier in the day, which saw the bassist insist the girls get a refund on their recently purchased tickets and be placed on his guest list, Helen and her chums positioned themselves at the edge of the stage directly in front of their hero. Helen has gone down in punk folklore for being the girl who head-butted Sid, but the truth is more mundane. During her interview for *Who Killed Nancy* (Soda Pictures), Helen revealed that she had actually been holding a cigarette up to Sid, but had clashed heads with him as he lent towards her, splitting Sid's still tender nose for a second time. Monk's team, being the only ones with official leave to strike Sid, moved in to eject Helen, but Sid waved them back and proceeded to smear the free-flowing blood across his face and chest.

Bob Gruen was standing less than six feet away from Sid at his side of the stage and captured the moment where the blood-splattered Sid calls off the security guard attempting to manhandle Helen away from the front of the stage. The photographer's privileged access-all-areas status came at a price, however. Whilst he'd been grabbing some shut-eye en route to Dallas, Sid, who'd obviously been coveting his neighbour's footwear, helped himself to Gruen's engineer boots to complete his trademark image. According to Joe Stevens, who witnessed the event, Sid held a knife to the sleeping Gruen's throat whilst enquiring of him and John whether he'd be able to keep said boots if he killed Joe's fellow photographer.

The penultimate pit-stop came in Tulsa, Oklahoma, a deeply religious city situated in the heart of the American Dustbowl. The already war-weary Sex Pistols arrived at the 600 capacity Cain's Ballroom in the midst of a violent snow storm, which merely served to set the mood. Upon disgorging from the bus, the band was greeted by a bible-thumping Baptist pastor, and thirty or so of his God-fearing congregation all carrying placards with the catchy: '**LIFE IS ROTTEN WHEN THE LORD IS FORGOTTEN**'.

John, Paul and Steve could have been excused for thinking they'd travelled through a time vortex back to December 1976, for the zealous pastor, like the Caerphilly clergyman, was handing out fire and brimstone leaflets which urged those going into the venue to repent of their punk ways. Caerphilly may have been a victory for the carol singers but the bible bashers were woefully outnumbered in Tulsa. The excitement-starved young Okies cared little that the Pistols put in another lifeless performance owing to John and Steve both suffering from flu.

Indeed, the only noteworthy incidents during the entire show both came courtesy of Sid. In a near repeat of San Antonio, Sid took umbrage with a heckler's goading, but fortunately for the obstinate Okie, Monk's eagle-eyed security team were on hand to prevent him from delivering another knock-out blow with his bass. The second incident came following the show, when Sid disappeared up to his room at the local Holiday Inn with a suspect blonde, both taller – and infinitely broader – than himself. It was only when Monk came a-knocking the following morning, and happened upon Sid's conquest in the act of reapplying her make-up, that he realised she was a post-op transsexual. 'I didn't know whether to suck her cock or her cunt,' the bassist admitted when later questioned by his bemused band mates.

#

Bob Regehr and the rest of the Warner Bros hierarchy were no doubt hoping the Sex Pistols' final US date at San Francisco's 5400 capacity Winterland Ballroom on Saturday 14th January – where the tickets had sold out in a single day – would prove a glorious finale, paving the way for the band to return to America in the near future for a more comprehensive tour. There was even talk of extending the current tour to perhaps incorporate shows in either Los Angeles or New York once news filtered through from London that the proposed 18th January show in Finland's capital Helsinki had fallen through owing to the band having been refused work visas by the Finnish authorities.

Roadent's brief incarceration within a 'house of many doors' had put the kibosh on his accompanying the Pistols on the US tour. He was therefore manning the Glitterbest office in Sophie's absence when the call came through from a tabloid journalist sniffing out a story that the Sex Pistols had been banned from Finland. Roadent had been party to booking the show at Helsinki's Worker's Hall and, although he'd sensed the journalist was telling the truth, he decided to find out for himself and put a call through to the Finnish embassy in Grosvenor Square. Instead of dealing with some junior lackey, however, Roadent found himself on the line with the ambassador who courteously – yet firmly – informed him that the Sex Pistols were no longer welcome in his country. The revocation of the visas was due to mounting pressure from the Finnish press beginning with a hostile anti-Sex Pistols editorial which appeared in the country's leading newspaper, the *Helsingin Sanomat,* on 3rd January.

The cancellation meant the band now had a five-day lay-off before the next scheduled show in Stockholm, Sweden. Regehr's hopes of persuading Malcolm into a rethink about further shows in the US though were thinner than a politician's promise as the wheels had fallen off the Pistols' war wagon by the time the tour rolled into San Francisco. Unlike John and Sid, Steve and Paul had long since tired of hour upon hour of watching the seemingly never-ending American landscape flash past the window, and elected to fly to San Francisco with Malcolm, Boogie and Sophie, who'd joined up with them in Baton Rouge.

Their arrival in the Golden Gate City well in advance of John and Sid gave the band's two longest-serving members plenty of time to consider their options. They had set out on their musical adventure with little ambition other than to get pissed, laid and paid after every show, and although they both recognised that without John they'd probably still be scrabbling for gigs on the London club circuit, they'd had enough of his high-handed attitude. And as for Sid …

By choosing to remain on the bus John also had plenty of time to consider his position. His vexation, however, wasn't with the Sex Pistols per se, but rather Malcolm's continuing mismanagement of the band. When he'd joined the group in August 1975, he'd had little option but to toe the party line in regard to Malcolm's manifesto. Now, though, 'El Dementoid' had come of age and was no longer willing to put up with Malcolm's bullshit. What John failed to realise was that mismanagement was Malcolm's greatest strength. Despite his brief dalliance with the Dolls, he'd never sought to be the manager of a serious rock 'n' roll band – which by this stage the Pistols had undoubtedly become – and had stumbled rather than swindled his way to pop prominence. His style was more 'anti-management' than mismanagement, or how else can one explain the soar-away success of Seditionaries – a shop which contradicted all the fundamentals of retail in having a store-front encased with opaque glass? Malcolm was happy to run with the ball with scant regard for the offside rule, and could John honestly expect him to change tack so far into the game?

Following the Pistols demise, Malcolm would accuse John of having been in collusion with Richard Branson, believing that the Virgin supremo was openly courting the singer with a view to a post-Pistols solo career. Although John didn't know it at the time, the song ideas he was working on during the US tour – 'Public Image' and 'Sod In Heaven' (a.k.a. 'Religion') – would both eventually appear on the first PiL album. Somewhat amazingly, given the incendiary subject matter of several songs within the Pistols' canon, when he presented 'Sod In Heaven' to the rest of the band during the Dallas sound check, Steve and Paul had baulked at the idea. Britain's ailing Establishment and its monarch were both legitimate targets, but religion was considered to be a step too far. John simply filed the song away for later use. Now that he was in a steady relationship with Nora Foster, 10 years his senior and the daughter of a wealthy German newspaper magnate, if he played his cards right there would be little need to worry about life beyond the Sex Pistols.

By electing to fly on ahead with Malcolm, Steve and Paul were afforded rooms at the plush five star Miyako Hotel located at 1625 Post Street, a few blocks up the street from the Winterland. Although remaining on the tour bus with a strung-out Sid had been marginally preferable to sharing airspace with Malcolm, John had fully expected to be afforded the same luxuries as the 'side men'. Yet when he arrived at the Miyako he was told there was no room at the inn, and he and Sid had to be content with bunking down with the road crew in the far less salubrious settings of the Cavalier Motel located out near the city's airport. After taking a stroll along the 'Dock of the Bay', John and Sid – with Bob Gruen – were escorted across town to the offices of K-SAN, San Francisco's leading radio station. It boasted *The Outcastes*, the country's first commercial station show entirely dedicated to promoting punk rock, where the boys were scheduled for an interview with the station's programme director Bonnie Simmons. As the Pistols' Winterland concert was to be broadcast live from midnight, as part of *The Outcastes*' two hour show, Steve and Paul had been invited into the station the previous evening to participate in a late night radio phone-in with the show's hosts, Norman Davis and Howie Klein.

Having its finger on the pulse of San Francisco's vibrant punk scene meant K-SAN was attuned to what was going on in London. It was therefore keen to get the Sex Pistols into the studio to talk about the tour, as well give their accounts of certain well-documented events in the band's colourful career to date. Davis and Klein were probably thinking that in the absence of John and Sid, Steve and Paul would enjoy being able to put their views and thoughts across without fear of contradiction. Unfortunately for them, things didn't quite pan out that way as the two slightly intoxicated Sex Pistols thought it would be fun to sidestep Klein's instructions as to what they could and couldn't say whilst on air by using English swear words to insult those calling into the studio.

John and Sid, on the other hand, confounded the station's crew by not only remaining courteous throughout the interview, they were happy to discuss dog-eared subjects such as 'why the band had been thrown off EMI and A&M', or 'why they'd elected to play down south rather than New York and Los Angeles'. Listening to Simmons' interview with Sid and John today, there's no indication of any friction between the two. Indeed, they both appear to be in good spirits, with Sid playfully slipping into Cockney rhyming slang and Jamaican patois to confuse his host.

The Winterland Ballroom was located on the corner of Post and Steiner in San Francisco's Marina District before being torn down in the mid-eighties to make way for the inevitable luxury apartments. Its first live music show was staged in 1966 when the Bay Area's legendary promoter Bill Graham, who was the then owner of the Fillmore Auditorium on nearby Geary Boulevard, booked the venue for San Francisco's psychedelic pioneers Jefferson Airplane. Following the closure of the Fillmore East in New York in 1971, Graham began booking the Winterland on a regular basis and staged shows by the likes of the Rolling Stones, the Who, Jimi Hendrix, Led Zeppelin and Cream.

When it first opened its doors on 29th June 1928 it was known as the New Dreamland Auditorium, a fabulous $1million ice-rink. However, the venue underwent a name change sometime during the late-thirties following redevelopment so that the rink could be converted to stage live entertainment. 1978 not only saw the venue celebrate its half-centennial, but the year also proved to be its last, and Winterland closed its doors for the final time on New Year's Eve following a show by the Grateful Dead.

As this was to be the last gig of the tour, Malcolm thought it might be fun to open the Winterland stage to any local band that cared to come along and play. Had the Sex Pistols' US swansong taken place in Dallas or Memphis, or any other of the venues on the itinerary, then Malcolm may well have had his way, but Graham – who would continue to hold sway over San Francisco's live music scene until his death in a helicopter crash in October 1991 – refused to even consider the idea. As far as he was concerned the doors would open at 5 p.m. as scheduled, and the only two Bay Area bands that would be setting foot on the stage, the Nuns and the Avengers, had already been confirmed.

It was only due to K-San's request to broadcast the Winterland gig as part of their *Outcastes* show that the Pistols start time was put back to the witching hour. This, however, was a recipe for disaster as it presented Sid with a seven hour window between door and show. Monk and his crew had relaxed their guard on the bassist now that their babysitting duties were almost at an end, so Sid was able to slip away unnoticed with Helen Keller and several local punkettes who led him up into Haight Ashbury to score some heroin.

Two months earlier, midway through the Clash's incendiary set at the King's Hall in Bellevue, Manchester, Joe Strummer had shrugged off an onstage fuck-up by rhetorically asking 'who wants it to sound like the record?' Yet while Joe made a good point, in that songs played within a live setting ought not to mimic the polished studio recordings, it doesn't half help if the audience can at least pick out the tune. Whilst reviewing the Winterland show for *Record Mirror*, Mark Cooper described the Pistols' set and playing style on the night as 'uncoordinated' and having 'absolutely no pacing or range.'

Cooper's eulogy was confirmed with the release of *Gun Control* (SP 2900), an American bootleg which emerged later that same year. Although the wonders of modern technology have since provided fans with several infinitely superior feedback free versions, *Gun Control* (which came housed in a blank cover with a stick-it-on-yourself flyer bearing a photo of John and Glen from the November 1976 Notre Dame Hall show), revealed to the world that the Sex Pistols were – as Malcolm rightly stated in *Swindle* – a horse that needed putting out of its misery. Yeah, sure the inadequate PA and the faulty monitors no doubt played their part in the monophonic miasma emanating from the stage, but the PA can't be held accountable for John's indifference and Steve's out of tune guitar.

Sid surprisingly made it back before midnight, even treating the crowd to a three song Ramones sing-a-long-a-Sid solo spot playing '(I Don't Want To Go Down To The) Basement', 'Sheena Is A Punk Rocker' and 'Blitzkrieg Bop', but he was still out to lunch, lumbering about the stage like Frankenstein's monster in need of a power surge.

#

As Paul beat out the staccato intro to 'No Fun' for the encore, John informed the Winterland crowd that they'd be getting 'one number and one number only' on account of his being a 'lazy bastard'. By this point he was also a disillusioned and disgruntled bastard, for here they were playing in front of 5400 people – the largest audience the band had faced to date – and yet Malcolm's insistence on keeping the ticket price to a paltry $5 (paltry by San Francisco's affluent standards) meant that by the time Bill Graham had trousered his sizable slice, and the other deductions were knocked off from the $21,800 door receipt, the band was left with just $66 to show for their hard-earned efforts. Little wonder it was a one song encore!

The wad of grubby dollar bills that the crowd had thrown up onto the stage and which were now nestling within the pockets of John's new leather waistcoat wasn't much by way of compensation. Before abandoning the stage, and unwittingly bringing the curtain down on the Sex Pistols' career first time round, John uttered his immortal line: 'Ever get the feeling you've been cheated?' *Record Mirror*'s Mark Cooper cited John's enigmatic jibe as 'a perfect strategy to convince the crowd that they've been had.' For years it was assumed that Cooper's analysis was on the money, and that John had been mocking the punters. When John finally got around to explaining the true meaning behind his perplexing poser in 1986, as part of BBC2's Def Jam series *That Was Then This Is Now*, we finally learn that the remark had also been aimed at himself and his fellow Sex Pistols for allowing Malcolm to drive a wedge between them and deny them their wedge.

#

With a five day lay-off before the Stockholm date on 19th January, and Warner Bros having agreed to issue the Sex Pistols with open-ended plane tickets to any destination of their choice, Malcolm's scheming mind went into overdrive. He came up with another headline-grabbing scam whereby the Pistols would fly down to Rio de Janeiro in Brazil to play a show and meet up with the Great Train Robber Ronnie Biggs.

Once again (come on, it's been a while), we find ourselves delving into the realm of 'ifs, buts and maybes'. *If* the Finnish authorities hadn't allowed themselves to be swayed by the country's newspaper vilification of the Sex Pistols and the Helsinki show had gone ahead as planned, *then* there wouldn't have been time for sailing down the Amazon with Uncle Ronnie. The band *may* well have gone on to complete their January-March 1978 touring commitments, either with or without Sid, and then take a much-needed couple of months off to recharge the old batteries before regrouping. This, of course, is just wishful thinking on our Northern parts, as one of the confirmed March dates was for the Manchester Mayflower: now there's an 'if' we'd like to have seen come to pass.

Although Biggs only played a minor role in the audacious robbery, his escape from Wandsworth Prison and flight to first Australia and then Brazil made him something of a folk hero amongst the British public. Malcolm thought it would be a hoot to have the fugitive join the band on stage and recite some poetry between songs. Steve and Paul, being fully paid-up members of the 'five-fingered discount club', held the Great Train Robbers in the highest esteem, and were well up for the trip. Sid was surprisingly amenable to the idea too, although his enthusiasm could have been due to the availability of cheap drugs within Rio's slums, rather than any genuine affection for Biggs. John, however, who claimed he only found out about the Rio proposal courtesy of Sophie, was livid at not having been consulted and refused to go.

In *No Irish, No Blacks, No Dogs*, John dismissed Biggs as an 'ageing tosspot robber', and said that he couldn't condone the idea of celebrating someone who'd taken part in a robbery that had resulted in the 'bludgeoning of a train driver', and 'the theft of what was basically working-class money'. The fact that the money in question was on its way to London to be destroyed, and that the train driver, Jack Mills, had received nothing more wounding than a glancing blow to the back of the head, and was bandaged up by the police to be used as a publicity pawn, seems to have passed John by. It looks more likely that his aversion to the Rio trip was his way of getting even with Malcolm. There was also the fact that he had just spent 10 days criss-crossing America cooped up on an air-conditioned bus in the midst of a harsh winter which had played havoc with his sinuses: 'I am spitting blood and they [Malcolm, Steve and Paul] expect me to sit on a plane for two days!' was how he succinctly put it at the time.

Although having the Sex Pistols sunning themselves on Copacabana Beach with Ronnie Biggs would surely have caused a sensation in Britain, Malcolm may well have come up with the Rio proposal as a means of breaking up the act. Joe Stevens told Jon Savage in *England's Dreaming* that Malcolm was 'fed up of managing an established band' and was looking for a way out. He would have known that by purposely keeping John out of the loop the singer would retaliate in kind by vetoing the proposal.

In his aforementioned 8th April 1978 *Record Mirror* interview Sid told Rosalind Russell that Malcolm had collected him from Haight Ashbury at 5a.m. on the 16th to deliver him to the airport – where Steve and Paul were already checking in – for the 7 a.m. Pan Am flight to Rio. Whilst en route to the airport, aside from voicing his displeasure at the idea of going down to Rio to 'play to a lot of Pakis who didn't understand us or know what we were about', the bassist had also expressed his disillusionment with what the Sex Pistols, particularly John, had become. He also claimed to have told Malcolm that he wanted to leave the band as he didn't think John was a worthwhile performer anymore. He then ordered Malcolm to take him back to Haight Ashbury where he spent a couple of hours getting wasted again whilst contemplating his own options, before calling John at the Cavalier Motel to tell his former old mucker that he now regarded him as a 'useless failure'.

Later that day, John headed over to the Miyako to finally have it out with Malcolm. When he failed to stir from his room, the singer went along the hall to confront Steve and Paul. As far as he was concerned, Sid had burned the last of his bridges, but he still believed the three of them could and should carry on. He tried to get them to see the error of their ways in siding with Malcolm, but it seemed the 'side men' had also reached the end of their collective tether, and they were also pissed off at John for being denied their holiday under the Rio sun. At some point during the debate, the three paid a visit to Malcolm's room

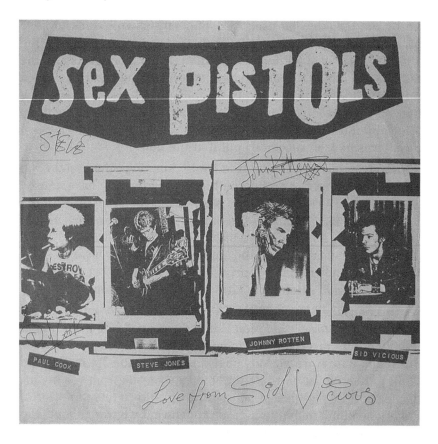

A gift to Alan from Malcolm McLaren

where John accused his manager of having only come up with the ludicrous Rio scam as a means of 'stitching him up' again. Malcolm retaliated by denouncing John for being in collusion with Richard Branson, who was surreptitiously grooming him to be the new Rod Stewart! And that was pretty much it. As John said, there was no punch-up or mass resignation; each one simply wandered off to lick their respective wounds. The 'war unit' that had risen above the mediocre to grab Britain by the bollocks had finally turned on itself and fragmented beyond repair. There was no Wagnerian fanfare, but the twilight of the 'Sods' was upon us and the Sex Pistols' Götterdämerung, which, if truth be told, had begun with Glen's forced departure some eleven months earlier, was now finally complete.

Three Sides To Every Story; Yours, Mine And The Truth!

'The fact that they are now in three different corners of the world could be construed as part of their continuing attempt to subvert authority and achieve world domination. It could also be construed as splitting up.'
Virgin Records Press Release

Egypt's President Anwar Sadat's decision to recall his peace delegation from Cairo on 18th January until his Israeli counterpart Prime Minister Menachem Begin reviewed his position on Palestine, sent a shock wave across the Middle East and beyond. *The Sun* though, God bless 'em, knew of a more important news story when they came across it and their front page headline for 19th January read: '**SEX PISTOLS SENSATION: PUNK BAND SPLITS UP AS ROTTEN WALKS OUT**'.

At the time, Britain's leading tabloid just happened to be serialising Fred and Judy Vermorel's *Sex Pistols* book, and in 'another *Sun* exclusive' tracked Malcolm down to Los Angeles for his version of events. 'It's all over. We will never perform again'. Malcolm told reporter Leslie Hinton who was calling him from New York. 'I have given up as manager and we will all go our separate ways.' When asked as to what had happened Malcolm replied: 'We had a long talk after our San Francisco concert and the other [band] members decided to kick out Johnny Rotten. He was just too destructive and was dragging us all down.' Hinton was in New York having uncovered John's hidey-hole. 'We all just sat down and agreed that the end had come,' John told Hinton.

'We have gone as far as we could go. Everyone was trying to turn us into a big band group, and I hated that.' Just so there could be no mistaking his intentions he added: 'I am sick of working with the Sex Pistols. I never want to appear with them again.'

Later that same day, Glitterbest issued the following press release: 'The management is bored with managing a successful rock and roll band. The group is bored with being a successful rock and roll band. Burning venues and destroying record companies is more creative than making it.' However, two hours later Glitterbest withdrew the statement. 'Yeah, the hasty retraction came on Malcolm's orders,' says Roadent, who was one of those responsible for the release's wording. 'You know what Malcolm's like,' he chuckles into his Guinness. 'He was worried that EMI and A&M's legal teams would seize on the bit about "destroying record companies" and attempt to reclaim some of their lay-out by suing us, or rather Glitterbest. Another reason was that he still thought he could get the boys back together. But everyone back at the office knew that was not going to happen any time soon. I'm pissed off that I missed out on going to America, but at the same time I was glad the band split up when they did, because even working for a successful rock 'n' roll band does become rather boring in the end, you know.'

#

Whether it was Joe Stevens who put Hinton onto John isn't known, but it was only through his munificence that John was able to get out of San Francisco. For although Warner Bros had honoured their commitments in taking care of the travel arrangements for Malcolm, Steve, Paul and Sid, there was no open-ended ticket waiting for John. The four Pistols had never been entrusted with their own bank accounts so the singer found himself stranded alone some six thousand miles from home with just $30 to his name. Stevens readily lent John $50 so that he could purchase a ticket back to London. But the photographer wasn't going to pass up an opportunity to get an insider scoop, and invited him to spend a few days as his guest in New York before returning to the UK.

Upon arrival in New York, John – at Stevens' behest – called Warner Bros' local office to request funds to get him home. It seems though that the label had either decided the sum of the Sex Pistols' parts was never going to be as great as the whole, or was refusing to believe it was John actually making the call. Seeing as John was staying with Stevens, at least until the blizzards subsided, the *NME*'s 4th February 1978 issue featured a special commemorative double-page centre-spread:

Section A: 'Four days in New York with dole-queue statistic Johnny Rotten' featured several of Stevens' photographs showing John relaxing with a few beers and porno mags at the photographer's apartment, as well as hanging out at CBGBs, tramping the city's snow-laden streets, and even posing outside the local Social Security office. The most telling photo, however, is the one of John sat huddled up against the reception desk in the San Francisco Miyako's lobby furtively eyeing his suitcase whilst Steve stands nearby purposely looking the other way.

Section B: 'An evening with Sid and Nancy: The Odd Couple Behind Closed Doors' featured a Chris Salewicz interview with Sid and Nancy at Pindock Mews with accompanying photos of the pair taken in Thin Lizzy frontman Phil Lynott's bathroom. Unfortunately for Chris, however, the interview should have been retitled 'Behind Closed Snores' as Sid, just as he did when Lech Kowalski came calling, kept nodding off in mid-sentence.

#

Whilst John was on his way to New York with Joe Stevens, and Steve and Paul were accompanying Malcolm and Boogie to Los Angeles, Sid had been left behind in San Francisco to recuperate from his latest heroin overdose. Having returned to the Haight Ashbury shooting gallery where he severed the last strand of his five year friendship with John, Sid had cooked up another Chinese rock and gone in search of the fabled dragon. There he may well have remained for all eternity had one of his distraught female fan club not put in a frantic call to the Miyako. Boogie and Steve headed round to the Haight Ashbury address and found the bassist lying lifeless on a grubby mattress surrounded by assorted San Franciscan low lifes. Having managed to revive Sid to a point where he was able to travel, the two then headed over the Golden Gate Bridge to an alternative doctor in Marin County who administered acupuncture to alleviate Sid's chronic withdrawal symptoms. But with Boogie having accompanied Malcolm, Steve and Paul to Los

Angeles, the task of collecting Sid the following morning fell to Sophie. Her instructions were to bring Sid to Los Angeles, but as she didn't know where Malcolm and the others were staying, she was forced to play wet nurse for another twenty-four hours before Boogie appeared like an angel of mercy to escort the bassist back to London.

By this time, of course, the acupuncture's anaesthetising effects had long since worn off. Sid couldn't face spending ten hours or so on an aeroplane with nothing to numb the pain; so before heading for LAX, Boogie first had to scour Los Angeles in search of a doctor with questionable ethics, who'd be willing to supply Sid with enough methadone tablets to last him until he was back in the UK. Unbeknownst to Boogie, however, Sid also had a stash of Valium secreted on his person and he slipped a few in with the methadone thinking the mix might help further ease the pain. As a result he overdosed again, and with his spindly frame no longer able to cope with the constant bombardment, he slipped into a drug-induced coma.

By the time the plane landed at JFK in New York his condition was so poorly that the airport's medical staff refused to allow him to make the connecting flight to London and rushed him to the nearby Jamaica Hospital in Queens, where he was kept in for observation. Had Sid simply succumbed to the methadone then Boogie might have showed a little more compassion and stayed at the Jamaica with him, but when he discovered the true cause of Sid's mid-air mishap he gave his hands a metaphorical rinse and headed into Manhattan, just as a raging blizzard descended upon the city. So, when Sid finally rejoined the land of the living sometime the following morning he would have had little or no idea as to his location, let alone how he'd got there.

John, of course, was in New York at the time, but even had he known of Sid's predicament, it's doubtful he would have made any effort to get in touch. Although Sid did have friends and acquaintances in the city such as Bob Gruen, John Holmstrom and Roberta Bayley, the blizzard had left New York at a near-standstill making it virtually impossible for any of them to get to the local 7-Eleven store, let alone off Manhattan to Queens. Sid's only contact with the outside world therefore came via a telephone conversation/interview with Roberta on 20th January. During the thirty-or-so minute chat, besides bemoaning his having been abandoned by Boogie and the resulting loss of his *Marvel* comics, the not-so-sanguine Sid inflated his own self-worth by casting a disparaging eye over his fellow ex-Sex Pistols. 'They'll probably try and get another band together – and fail,' he said in response to Roberta's query on Steve's and Paul's future musical prospects. 'And John is completely finished,' he added after criticising his former friend's recent on-stage efforts. 'He's finished as a person; he's just not what he used to be. Nobody will even want to know him. They'll say "oh, didn't you used to be Johnny Rotten?"' When Roberta asked of his own future plans, Sid expressed a desire to hook up with Johnny Thunders: 'Just think what that group [Heartbreakers] would be like with me, Thunders, Nolan and Walter Lure,' he mused. 'And that would be an incentive for me to get healthy as well.'

John arrived back in the UK on 23rd January and threw another red herring into the shoal of myths and mistruths that had been swimming around the Sex Pistols since their appearance on *Today* some thirteen months earlier. He informed the reporters waiting to greet his arrival at Heathrow that 'The Sex Pistols haven't broken up; it's all a publicity gimmick. I am totally amused by the whole business. I still exist and am enjoying myself.' While certain headline hungry scribes less au fait with the Sex Pistols, and the Glitterbest propaganda machine – papers such as the *Daily Telegraph* and the *Daily Mail* – took the bait and ran with it all the way back to Fleet Street, seasoned reporters who'd kept their ear to the ground were not so easily fooled. When one of the latter enquired as to his future plans, John quipped 'I haven't even had time to comb my hair. Give a girl a chance.'

As the music papers had already gone to press when the story broke, it wasn't until the following week that they were able to comment on the split. *Sounds'* 28th January issue left its eulogy to John's reggae-loving friend Vivien Goldman who expressed what many of the band's early followers were also thinking: 'The Pistols had to end with a bang if they really meant it, man.' Having cited John and Sid's ailing friendship, the strain in relations between John and Malcolm, and John, Steve and Paul's collective disenchantment with Sid's 'over the top self-destruction binges' as the main reasons for the break-up, Goldman provided what would prove to be a prescient piece of journalism: 'Whatever they say about one another publicly, John works in a tight team with Steve;

and Paul and Steve are an equally strong unit.' She went on to add that 'Rumours close to the band suggest that it's not inconceivable that John, Paul and Steve may yet hook up again.'

Record Mirror's Sex Pistols 'overkill' issue, which featured a Sex Pistols colour photo centre-page spread, reviews of Fred and Judy Vermorel's book *The Sex Pistols*, and the Winterland show, covered the latest developments surrounding the split in its News-desk page; while the paper's 'tongue-in-cheek' Off Centre column – accompanied by a rather unflattering cartoon – opined: 'The reported break-up of the internationally acclaimed Punk Rock group, The Sex Pistols, has so far failed to arouse public outcry, the imposition of a curfew in Bromley ... or a drought in India'. Having described the Sex Pistols sensation as 'one step away from a damp squib', *Record Mirror* decided to poll 'some prominent figures in the public eye' for their views on the Sex Pistols demise. Somewhat surprisingly, none of those canvassed appeared all that shocked by the news, but then again, nihilism does tend to have a short shelf life: with the Sex Pistols having seemingly run out of targets, it was inevitable that the band would turn on themselves.

When ex-Sex Pistol Glen Matlock was asked for his opinion he expressed bemusement: 'Is it for real then? I only know what I've read in *The Sun*.' he quipped. 'It could be just a publicity stunt. It's been done before. But it's getting beyond a joke now.' Another bassist asked for his opinion was The Jam's Bruce Foxton: 'Well, I reckon it's just one of Malcolm McLaren's publicity stunts,' said Bruce also picking up on the 'publicity stunt' vibe. 'If it's true I'm not that bothered. They made great records, but their breaking up won't affect me any other way.' One who definitely wasn't saddened by the news was Radio One DJ Tony Blackburn: 'I'm sure we'll all survive very happily without them,' he gloated. 'New Wave is on the way out anyway. I'm not going to cry about it.'

Aside from offering quotes from John and Malcolm purloined from *The Sun*'s front page, Off Centre collared Virgin Press Officer Al Clark: 'The Sex Pistols are taking a rest from each other at present,' they reported Clark as saying. 'A situation prompted largely by their American tour and by the fact they were in danger of becoming Rock Celebrities which is precisely the kind of stereotype they resist. Besides, bands with built-in detonators burn brightly in brief bursts. Rotten and Sis (sic) Vicious and Malcolm McLaren are in London. Steve Jones and Paul Cook are in Rio de

Janeiro. Until all the band are talking together in the same place there is not much more to say. They're all under contract to us for severeal (sic) albums still to come.'

#

On 21st January, with his visa due to expire the following day – and the Jamaica's staff having no desire to extend his stay – Sid discharged himself from the hospital and boarded a plane back to London. Whilst there were no reporters waiting to greet his arrival at Heathrow, he was back in the arms of his beloved Nancy. Aside from surfacing to fulfil his contractual obligations as a Sex Pistol in order to collect his weekly £60 Glitterbest stipend, or to conduct the odd interview, he retreated behind the walls of his Maida Vale bolthole, where 'Bonny and Snide' slipped deeper into the narcotic nightmare from which neither would escape.

On 24th February, however, Sid found himself back under the media microscope following his and Nancy's drugs-related court appearance the previous day. *The Sun* led the witch-hunt with its front page headline '**SEX PISTOL AND GIRL IN DRUGS PROBE**' accompanied by a photo of Sid taken by Bob Gruen during the band's promotional trip to Luxembourg back in November. And a witch-hunt it undoubtedly was. For although Sid and Nancy had been caught in possession of Methamphetamine, a psychostimulant more commonly known by its street name 'Crystal Meth', the amount found on their person was, according to the couple's solicitor, 'the smallest ever known, and invisible to the human eye'. February also marked Sid's return to the spotlight when he was invited to take the drum stool in Johnny Thunders' aptly named ad hoc outfit The Living Dead on stage at the Speakeasy. The scene had moved on since September 1976, however, and this was no 100 Club Punk Fest fuck-about. Thunders might have been a junkie, but he took his music very seriously and Sid's triumphant return ended in ignominious failure when Johnny ejected him from the stage after he collapsed into the drum kit.

Under normal circumstances, being ejected from Junkie Johnny's court would sound the death knell on anyone's musical aspirations. However, Sid wasn't just 'anybody', and the Sex Pistols having grabbed the headlines in nineteen languages meant he wouldn't be left licking his wounds for long. So it proved when

Virgin released his punked-up rendition of the timeless Frank Sinatra classic 'My Way' as a Sex Pistols double A-side coupled with 'No One Is Innocent' (VS220), which was the first post-Johnny Rotten Sex Pistols single when it was released on 30th June 1978.

Somewhat surprisingly, given its now iconic status, when 'My Way' was first released in 1969, it stalled at No. 27 on the Billboard chart. It would, however, fare much better in the UK, where it climbed to No. 5 and went on to become that year's best-selling single. The song's composer Paul Anka, having purchased the publishing rights to the French song 'Comme d'habitude' two years earlier with no specific use in mind for its soulful melody, set about penning the reflective lyric destined to become Sinatra's 'signature song' after dining with 'Ol' Blue Eyes' in Florida. Whilst being interviewed for a 2007 'My Way' retrospective, Anka said that he'd been left 'somewhat destabilised' by Sid's version, but was willing to concede that he believed Sid to have been sincere in his delivery.

Sid had recorded the song in Paris on 10th April at the Studio de la Grande Armée in Porte Maillot in the French capital's European Quarter. Although Chris Thomas' services weren't called upon, the final mix included a strings arrangement by Simon Jeffes of Penguin Café Orchestra fame. He wasn't actually informed what his arrangement was being used for until weeks later in case he got cold feet! Steve's now trademark chugging riffs gave 'My Way' a distinct Sex Pistols flavour.

Despite the to-be expected blanket ban on airplay, as well as the equally predictable veto by high street chain stores/guardians of the nation's morals Woolworths, Boots and W.H. Smith – all of whom refused to stock the Sex Pistols' latest offensive offering – the single slammed into the Top 10. Both songs, of course, would feature in *The Great Rock 'n' Roll Swindle* film, as well as appearing on the accompanying double album soundtrack. In a repeat of the fiasco surrounding the release of *Never Mind The Bollocks* eighteen months earlier, Virgin would be forced to rush-release the soundtrack on the 26th February 1979 to counter Barclay's imported version.

Rumours began circulating that Ronnie Biggs was to be flown in by helicopter to perform 'No One Is Innocent' alongside Steve and Paul on the roof of the TV studio, where ITV's Saturday night punk/new wave-orientated music show *Revolver,* hosted by Peter Cook, was being broadcast. Sadly, the rumours proved unfounded.

While the show's studio audience were being treated to the promo video, those of us glued to our TV sets were to be denied that particular cinematic delight until *Swindle* hit the big screen some two years later.

Had 'My Way' been selected as the single's sole A-side – as it was in France – then it is likely the accompanying promo video (which was shot at the Paris Olympia music hall on the Boulevard des Capucines, on 23rd April 1978), would have been given radio airplay and possibly resulted in the tape being used on *Top Of The Pops*. As it was, Malcolm had to rely on an old pals' act from Tony Wilson, who must have used his influence with the powers that be at Granada to see that enough strings were pulled to get the video premiered on the regional station's news magazine programme *Granada Reports* on Wednesday 5th July.

Three years might have passed, but Vivienne's intuition about Sid's frontman capabilities had finally come to pass. Although Sid's vocal style was a pale imitation of Johnny Rotten's caustic rant, Malcolm, Julien Temple, Boogie, and everyone else who witnessed tuxedo-clad Sid's swaggering performance at Paris' oldest – and most illustrious – music hall, knew the bumbling bassist had finally found his forte. Unfortunately for Malcolm, however, Sid had only agreed to record 'My Way' in return for his signing a piece of paper relinquishing his managerial responsibilities over Sid. After filming his remaining scenes for the *Swindle* film – most notably the videos for 'Something Else' and 'C'mon Everybody', as well as the deleted Jubilee kiosk scene – Sid clambered aboard his motorcycle and rode off into the Sex Pistolian sunset to seek fame and fortune under the guidance of his new manager, Nancy.

One might have expected Sid's resurrected status to see a plethora of his rock 'n' roll peers beating a path to his door offering to put a new band together. However, with the exception of Roadent and Steve English, the only visitors to Pindock Mews were fellow junkies living on nearby Sutherland Avenue and Harrow Road, looking for a free fix and somewhere to rest their head for the night. 'We had some good nights at Pindock Mews,' Roadent says today. 'That's, of course, when I managed to get inside.' he adds. 'There was many the time that I'd get a call from Sid inviting me round for a few drinks and a chat. And all the while getting over to Maida Vale I'd be thinking "well, he sounded quite lucid and in good spirits, so we should be all right". But more often than not I'd get there and spend twenty minutes pounding on the front door before giving up and going home again as one of his dealers had already made a house call.

In late June, Helen (Killer) Keller, who'd arrived in London from New York several weeks earlier, moved into No. 3 Pindock Mews and remained there until Sid and Nancy left for New York. Helen, having already made the 3,000 mile journey from California to check out the New York punk rock scene, decided that as she was now halfway to London she might as well go the whole hog and cajoled her mother into funding her one-way ticket to the UK.

Upon arrival in the capital, the penniless Helen had phoned Malcolm only to be told to call back later as he was in a meeting. However, as she was walking along the King's Road later that same afternoon she'd happened upon a female acquaintance from Los Angeles who invited her to move into the squat where she was living with several home-grown punks. Although Helen had regaled her fellow squatters with tales of her adventures with the Sex Pistols, especially with Sid, in Dallas and San Francisco, it wasn't until several weeks later that she discovered the English punks didn't believe her story. Said discovery came one Saturday afternoon on the King's Road when one of her detractors stopped and pointed into BOY, where Sid and Nancy were perusing the shop's wares. 'Why don'tcha go inside and say hello to Sid?' they'd sneered. Helen had no reason to fear entering the shop, although five months had passed since her last meeting with Sid, and she had no reason to assume that he'd even remember her; there was also Nancy to contend with. She needn't have worried, though, as Sid took one look at Helen, bounded towards her and gave her a hug, and the detractors could only look on in shame-faced silence as Nancy welcomed her fellow American with open arms and insisted she move into Chez Vicious.

'They did ordinary stuff like go out to the cinema,' Helen told us. 'And they went to the stores to buy groceries or go to the chip shop. It was only their bedroom that was painted black, the rest of the place was entirely normal.' Sid and Nancy also took Helen out to see bands at venues such as the Music Machine and the Electric Ballroom in Camden Town. Helen's abiding memory of Sid during her two month stay at Pindock Mews is of him leaping around the living room to Eddie Cochran records dressed in only his leather jacket and leopard-skin underpants.

One of the by-now regular attendees at Pindock Mews was 19-year-old studio assistant John Shepcott who spent the evening of 12th August naively believing he could match the tolerance levels of his more illustrious neighbours and OD'd on a cocktail of cocaine and heroin; legend has it that Sid and Nancy woke sometime the following day to find young Shepcott lying dead on the bed beside them. Shepcott's untimely death was enough to galvanise Sid and Nancy into seeking help by entering a methadone programme at the private hospital Bowden House in Harrow-on-the-Hill, North West London. According to the *Collins English Dictionary*, methadone is a 'narcotic analgesic drug similar to morphine but less habit-forming'. But the 'less habit-forming' bit depends on the patient's willpower. What the dictionary also neglects to mention is that methadone withdrawal can actually be much worse than coming off heroin.

#

Virgin might have been keeping tight-lipped with regard to its contractual commitments to the Sex Pistols, but it was obvious the label would follow the talent. John had barely had time to unpack his suitcase before Richard Branson whisked the singer, along with his buddies Don Letts, Dennis Morris and Vivien Goldman, on a three week all-expenses-paid trip to Jamaica. The idea being that John, serving in an unofficial A&R capacity, would cast his discerning ear over prospective local reggae acts with a view to signing them to Virgin's new subsidiary label, Front Line.

Many onlookers saw the trip as little more than a means for Branson to curry favour with John. The Virgin boss has since denied any ulterior motive behind the Jamaica trip, although some people at the time doubted this. John might well have acquired a love of reggae through his mid-'76 jaunts to clubs such as The Four Aces in Dalston courtesy of Don Letts, but he was hardly an expert on the genre. And what other purpose did Don, Dennis and Vivien serve during the three week reggae reconnaissance mission other than to keep their mate company?

Aside from listening to demo tapes whilst relaxing by the pool at the Kingston Sheraton Hotel (which would be name-checked in the Clash song 'Safe European Home') John headed into Trench Town to hang out and smoke chalice with reggae stars such as Peter Tosh, Big Youth, Burning Spear, U Roy and Prince Far I. John wasn't black and he didn't have dreadlocks (you may have noticed), but the local rastas recognised a kindred 'anti-colonial' spirit. Don says upon receiving John's late night invite to Jamaica he packed his passport, Super-8 camera (the same one he used to make his now-legendary *Punk Rock Movie*), and a spare pair of underpants into a carrier bag and headed for Heathrow.

Jamaica was the land of Don's forefathers, but this would be the first time he'd ever been to the island and, by his own admission, it was as alien to him as it must have been for John. A surprise visit to his grandparents' home ended in farce as he and John made the trip to the small shanty town, where the old couple lived, in a chauffeur driven white Cadillac stretch limo. Another ill-fated house call came when Don accompanied John to Joni Mitchell's island retreat, and the two were forced to curtail their visit after inadvertently dissing Joni's latest album. Social faux pas apart, the Jamaica trip was a great success with several major reggae acts signing to Branson's Front Line label, which suggests that the Virgin boss was vindicated in sending Rotten and Co. on the jaunt.

#

While John was enjoying his holiday in the sun, Malcolm arrived back in London principally to sort out a film crew to meet up with Steve and Paul in Rio, as well as to attend a meeting called by Bob Regehr. The Warner Bros bigwig had come over to voice concerns over having laid out a large sum of cash on the Sex Pistols; a band which no longer appeared to exist anywhere other than in Malcolm's mind.

An unwanted legal distraction came via Ray Stevenson's solicitor, who was threatening litigation over Glitterbest having halted the photographer's book: *Sex Pistols Scrap Book* (Ray was forced to self-publish whilst the legal wranglings went on, before Omnibus Press picked it up and retitled it *The Sex Pistols File*). Malcolm was desperate to hang onto the Warner Bros £200,000 film advance, but it seemed the only way he could do so would be to resolve his differences with John. So when he heard about John's Jamaican jaunt he handed Boogie a cache of blank sheets of paper, each one bearing his signature, and ordered him to book a seat on the next available flight out to the island.

Boogie's mission was twofold: the signed sheets of paper were to be used to make promises, albeit false ones, to John if the singer would agree to a truce and cooperate on the ongoing

Promotional poster for Swindle *film*

Swindle film. If this ruse failed then Boogie was to snap some pictures of John smoking a spliff by the swimming pool in order to discredit him back home. John, of course, was savvy enough to know that whatever promises Boogie was making on Malcolm's behalf wouldn't be worth the paper they were written on and gave his former road manager extremely short shrift. After all, what possible reason was there to smoke the pipe of peace with Malcolm when he had the ear of Richard Branson? So Boogie, rather than return to London empty-handed, set up an observation post within the Sheraton's grounds in the hope of catching John 'ganja *in flagrante'*. His Anglo-Italian heritage may have given him the countenance of a Red Indian when the sun tan took effect, but Boogie still stuck out like a snowball in a coalhole and the locals didn't take kindly to interlopers; especially those carrying cameras. When the hapless Boogie was discovered lurking in the bushes with his lens aimed squarely at John's room he was summarily dumped into the swimming pool.

⌗

Steve and Paul also enjoyed a 'business holiday' of sorts in Rio de Janeiro with Ronnie Biggs. On the morning of 17th January, with all forthcoming dates having been cancelled and their immediate calendar empty, the two 'side men' had accompanied Malcolm and Boogie to Los Angeles to see what the City of Angels had to offer, before then flying down to Rio to hook up with Biggs. Despite living in exile, Biggs was aware of the Sex Pistols thanks to a friend having played him the 'God Save The Queen' single. The affable emigre was happy to have a couple of 'good old London boys' drop by for a chinwag. As John says in *No Irish, No Blacks, No Dogs*, their decision to remain with Malcolm rather than side with him wasn't done out of malice, but rather it being the easier ride at the time.

For unlike John, who'd insisted that his name went on the land registry deeds of the recently-purchased house on Gunter Grove in Chelsea, Steve and Paul had naively allowed Malcolm to sign the lease on their Bell Street flat, and were therefore left with little option but to dance to Malcolm's tune. Sid, of course, was in a similar position as the tenancy lease at Pindock Mews was in Sophie Richmond's name.

Malcolm having managed, albeit temporarily, to assuage Regehr's concerns by sending Boogie on his ill-fated reconciliation mission to Jamaica, flew out to Rio to join up with Steve and Paul and the film crew. In order to keep his pale features from being frazzled by the scorching heat he took to wearing a baseball cap and sunglasses, which gave him more than a passing resemblance to the renowned Formula One racing driver Niki Lauda and led to the locals dubbing him 'Niki'. Lauda, of course, had been forced into wearing a cap to hide the facial scarring he'd suffered in the accident which had nearly claimed his life at the German Grand Prix in August 1976.

Aside from soaking up the sun and ogling the bevy of bronzed Brazilian beauties parading along Rio's legendary Copacabana Beach, Steve and Paul went into a local studio to record two songs, with Biggs (whom the Virgin press team would inevitably dub 'Ronnie Rotten') providing the vocals for inclusion on *The Great Rock 'n' Roll Swindle* soundtrack. One of these was the aforementioned 'No One Is Innocent (A Punk Prayer' by Ronnie Biggs), while the other was a reworking of 'Belsen Was A Gas'. Malcolm had originally wanted to call 'No One Is Innocent' (in which Biggs purports to exonerate the crimes of Moors Murderers

Ian Brady and Myra Hindley, Ugandan dictator Idi Amin, and his fellow fugitive Reichleiter Martin Bormann), 'Cosh The Driver' in a twisted reference to the train robbers' assault on driver Jack Mills. Virgin had baulked at this proposal which forced Malcolm into a rethink for the title. There was also an issue concerning Jamie Reid's original advertising art for the single, which along with the title 'No One Is Innocent' featured a picture of Branson himself with his arm around a school age prize winner, alongside the wording 'three cheers for the child molesting public school boy!'. This image of course would also be shelved until many years later.

In an exclusive phone interview conducted with *Record Mirror*'s editor Tim Lott, which appeared in the paper's 15th July 1978 edition – by which time 'No One Is Innocent' was riding high in the UK chart – Biggs said his 'punk prayer' was at least 'half serious' as he'd put a lot of his own sentiments into the lyrics. 'Whether it's in bad taste or not depends on how you look at it.' a philosophical Great Train Robber told Lott over a crackly transatlantic line. 'The message of the song is simply this: if God is going to save the Queen, then he should save Myra Hindley, and Martin Bormann, and Ian Brady. He has to save everybody or nobody; because no one, absolutely no one, is innocent.' he added, taking on the role of theologian. When Lott questioned Biggs over his having written several new – equally tasteless – verses for 'Belsen Was A Gas' to replace those originally penned by Sid, the train robber denied that he was cashing in on one of history's more shameful episodes: ' "Belsen Was A Gas" was already recorded by the Sex Pistols before I got involved with them,' he said by way of defence, before glibly adding: 'Anyway, Belsen was a gas. People got gassed.' (Ronnie should have paid more attention in history class at school as the Bergen-Belsen concentration camp – which claimed the life of Dutch diarist Ann Frank – didn't actually possess a gas chamber).

Just in case there was anyone who hadn't picked up on the right wing vibes emanating from Rio, Malcolm hired American actor James Jetters –perhaps best known for starring in John Carpenter's 1976 original version of *Assault On Precinct 13* – to strut around sporting a Nazi uniform posing as Martin Bormann; a role he had already played for Russ Meyer.

Lott concluded his interview by asking Biggs what he hoped to gain via his unexpected venture into pop music: 'I have high hopes that I stand to make a great deal of money.' Biggs replied. 'But I've been involved in so many rip-offs, so many promises that haven't gone right,' he added wistfully, 'that I now take everything with a pinch of salt.' And 'Rockin' Ronnie' was right to reach for the Saxa, for although he managed to wangle a few grand out of Malcolm, no recording royalties would ever find their way into his Rio account.

Malcolm was forced to interrupt his filming schedule towards the end of February to fly to Los Angeles to attend a reconciliatory meeting with John, arranged by Bob Regehr in an attempt to reach a compromise over *Swindle,* so that Warner Bros might recoup some of its six-figure Sex Pistols outlay. This time Warner's wanted both estranged protagonists where they could see them, and even provided John with sufficient funds to bring his mum Eileen out to Los Angeles for a holiday. The intervening month since their last acrimonious meeting at the Miyako in San Francisco had done little to assuage John's feelings towards his erstwhile manager. Even before taking his seat at the negotiating table with Malcolm, John let it be known that he had no intention whatsoever of working with the Sex Pistols again. He was even of the opinion that Warners should instead consider funding his future musical projects. Regehr's hopes of at least getting John to reconsider giving his consent to the *Swindle* project were crushed the following morning as John and Malcolm came face-to-face at the Continental Hyatt House Hotel. The singer purposely imposed several non-negotiable content stipulations with which he knew Malcolm could never comply .

#

Aside from seeking help to cure his chronic drug addiction during the summer, Sid also made moves to rekindle his friendship with John in the hope that they might work together at some point in the near future. Despite Sid publicly ostracising John as 'useless' several months earlier – and the character assassination he'd received at Sid's hands in Rosalind Russell's *Record Mirror* interview – John was surprisingly amenable to the idea of a musical collaboration; his only concern being that now Sid had tasted success in front of the microphone what would his own role in the venture be? In her own inimitable way, Nancy put the kibosh on the collaboration, as well as any hopes Sid had for the reconciliation, by informing John he could be the drummer in her beloved's new band!

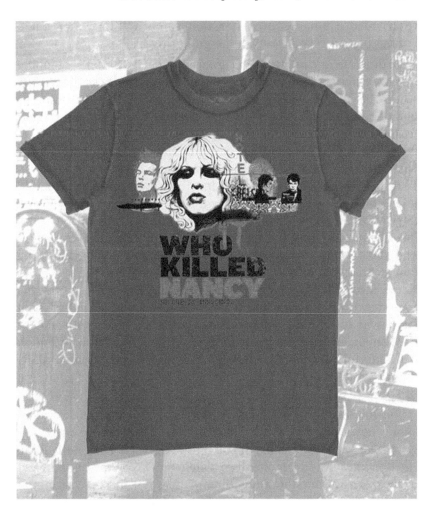

Who Killed Nancy *T-Shirt from the film*

One evening in early August, Sid and Nancy paid another visit to Gunter Grove. Now, while we'd like to think it was so that Sid could apologise for Nancy having insulted John in his own house, it's more likely that he was calling round with aftershow invites for his forthcoming solo show at the Electric Ballroom in Camden Town on the 15th. Although the couple could hear noises coming from the upstairs room, where John liked to hold midnight court, no one responded to their incessant knocking, so they eventually gave up the ghost and returned to Pindock Mews. Sid, however, must have had a pressing need to speak to John for he and Nancy returned to Gunter Grove later that same evening; once again failing to get a response from the gathering inside.

Sid didn't take kindly to being ignored, especially after schlepping half-way across London, and headed for the nearest phone box where he vented his spleen into the phone for several minutes before returning to John's lair and kicking in the front door. What followed next has always been shrouded in mystery and intrigue, but what we do know is that Sid and Nancy came under attack from either Wobble or Paul Young or another of John's Finsbury Park cronies, as they were making their way up the stairs. Sid later claimed he'd been struck with an axe, but Wobble, who'd answered the phone and inadvertently suffered Sid's vitriolic rant, has always disputed this and says that Sid tripped on the stairs and smashed his head against the metal thresher fitted into the door frame. Axe or accident made no difference in Sid's eyes, as Nancy also suffered injuries during the assault: needless to say, the aftershow passes remained in Sid's pocket. The Electric Ballroom show was to be Sid's UK swansong; a benefit show with him as the beneficiary, to raise funds for a new life in New York. Although it's doubtful that John would have attended the Camden show anyway, little could he have known that he would never again see or speak to Sid.

One ex-Sex Pistol who was present at the Electric Ballroom show, however, was Glen Matlock. Glen had never held any grudge towards Sid, as his argument had always been with John. He happily offered his services when Sid broached the subject of their doing something together, over a pint in the Warrington pub (located at the end of Warrington Avenue in Maida Vale), close to where they were both living at the time. Once it had been established that Glen would be playing bass leaving Sid free to sing, Glen brought in his fellow soon-to-be ex-Rich Kid Steve New on guitar and he and Sid's mutual chum Rat Scabies on drums. Following the Damned's demise earlier in the year, Rat had put together his own band The White Cats and so the four decided upon an amalgamation of their names and the Vicious White Kids were born.

Glen had booked a week at John Henry's Rehearsals in Islington, but as the show was intended as a one-off there was little need to write new material. Instead the makeshift combo worked up a nine song set consisting of 'My Way', as well as Eddie Cochran's 'Somethin' Else' and 'C'mon Everybody' (which would become

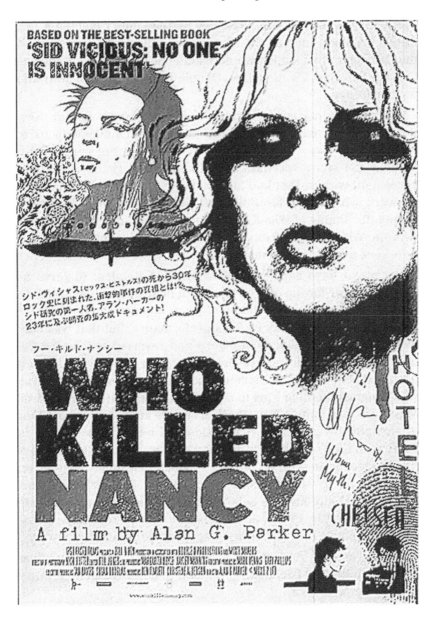

Who Killed Nancy *Film poster*

posthumous hits for Sid), 'Belsen Was A Gas', and a few rock 'n'
roll standards including the Monkees' '(I'm Not Your) Stepping
Stone', and Dave Berry's '(Don't You Gimme) No Lip', both of which
had been early Sex Pistols set perennials. With two ex-Sex Pistols

in the line-up, one has to wonder why they didn't include a few Pistols originals such as the Glen-penned 'Pretty Vacant' to send the Camden crowd (which would include punk aristocrats such as Captain Sensible, Viv Albertine, Debbie Harry and Joan Jett) into further frenzy.

Why not use the Damned connection as an excuse to play 'New Rose' too? After all, Sid had almost joined the band back in 1976. Helen Keller was also at the gig and, perhaps not surprisingly, thought the show was fantastic. Incidentally, Helen is in total agreement with us that had Sid lived then there would have been no work whatsoever for Billy Idol. She also let slip off camera during the filming of *Who Killed Nancy* that Sid had presented her with the white tuxedo from the 'My Way' video before leaving for New York (it was later stolen).

One might have expected Sid to bring in Roadent to serve as stage manager for the one-off show, but instead that honour fell to the Clash's road manager Johnny Green. Johnny readily admits to having been blown away by Sid's performance, but that was only during the soundcheck as our hero had reverted to form by the time the curtain went up. Several years later, Glen found himself having lunch with Rob Dickens, the then head of Warner Bros who'd signed the Rich Kids to a publishing deal with Warner Bros Music. He was quite taken aback when Dickens commented that in his opinion the Vicious White Kids had been the best band to feature on Glen's CV. When Glen had enquired as to why Warners hadn't stepped in with a contract – which just might have given Sid cause for a rethink about relocating to New York – Dickens told him that although he believed Sid to be a natural performer, he'd also been in the business long enough to recognise a lost cause: or maybe that should read 'lost corpse', when he saw one.

And so on 23rd August 1978, after bidding a fond and final farewell to the few friends they had left in London, Sid and Nancy headed for New York.

CHAPTER fOuRTeen

And Now,
The End Is Near ...

'When they arrived in New York they were not stars, they could walk around anywhere, precious few people even knew who they were! If anything they were 'famous' on the underground'
Sturgis Nikides

Upon arrival in the Big Apple, Sid and Nancy booked into the Chelsea Hotel on West 23rd Street under the names Mr and Mrs John Ritchie. Nancy had called home several weeks earlier requesting money from her mother Deborah so that she and Sid could get married, but Deborah refused suspecting, quite rightly, that the money would be spent on drugs. Before heading for Heathrow, Nancy had followed the Boy Scouts' motto of 'be prepared' and had secreted the couple's methadone stash inside a plastic Fairy Liquid container. Not that there was any need to worry about where their next fix was coming from as most of the 'Heroin Hotel's' clientele were hapless drug addicts. And if none of the residents happened to be holding, then the Chelsea's bellboys would happily oblige.

Until 1899 the twelve storey red-brick fronted Chelsea Hotel had the honour of being New York's tallest structure. It had first opened its doors in 1884 to serve as the city's first artist's co-operative. The venture lasted ten years before going to the wall but, following a refurbishment, the Chelsea reopened as a hotel in 1905. Over the ensuing decades it became something of a home from home for writing luminaries such as Mark Twain, Thomas Wolfe, Brendan Behan and Eugene O'Neill. By the late seventies, however, the hotel – like New York itself – had fallen into serious decline, and was now the refuge for wannabe actors hoping for a break on Broadway, as well as down-at-heel musicians.

'It wasn't the worst place in town by any means,' ex-Chelsea resident (and Neon Leon's one-time guitarist) Sturgis Nikides told us. 'You couldn't even book a room for any longer than a night at a time at St Mark's (St Mark's Hotel on St Mark's Place in the East Village),' he adds. 'The walls would be covered with blood from where the previous guests had removed the air bubbles before administering their goodnight fix.' John Holmstrom endorses that view. 'When I moved to New York from Connecticut around the summer of 1973 I couldn't afford to stay at the Chelsea because $100 per month was a lot of money back then. And to put that into perspective there were plenty of places in Manhattan where you could stay for $10 per week.'

Before leaving London, Nancy would have no doubt filled Sid's head with stories about New York's thriving punk rock scene and how a rock star of his standing would be welcomed with open arms. However, the Big Apple was still smarting over having been snubbed by the Sex Pistols back in January, and the city took its revenge by largely ignoring Sid's arrival – regardless of the fact that his lover/manager/surrogate mother was one of their own. Fortunately for Sid, however, Nancy's talent for oral handshakes meant she was able to secure her lover several dates at Max's Kansas City located on Park Avenue South.

The legendary two storey restaurant/nightclub, which is now a Korean deli, was generally regarded as Manhattan's premiere watering hole for the weird and wonderful. When its colourful owner Mickey Ruskin first opened Max's in December 1965, it predominantly served as a hangout for the New York School collective of artists, poets, musicians and sculptors, before gaining prominence thanks to Andy Warhol's patronage. Over the ensuing decade, Max's had staged shows by the likes of Bruce Springsteen, David Bowie, and Bob Marley, as well as punk progenitors the Velvet Underground, the Stooges and the New York Dolls.

Sid's adoration of the Dolls and the Ramones, coupled with Nancy's assurances that heroin would be available on tap, meant that New York was the obvious location for him to try and establish himself as a solo artist. However, whereas Johnny Thunders and Dee Dee Ramone could function whilst under the influence, and knock out catchy rock 'n' roll tunes into the bargain, all Sid had to bring to the party was his stash. Nonetheless, his celebrity status as an ex-Sex Pistol ensured there were plenty of local musicians willing to offer their services. First to put his name in the frame was Dead Boys guitarist Cheetah Chrome, after inadvertently encountering Sid and Nancy in the office of Max's manager Peter Crowley. Chrome cemented the proposal by inviting them back to his apartment to sample some of his stash, where the guitarist's roommate and Dead Boys' bassist Jeff Magnum was co-opted into service. Having recruited fellow Dead Boy Jimmy Zero, as well as Jerry Nolan, Chrome and Magnum got as far as booking rehearsals before Nancy summoned the pair to a meeting at Max's to inform the two Dead Boys that they – and Zero – no longer featured in Sid's plans. Having been in the New York Dolls and the Heartbreakers, as well as between Nancy's legs, meant that Nolan was always going to feature and he was occupying the drum stool when Sid – with his ad hoc backing band, the Idols – made his debut at Max's on 7th September.

Aside from Nolan, the Idols consisted of the drummer's ex-New York Dolls rhythm section partner Arthur 'Killer' Kane (who borrowed Sid's blood-splattered Fender bass for the show), and Sid and Nancy's drug-buddy from London, Steve Dior (Stephen Hershcowitz) on guitar. Steve, himself a heroin addict, had first encountered Sid whilst hanging out with the Warrington Crescent crowd just prior to the UK punk explosion. A friendship with Glen saw him become something of a regular visitor to Denmark Street where he often jammed with Glen, Steve and Paul. John's unexplained enmity towards the younger middle class Jewish kid from Kensington meant that Sid also initially took a dislike to him. But once Sid developed a taste for heroin, courtesy of Nancy, the two became friends; Sid even entrusting Steve to keep an eye out for Nancy whilst he was away on tour with the Pistols.

He was present the night Sid called from Tulsa to tell Nancy that he'd just fucked a transvestite, and was amused to hear Nancy tell her lover that it was okay just so long as he didn't fuck any girls. Steve, of course, is one of the few people who has anything nice to say about Nancy. 'Sure, she could whine,' he says mimicking Nancy's New York nasal twang. 'But she really did have a heart of gold. I remember bumping into them on Canal Street shortly after their arrival in New York, and I happened to be wearing a pair of Chinese slippers that had seen better days; in fact my big toe was sticking out through one of them. Nancy insisted on buying me a brand-new pair of motorcycle boots, and would never let me repay her even though I made good money from the Max's shows.'

According to Steve, whose younger sister Esther was also close to Sid and Nancy as she was going out with Jerry Nolan at the time, Johnny Thunders was also approached for the Max's shows. However, an altercation between the guitarist and Nolan the day prior to the opening show led to Steve calling on Mick Jones, who happened to be in town with Joe Strummer overseeing the mixing of *Give 'Em Enough Rope*. Mick was initially reticent to get involved but eventually acquiesced following pressure from Joe. Although the Clash six-stringer was himself no stranger to drugs, Mick might have been tempted to suggest renaming the Clash's forthcoming second CBS album '*Give 'Em Enough Dope*', as he later commented that he'd been sharing the stage with people who were as far out of it as one could possibly be without being dead.

Despite his reservations, Mick had been happy to play the gig and was therefore peeved at not being asked to play the following night's show. Somewhat surprisingly, the rebuttal came courtesy of Sid who'd grown accustomed to playing with one guitarist and had criticised his old mate's fancy guitar style. Steve also remembers Sid giving him and Mick some stick over their failing to work out the chord changes to 'My Way'. He and Mick had spent the afternoon of the debut show listening to the single over and over again without managing to figure out the key change midway through the song, but the song couldn't be dropped from the set: not play 'My Way'? No way! So a true punk rock compromise was reached whereby they would play the song up to the elusive key change before stopping dead and fleeing the stage. Several months would pass before Steve and Mick's paths crossed again, and the first words out of Mick's mouth were to enlighten Steve that there hadn't been a key change at all; he'd simply been thrown by Steve Jones' improvisation.

In all, Sid made eight appearances at Max's that September. Whilst Steve readily admits that several shows were shambolic affairs – largely due to Sid's inability to stay straight until after he'd come off stage – the guitarist says that the last two gigs, the 28th and 30th September (both of which appear on the CD *Sid Lives)*, were really great performances. Two from eight, however, isn't a good hit rate, and the majority of the New Yorkers that had allowed their curiosity to get the better of them must have wondered what the fuck all the fuss was about as they watched Sid lumbering about the stage like a lobotomised zombie struggling to remember the lyrics to the songs. 'The show I saw was pretty bad,' the colourful and highly engrossing Sturgis told us for *Who Killed Nancy* (Soda Pictures) 'Sid was totally off his head on smack that night and couldn't even remember the words to the songs! People still talk about Sid Vicious being regarded as a rock star in New York, but that was only amongst the punk rock fraternity which was a fairly small crowd. To put it another way, he couldn't have got a motel room in Cleveland.'

Sid was barely into his twenties, but twelve months of excessive substance abuse had aged him prematurely and left him a shadow of his former sprightly self. Heroin had also taken a heavy toll on his once brooding good looks. During the 'God Save The Queen' photo-shoot just fifteen months earlier, he'd been so conscious about a spot on his cheek that he covered the unsightly blemish with a strategically placed Jubilee souvenir plastic windmill. Pride in appearance, of course, is one of the first casualties of heroin addiction, and his emaciated track-marked frame and parchment-like pallor was akin to that of the Belsen inmates he'd once derided. In addition, a late-night woefully one-sided altercation with an off duty marine back in March had left him with a permanently half-closed right eye. Nancy was in her element, though. It didn't matter that her boyfriend was dying on his arse every night, because to her mind having Sid appear at Max's Kansas City had elevated her status amongst her peers. On previous visits to the club she'd just been another groupie looking to fuck whoever happened to be playing that particular night. But now she was Mrs Sid Vicious and could take pride of place at the side of the stage.

Having found out the hard way that New York didn't suffer fools gladly, the Big Apple must have appeared even sourer when Sid discovered that methadone wasn't available on prescription. So once the Fairy Liquid had run dry, he and Nancy were forced to stand in line at the nearby Spring Street clinic to get their daily fix. By this time, of course, methadone was no longer the couple's only drug *de jour*, as Sid and Nancy were both also hooked on barbiturates such as Tuinol and Dilaudid (a synthetic morphine normally given to terminal cancer patients). It has often been said that Americans don't have a sense of perspective; to them everything is black and white, with no shades of grey between. The assorted junkies and low-lifes standing in line to get their daily fix to oblivion, having recognised Sid from seeing his photo in the *Village Voice*, took him at face value. Had he been called Sidney

Stupid or Sid Sarcastic then he might only have been challenged to make them laugh but after one Bowery beating too many Sid began carrying a knife for protection.

#

The Max's Kansas City dates were reasonably well-attended but, if truth be told, the majority of the five or six hundred strong audiences were there to see if this would be the night the Sid Vicious train wreck finally came off the rails. Having completed the final Max's date on 30th September – and with no other shows until the first of two dates at the Artemis in Nancy's home town Philadelphia on 18th October – Sid and Nancy withdrew from public view spending each evening holed up in the Chelsea blotting out their miserable existence with a cornucopia of drugs procured with Sid's money from the Max's shows. Sid's celebrity status as a *bona fide* Sex Pistol ensured there was a steady stream of visitors to room 100, to which the couple had recently relocated after having accidentally set fire to the mattress in their old room up on the third floor. During the first week of October, Sid and Nancy's survival fund received a sizable boost following a $20,000 royalty payment from Virgin Records for 'My Way'.

Seeing as neither of them had a US bank account, they stashed the bundles of $100s into the bottom drawer of a bedside cabinet. Having $20,000 – some $100,000 in today's money – burning a hole in their collective pocket meant Nancy was soon on the phone to the drug dealers plying their wares in the El Coyote restaurant, which served as the Chelsea's residents' bar. One of these was hairdresser and wannabe actor Michael 'Rockets Redglare' Morro. Sometime during the early hours of the following morning, Rockets arrived at the Chelsea and made his way up to room 100 where Nancy placed an order for 40 Dilaudid capsules – known as D-4s on the street – and handed over $1600.

For a more detailed account of what happened during the next six hours let us be the first to recommend *No One Is Innocent* (Orion Books). But basically, Sid – who'd been blissfully out for the count having taken enough Tuinol to fell a triceratops on heat – awoke to find a snail-trail of blood leading through into the tiny en-suite bathroom where Nancy, dressed in just her black knickers and bra, lay slumped on the floor between the toilet and washbasin: a knife – his recently-purchased Jaguar K-11 – protruding from her abdomen. The money, of course, was missing.

'Sid was totally out of it that night,' says former Sopranos star Victor Colicchio, who was living at the Chelsea, and actually supplied Nancy with the Tuinol capsules. 'My girlfriend at the time, who was paying the rent, told me that Sid wanted some Tuinol. I was getting them on prescription, you know, and had plenty to go around, so I went down the hall to Sid and Nancy's room where Nancy gave me $60 for a dozen or so capsules, which was way over the current street value. When I happened by some time later, whilst on my way to Neon Leon's room to try to get some pot, I noticed that the door to Sid and Nancy's room was open about six inches and I saw Nancy in discussion with a drug dealer [Steve Cincotti] whom I'd see hanging around there occasionally. Sid was just lying motionless face down on the bed and I kinda figured we wouldn't be seeing much of him until the morning.'

No one has ever been brought to book for Nancy's murder, and for 30 years the events of the 11th and 12th October 1978 have been shrouded in myth, mistruths and mystery; a 'whodunit' for the punk rock cognoscenti. In *No One Is Innocent*, we pretty much laid the smoking gun – or blood-stained knife – at Rockets' door, largely due to his having later boasted to anyone willing to listen – including underground filmmaker Nick Zedd – that he'd killed Nancy to get his hands on Sid's royalty cash, and the $20,000 was certainly missing from the hotel room. Also, the day following Nancy's murder he was seen swanning around the East Village dressed in brand new leather trousers and cowboy boots, buying drinks for everybody, as well as talking about starting up a record label. So it's fair to say that whether he was 100% guilty is up for debate, but certainly his hands weren't totally clean either; after all he had been penniless that previous day. Rockets died in 1999 and never did get around to starting up that record label, while his acting talent never extended beyond a bit part in Madonna's 1985 cinematic debut *Desperately Seeking Susan* (he's the overweight taxi driver that gets stiffed by Madge's character). Many of Rockets' former associates, however, are adamant that he had nothing to do with Nancy's murder and that he actually served as Sid's unofficial bodyguard. The money he was seen throwing around the day following Nancy's murder could have been the $1600 that Nancy had given him for the Dilaudid capsules.

Redglare, of course, wasn't the only Michael in the frame for Nancy's murder. Whilst being interviewed for the *Who Killed Nancy* film, Steve Dior told us that when he was questioned by the NYPD the detectives leading the murder enquiry had more or less admitted to him that they were pretty sure Sid didn't kill Nancy, and were keen to speak to a Michael whom Nancy had apparently befriended shortly before her death. Steve told us exactly what he told the NYPD: he had no idea where this mysterious Michael – whom he described as a skinny blond haired punk kid with a hair-trigger temper and a penchant for blue plaid shirts – came from, or what his relationship was to Nancy. And the guitarist even brought along a recently drawn pencil sketch of the suspected killer for our perusal.

Los Angeles recording studio owner Kathleen Robinson Wirt, who herself attempted to make a documentary about Nancy's murder in the late 80s – and interviewed Elliott Kidd and Arthur Kane for her eventually-shelved project – revealed that shortly after the murder Michael was seen clutching a wad of $100 bills wrapped up in Nancy's crimson hair band. Kathleen also claimed that Michael was still alive and that he had attacked her friend Ned shortly after the murder, and she provided interview footage of Ned – who refused to utter Michael's name to the camera for fear of reprisals – speaking about the attack.

Another possible suspect was Sid and Nancy's colourful Chelsea neighbour 'Neon Leon' Webster, a wannabe rock star and drug addict, who managed to pay the rent by playing the occasional gig at CBGBs and Max's. It was Webster who first planted the suicide pact seed by informing the police that Sid and Nancy had visited him and his go-go dancer/stripper girlfriend Cathi 'Honi' O'Rourke in room 119 at around 9.45 p.m., remaining there until midnight, the time Cathi normally left for work. According to Leon, Sid and Nancy had both appeared overly despondent during their visit and Sid kept dismissing himself as 'a nothing', and that he had 'no future'. Webster's version of events also has the couple bequeathing him their worldly possessions, including Nancy's portfolio of newspaper clippings, several Sex Pistols gold discs and Sid's prized leather motorcycle jacket.

This – like much of what he said about that fateful night – simply doesn't stand up under scrutiny. Even if Sid and Nancy were contemplating suicide, there is no evidence to suggest that his relationship with Sid extended beyond their being neighbours with a shared fondness for drugs, let alone that Sid would choose him as the beneficiary for his worldly chattels before departing for Punk Paradise. Leon told police that following Cathi's departure, Sid and Nancy had returned to their own room and that he'd then gone out to meet up with friends at Max's. Now, Max's Kansas City was something of a second home to Leon and yet no one – not even the bar staff – could validate his story. Fortunately for him, however, one of his friends crawled out of the woodwork to provide an alibi, swearing Leon was with him at another well-known punk rock hangout called The Nursery on 3rd Avenue; otherwise his being in possession of Sid's belongings might have raised some uncomfortable questions down at police headquarters. And Victor Colicchio claims that Leon tried to coerce him into lying to the police about which night Sid had supposedly handed over said items. Leon has pointed out that he could not have been more hassled in the weeks following Nancy's murder, by both the NYPD and the New York Punks, yet his prints are NOT among the six sets of unidentified dabs found by the cops in room 100.

Leon's claim of a suicide pact is supported by Sid's suicide note which referred to a death pact, and that he was simply keeping to his side of the bargain. But was the note – which was conveniently found tucked away in the back pocket of Sid's jeans sometime later – actually penned by Sid?

Yes, we know Sid had already tried to kill himself by slashing his wrists with a broken light bulb whilst staying with his mum at the Hotel Deauville on East 29th Street, and that his letter to Deborah Spungen, written on 30th October, spoke of him killing himself if anything ever happened to Nancy. Also, we mustn't forget his telling *Nationwide*'s on-the-spot reporter Bernard Clarke on 28th November that he wanted to be 'under the ground'. However, the use of generic block capitals as written in the pact note was very uncharacteristic of Sid. Plus, where are the tell-tale girlish curlicues above the 'i's that readily identify Sid's handwriting?

The suicide theory is also supported by the fact that Nancy died from a single one-inch hari-kari-esque stab wound to the lower abdomen. This type of wound is consistent with a self-administered cut, whereas a heat of the moment thrust from Sid, Rockets Redglare, the elusive 'Michael', or any other third-party male would surely have been more severe. Which begs the question, why would Sid and Nancy have been contemplating suicide when they had $20,000 to blow on drugs? Nancy's autopsy, conducted by New York's Associate Medical Examiner Dr Geeta Natarajan, confirmed that she'd died from external and internal haemorrhaging as a result of the stab wound. The wound itself though was not immediately fatal, and Nancy might well have been saved had someone raised the alarm. If a semi-coherent Sid or a third-party intruder had stabbed Nancy then why did she crawl or drag herself into the en-suite bathroom – from where there was no means of escape – instead of calling down to reception to summon help?

Although Dr Natarajan's report failed to provide a specific time of death, it is generally assumed that Nancy was stabbed between 6-7 a.m. and died sometime between 8-10 a.m. In other words, Nancy took two hours to bleed to death, and yet she made no tangible attempt to raise the alarm. The couple's next door neighbour, 48-year-old sculptor Vera Mendelssohn, told police that she'd been wakened at around 7.30 a.m. by strange whimpering sounds emanating through from room 100, yet didn't get up to investigate nor raise the alarm. Then again, Sid's celebrity status as an ex-Sex Pistol, coupled with his and Nancy's penchant for illegal substances, meant strange comings and goings and untoward noises were hardly uncommon in room 100. Were the whimpering noises heard by Mendelssohn Nancy's final death throes?

#

Upon their return from Rio, Steve and Paul had continued working on *Swindle*. Paul's shy and retiring nature meant that his appearances in the film were few and far between; his main moment being the car rape scene featuring Gordon Sumner, a.k.a. Sting from The Police; who used a significant slice of the band's A&M advance to hire a solicitor to have the scene removed. Steve, on the other hand, took to acting like a cat to kippers, playing the film's underpinning role of 'The Crook' dressed like a fictional film-noir detective *à la* Philip Marlowe, whilst trawling through the streets of Soho in search of the elusive Malcolm and the Sex Pistols' missing millions.

When they weren't busy in front of the camera, the two cashed in on their ex-Sex Pistol status by becoming serial liggers on the London live circuit; with Steve going so far as to follow the Clash's 'Out On Parole' tour bus out into the provinces in his newly-acquired BMW. At first, Mick Jones didn't stop to question what his namesake was up to. However, after several such spur of the moment encore appearances he cornered Steve for an explanation and was alarmed to hear that the ex-Sex Pistol was in cahoots with Bernie Rhodes to replace him as guitarist. Nothing ever came of the mooted move, of course, and when the *Swindle* project moved into the editing suite, Steve and Paul accepted Johnny Thunders' invitation to join him in the studio to add their distinctive sound to several songs intended for his debut solo album, *So Alone*. One of these was 'London Boys', which Johnny had penned in response to the Pistols' eponymous anti-New York [Dolls] rant, and contained several less than flattering references to their former band. The pair also guested as part of Thunders' All Stars line-up at London's Lyceum Ballroom on 11th October.

#

On Friday 13th October 1978, whilst Sid was kicking his heels in a holding cell at New York's 51st Precinct station house, having been charged with 2nd degree murder, John's new band Public Image Limited a.k.a. PiL released their eponymous debut Virgin single *Public Image* (VS228). The single was housed in a folded-up newspaper – designed by Dennis Morris – filled with far-fetched and fabricated stories about John and the rest of the band lampooning the tabloids which had wilfully weaved tall tales about John and the Sex Pistols. Those same tabloids – as well as the music press – had been waiting with bated breath for John to emerge from his Gunter Grove parapet and reveal his future plans.

When he finally did so in July he was barely recognisable as the manic-eyed Antichrist that had terrorised the British Establishment twelve months earlier. Not only had he reverted back to his real name, John Lydon, but he'd also shed his spiky ginger locks and put away the Destroy muslins and leather trousers.

Although he'd teamed up with ex-Clash guitarist Keith Levene, John made it abundantly clear to the music press – and anyone else hoping for a Sex Pistols Mark 2 – that the new band's sound would be far removed from punk rock in both style and content. While John had undergone a musical metamorphism, he'd not lost his sense of humour and at one point was considering naming his new band 'The Royal Family'. Another name rumoured to being given some serious consideration at the time was the Carnivorous Butterflies, before he finally settled upon Public Image Limited from the 1968 Muriel Spark novel *The Public Image*.

Despite having had his feeding hand badly mauled once already, John again called upon one of the 'Johns' to play bass in his new band. This time it was Wobble who, like Sid, had never before played the cumbersome instrument. On this occasion John's intuition paid dividends as Wobble proved to be a gifted natural. Their Canadian born drummer, Jim Walker, however, was recruited the time-honoured way via the *Melody Maker*'s 'Musicians Wanted' classifieds. 'He [Walker] was the only drummer I liked from the auditions,' John is quoted as saying on the Fodderstompf website. 'He sounded like Can's drummer [Jaki Liebezeit], all double beats …'

In an interview on the same site, Walker, who was known as 'Donut' having been named James Donat after his French/American grandfather, says that shortly after his arrival in London in October 1977 he was offered the job of replacing Rat Scabies in the Damned. When that particular venture didn't work out he'd laid low through the winter and had then kept tabs on John's movements following the Pistols split. 'I figured he'd be needing a drummer at some point,' he says. Yet, whilst being quizzed about his tenure in PiL by one of the authors backstage at the Marquee in January 1981, while he was playing with the Straps, Walker said that he'd responded to the *Melody Maker* ad having never actually heard of either the Sex Pistols or Johnny Rotten. He was therefore totally nonplussed when he arrived at John's house for a meeting with his new band only to find the place teeming with journalists, all of whom were fawning around the band's frontman. Walker wasn't only a founder member of Public Image Limited, however, he was also a PiL company director. When he quit the band in January 1979 he refused to give up his quarter ownership of the company and continued to collect a share of the profits for several years thereafter until John – and whoever else happened to be on the board at the time – were able to vote him off.

#

Instead of recruiting like-minded musicians to form a band, Steve and Paul chose to keep themselves occupied by joining forces with Thin Lizzy's Phil Lynott, Scott Gorham and Brian Downey to form the Greedy Bastards. The idea was that they would play a few shows in and around London during the summer, but the collaboration carried on throughout the remainder of the year. Industry rumours that the two Sex Pistols 'sidemen' were seriously considering putting a new band together came following the success of 'Silly Thing' (VS256), which Virgin released on 30th March 1979; the third Sex Pistols single lifted from *The Great Rock 'n' Roll Swindle* soundtrack. Somewhat amazingly, the rumours turned out to be true. It wasn't so much a new band, more of a punk supergroup, for Steve and Paul had teamed up with want-away Sham 69 frontman Jimmy Pursey along with the Hersham Boys' bassist Dave 'Kermit' Treganna.

On 29th June, the two joined Sham 69 on stage at the Glasgow Apollo (the show was billed as 'Sham's Last Stand') to perform a three song encore of 'Pretty Vacant', 'White Riot' and 'If The Kids Are United'. The prospect of a 'Sham/Pistols' supergroup ensured plenty of excitement amongst press and fans alike. The four musicians made it as far as the studio and recorded two – officially unreleased – songs together (there is a bootleg in existence): 'Some Play Dirty' and 'Natural Born Killer'. However, the venture fell foul to ego, with Steve and Paul walking out of a recording session having cited the relationship with Pursey as 'worse than working with fuckin' Rotten.'

Speaking of Rotten, Public Image Limited released their debut album *First Issue* (VS114) on Friday 8th December 1978. Somewhat surprisingly, the eight track record – a masterful fusion of funk, reggae and rock – stalled at No.22 on the charts, and was also given a rough ride by the music press: 'And the boy looked at Johnny and shouted "look, ma, the emperor's got no clothes"' was how Pete Silverton over at *Sounds* put it. Needless to say, the fans still turned out in their droves to buy the album, and when rumours began circulating that PiL would be making their live debut with a secret show on the Beaufort Street market roof the following day, hundreds of punks descended upon the place. The police also arrived in numbers, which led to the show being cancelled at the eleventh hour and so the several hundred strong throng headed up the King's Road to Seditionaries in response to another rumour – reportedly started by Malcolm – that the shop was set to close and all the remaining stock would be given away.

The shop was indeed closed, but this was simply due to Vivienne's *blasé* attitude towards business rather than imminent foreclosure.

When Vivienne came out to inform the bargain hunters that there was no foundation to Malcolm's tales and that it would be business as usual at 430 King's Road, a section of the crowd turned angry and looted the shop, making off with £3,000 of stock. It is probably fair to assume that much of the purloined clothing was on display when PiL made their UK live debut fifteen days later on Christmas Day at the Rainbow Theatre, Finsbury Park. The show was marred by sporadic outbursts of not so festive in-fighting between the warring football cliques that made up the thousand strong audience. Despite John haranguing the crowd for continually shouting out for Sex Pistols' songs, the set did include 'Belsen Was A Gas'.

Jim Walker had left the band by the time PiL ventured out into the provinces to headline the Creation for Liberation Concert in aid of Race Today Friendly Society, staged at Manchester Bellevue's King's Hall on Friday, 23rd February 1979. His stand-in for the evening was Vibrators' drummer John 'Eddie' Edwards. As they had in London two months earlier, the band's seven song set featured 'Belsen Was A Gas'. It was three weeks to the day since Sid's death yet John callously chose to ignore his mate's contribution to the song by introducing it, as he had done at the Rainbow, as a 'song that me an' Keith wrote'. Sid was obviously looking down from above, as no sooner had Keith begun to strum the opening chords than he was forced to stop due to problems with the sound.

#

In America, the second day of February is traditionally known as 'Groundhog Day'; the day when Uncle Sam's most fickle furry inhabitant – also known as the woodchuck – emerges from hibernation to determine the coming spring. Should the groundhog happen to see its shadow upon the ground then it would scurry back into its burrow and winter would continue to drag its icy claws across the landscape for another six weeks. For Sid, however, 2nd February would be forever winter. The previous day, like the groundhog, Sid had emerged from the darkness thanks to his lawyer, James 'Jimmy' Merberg, having presented presiding Judge Betty Ellerin with enough evidence to suggest several major inconsistencies in the prosecution's case.

Sid had spent Christmas and New Year in Riker's prison following his assault on Patti Smith's brother Todd in the trendy Manhattan discothèque Hurrahs on West 62nd Street. Smith had taken offence to Sid chatting up his girlfriend and had received a beer glass in the face for his troubles. 'We got him out of there and into a taxi pretty quickly,' Pete Kodick told us. 'But it was a pointless exercise, as there were a dozen witnesses who'd all seen Sid do it. The police arrested him the next morning.' Merberg's diligence, however, would prove to be Sid's downfall. Malcolm was due to fly out to New York on the Sunday, with Steve and Paul, to collect Sid before then heading down to Miami to record an album of rock 'n' roll standards to raise funds for the forthcoming trial. Malcolm had expected the bail hearing to last until late Friday when Sid would then be released into the care of his mother Anne, who would keep him out of trouble over the weekend. As it turned out, Sid was freed by Thursday lunchtime, giving the devil more time to find work for his idle hands.

One of those waiting outside the courthouse with Anne and Michelle Robison (an aspiring actress and low-maintenance groupie with whom Sid was now living despite it contravening his strict bail conditions) was photographer Pete Kodick. 'Sid emerged from the court-house dressed in just his jeans and a grubby I Love New York T-shirt. It's fucking freezing in February in New York and the hotel where his mother was staying was a good ten blocks away. Yet all Sid was interested in was whether Anne had got anything for him. She had, of course, but the stuff she'd got for him was total crap and he asked me to go out and get him something a little bit stronger.' Pete arrived at Michelle's brownstone apartment at 63 Bank Street in Greenwich Village at around 8 p.m., by which time Sid was climbing the walls, despite his latest Riker's Island detox. Also present that fateful evening was Sid and Nancy's friend, photographer Eileen Polk, Jerry Nolan and his girlfriend Esther (Steve Dior's sister), and musicians Howie Pyro and Jerry Only.

Having introduced Pete to his mum as 'the guy who'll be doing my solo album cover' Sid – closely followed by Jerry – whisked Pete off to the bedroom at the end of the lobby. According to Eileen, this was her cue to leave, but as she, Howie and Jerry were heading for the door they heard strange – yet somehow familiar – noises emanating from behind the bedroom door. Upon entering the bedroom Eileen found Sid lying prostrate on the bed. Anne, being little more than a glorified tourist, meant she'd had no idea who was holding, whereas Pete had served his rock 'n' roll apprenticeship as Keith Richards' personal drug mule and knew exactly where to score some quality brown sugar. Therein lay the problem, as the heroin Pete had procured was almost 100% pure, and although he only gave Sid a small dose, Sid's freshly detoxed body couldn't cope with the hit and he OD'd. 'He was as sick as a dog,' Pete told us. 'We managed to revive him by plying him with cups of tea and cigarettes and frog-marching him around the room. I stayed until around 2 a.m., and he certainly didn't do any more drugs whilst I was there, because I'd given the rest to his mum.'

The official version of what happened during the small hours of Friday, 2nd February 1979, is that Sid woke up and, having filched the heroin stash from the sleeping Anne's pocket, he returned to the bedroom to cook up the hit which sent him into the gossamer-winged hereafter. Another, rather more disturbing, version is that Anne – fearing that Malcolm wouldn't be able to clear her son of the 2nd degree murder charge – purposely gave Sid the heroin to spare him the horrors of America's harsh penal system. Although Anne never actually came out and said 'yes, I gave him the fatal dose', she more than hinted at such over many a long night drinking.

The evidence that she at least helped Sid on his way was provided by New York's Chief Medical Examiner Dr Michael Baden, who carried out the autopsy. Upon arriving at the scene and examining the body, Dr Baden quickly ascertained that the fatal dose had to have been administered much more recently than either Michelle or Anne had stated. Michelle, who'd woken up to find Sid dead in bed beside her, was still hysterical and had been sobbing uncontrollably since Sergeant Richard Houseman – the first police officer at the scene – responded to the call, whereas it was only when Baden threw doubt on the women's version of events that Anne's veneer cracked. Much to Houseman's astonishment, Anne became aggressive and launched into a seemingly well-rehearsed mantra about her now being the sole executive for her dead son's estate. Instead of charging Anne with at least 'aiding and abetting a suicide', as Houseman was seriously considering, the NYPD listed Sid's death as suicide which also, all too conveniently, closed the book on Nancy's murder.

Thanks to the endeavours of a diligent young female Philadelphian – who wishes to remain anonymous for obvious reasons – we have a copy of the NYPD's case file on Nancy's murder. The file,

Gold Who Killed Bambi – French Swindle *back cover*

which is woefully incomplete and riddled with typographical errors, contains reports from the officers at the scene as well as several never-before-seen photographs. Two of these – listed as 'suspect arrest' photos – show Sid standing within the door frame of room 100 with bloodied hands and a bemused look on his face; a horrific close-up of Nancy's bloodied body slumped between the sink and toilet, and three shots of the room's dishevelled interior. Had Sid lived long enough to go to trial then the NYPD would have followed three main avenues of investigation: was it Sid, suicide, or someone else? The Bellevue's medical records – along with the recently ordained minister Victor Colicchio's testimony – reveal that Sid was away with the Tuinol fairies at the time of Nancy's demise. And, unless New York's finest helped themselves to Sid's royalty advance then the missing money blows a magnum-sized hole in the suicide theory; which leaves us with 'someone else'.

Here's where the speculation is never-ending. Rockets Redglare was a low-rent drug dealer, not a chemistry major, and forty

Dilaudids wasn't your average run-of-the-mill order. He would have had to put the word out beyond his usual suppliers, and news of Sid and Nancy's royalty nest egg would have hit the streets in a New York minute. Whilst *Who Killed Nancy* doesn't solve the case by conclusively laying the blame at any one particular door, what it shows is that Sid is entirely innocent of the crime. Nobody deserves to go to their grave accused of a murder they didn't commit: not even a strung-out Sex Pistol.

#

December 1979 saw Steve and Paul again team up with the boys from Thin Lizzy to resurrect the Greedy Bastards. This time the five wise men went into the studio to record the Christmas single 'A Merry Jingle', which was released that same month through Vertigo Records, a subsidiary of Thin Lizzy's label Phonogram. In order to ensure plenty of festive airplay during the build-up to Xmas, they prudently truncated their name to 'The Greedies'. Now that Steve and Paul had finally shed their Sex Pistols' personas, they had no objection to making a 20th December 'live' studio appearance on *Top Of The Pops*. On 31st December, with the Lizzy boys due to return to their day jobs, the curtain came down on The Greedies career with a final appearance on Kenny Everett's New Year's Eve TV Special: *Will Kenny Everett Make It To 1980?*

The New Year saw Steve and Paul dust off their equity cards and accompany Clash bassist Paul Simonon out to Canada to star in the Lou Adler film: *Ladies And Gentlemen – The Fabulous Stains*. The Fabulous Stains were a fictional all-girl teenage punk band (featuring future Jurassic Park star Laura Dern) who go out on the road opening for The Looters, a 'washed-up dirty Punk Rock band' played by Steve, the two Pauls, and Scum star Ray 'Johnny Strummer' Winstone.

In July 1980, Steve and Paul teamed up with Lightning Raiders' bassist Andy Allen, to form the Professionals. Despite failing to trouble the charts, the three-piece band's debut single 'Just Another Dream' (VS353) received favourable reviews, but by this time Steve was dabbling with heroin, which meant inevitable delays with the album. The follow-up single, '1-2-3' (VS379), was released at the beginning of October, and gave the Professionals their one and only chart placing; a lowly No. 43.

By the time that the band went out on tour later that same month, Allen had been replaced by ex-Subway Sect bassist Paul Myers, and Ray McVeigh was brought in as an additional guitarist. Allen wouldn't have to wait long to get his revenge, however, for that November Virgin issued *Cash Cows*, a budget priced sampler album featuring one promo track from each of the twelve records the label intended to release during the opening months of the coming year. The album's first track was the Professionals' 'Kick Down The Doors', and the bassist not only won an injunction against Virgin for releasing the song without his permission, but also received overdue payment for his contribution to 'Silly Thing'. Virgin was forced to reissue *Cash Cows* with the Magazine number 'A Song From Under The Floorboards' replacing 'Kick Down The Doors', as well as having to amend the album's artwork.

Nothing was heard of the Professionals until the following June when Virgin released the single 'Join The Professionals' (VS426), which was hardly new material as the tune was a reworking of one of the songs Steve and Paul had contributed to the *Fabulous Stains* film. In October, after making a rare UK appearance at the Leeds Futurama Festival, the band embarked on a US tour, which was derailed indefinitely when the two Pauls and Ray McVeigh were all supposedly seriously injured in a car smash in Minnesota on 5th November. Rumour has it that this was merely a smoke and mirrors ploy to mask the true depth of Steve's heroin addiction, as two days after the alleged crash a perfectly healthy Paul Cook strolled into Virgin's London offices on the hunt for an overdue Sex Pistols royalty cheque. And if the drug rumour is nothing more than a fallacy, then why is it that three band members sustained serious injuries yet Steve walked away from the accident without so much as a scratch? Somewhat ironically, given what was purported to have occurred in Minnesota, the Professionals long-awaited album *I Didn't See It Coming* (V2220) had been released at the beginning of the month. The album received positive reviews, but with three members supposedly recovering from their injuries the band was unable to go out on tour to promote the album.

In April 1982, the Professionals kick-started their second US tour with a show at the Keystone Berkeley in Los Angeles. The Clash, who also happened to be touring America to promote their fifth studio album *Combat Rock*, had invited the band to open for them on several dates. The Clash were enjoying mainstream success in the US, and this was an opportunity for the Professionals to play in front of sizable and appreciative audiences, but Steve and Paul were too proud to accept what they considered to be a hand-out from a band that had once played second fiddle to them. That, of course, had been way back when, and this was very much now. So, whilst the Clash continued to rock the colonial Kasbahs, the Professionals were left to wallow in their wake. Following the band's final low-key US date in New York, rather than return to the UK with the others, Steve decided to chance his arm in America which effectively called time on the Professionals.

#

Saturday 31st May 1979, saw John return to centre stage when he was invited to appear on the BBC's rejuvenated '60s music show *Juke Box Jury* hosted by Noel Edmonds. Aside from flirting with fellow judge Elaine Page, John cast his caustic opinion on several of that particular week's single releases; including 'Playground Mystery', the latest offering from Siouxsie and the Banshees, which wasn't all that far removed from PiL's supposedly innovative sound. The BBC had invited John onto the show to boost ailing viewing figures and purposely chose to introduce him as 'Johnny Rotten' rather than John Lydon. The director was willing to turn a blind eye to John keeping a pint of Guinness nefariously nestled out of site of the camera, but he took exception to the singer donning his straw boater. John, however, took equal exception to one of the studio hands attempting to take back the offending headgear and stormed off set. 'I set out to end that programme and I thought I succeeded.' He later commented. 'They didn't like me at all. I was meant to look a fool. They cut the bit where I was talking to the audience; didn't like that. Quite frankly, it's the most awful goddamn programme in the world.'

On 29th June 1979, by which time former 101'ers drummer Richard 'Snakehips' Dudanski had joined the line-up, Virgin released PiL's second single *Death Disco* (VS274). John may have penned the song as a lament to the recent passing of his mother Eileen, but to the press it was little more than a meandering tuneless dirge. The *NME* rather uncharitably described the tune as 'a dog-eared disco-reggae fusion [that] emerges as a lethal dose of psychedelic eclecticism which makes the Plastic Ono Band's doodlings sound positively sing-a-long'. The band's third single *Memories* (VS299), released on 10th October – by which time Dudanski had left the revolving drummer's stool to be replaced by Martin Atkins – also failed to trouble the charts, but was enthusiastically received by the music press; *Sounds* going as far as to cite *Memories* as 'PiL's most aggressive record to date'.

Their second album *Metal Box* (Metal 1), which consisted of three 12" singles housed within a metal film canister, fared only slighter better than its predecessor by reaching No. 18 on the UK album chart. The music press was also impressed, with the *NME*'s Angus MacKinnon stating 'All this forward flow in twelve months – it's almost frightening. PiL are miles out and miles ahead. Follow with care.' The album was reissued in the usual format on 22nd February 1980 as *Second Issue* (VD2512) and reached a respectable No. 46 on the chart.

On Monday, 5th February 1980, nearly three years after Bob Harris came under attack at the Speakeasy for refusing to have the Sex Pistols on his show, John finally got to make his appearance on *The Old Grey Whistle Test*'s stage. The band performed two numbers: 'Poptones' and 'Careering' with John reading the lyrics straight from the *Second Edition* album sleeve. Had Harris relented? Had he heck as like. He wasn't presenting the show by this time, but his successor, Ann Nightingale, described their appearance as 'the most powerful performance I ever saw on Whistle Test'.

In April, PiL flew out to Boston for the opening concert of a 10 date US tour. As it was their first foray to the US, Warner Bros wanted the band to play 40 shows but by this time John had developed a deep loathing for touring and refused to play ball. In June, the band suffered a setback when drummer Martin Atkins announced he was leaving PiL to concentrate on his own band, Brian Brain, but fans were in for a bigger shock when Jah Wobble announced his departure from the fold on 5th July. John may have grown tired of touring, but Wobble believed it was an integral part of being in a band and headed off to do his own thing. The first post-Wobble PiL single, 'Flowers Of Romance' (VS397), was released on 27th March 1981. Whilst John may have delved into his past for the song's title, its cutting-edge cello'd bass and drum sound was definitely of the now and augured well for the future. On 5th September 1983, PiL released 'This Is Not A Love Song' (VS529), which would not only give the band its biggest UK chart hit, but would also prove to be Keith Levene's swansong.

On 26th October, by which time Levene had departed the band, John held a press conference at the Royal Lancaster Hotel in

London to promote the film *Order Of Death* [a.k.a. *Copkiller*] in which he starred alongside Harvey Keitel, as well as to announce PiL's forthcoming UK and European tour commencing on 2nd November at Brighton's Top Rank. Two days later, fans got the chance to sample PiL's new 'keyboard cabaret' sound when the band appeared on Channel 4's flagship music show *The Tube*. Amongst the songs performed was a less than par version of 'Anarchy In The UK'.

CHAPTER FIFTEEN

Who Killed Russ Meyer?

'In the final analysis you have to be a man ...
Otherwise you ain't worth shit if you don't really finally
stand up to something; something you believe in'
Russ Meyer

On Sunday, 25th May 1980, Malcolm's cinematic dreams finally came to fruition when *The Great Rock 'n' Roll Swindle* was premiered at the Sex Pistols' former stomping ground, the Screen On The Green cinema in Islington. The first draft of what ultimately became *The Great Rock 'n' Roll Swindle* was registered with The Screen Writers Guild of America, West, Inc, during the first week of July 1977 under the fairly obvious title of *Anarchy In The UK*. The screenplay was credited to Pulitzer Prize-winning American movie critic and screenwriter Roger Ebert, from an original story by Malcolm McLaren, Rene Daalder, Rory Johnston, Russ Meyer, Johnny Speight and Ebert himself.

According to Malcolm's biographer, Craig Bromberg, Malcolm's first port of call had been comedian Peter Cook, whom he had encountered the previous summer at the Granada TV studios in Manchester when Cook and the Sex Pistols had appeared on *So It Goes*. However, no mention is ever made of Graham Chapman's involvement in the initial scriptwriting process, but the ex-Monty Python member was brought in to work alongside Johnny Speight on a storyline earlier that summer, while Malcolm was otherwise occupied in trying to do a deal with Shepperton Studios. The deal was in regard to the studio's ownership of the sets used in the Oscar winning 1968 musical version of Charles Dickens novel *Oliver*, which bizarrely enough were still standing on the studio's back lot. As *Anarchy In The UK* told the tale of a gang of street urchins who form a rock n' roll band – with Malcolm typecast as the band's Fagin-esque manager – he saw the old Dickensian sets as the perfect backdrop for his film.

Having decided to put the Sex Pistols' tale up on the silver screen, Malcolm set about looking for someone to direct his opus. He thought he'd found his man in 28-year-old London Film School graduate Don Boyd. He ran his newly established production company Boyd's Co. from Berwick Street in Soho; a stone's throw away from the Sex Pistols' Denmark Street HQ. Upon graduating from the LFS in 1970, Boyd had landed a job working on the BBC's long-running science and technology series *Tomorrow's World*, and then moved into directing TV commercials for a couple of years, before making his first full-length feature film *Intimate Reflections*, which premiered at the London Film Festival in 1974.

However, it was his follow-up film 1976's *East Of Elephant Rock* starring John Hurt that brought him to the attention of his peers with trade magazine *Variety* going so far as to hail him the '**WHIZ KID IN BRIT PIX BIZ**'. Boyd was aware of the Sex Pistols long before their appearance on *Today* thanks to his associate Michael Dempsey's friendship with Jamie Reid. Boyd reckons Malcolm was only interested in making the most commercial movie possible: something along the lines of Frank Tachlin's 1956 rock 'n' roll rom-com *The Girl Can't Help It* starring Jayne Mansfield and Tom Ewell. He also wanted a script brimming with bawdy British working-class humour as typified by the recently defunct BBC series *'Til Death Us Do Part* starring Warren Mitchell and Dandy Nichols. Indeed, it was Boyd who put Malcolm in touch with the series' creator Johnny Speight who readily agreed to write a script for £25,000. Boyd's involvement in the film, however, proved short-lived for he'd insisted on complete creative control over the project, and Malcolm – despite giving assurances – was never going to be able to comply. This parting of the ways also called time on Speight and Chapman's brief encounter with the Sex Pistols.

#

It was Boyd's departure that paved the way for legendary American soft-porn filmmaker, and ex-US Army combat photographer, Russ Meyer to enter the post-production picture. The then 55-year-old Meyer – who died in September 2004, aged 82 – had first started out making industrial short films for clients such as Southern Pacific and Standard Oil, before making his first feature-length film *The Immoral Mr. Teas* in 1959. The film, which was inspired in part by Jacques Tati's *Monsieur Hulot's Holiday* of six years earlier, was shot like an old silent picture with a mock-documentary feel, which led one reviewer to label the film 'Tati with tits!' By this time, of course, Meyer had also established himself as something of a photographer with his work appearing in both *Playboy* and the long-defunct *Adam* magazine; his stock-in-trade being known as 'nudie cuties'.

Over the ensuing years, Meyer had written, directed, and distributed a further twenty-four 'sexploitation' films including *Mudhoney* (1965), *Faster, Pussycat! Kill! Kill!* (1965), *Mondo Topless* (1966), *Vixen* (1968) and *Beyond The Valley Of The Dolls* (1970), each of which featured an abundance of naturally large-breasted honeys such as the 39DD-cupped Anita Ekberg, and the equally well-endowed Tura Santana, which earned him the title: 'King Of The Nudies'. His most recent offering, *Up* (1976), however, was the first Meyer film to feature girls with surgically-enhanced boobs.

The original *Anarchy In The UK* script, which runs to just eighty pages, credits Meyer as director with Malcolm named as producer. The original script also lists the film as a Matrixbest production, which is the first mention anywhere of the new company Malcolm had set up to incorporate Glitterbest's cinematic projects. Accompanying the first draft is a simple two page biography. Not of the Sex Pistols or Russ Meyer, as one might have expected but of Malcolm himself; his rise from humble beginnings as a King's Road haberdasher, through to his having effectively swindled three record companies out of substantial amounts of cash for a band that couldn't actually play (yes, that old chestnut!), and who was now finding his feet in the film industry.

'Malcolm had pretty much lost interest in the band as a working unit once they'd inked a deal with Virgin,' ex-road manager Nils Stevenson recalled shortly before his unexpected death in 2002. 'He knew full well that he'd burned his bridges in terms of scamming record companies and so he handed the mundane day-to-day running of the band over to Sophie Richmond, Boogie, Sue Steward and Roadent. The shop [Let It Rock/SEX/Seditionaries] had always been regarded as Vivienne's baby anyway and anyone who knew Malcolm knew his dream had always been to make a film. He was determined to follow the example of Brian Epstein and Peter Grant by turning his boys [Sex Pistols] into film stars. After all, bands come and bands go, but film stars last forever.'

Russ Meyer may have been interested in adding some tits and Tinseltown to the Sex Pistols' already salacious tale, but much of the initial script was simply unusable and ended up being shelved. The most notable scene, of course, being the one where Sid shot heroin with his mother – to be played, if legend is to be believed, by '60s siren Marianne Faithful – before then shagging her on the family bed. But while Sid was happy for any excuse to cook up a little brown sugar, he – probably at Nancy's insistence – drew the line at bonking the woman who was Mick Jagger's old flame.

#

On Sunday 3rd July 1977, the day following the release of 'Pretty Vacant', Malcolm flew out to Los Angeles to meet up with Russ Meyer at the producer's palatial home nestled high up in the Hollywood Hills. With the Sex Pistols about to embark on a two week tour of Scandinavia, Malcolm was free to stay in LA for as long as it took to knock a script into shape. However, instead of booking himself into a hotel, he arrived at LAX fully expecting a little southern Californian hospitality. Whilst Meyer was happy to work with Malcolm, he felt his prospective British business partner would be better suited staying with someone closer to his own age; someone with similar interests.

That someone was his screen-writing protégé Rene Daalder, a 32-year-old blond-haired Dutch *émigré*, who, like Malcolm, had a passion for fashion and vintage rock 'n' roll. The two got on well together and quickly put together a sixty page treatment for Meyer's perusal. However, the tale of a supposedly incorruptible band [Sex Pistols] being led astray by a smooth-talking, beguiling manager [Malcolm] set against a backdrop of dole queues and dark depression [Britain *circa* July 1977] was not to Meyer's liking. He therefore enlisted the services of old friend Roger Ebert, the *Chicago Sun-Times* film critic. Ebert – who'd written Meyer's most successful film to date: *Beyond The Valley Of The Dolls* – was to add a little voyeurism and violence to the script. The then 35-year-old Ebert duly accepted the challenge and invited Malcolm to his suite at the legendary rock 'n' roll guest house, the Sunset Marquis Hotel on North Alta Loma Road in West Hollywood, where the pair knocked up a script tentatively called *Who Killed Bambi?*

Beyond The Valley Of The Dolls featured a fictitious all-girl rock band, the Carrie Nations, which Ebert used to attack Hollywood's hierarchy (read: Meyer's directorial detractors). Although his amended treatment of the Pistols' film loosely followed their rock 'n' roller-coaster rise from the London gutter to battle Britain's establishment elite, it contained several typical Meyer subplots to titillate and tantalise a wider-reaching audience. As Meyer's film characters were often larger than life, Ebert exaggerated each Sex Pistol's on-screen persona; particularly that of Sid, who was transformed into a cartoon-esque caricature. This may have added a kick to the mix, but would ultimately prove too demanding an image for the bassist to live up to.

Malcolm's Machiavellian qualities were also expanded for the band's fictitious manager, P.T. Proby – a talent spotter *à la* Simon Cowell – which no doubt planted the seed in Malcolm's egotistical mind that he was the manipulative puppet master in control of all the strings. And as every film has to have a 'baddie' for the audience to hate, Ebert conceived the character M.J. [Mick Jagger?], a famous rock star – and P.T. Proby's leading client – who earns the audience's enmity by attempting to co-opt the Sex Pistols' act to salvage his own ailing career. The idea to name the character M.J. might have related to a real-life incident where Mick Jagger had paid a visit to Seditionaries. According to John, the Stones' flamboyant frontman had spent several minutes pacing up and down along the King's Road directly across from the shop as though summoning up the courage to cross the threshold, only for John to slam the door in his face.

It is fair to say that had Russ Meyer remained at the directorial helm then *Who Killed Bambi?* would probably be regarded as something of a 'cult classic' amongst today's cinema cognoscenti; a sort of *Rocky Horror Show* for the punk generation. This eventuality, of course, never came to pass, yet despite reports that Meyer only oversaw one day's filming, the truth of the matter is that the American was on set for four days during October 1977. He only got one finished scene in the can though; that of M.J. (now renamed B.J. to avoid a potential libel suit), slaying a fawn with a steel-tipped arrow. This was filmed at the Queen's Game Reserve in the picturesque Wye Valley nestled on the border between England and Wales. In this now-legendary scene, a wide-eyed young innocent cries out: 'Mummy, Mummy, come quickly, they've killed Bambi!'. Actually, the little girl wasn't the only one horrified at the slaughter, as several members of the crew walked off set in protest at what they saw as little more than gratuitous bloodletting.

Young Flesh Required

By the time the crew had been appeased, however, Meyer – having discovered there was no more cash in the kitty – had stormed off the set, returning to the plush river-view flat in Chelsea's Cheyne Walk that Malcolm had leased for him and his girlfriend. He only stayed long enough to pack his bags, and headed for Heathrow vowing to 'sue Malcolm's ass!' Upon returning to Hollywood, Meyer promptly forgot all about Malcolm (whom he uncharitably nick-named 'Hitler'), the Sex Pistols, and whoever it was that was supposed to have killed Bambi, instead concentrating all his efforts on editing his latest nudie flick *Beneath the Valley of the Ultra Vixens* for cinema release. Shortly before the film was due to be released (1979), rumours began circulating along the grapevine about how Meyer had supposedly 'borrowed' certain ideas from the aborted *Bambi* script. However, these rumours were totally unjustified as Meyer had shot the entire film before leaving for London. Although the American never saw so much as a penny-piece of his £30,000 fee he, somewhat surprisingly, never followed through with his legal threat.

Malcolm would later attempt to belittle Meyer by circulating a tale about how he'd been forced to part company with the American on account of the latter's intent on making *Who Killed Bambi?* into a 'soft, soapy, kinda sexy *A Hard Day's Night*'. At the time though he was desperate to appease Meyer at any cost and frantically urged Sandy Lieberson – head of London-based international production and marketing at 20th Century Fox, who had taken over the film when Meyer got involved – to procure the requisite funds by any means necessary. Unfortunately for Malcolm, however, Meyer wasn't the only American to become disillusioned with the project. Lieberson may have managed to cajole his stateside boss Alan Ladd Jr (son of diminutive *Shane* star, Alan Ladd) to approve the initial £150,000 funding by purposely playing down the by-now omnipresent controversy surrounding the Sex Pistols in the UK, but when the costs began to rise so did Ladd's blood pressure.

Indeed, several prominent members of Fox's board – including former actress Princess Grace of Monaco – were unwilling to risk having Fox's name tarnished by a pop group, and told Ladd in no uncertain terms to pull the plug on the film. The UK press, of course, had a field day with the news that the Sex Pistols had managed to ruffle royal feathers, albeit those of a princess from a Mediterranean principality, for the second time in six months: **'PISTOLS SEXY FILM HAS PRINCESS IN A RAGE'** the Evening

Toyko Shinkiba Sex Pistols tour poster

Standard gleefully reported. 'You have to admit it made great copy,' Roadent cackles today. 'I mean, it's not every day you get your wings clipped by a princess, is it? She [Princess Grace] might have once dialled *M for Murder* [the 1954 Alfred Hitchcock classic in which she starred alongside Ray Milland], but she wasn't likely to be dialling M for Malcolm.'

#

Malcolm may have had Fox's £150,000 pay-off nestling within Glitterbest's coffers, but he was still forced to put the film on temporary hiatus until fresh funding arrived following the release of *Never Mind The Bollocks*. There was also the small matter of finding a new director now that Meyer was out of the frame. His initial idea was to tempt Rene Daalder over to London, but the Dutchman was savvy enough to know where his loyalties – and future pay cheques – lay, suggesting that Malcolm try pitching the idea to American director Jonathan Kaplan and screenwriter Danny Opatoshu, both of whom he'd worked with on various projects in recent years. Kaplan and Opatoshu were both graduates of the New York University (NYU) Film School where they'd studied under the tutelage of now-legendary director Martin Scorsese. Upon graduation, the two had followed the master out to Hollywood and had worked with Roger Corman's New World Pictures on films such as *Night Call Nurses*.

Despite having been sent several Sex Pistols demo tapes – as well as various newspaper clippings detailing the band's anarchic antics – Kaplan and Opatoshu arrived in London on 5th November with little understanding of the Pistols, the English punk scene, or what kind of film Malcolm was intent on making. Several days in Malcolm's company, and being what they would latterly describe as 'Malcolmised', the duo quickly realised that there was to be but one star of the Sex Pistols show – that was Malcolm himself.

With newly incumbent producer Jeremy Thomas ready to roll, and Kaplan checking out the studio sets, Opatoshu locked himself away in his hotel room and set about knocking up an eleven page treatment for the now untitled film. This, however, was far easier said than done, because with the possible exception of Elvis and Cliff Richard – who were both groomed for their roles – rock stars are musicians, not actors, and therefore can't be expected to learn reams of dialogue to be delivered on cue. John, Paul, George and Ringo may have enjoyed seeing themselves up on the silver screen, but the Sex Pistols were an entirely different proposition altogether. Opatoshu also had to come up with a script that would prove acceptable to the band and their burgeoning fan base, if the film's new financiers were ever going to see a return on their investment.

With this in mind, Opatoshu kept the new treatment close to Meyer's and Ebert's original script. But with *Bambi* having literally been laid to rest, the new treatment opened with a commercial extolling the delights of Swinging London, before dissolving into a shot of the four Sex Pistols loitering with disinterested intent within the fictional setting of 'Dead End', a Dickensian-esque slum area where ragged-arsed kids roam the streets in search of their next meal, while tourists snap their cameras from atop a double-decker bus. In the rewrite, B.J., the artist formerly known as 'M.J.' has been renamed Rod Bollocks, and the ageing rock dinosaur returns from his tax exile hideaway to find his plush pad has been taken over by the Pistols. When he complains to 'Derek', the chief executive of his record company, Mamie Records, the savvy Derek forlornly attempts to sign the Pistols to his label.

To a certain extent, Opatoshu's treatment mirrors the Pistols meteoric rise to stardom, as well as the band's brushes with the

Establishment. Unlike Whitehall's shadowy powers-that-be who attempted to neuter the Sex Pistols' threat to the status quo by prohibiting them from playing live and banning their records, Opatoshu's fictional oligarchs – realising they couldn't stamp punk out – elected to absorb it into the system. They arrange for the subservient Derek to kidnap Rotten, thereby fragmenting the band to maximise its commercial value, but, as in real life, the singer proved he was nobody's puppet by hurling himself out of Derek's office window.

Opatoshu's pen would prove uncomfortably prophetic, for as Rotten plummets to his death the screen fills with a montage of images of what will happen once punk is assimilated into the system: American TV moneymen selling punk kits to the masses; over the hill actors donning punk paraphernalia whilst performing 'Karaoke In The UK' at the local Holiday Inn; a stereotypical British nuclear family with mum and dad sporting spiky hair, safety pins and bondage apparel; and finally, the four Sex Pistols being knighted by the Queen at Buckingham Palace. Needless to say, Rotten's blood and brains don't end up redecorating the pavement as the singer is inadvertently saved by the Union Jack flag hanging outside Mamie Records. When he finally drops to the ground, to find himself back in Dead End, the other Pistols inform him that this was no dream, and that the Queen would be unveiling a statue in the band's honour in the newly-dedicated Pistol Park. Rotten, however, has other ideas and as the credits roll, he and the other Pistols – having commandeered the tourists' double-decker bus – hurtle through Pistol Park spraying the ceremonial gathering with machine-gun fire and hand-grenades.

Opatoshu's treatment got the seal of approval from both Malcolm and Jeremy Thomas, and he and Kaplan met with all the interested parties to start planning pre-production. Up until this point, the Americans had acted on trust, but as things were about to move up a gear they felt they should get something down on paper. However, despite Malcolm's assurances that the contracts were being drawn up and that the pair would be paid the $10,000 they felt they were owed for their efforts thus far, they – like Russ Meyer – were to be left disappointed and equally empty-handed. For Malcolm no longer felt a narrative film was the way forward and suggested having the Sex Pistols play a concert in some remote northern outpost such as Northumberland, warn the local constabulary in advance, and film the inevitable confrontation between fans and police. Kaplan and Opatoshu were dumbfounded at the idea. They may have been relatively new to movie-making, but they recognised a shyster when they saw one. For Kaplan it was the final straw: 'At that point I knew I had to leave,' Kaplan told Craig Bromberg in *The Wicked Ways of Malcolm McLaren*. 'I flew back to Los Angeles and left Danny to deal with the last details.' But before departing for Heathrow he suggested Malcolm give the project to Julien Temple.

#

Temple, whose follow-up feature film was the 1986 musical *Absolute Beginners* (based on Colin MacInnes's book of the same name, set amid the London race riots of September 1958), may have been a novice in terms of directorial experience, but the then 22-year-old was a veteran in terms of understanding Malcolm's mindset, having spent the previous eighteen months filming the Sex Pistols in one capacity or another. Although the film's financial backers were understandably anxious at the decision to let an absolute beginner loose on set, Malcolm was content to sit back and see what Temple would bring to the party. After all, he'd been equally naïve in terms of managerial experience when first taking the Sex Pistols under his wing, and yet now they were currently the most famous band on the planet. Of course, by the time Temple came on board the Sex Pistols had already imploded, there was no script to speak of, and very little money in the kitty despite Malcolm having secured a £100,000 publishing deal with Warner Bros before the band embarked on their fateful US tour.

Nevertheless, the Young Turk readily accepted the carrot and accompanied Malcolm to Rio de Janeiro to join up with Steve and Paul in late January 1978. As he filmed Steve and Paul sailing down the Amazon with a punked-up Ronnie Biggs crooning his amended lyrics to 'Belsen Was A Gas', he could never in his worst nightmare have imagined that he would end up being held as 'human insurance' by the local mafia for four nerve-racking weeks, until Malcolm stumped up the cash for the hired instruments the trio had thrown overboard at the song's finale. When he finally made it back to London he discovered that in his enforced absence Malcolm had scrapped the feature-film idea and reverted back to his original idea of making a documentary.

With Danny Opatoshu's idea left to gather dust alongside those for *Anarchy In The UK* and *Who Killed Bambi?* Malcolm and Temple set about ferreting out every bit of footage relating to the Sex Pistols. Once the pair returned from Paris with footage in the can of Sid performing 'My Way' and generally making a nuisance of himself in the French capital's Jewish Quarter, they settled down to begin work on a new treatment. Malcolm's initial idea was to tell the Sex Pistols story – with Rotten reduced to a virtual-reality figure only appearing in the live footage – from the band's humble beginnings through to their tumultuous US tour finale at Winterland; bringing the film to a triple-whammy climax by metaphorically killing off each of the other three members in risible turn. Sid was to bow out in a blaze of glory crashing his motorcycle whilst flashing 'v's to the cows in the surrounding fields; 'Serial Shagger' Steve was to lose his manhood whilst parachuting from an aeroplane, while poor old Paul was to be car-jacked – in more ways than one – by the members of a rival, and fictional, band the Fabulous Blow-Waves, fronted by the not-yet-famous Sting.

Indeed, Temple actually got as far as shooting the car-rape scene before Malcolm turned on an unexpected tangent by deciding he was the one best-suited to tell the Pistols' story. After all, he'd been present at the band's inception, and he was there to witness its demise. He, more than anyone, was aware of how the myths, legends and mistruths surrounding the Sex Pistols meant that the majority of the band's fans – not to mention the Great British public at large – had only a vague idea as to what had really gone on behind the scenes during their short yet highly eventful career. History was written by winners, and with scant regard for the efforts of John, Paul, Steve, Sid, or indeed Glen, he handed Temple a revised treatment tentatively titled *The Great Rock 'n' Roll Swindle.* In this version Malcolm, the self-styled 'Embezzler' told a (ludicrously embellished) tale of how he, through his manufactured creation the Sex Pistols, invented 'the Punk Rock', and swindled the record industry out of £1 million.

In order to deliver his on-screen revised version of events, which saw Steve recast as 'The Crook', Sid 'The Gimmick', Paul (rather uncharitably) dubbed 'The Tea-Maker', and John vilified as 'The Collaborator', Malcolm chose to wear a full-body rubber gimp suit complete with inflated headwear. The on-screen image was mesmerising, but the Seditionaries gimp suit wasn't designed to be worn under harsh studio lighting and Malcolm could only deliver a few lines at a time for fear of being slowly broiled in his own sweat.

#

Fans would have to wait twenty-one years until the release of *The Filth And The Fury* in 2001, also directed by Temple, to get an 'in-house' accurate account of how the Sex Pistols earned, not swindled, close to £1million. *The Great Rock 'n' Roll Swindle* would be panned by both purists and critics alike but to us humble fans, entering our local cinema to watch a feature film on the Sex Pistols was akin to crossing the threshold of Willy Wonka's fabled chocolate factory. Whilst we readily concede that at least ten per cent of TGRNRS is utter shite, where else were we going to get to feast our eyes on previously unseen footage, such as that of the Pistols performing at Andrew Logan's Valentine's Party from February '76, the Jubilee Boat Party and the '78 US tour? Not to mention the promo videos for both 'God Save The Queen' and 'Pretty Vacant'.

With John refusing to have anything to do with TGRNRS, and Sid barely able to function without either Nancy or a needle, the in-house acting was – aside from occasional Cookie cameos which included providing the vocals on 'Silly Thing' – largely left to Malcolm and Steve. Indeed, Malcolm proved himself something of a natural in front of the camera, and his performance – which included his rendition of Max Bygraves' 1958 hit You Need Hands – was highly amusing. As the Sex Pistols were pure Vaudeville, as John likened the band in the opening segment of *The Filth And The Fury,* TGRNRS – Sid's death apart, of course – was always going to be a slapstick comedic offering.

Malcolm ensured more mirth by bringing in renowned British comedy actress Irene Handl to play the doddering cinema usherette who gets more than she bargains for when she attempts to dampen Steve's ardour for his latest conquest, played by porn star Mary Millington. A self-confessed Bee Gees fan, Mary had no idea who the Pistols were, even after her agent John M East had given her the low down! But Mary was hired to get naked and learn a few lines, a role which she'd been playing for years.

The then 77-year-old Irene, who was best known for her role as the malapropism-prone Ada Cresswell in the early '70s Thames

TV sit-com *For The Love Of Ada*, was seen as everybody's favourite grandma. Fans could be forgiven for thinking Steve's outburst: 'What do you want, you cunt?' upon emerging from between Mary's suspender and stocking-clad legs was later added to the scene so as not to offend the sensitive ears of the septuagenarian actress. Not so, according to Temple. Irene, whenever off camera, regularly regaled cast and crew alike with bawdy tales about her acting past. Irene passed away in November 1987, and her last film role was playing Mrs Larkin in Temple's *Absolute Beginners*. *The Great Rock 'n' Roll Swindle* would sadly prove to be Mary Millington's final film appearance as the actress took her own life with a lethal cocktail of paracetamol and alcohol at her home in Walton-On-The-Hill, Surrey, on 19th August 1979. She was aged just 33.

With Ronnie Biggs having already established that anyone – even a fugitive Great Train Robber – could be a Sex Pistol, Malcolm attempted to further denigrate John's achievements by staging open-mic auditions at the Duke of York's Theatre on St Martins Lane. Anybody fancying themselves as a 'Johnny Wannabe' could wander in off the West End streets and give their all on the film's title track. And let's face it, who wouldn't want to grab their fifteen minutes of fame by having a sing-a-long with Sid, Steve and Paul? After all, the last time the remaining three Sex Pistols had appeared on stage together was at the Winterland.

Needless to say, none of the applicants were worthy of assuming John's mantle, but the auditions did unearth a rare gem by the name of Edward Tudor-Pole. Legend has it that the aspiring thespian, and future *Crystal Maze* presenter, had been making his way to another audition when he was stopped in the street by Malcolm and Julien and invited to accompany them to the stage of the Duke of York's. Eddie's main recollection of the day is how the other applicants were in total awe of Sid and Nancy, crowding around the couple at any given opportunity. He himself had no real interest in Sid, the Sex Pistols, or even punk rock for that matter, but he was determined to land whatever gig Malcolm and Julien were offering. Although his improvised stage shenanigans would have seen off the competition, he got Malcolm's seal of approval by performing his party trick which involved placing a lighted cigarette at the front of the stage and then flicking it up into the air with the tip of his shoe and catching it in his mouth. Besides being invited to sing two tracks, 'Rock Around The Clock' and 'Who Killed Bambi?', Eddie was given the role of Tadpole, Irene Handl's cinema sidekick. It could only have been Irene's professionalism that kept her from smirking as Eddie bounded about the cinema foyer like John Cleese on acid using a vacuum cleaner as an improvised microphone whilst performing the latter song.

Although Eddie knew there was never any serious consideration being given to his actually replacing John in the Sex Pistols long term, the gangly thespian put aside his acting aspirations temporarily and resurrected his old band Tenpole Tudor. Thanks to his involvement with the Pistols, the band signed a deal with Stiff Records and released two albums, enjoying a modicum of mainstream success, most notably with the 1981 hit single 'Swords Of A Thousand Men' (STIFF-BUY109), which reached No. 6 on the UK chart. Since posing the enigmatic question: 'Who Killed Bambi?', Eddie has appeared in numerous films and plays including the aforementioned *Absolute Beginners*, Alex Cox's *Sid And Nancy* (1986), Clint Eastwood's *White Hunter Black Heart* (1988), *Quills* (2000), *The Queen's Sister* (2005), in which he played royal portrait photographer Cecil Beaton (whose official Silver Jubilee photograph of Queen Elizabeth II was famously utilised by Jamie Reid), and most recently in the latest remake of the Dickens' classic *Oliver Twist* (2007). When he's not appearing on the big screen, Eddie mainly focuses on his live act, which he describes as his 'One Man Stadium Show'. On special occasions he goes out with the Sex Pistols' tribute act, the Sex Pistols Experience, to belt out the old *Swindle* and Tenpole Tudor classics. It is, in a good many ways, a match made in heaven.

#

Malcolm had seen his cinematic dreams come to fruition, but on 13th January 1986, the clapperboard finally sounded on his 10 year Glitterbest Empire when he lost his seven year long court case and agreed an out of court settlement. He relinquished control of Glitterbest and Matrixbest in favour of John, Steve, Paul, and the Sid Vicious estate (initially looked after by Anne Beverley and, since her suicide in 1996, by Sid's cousin, David Ross). The initial Lydon v Glitterbest court case, court action 1152 in the 1978 list, had got underway on Wednesday, 7th February 1979; the same day that Anne Beverley would scatter her only

Satellite *book launch. Paul Cook and Eddie Tenpole Tudor*

son's ashes on to the top soil of Nancy's grave at King David's Cemetery in Philadelphia, following a low-key cremation service at the Garden State Crematorium in North Bergen, New Jersey. By 1986, however, despite the Sex Pistols still being lauded as the band every aspiring rock 'n' roll rebel should emulate, the world had moved on.

Although the new decade had seen real anarchy in the UK with unemployment topping three million, and the nation's disaffected youth taking to the inner-city streets, Prime Minister Margaret Thatcher – who'd survived an assassination attempt by the IRA in October 1984 – had stood firm and won her war against the unions. The 'Iron Lady' had also proved victorious in the war with Argentina over sovereignty of the Falkland Islands. The music industry had also undergone a metamorphosis: punk had initially been usurped by the New Romantics, spearheaded by the gender-bending Boy George, a one-time devotee of 430 Kings Rd himself. This in turn had given way to the Indie (Independent) music scene fronted by student faves, misery-monger Mozzer's the Smiths.

The two main protagonists in our story had also evolved from their previous incarnations. John, who by this time had relocated to New York, had established PiL as a successful band/brand. Malcolm had returned from his self-imposed Parisian exile to launch another attack on the British music industry with the piratical prancing Bow Wow Wow, fronted by the then 14-year-old Anglo-Burmese schoolgirl Annabella Lwin (born Myint Myint Aye). Instead of attacking the industry from within as he had done with the Sex Pistols, Malcolm attempted to bring it to its knees by advocating home taping. The band's debut single 'C30 C60 C90 Go' was released in cassette format only, with the flip side left blank so that kids could use it to tape their favourite songs free and deny the record companies their profits.

Steve and Paul had initially sided with Malcolm, but switched sides at the eleventh hour. Although they'd long accepted that Malcolm loved to run with the ball with scant regard for the offside rule, this was the money shot and they no longer held any confidence in their ex-manager's aim. Each passing day they'd sat stony-faced as John's Q.C., Mr John Wilmers, effortlessly chalked up point after point against Malcolm and co-Glitterbest director Stephen Fisher. The iceberg that finally sunk the Good Ship Venus came when Wilmers guestimated that of the £880,000 which Glitterbest had received in the Sex Pistols' name between September 1976 and March 1978, only some £30,000 could be accounted for. The slipshod accounts that Malcolm had been able to provide revealed that only £343,000 had been spent on *The Great Rock 'n' Roll Swindle*, which still left a whopping £537,000 unaccounted for.

When the presiding judge, Mr Justice Browne-Wilkinson, had delivered his verdict back on 14th February 1979, he was unwilling to get enmeshed in a lengthy trial by attempting to unravel Glitterbest's Gordian-esque managerial knot, or the legality of the Sex Pistols/Glitterbest contract; restricting himself instead to ruling only on Glitterbest's fiscal dealings. The company's only remaining viable assets were *The Great Rock 'n' Roll Swindle* film and the accompanying soundtrack album, and the justice appointed a third-party receiver – Mr Russell Gerald Hawkes of the London accountancy firm Spicer & Pegler – to administer said assets. Although he dissolved both Glitterbest and Matrixbest, the justice suggested that Malcolm should help to exploit the film. But you know Malcolm, he had no interest in playing second fiddle on a project which he had orchestrated. Later that same day, after one final raid on the Glitterbest piggy bank, he boarded a plane to Paris.

However, the justice's reluctance to deal with the Glitterbest/ Sex Pistols contract had left the ruling inconclusive, and the case dragged on for another seven years, costing an estimated £250,000 in legal fees. John had finally got his day in the sun and would forever more bask in its reflected rays. He, Steve and Paul, along with the solicitor acting on behalf of Anne Beverley, were to set up 'Sex Pistols Residuals' to handle all future Sex Pistols business dealings. Having finally got his wallet back, John was able to turn his attention to Public Image Limited, and later that year the band enjoyed both critical and commercial success with the single 'Rise' and its parent album, imaginatively titled *Album*. To all intents and purposes the Sex Pistols were finally a museum piece ...

CHAPTER Sixteen

Fat, Forty, And Very Much Back!

'In 1976 concert promoter Sid Bernstein offered his biggest cheque to date for a Beatles re-union. An unprecedented ten million pounds sterling for one live show. The only thing he hadn't bargained for was the 'fab four' themselves. You see despite years of press interviews saying they had some level of fondness for their time together, the only way you're ever really going to bring about a re-union is if everyone actually wants to do it!'
Beatles Monthly Magazine – 1990

At 11.06 a.m. on Saturday 15th March 1996, the Provisional IRA detonated a massive 3300lb bomb within the heart of Manchester's commercial centre causing widespread destruction to some 75,000 square metres of retail and office space. The device, which was secreted in the rear of a Ford lorry left on Corporation Street outside the city's Arndale Shopping Centre, was the largest bomb ever detonated by the IRA, and the largest to explode in Britain since the Second World War. Although the terrorists issued a coded warning giving the authorities plenty of time to evacuate the immediate area, some 206 people were injured due to flying glass.

Three days later, the Sex Pistols dropped a bombshell of their own in London's Oxford Street when the band's founding line-up held a press conference at their old stomping ground, the 100 Club, unveiling plans for an extensive world tour. Sardonically titled the 'Filthy Lucre Tour', after the 2nd December 1976 *Daily Mail* headline: **PUNK: CALL IT FILTHY LUCRE,** it was due to kick off at the Messila Festival in Hollola, Finland, on 21st June, taking in Europe, including three UK dates, as well as the USA, South America, Australasia, and Japan.

#

For those of you who don't own a copy of the Neurotic Outsiders' eponymously-titled 1996 album, track nine is a Steve Jones penned offering entitled 'Union'. The song is nothing special in terms of the tune, but it came as a something of a surprise to hear the ex-Sex Pistol lamenting over his, and his fellow Sex Pistols, collective failure to set aside their personal differences and reach a compromise that would see the band back on stage together. Steve, of course, wasn't the only one wishing for a Pistols reunion and, as we now all know, several substantial offers were tabled over the years to get the band's original line-up back together. Hell, on occasions if the music press is to be believed offers were even made for line ups that would feature replacements for either Rotten or Matlock! Anyone remember the famous Axl Rose re-union? We also now know that it was John who was the only one of the four steadfastly refusing to come to the negotiating table as Steve, Paul and Glen would have all have happily put pen to contractual paper way earlier than 1996.

In his autobiography, *No Irish, No Blacks, No Dogs*, John was adamant that there would never be a Sex Pistols reunion, and that he was content to let sleeping dogs lie. This, of course, was said with publisher Hodder & Stoughton's weighty advance safely nestled in his bank account. By 1996, PiL was floundering on the rock 'n' roll reef, dormant since 1992 in fact. John, however, still believed he was a viable entity as a recording artist. At the time he was busy working on the songs that would eventually appear on his, dare we say, 'less-than-successful' 1997 debut solo album *Psycho's Path*. Although John would probably deny it, there are those close to the band's inner circle who are convinced that had Nora's multi-millionaire father passed away several months earlier then we'd probably still be wishing for any kind of Sex Pistols reunion .

So when the latest rumour of a possible Sex Pistols re-formation began circulating amongst the party faithful back in February 1996, despite said rumour coming from Jim Henderson, editor-in-chief of the highly informative Sex Pistols' fanzine *Never Trust A Hippy*, the cynics amongst us still treated it as just another deluded pipe dream and got on with our daily grind. This time, however, it was different. Jim had been given the nod by Steve's management company, who were requesting a biography on the ex-Pistol for a forthcoming press conference when all would be revealed. The national press soon picked up on the story, and more grist was added to the rumour mill when John – instead of rubbishing said rumour as he had done in the past – told reporters to hold their respective front pages in anticipation of an official announcement.

On Tuesday 18ᵗʰ March 1996, the improbable came to pass when John, along with Steve, Paul, and Glen, made their way up on to the stage at the once familiar 100 Club and took their seats at the Union Jack-draped podium to unveil plans for an extensive world tour. According to Paul, the four mischievous band members had succeeded in getting hold of Malcolm's home telephone number in Paris and contacted their former manager to offer him his old job back. Although Malcolm had caustically likened the Pistols' reunion to that of 'dray horses out for one last ride before being put out to pasture', he surprisingly accepted the offer only to be told, amid a collective fit of the giggles, to 'fuck off'.

The 350 or so journalists gathered inside the basement club, waiting to grill the four ageing Sex Pistols over their decision to reform after twenty years, must have wondered what the fuck was going on as five skimpily-clad transvestites served them cheese rolls and jellied eels, whilst the Union Jack draped PA blasted out rousing WW11 anthems. During a July 2008 *Mojo* interview John readily admitted that he'd arrived at the venue knowing he was in for a rough reception at the hands of the press. Rather than suffer a sleepless night worrying about the line of questioning he and the other Pistols could expect, he preferred to while away the night building up Dutch courage in some of London's less than salubrious drinking establishments.

The majority of the assembled press pack probably hadn't been born or were too young to remember the late '70s zeitgeist, when the Sex Pistols were terrorising the tepid British music scene with their anarchistic 'Bible Quotation No. 1'. You might think though that they would have done their homework on the band. But no, they foolishly chose to engage John in a game of verbal chess, which was akin to asking Arnold Schwarzenegger if he fancied a spot of arm-wrestling, and they were soon squirming in their seats wishing they'd chosen another assignment.

For two decades the Sex Pistols had been considered sacrosanct in terms of rock 'n' roll rebellion, and many people considered their decision to get back together a cardinal sin. However, as John told Jim Henderson for *Never Trust A Hippy* (issue 12): 'I know that a lot of the bitching and moaning will be about "they're only in it for the money", but quite frankly we've never been paid well for what we done in the first place. And that would only be to right a wrong.' Let's be honest, why should the band that (albeit inadvertently) brought about the English punk scene, and lined many an entrepreneurial pocket in the process, be expected to stick to their principles? After all, every other British punk band, with the notable exceptions being the Clash and the Jam, has re-formed for the money, and been free to do so whenever the mood suited without fear of ridicule or retribution. When it came down to it, the money aspect of the reunion was irrelevant as the burning question upon every fan's lips wasn't whether the Sex Pistols would still find relevance in the mid-'90s music scene, but whether the four middle-aged musicians could still 'mean it, man ...'

On Sunday 23rd June we got the opportunity to find out for ourselves when the band played the first of the three aforementioned UK dates at Finsbury Park in London.

#

As John had glibly informed reporters at the 100 Club press conference, Finsbury Park isn't a stadium, it's a 112 acre public park situated within the London borough of Haringey; a mere stone's throw from the Poole Park council estate which the Lydon family once called home, and where the singer had spent his formative years. The park's facilities include open grounds, formal gardens, and an arboretum (that's a collection of trees to you and me); while the park's sports facilities include an athletics stadium, several football pitches, tennis and basketball courts, and a bowling green for those nearby residents whose salad days are well and truly behind them. However, as with most things in London during the 'Decade of Discontent', the park fell into serious decline during the mid '70s, and its future remained in doubt until funding from the National Lottery – in the early 1990s – brought about something of a renaissance in its fortunes. Said regeneration also led to Finsbury Park becoming an established music venue – most notably for the Madstock and Fleadh festivals spearheaded by Madness and The Pogues respectively.

Although John and the other three Sex Pistols had all reacted negatively to any suggestion of turning the Finsbury Park show into a 'Punkstock' by clogging the bill with ageing punk bands from yesteryear (a 'geriatrics day out' as John likened the proposal), both the Buzzcocks and Stiff Little Fingers appeared on the bill alongside 60 Foot Dolls, Three Colours Red, Skunk Anansie, The Wildhearts (who can forget their incredible yellow and pink T-shirts 'Never Mind the Headliners Here's the Wildhearts'?), and Uncle Iggy Pop. Although the Buzzers and SLF put in solid performances, the on-stage demeanour of both bands suggested they knew their efforts were always going to be superfluous on the day; London's original outrage was back in town, and no one was going to steal their thunder.

Indeed, many of the musicians on the bill were as much in awe of the headliners as the audience was. Wildhearts' then bassist, Danny McCormick, whose brother Chris was the guitarist in Three Colours Red, was in seventh heaven hanging out in the backstage VIP area within touching distance of the Sex Pistols. Although the garrulous Geordie readily engaged Glen and Paul in conversation, and Steve to a lesser degree, he purposely chose to avoid John: 'You've got to be mindful of your heroes,' he told us one sunny June afternoon back in 2002 whilst we were sailing down the Thames with the Sus-Sex Pistols tribute band. 'Because every fucker and his dog were trying to get their five minutes with John, and it would have been just my luck to catch him in a lousy mood. And that would have ruined me fuckin' day, like!'

Twenty years had passed since that glorious summer of 1976, and John, Steve, Paul, and Glen were no longer angry young men with an axe to grind. But the 30,000 punters in attendance didn't give a fuck about the furrowed wrinkles on Paul's receding brow, or John's and Steve's ever-expanding waistlines when the stage lights dimmed and the band burst through the paper backdrop depicting the now all too familiar outraged headlines from 2nd December 1976 following the band's appearance on *Today*. It's fair to say that if there had been a roof covering Finsbury Park that day then the collective roar would have blown it from its stanchions as Steve slung on his trusty Les Paul and cranked out the opening riff to 'Bodies'. The portly guitarist's black shirt may have been straining at the seams owing to another visit to his favourite London eatery – Cooke's pie and mash shop in Shepherd's Bush – but he still knew how to strike the 'guitar hero' poses we remembered from the 'God Save The Queen' video shoot.

Although no one was really expecting John to take to the stage dressed in the once-familiar leather jeans and Destroy muslin, the green-checked jacket covering his own girth looked as though it had been cut from one of Cooke's tablecloths, and the less said about his pantomimic green-tinged spiked crown the better. Glen, of course, who'd never really looked all that comfortable in the SEX gear back in the day, was never likely to get 'punked-up' for the occasion and chose to play it safe in black jeans and a striped T-shirt. Now even the most naïve music fan could have guessed that the Pistols would be serving up a setlist comprising of 'Bollocks and B-Sides' (and possibly 'Belsen Was A Gas'), but each number – especially the four singles – was greeted like a long lost relative. Whilst John's voice had lost much of its vitriolic venom, Steve, Paul and Glen had all matured as musicians, which added an extra dynamic to the performance.

#

Following on from their triumphant homecoming, the band flew to Sweden for a show at the Stockholm Naval Museum on 26th June, before then making the relatively short hop across the Baltic border into Denmark for their ill-fated appearance at the Roskilde festival two days later. The four day jamboree – which is regarded as one of Europe's 'big four' summer festivals – was celebrating its 25th anniversary that year, but a small percentage of the 115,000 crowd decided to take umbrage with the Pistols (or more likely John's psychedelic shell-suit) and began lobbing bottles at the stage; not all of them plastic. Despite repeated warnings from John that he and the rest of the band would leave the stage, several troublemakers kept up their barrage. Said warning was duly carried out when a low-flying bottle almost took Steve's head off at the end of 'Did You No Wrong'.

Thankfully, the rest of the European shows passed without serious incident, including an unexpected second London show at the Shepherd's Bush Empire on 17th July following the cancellation of the show at Dublin's Point Depot scheduled for the following evening. For many of us, the Shepherd's Bush Empire show was even better than the one at Finsbury Park, primarily owing to it being staged indoors rather than a field and therefore more intimate. Indeed, Creation's head honcho – and punk aficionado

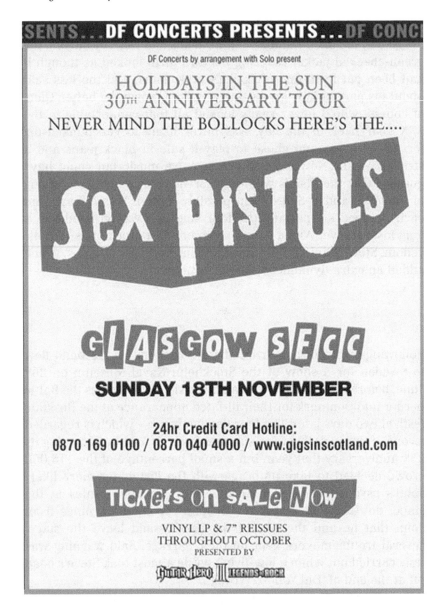

Glasgow SECC flyer 2007 tour

– Alan McGee, was sufficiently moved by the band's performance to shell out £20,000 to secure the back pages of every leading music magazine for his 'on-the-money' press release extolling the Sex Pistols true worth within the then stolid music scene. Unfortunately for the band, however, such close proximity to the audience put them within gobbing range. Not surprisingly, John took exception to being spat at by a few sweaty oiks (who should have known better) and threatened to come down and knock a few heads together unless the spitting stopped.

Gobbing has to be the most idiotic, not to mention abhorrent, aspect of punk rock, so why these morons thought it would somehow still be acceptable some twenty years later is anyone's guess. Why they believed John would allow his stage to be used as a spittoon is even more of a conundrum. Once again 'I Wanna Be Me' was again inexplicably left out of the set, but we were given an unexpected treat in the form of 'Roadrunner', the Jonathan Richman classic written in 1972, which the embryonic Pistols had co-opted for their early repertoire. And this time, John knew the words ... or at least enough of them to pass muster. The feeling the next day was one of 'wow'! That was probably just like seeing the Pistols in their prime; no fields, no cheap watery beer, a perfect view of the group on stage and an incredibly tight set.

The previous evening's show at Glasgow's SECC (Scottish Exhibition and Conference Centre), however, had proved something of a damp squib. This was only the second time the Sex Pistols had ventured north of Hadrian's Wall, but it seemed the Scots were somewhat less overawed about the reunion than their English counterparts and, come the day of the show, there were still plenty of unsold tickets. With the eleventh hour, and possible embarrassment, fast approaching someone within the promoter's camp hit upon the face-saving idea of inviting Stiff Little Fingers onto the bill. The Fingers were, and still are, held in the highest esteem amongst Scottish music enthusiasts, and could therefore be relied on to shift a bucket full of surplus tickets in no time. Although SLF's last-minute inclusion saved face at the box office, the plan ultimately backfired on the Pistols as the 'Fingers Faithful' decamped as soon as their heroes had departed the stage leaving sizable gaps about the 12,500 all-seater hall. Thankfully, this proved to be the exception rather than the rule, and the Pistols brought the European leg of the tour to a rabble-rousing finale at the Phoenix Festival on 21st July.

One might have thought that the opportunity to see the Sex Pistols playing live would have been enough to whet the driest of whistles, but certain individuals (no doubt having been let out on day-release for the occasion) took it upon themselves to stand directly in front of Glen and spend the entire show championing

Sid. Now, while we all love watching videos and DVDs of Sid and his on-stage antics, in musical terms, he was – as John rightly, if cruelly, pointed out at the press conference – little more than a 'coat-hanger on stage'. Instead of barracking Glen, these morons should have been throwing flowers at his feet for it was he who was instrumental in bringing about the long-awaited reunion.

Glen just happened to be in Los Angeles earlier in the year sounding out a possible vocalist for his solo band The Philistines, and finding himself in Steve's neighbourhood he decided to drop by and see what his old 'guitar hero' mucker was up to. Steve was not only happy to see Glen, but suggested they should make the short journey down to John's Venice Beach-fronted home. Prior to this, Glen's communications with John had been reserved to brief transatlantic telephone conversations, and he was understandably apprehensive about coming face-to-face with his erstwhile nemesis; especially given John's predilection for bad-mouthing him at any given opportunity. The get-together went surprisingly well, however, and when the conversation drifted – as it surely would – onto the Sex Pistols, the loved-up trio decided to put in a transatlantic call to Paul in London. And the rest, as they say, is history …

#

After a ten day break to recharge the batteries, the boys kicked off the US leg of their Filthy Lucre world tour with a show at the Red Rocks Amphitheatre in Denver, Colorado on 31st July. It had been eighteen long years since the Pistols had last darkened America's doorstep, and although the Centennial State was home to enough Green Day and Offspring fans to ensure the band got a rapturous welcome, the critics were less than enthusiastic about the reunion: 'Glitter City folks, welcome to the birth of lounge punk', as one caustic colonial unkindly put it. From there the tour headed south into Texas, which, having played host to the Sid-era Sex Pistols on two occasions first time round, must have been left somewhat underwhelmed at seeing the sanitised version roll into town. Unlike January '78, the Pistols had no compunction in playing New York and Los Angeles, but having said that, as far as John and Steve were concerned, the three LA shows (22nd, 23rd & 25th August) would have been considered 'home games'.

Following on from the final North American date at Vancouver's Pacific National Exhibition Centre on 31st August, the band took an

John Lydon at Hammersmith Apollo

extended vacation before regrouping in early October and flying out to New Zealand to undertake a ten date tour of Australasia. From there they flew to Japan, another Sex Pistols 'first', and commenced an eighteen date 'holiday in the land of the rising sun' with the first of two shows at Club Citta, Kanagawa. The Pistols near-iconic status amongst Japan's youth (we know from our own experience that Sid is like the 'fourth prophet' over there!) saw them play three nights at Tokyo's 14,000 capacity Nippon Budokan. The fifth and final leg of the tour saw Steve and Paul make a return to Rio de Janeiro in a Sex Pistols capacity (although there would be no reunion with Ronnie Biggs), when the band played Brazil's second city's Plaza Da Apoteose on 29th November.

After a second Brazilian outing in Sao Paulo, the band took a short five day break to catch their collective breath before heading down to the Argentinian capital Buenos Aires for two shows over consecutive evenings – 4th and 5th December – at the city's Arena Obras Sanitarias. Two days later, Johnny and the boys brought their Filthy Lucre world tour to its anarchic climax with a show at a basketball stadium in the Chilean capital Santiago. 'It was fucking mad! Like being a gladiator,' Glen told *Mojo* in July 2008.

Yet despite the mayhem, the bassist cited this show as his favourite ever Sex Pistols gig.

And that, boys and girls, was supposed to be that. John, Steve, Paul, and Glen had basked in the spotlight, taken their bows, and finally collected their substantial pay cheques. More importantly, they had been able to give the Sex Pistols a well deserved send-off, and in doing so, finally laid the band's ghost to rest. The world, except in a solo project capacity, would hear from them no more. Although one could argue the merits of whether the Pistols were right to reform, there can be no disputing that the reunion shows – most notably Finsbury Park, and Shepherd's Bush Empire – were fucking fantastic, and will live long in the memory. The Filthy Lucre tour not only enabled those of us who were born a tad too late to catch the Sex Pistols first time round and to finally see for ourselves just how awesome the original line-up was when they were firing on all cylinders, but also provided the band with a fitting closure.

#

So, imagine the surprise when it was announced in April 2002 that the Sex Pistols were coming out of retirement for another one-off – and no doubt highly lucrative – reunion to help Queen Elizabeth II, Gawd bless her, commemorate her Golden Jubilee.

It is possible that the Queen hadn't even been aware that a pop group had dared to stick a safety pin through an image of her noble phizog twenty-five years earlier, but if she had known of the affront then dear old Liz had obviously mellowed with age in the intervening years, for on 3rd June she consented to the staging of a pop concert – billed as the 'Party at the Palace' – at Buckingham Palace. The event was touted as the greatest concert to be staged in Britain since Live Aid, and the 12,000 tickets were determined by way of a lottery. Aside from those 12,000 beneficiaries, an estimated one million people were gathered outside on the Mall, with another two hundred million watching on television. Amongst those performing on the day were Sir Paul McCartney, Dame Shirley Bassey, Sir Elton John, Phil Collins, Sir Cliff Richard and Ozzy Osbourne (with the exception of Ozzy you see the pattern). The Sex Pistols services were not sought, needless to say.

Although the band was no longer 'banned from the land', and wouldn't need to cruise up the Thames like river-boat pirates, the

Argentinian Flogging A Dead Horse *cover*

question on most lips was: was there really any need for them to bother at all? As catchy as 'Pistols at the Palace' sounded, didn't anyone within the band's inner caucus give any thought to the fans, and the logistical ball-ache of having to trek out to the Crystal Palace National Sports Centre, a dilapidated athletics stadium stuck out in the arse-end of nowhere (with all due respect to readers of the book who live in Sarf London)? Although some die-hards (and you know who you are!) greeted the news with gusto and reached for the Vaseline and hair dye, along with that T-shirt that still fits (if you breathe in), the rest of us were totally nonplussed. Especially so in view of John having already reverted to type by slagging off Glen in *The Filth And The Fury;* a backlash nobody was expecting, least of all Glen, who refused to sign merchandise related to the film.

It is often said that a good idea only usually works first time and unfortunately for the Sex Pistols this reunion proved no exception to that particular rule. The novelty value from 1996 had long since been dispelled and the re-release of 'God Save The Queen' wasn't going to change the groundswell of opinion. While there were a goodly number of fans poised by the phone with their credit card details at the ready when the tickets – priced at a whopping £32.50 + £3.50 booking fee – went on sale, Crystal Palace is a large venue to fill. As Saturday 27th July loomed ever closer and the ticket sales showed little signs of improving (and with a guest list as long as the London Yellow Pages too) John was forced to do the unthinkable by appearing on several naff TV talk shows to drum up publicity and make a personal appeal to those fans still wavering over how to spend their Saturday evening, along with anyone else wanting to stick two fingers up at Queen Liz. *The Guardian*'s Alexis Petridis, who'd also been unimpressed by the official Palace Party of six weeks earlier, was even less impressed with the Pistols, and saved his harshest critique for John's chat show shenanigans: 'He [John] cuts a strangely pathetic figure, a 47-year-old trapped in perpetual sneering adolescence, unable to grow up because he has nothing new to offer'. Ouch!

We can only assume that the failure to shift the allotted tickets had a knock-on effect on the band's morale, for while it's one thing for Joe Public to show apathy to what's on offer, it's quite another for a band to show total disinterest in the proceedings. Yet that's precisely what happened at Crystal Palace. Any lingering doubts we had about the disaster waiting to unfold came to the fore upon seeing our beloved Pistols take to the stage and open with Hawkwind's 1972 hit 'Silver Machine'. On the train ride through darkest South East London we had amused ourselves by eavesdropping on our fellow punters who were all feverishly debating which 'classic' *Bollocks* track the Pistols would chose to kick-off the proceedings. The obvious favourite – given the occasion – was 'God Save The Queen', but there were those who were still willing to put their money on 'Bodies', while the other frontrunners were 'Anarchy In The UK', 'Pretty Vacant' and 'Holidays In The Sun'. But no one, absolutely no one, aboard that train would have believed in their wildest nightmares that their heroes would – after a few lines of unpatriotic patter from Chairman John – open the set with a whimsical ode to a silver bicycle. And falsetto-segueing into 'God Save The Queen' midway through wasn't going to spare any blushes!

Although it's fair to say the 1996 reunion tour had already laid waste to the Sex Pistols' myth, in those five shameful minutes John, Steve, Paul and Glen became their own tribute band. While our own mindset may well have been predetermined owing to our having spent the preceding hours holed up in a salacious bar in Shoreditch, to be brutally honest, things didn't get any better from there on in. So, midway through the show, having decided it was indeed 'No Fun', we headed for the exit; we weren't on our own. As we joined the meandering procession of yellow and pink clad disgruntled fans heading back down to the train station a bemused on-duty WPC enquired as to why we were all leaving so soon. 'It's not very good,' one lad offered with a resigned shrug. 'It wasn't any good twenty-five years ago either,' came the retort. Given the meandering dirge emanating from the stage behind us, it proved one to which we could provide no justifiable answer. Of course, those who stayed until the end will insist that things got better, but the DVD suggests otherwise. And what the fuck were they thinking of playing 'My Way'? It may have been designated a Sex Pistols single back in June '78, and Steve may have participated in the sessions, but the glory and kudos belonged to Sid and Sid alone. They might have got away with it had John chosen to dedicate the song to his supposed best mate's memory, but no, he even forgot the words and how ironic that Glen – who'd been supplanted by Sid – had to step up to the microphone.

It also seems the 50,000 American punters who sweltered in the 100 degree desert heat to witness the Pistols headline performance at the KROQ Inland Invasion on 14th September were left equally underwhelmed by their lacklustre showing. The Pistols weren't the only disappointment on the day, however, for despite being billed as a 'low dough show' the admission price was a hefty $35. Although the festival, which was staged at the Hyundai Pavilion in Devore, California, was supposedly to celebrate '25 years of Punk Rock', no band or act from the New York scene was invited to attend. Aside from the Pistols, the Damned and the Buzzcocks were there to represent the UK, with Californian punksters the Offspring, Social Distortion, Blink 142, and Bad Religion making up the bill.

#

According to the famous wartime song made famous by 'Forces Sweetheart' Dame Vera Lynn DBE, 'There'll Always Be an England'. It also seems there'll always be one excuse or another for a band to reform just as long as the bunce is good: the Sex Pistols proving no exception to this rule. The arthritic anarchists were back together again the following year for a topping-up-the-pension-fund three week US tour, billed as the 'Piss Off Tour 2003'. Aside from a stop-off in Toronto, Canada midway through, the tour saw them take in shows on both US seaboards. Americans are obviously more tolerant of their heroes' musical shortcomings, but the general consensus on this side of the Atlantic, however, was that the Pistols would never dare to darken London's doorstep again after their lame and lethargic showing at Crystal Palace. But we were wrong, old bean, because in November 2007 – twelve months after telling the Rock 'n' Roll Hall of Fame where they could shove their induction – they were back with a vengeance.

By this time, of course, John had endeared himself to the nation by appearing on ITV's celebrity survival show *I'm A Celebrity, Get Me Out Of Here* early in 2004. Unlike his fellow contestants, who – with the possible exception of Alex Best – were all intent on salvaging their TV careers or building up their media profile, John was happy to be at one with nature. Indeed, many people thought he would go on to win the show had he not opted to throw in the towel midway through. His jungle capers – which included wrestling with a pack of irate ostriches – were not entirely in vain, however, as the powers that be at the Discovery Channel offered him the chance to present his own TV series, *John Lydon's Megabugs*, later that year.

It was clearly a case of 'Amnesia in the UK' as the fans, many of whom must have been present at the Crystal Palace debacle, welcomed the band back with open arms. The original three dates sold out in fifteen minutes, and what started out as a one-off show at the 5,000 capacity Brixton Academy quickly escalated into a five night residency, followed by two more sell-out shows at Manchester's G-MEX Centre on 17th November and Glasgow's SECC. The previous day, John, Steve and Glen had attended the press launch of the new Guitar Hero III computer game (which allowed would-be Steve Jones's to riff along to both 'Anarchy In The UK', and 'Pretty Vacant'), at the Hoxton Square Bar in Shoreditch, East London.

Secure in the knowledge that our entry was guaranteed that evening at Brixton, we spent an enjoyable afternoon meeting and greeting friends and fellow punters in the Spice of Life pub (or 'The Glue Pot', as it's more commonly known) in Cambridge Circus, before then heading down to the venue. Try as we might though, we couldn't tempt Roadent into accompanying us. 'I don't do pantomime,' he sneered sardonically before waving us out the door.

There was already a large crowd gathering on Stockwell Road, and we'd barely got out of the taxi when Steve English beckoned us towards the Academy's backstage door. Steve, who now earns his crust as a painter and decorator, was once again acting in his official capacity of looking after Steve and Paul. Selling out five nights at the Brixton Academy is no easy feat, especially for a band supposedly well past its sell-by date and at various times both loved and hated by the media. The reports from Los Angeles, where the band had performed a private Indie 103.1 sponsored warm-up show at The Roxy on 25th October, had been favourable. Although the memories of Crystal Palace were still loitering at the back of our minds, we were both willing to give the Pistols the benefit of the doubt.

We even allowed ourselves to get caught up in the punk party atmosphere – despite DJ Goldie's best efforts to numb our collective senses – and felt the butterflies swarming in our stomachs as the lights dimmed and Dame Vera's dulcet tones drifted along on the smokeless air. The sight of John's personal manager/valet/minder, John 'Rambo' Stevens strutting out beside his employer – and ahead of Steve, Paul and Glen – should have set huge alarm bells ringing. If further proof were needed that this was going to be Crystal Palace revisited it came with John's ludicrous stocking and gartered tweed hunting ensemble. Yes, we know 'individuality' has always been John's watchword, and while we would never dare to question his right to wear whatever the hell he chooses away from the spotlight, he's a Sex Pistol for fuck's sake! This time we had to endure several minutes of Lord Lydon's patriotic patter. While we are sure John is proud to be British, he spends so little time in the UK that his 'best of British' breast-beating reverberates with a decidedly hollow ring.

With the Pistols party political broadcast over it was on with the show. For several self-delusion-filled moments we thought the Pistols were opening with a new song until we realised it was actually 'Pretty Vacant', only without it's instantly recognisable A riff intro. We later learned that Steve was suffering from a bout of flu, which in turn had a knock-on effect with his playing, but that's still no excuse to mess up so badly. When the follow-up number, 'Seventeen', failed to raise expectations it was taxi time for O'Shea and Parker, and for a moment it looked as though Steve English was also up for throwing in the towel and coming for a curry. Of course, by the following morning we were both wondering if we might have been a tad previous in beating such a hasty retreat, but our anxiety proved unfounded. When everybody met up again in the Spice of Life later that day, even Brian Jackson, the self-styled 'Sixth Pistol', was struggling to put a favourable spin on the previous night's proceedings. Radio One DJ Chris Moyles, however, had no such compunction and was willing to call a spade by its name. Each morning of that week the portly breakfast show host had played a different Sex Pistols single to get the fans in the mood, but that morning he'd apparently played an Oasis track instead.

It seems that Steve, upon being given an honest opinion of the opening night's fare by Steve English, was all for cancelling the remaining shows and legging it back home for some California sunshine. However, his namesake had the presence of mind to whisk him off to a nearby café where he was able to talk some sense into him; either that, or it was the prospect of the venue's owners, Academy Music Group, calling in their legal team that got the disgruntled guitarist back in the saddle. Needless to say, the Pistols came in for some unsavoury flak at the hands of both the music and tabloid press, although they would have probably done so regardless of their performance. While the die-hards insisted that the band improved with each show, the neutrals – who had nothing to lose or gain by offering their opinions – left us in little doubt that the horse had been well and truly flogged to an ignominious demise.

＃

Were we foolish or naïve enough to think the world would hear of the Sex Pistols no more? Of course, we weren't. Then again, neither would we have put our money on the by now perennial re-formists coming back to the fore six months later to undertake a summer festival tour –ludicrously entitled the 'Combine Harvester' Festival Tour 2008 – kick-starting on Saturday, 7th June 2008 with a sell-out show at The Joint in Las Vegas, Nevada. On 11th June, the Pistols were back in the UK to play a warm-up show for the Isle of Wight Festival, scheduled to take place three days later, at the Birmingham Carling Academy. This was the first time the band had performed in England's second city since their appearance at Bogart's on 20th October 1976, and given the size of the Academy – a mere 2,700 capacity – the band could have been forgiven for thinking they'd stepped back in time, had it not been for the dressing room mirrors reflecting their collective ages of 207.

The Isle of Wight Festival would see the Pistols perform in front of their largest UK audience to date; some 55,000 punters. The band appeared totally unfazed by their surroundings – or the occasion – and put in a solid performance. Although John bemoaned his not being able to hear himself through the monitors he refrained from smashing anything as he had done at the Marquee and High Wycombe back in February 1976, merely keeping his displeasure vocal. Following on from here, the band took in festivals around Europe, as well as chalking up another Sex Pistols first by performing in Russia.

They returned to the UK for a 'Never Mind the Ballachs' headline appearance at the Loch Lomond Festival on Saturday, 3rd August. What should have been a grand day out for all concerned within the sedate setting of Ballach Castle, however, was marred by the site having been reduced to a sprawling mud bath following several days of torrential rain, and inadequate amenities left an unpleasant odour hanging in the air. Midway through the set John chose to put the record straight on his supposed racial slurs that had appeared in several British tabloids. John – like most people in the public eye – has been, and will continue to be, accused of many things, but to call him a racist is beyond ludicrous.

#

Following on from their festival frolics, the Pistols announced an indoor show at the Hammersmith Apollo on 2nd September. This venue, of course, was a pivotal landmark in the Sex Pistols' myth, for it was here – back when the venue was trading as the Hammersmith Odeon – that Steve and Wally took advantage of some lackadaisical security and made off with David Bowie's entire backline PA. As that also happened to be the night when Bowie called time on 'Ziggy Stardust', speculation began to mount amongst the Pistols' faithful that John – with the Pistols having

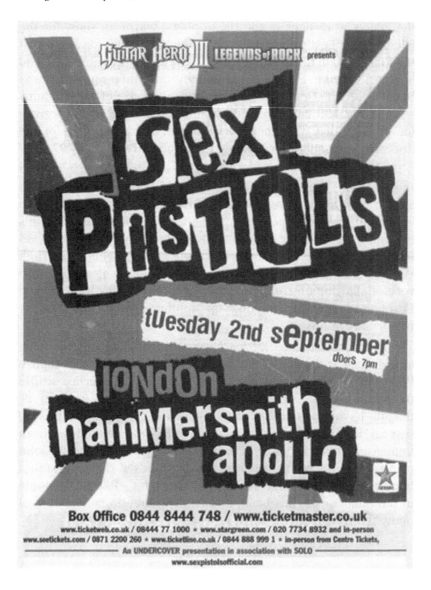

Hammersmith Apollo Union Jack poster 2008 tour

gone full circle, so to speak – would be calling time on his own colourful alter ego. Writers, of course, are known for their romantic disposition, and although we'd both happily turned a blind eye to the festival tour, we talked the idea of Hammersmith through a lot. The final outcome was that Alan didn't feel the need to attend, nor it seemed could he have been talked into it by anyone.

Mick did take a look on the final night though. Come the day of the show itself, Hammersmith Broadway was a sea of colour as the weird and wonderful – some of whom had travelled thousands of miles to be there – descended upon the venue. By the time Mick and friends took their seats – in the figurative sense only, as who was gonna sit through a Sex Pistols gig? – the band were already on stage ambling through a quirky 'Pretty Vacant' country hoedown, and for those two or three cringe worthy minutes shades of Brixton were feared. Those fears were blown into the ether as Steve launched into the song for real. The opening Brixton show – as with Crystal Palace five years earlier – had suffered owing to John's refusal to put in the necessary rehearsal time, but the summer schedule had seen the Pistols tighten up their collective act. Steve, Paul and Glen were seamless in delivering their pile-driving sound, and even John's voice held strong for most of the evening. It was also nice to see him sporting PiL-esque attire – tartan trousers and a long white shirt – instead of the ridiculous tweed and garter ensemble of ten months earlier. Indeed, our only criticism is why he insists on having Rambo standing on stage during the show. The minder's domineering presence so close to the action must make poor old Glen feel like he's in detention for some behind the scenes misdemeanour.

We were treated to two encores, but for some inexplicable reason, known only to the band, they chose to end the first encore with 'Anarchy In The UK'. Did they really think they could top their '76 call to arms with either 'Silver Machine' or 'Roadrunner'? Everyone in attendance knew that the Pistols wouldn't be bringing any new songs to the party, but were undoubtedly ignorant as to why they would choose to omit two of their stronger songs: 'I Wanna Be Me' and 'Satellite' from the setlist. Back in 1996, John excused the omission of 'I Wanna Be Me' by saying the song contained too many words, which is hard to fathom given that the lyrics were penned by one J. Lydon in the first place. We have it on good authority that 'Satellite' – which did feature in the Filthy Lucre set – was cut owing to it having too many verses. Memo to John: if Steve, Paul and Glen are happy to play these songs, and the crowd want to hear them, then why not make someone's day by choosing a member of the audience to come up on stage and sing them for you while you go and have a beer and a fag backstage? On a lighter note, John brought the proceedings to a temporary halt midway through the set to ask the crowd to join him, Paul and Glen in wishing Steve a happy 53rd birthday, which at the time was but a couple of hours away.

#

With the 2008 festival season at an end, and no more gigs in the pipeline, the four Sex Pistols have once again gone their separate ways. With no commemorative anniversaries on the horizon who knows when, or indeed if, we'll ever see them again. However, that doesn't mean to say that they've slipped off the radar entirely.

Paul is still providing the beat for Man Raze (along with Phil from Def Leppard) whose debut album, *Surreal*, has received favourable reviews. Glen has teamed up with David Bowie's one time guitarist Earl Slick, and Blondie's Clem Burke to form Glam-tinged outfit Slinky Vagabond. Even more recently he has, somewhat ironically, become a member of the re-formed Faces. And all this with his on-going solo project The Philistines still very much in existence, a new album was released in 2010.

Steve has returned to his day job spinning the platters at Indie 103.1 in Los Angeles and playing in any number of super-groups, while speeding around the hills of LA alongside Billy Morrison (The Cult/Billy Idol) as part of their own celebrity motorcycle club.

John would no doubt tell us he has various solo projects to fill his day, with PiL taking up the position of most importance (once again) for the time being. However, he still had time to accept Dairy Crest's offer to be the new face of Country Life for a TV advertising campaign extolling the delights of butter. 'He [John] is seen as a great British icon,' Dairy Crest said via an official statement announcing the singer's appointment. 'His independent views are part of his consumer appeal, and his tongue-in-cheek sense of humour shines through in our TV advertising.' Now hands up who would have thought that possible back in Silver Jubilee year?

Alan's Afterword

Who Breaks A Butterfly On A Wheel?

'My dreams are awakening; somebody is making me the only one in the room. Which nobody could do, nobody till you ...'

From 'Nobody Till You' by Lindsay Lohan

For Alexa Morris

Since we completed the draft of this book John has reformed Public Image Limited, and despite initial press stories regarding a union of the old Lydon, Wobble & Levene firm, it turns out that Jah wanted too much money. We know that Keith just wasn't interested, as he was sitting with me when the call came through from John's people. Though to be honest once he'd put the phone down we ordered a shot and toasted PiL. Since then, of course, Keith did make an appearance on stage at The 100 Club with the Sex Pistols Experience (in their guise as Public Imitation Limited) for a few numbers that went down a storm with the party faithful. To John's credit, PiL's original mission statement always talked about an ever evolving organisation. The new look PiL has completed two very successful tours and released a live album, with talk of a return to the studio. In the cold light of day it looks like he's finally found his way home: just don't call him a 'national treasure'!

In February of 2010, The Rich Kids took to the stage at The Academy in Islington, London. An evening arranged and played out because Steve New, the original 'Whizz Kid Guitarist' who was almost a Pistol, had been diagnosed with terminal cancer. On stage the four original Rich Kids (Ure/Matlock/New/Egan) were joined – for one of the greatest, most fun, gigs I've ever witnessed – by Mick Jones, Tony James, Viv Albertine, Gary Kemp and Patti Pallidan. Myself, and the usual crowd of suspects met up first in Soho (bet you're surprised by that bit!) before the show, drank a few beers and shared a lot of stories of meeting Steve over the years. A matter of months later Steve New was no longer with us, another of the good guys gone before his time. Elvis had once again left the building ... though I'm sure he was aware that his last stand was a fitting tribute to his whole life.

On 8th April 2010 I was sat outside another Soho boozer with Steve Diggle and Steve 'Roadent' Connolly enjoying the afternoon sun and a cold beer, when my mobile rang. It was Brigitte, one of Vivienne Westwood's best designers; she told me she was ringing to let me know before the news broke that Malcolm had just passed away. Roadent could tell by my face that something was wrong. Once I'd told him he rang his ex-wife straight away. I rang Alan 'Leather & Bones' Jones and John 'Boogie' Tiberi, not wanting either of them to find out first on the evening news. Twenty minutes later my phone rang again, it was BBC Radio 6, they wondered if I'd like to comment on Malcolm's death 'Just to say that he was an incredible person and he always supported me in all my Pistols related projects,' I said adding 'You know what, he'll be sadly missed.' I thought of the fun I'd had with him, hanging out in Paris, and remembered for a moment the words of the late Nils Stevenson: 'Despite what they've all said since, he really is fun to be with, is Malcolm. He might not be the best manager in the world, but he's a laugh!'

The next morning Malcolm made all the newspaper covers. He had died from cancer, aged 64, in Switzerland surrounded by his loved ones. The same tabloids that had screamed 'The Filth & The Fury' in 1976, now proclaimed him 'The Godfather of Punk' and 'The best known manager since Epstein' – how he would have loved to have read those words. He was working to the end, trying to finish a 13 part series for the BBC on popular culture. John Lydon issued an immediate statement that 'For me Malc was always entertaining, and I hope you remember that. Above all else he was an entertainer and I will miss him, and so should you'. Malcolm was buried in Highgate Cemetery following a funeral service that brought parts of London to a standstill. It was attended by two of the Sex Pistols in the form of Glen Matlock and Paul Cook.

In the days that followed Malcolm's death I was offered the chance to write a book on his life, as well as to direct a DVD documentary based on a two hour interview I'd done with him in 2007, of which to date we've only used about 25 minutes. I turned down both projects without hesitation. My friend Nick Reynolds did make a bronze death-mask of Malcolm at the mortuary for Malcolm's son Joe. The last time I saw Malcolm we were walking

Satellite *book launch. Alan with the late great Steve New*

down Dean Street in Soho, laughing and joking about some of the later T-shirts that were sold at 430 Kings Rd. It had been the plan to hook up with Roadent later that night and re-kindle a few old war stories in a Soho wine bar, but Roadent was late finishing work so I hung on for him while Malcolm left for dinner with some TV executive. We'd both laughed to ourselves there would be another time, another place, and of course as it turned out there wasn't ... God save Malcolm McLaren ...

As I write this afterword, *Who Killed Nancy* has finally opened in America to pretty much rave reviews. In Japan they almost declared a public holiday upon its release! You'll always get the odd one who doesn't understand what your point is. But screw 'em! I've also been doing quite a few telephone interviews with various newspapers and radio stations, fuelled on, no doubt, by the fact that the movie we followed up with, *Monty Python: Almost the Truth*, has recently been nominated for an Emmy Award.

So, it only leaves me to say, if you've enjoyed the Pistols books I've been involved with over the years, the radio documentaries, CD re-issues or indeed the films then 'thank you'. If you didn't, then I guess there is no way you'll be reading this anyway. Writing *Young Flesh Required* seems like a long time ago now as it was originally completed in 2005 but it has been updated twice since the sad death of Sean Body, who was to have published it. For my part I now intend to tread a very different path as a film director, with books becoming very much a secondary part of my career. Mick has just had his first film script commissioned in the shape of *The Wonderland Gang* which is set to star Frank Harper. So who knows what lies ahead for both of us? But from me alone it's 'Goodbye A&M' and goodnight from him ...

Alan G. Parker
- Looking at Abbey Rd through rose tinted glasses.

Sex Pistols Discography

UK Releases: singles

Anarchy In The UK/I Wanna Be Me (EMI Records EMI 2566)
Released 26th November 1976
Highest Chart Position No. 27
Personnel: Johnny Rotten/Steve Jones/Glen Matlock/Paul Cook

God Save The Queen/No Feeling (A&M Records AMS 7284)
Never officially released
Highest Chart Position: N/A
Personnel: Johnny Rotten/Steve Jones/Glen Matlock/Paul Cook

God Save The Queen/Did You No Wrong (Virgin Records VS 181)
Released 27th May 1977
Highest Chart Position No. 1?
Personnel: Johnny Rotten/Sid Vicious/Steve Jones/Paul Cook

Pretty Vacant/No Fun (Virgin Records VS 184)
Released 2nd July 1977
Highest Chart Position No. 6
Personnel: Johnny Rotten/Sid Vicious/Steve Jones/Paul Cook

Holidays In The Sun/Satellite (Virgin Records VS 191)
Released 15th October 1977
Highest Chart Position No. 8
Personnel: Johnny Rotten/Sid Vicious/Steve Jones/Paul Cook

No One Is Innocent/My Way (Virgin Records VS 220)
Released 30th June 1978
Highest Chart Position No. 7
*Personnel: Ronnie Biggs (vocals on No One Is Innocent)/Sid Vicious
(vocals on My Way)/Steve Jones/Paul Cook/Simon Jeffes*

Something Else/Friggin' In The Riggin' (Virgin Records VS 240)
Released 23rd February 1979
Highest Chart Position No. 3
*Personnel: Sid Vicious (vocals on Something Else)/Steve Jones
(guitar & vocals on Friggin' In The Riggin')/Paul Cook (drums)/
Andy Allen (bass)*

Silly Thing/Who Killed Bambi? (Virgin Records VS 256)
Released 30th March 1979
Highest Chart Position No. 6

Personnel: Steve Jones (guitar & vocals on Silly Thing*)/Paul Cook (drums)/Tenpole Tudor (vocals on Who Killed Bambi?)/Andy Allen (bass)*

C'mon Everybody/God Save The Queen (Symphony)/Watcha Gonna Do About It? (Virgin Records VS 272)
Released 22ⁿᵈ June 1979
Highest Chart Position No. 3
Personnel: Sid Vicious (vocals on C'mon Everybody)/Johnny Rotten (vocals on Whatcha Gonna Do About It?)/Steve Jones (guitar)/Paul Cook (drums)/Glen Matlock (bass on Whatcha Gonna Do About It?)/Andy Allen (bass C'mon Everybody)

The Great Rock 'n' Roll Swindle/Rock Around The Clock
(Virgin Records VS 290)
Released 4ᵗʰ October 1979
Highest Chart Position No. 21
Personnel: Steve Jones (guitar)/Paul Cook (drums)/Tenpole Tudor (vocals)/Andy Allen (bass)

(I'm Not Your) Stepping Stone/Pistols Propaganda
(Virgin Records VS 229)
Released 5ᵗʰ June 1980
Highest Chart Position No. 21
Personnel: Johnny Rotten (vocals I'm Not Your Stepping Stone)/ Steve Jones (guitar)/Glen Matlock (bass)/Paul Cook (drums)/Jon Snagg (vocals Pistols Propaganda)

UK Releases: Albums

Never Mind The Bollocks Here's The Sex Pistols
(Virgin Records CDVX2086)
Holidays In The Sun/Bodies/No Feelings/Liar/Problems/God Save The Queen/Seventeen/Anarchy In The UK/Submission/Pretty Vacant/New York/EMI Unlimited Edition
Released 28ᵗʰ October 1977
Highest Chart Position No. 1
Personnel: Johnny Rotten (vocals)/Steve Jones (guitar & bass)/ Paul Cook (drums)/Glen Matlock (bass)/Sid Vicious (bass)

The Great Rock 'n' Roll Swindle
(Virgin Records CDVDX2510)
The God Save The Queen Symphony/Rock Around The Clock/Johnny

B Goode/Road Runner/Black Arabs/Anarchy In The UK/Something Else/Anarchie Pour Le UK/Ein Mal War Belsen Bortrefflich/Belsen Was A Gas/No One Is Innocent/My Way/Watcha Gonna Do About It?/Who Killed Bambi?/Silly Thing/Substitute/No Lip/Stepping Stone/Lonely Boy/C'mon Everybody/EMI (Orch)/The Great Rock 'n' Roll Swindle/You Need Hands/Friggin' In The Riggin'
Released February 1979
Highest Chart Position No.7
Personnel: Johnny Rotten (vocals)/Sid Vicious (vocals)/Steve Jones (guitar & bass & vocals)/Paul Cook (drums & vocals)/Glen Matlock (bass)/Ronnie Biggs (vocals)/Malcolm McLaren (vocals)/Tenpole Tudor (vocals)/Black Arabs (vocals)/Jerzimy (vocals)/Andy Allen (bass)/Simon Jeffes (strings)

Some Product ... Carri On Sex Pistols
(Virgin Records CDVR2)
The Very Name 'Sex Pistols'/From Beyond The Grave/Big Tits Across America/The Complex World Of Johnny Rotten/Sex Pistols Will Play/Is The Queen A Moron?/The Fucking Rotter
Released August 1979
Highest Chart Position No. 6
Personnel: Johnny Rotten/Steve Jones/Sid Vicious/Paul Cook/ Malcolm McLaren/Glen Matlock

Flogging A Dead Horse
(Virgin Records CDV2142)
Anarchy In the UK/I Wanna Be Me/God Save The Queen/Did You No Wrong/Pretty Vacant/No Fun/Holidays In The Sun/No One Is Innocent/My Way/Something Else/Silly Thing/C'mon Everybody/ (I'm Not Your) Stepping Stone/The Great Rock 'n' Roll Swindle
Released February 1980
Highest Chart Position No. 21
Personnel: Johnny Rotten (vocals)/Steve Jones (guitar & bass & vocals)/Paul Cook (drums)/Glen Matlock (bass)/Sid Vicious (vocals)/Ronnie Biggs (vocals)/Tenpole Tudor (vocals)/Andy Allen (bass)

Kiss This (Virgin Records 07777 8 648925)
Anarchy In The UK/God Save The Queen/Pretty Vacant/Holidays In The Sun/I Wanna Be Me/Did You No Wrong/No Fun/Satellite/ No Lip/(I'm Not Your) Stepping Stone/Bodies/No Feelings/Liar/ Problems/Seventeen/
Submission/New York/EMI Unlimited Edition/My Way/Silly Thing

Released 5th October 1992

Released 5ᵗʰ October 1992
High Chart Position No. 8
Initial copies came with a free live album, 'Live in Trondheim' (21ˢᵗ July 1977) which featured; *Anarchy In The UK/I Wanna Be Me/ Seventeen/New York/EMI Unlimited Edition/No Fun/No Feelings/ Problems/God Save The Queen.*

Filthy Lucre Live (Virgin Records CDVUS 116)
Bodies/Seventeen/New York/No Feelings/Did You No Wrong/God Save the Queen/Liar/Satellite/ (I'm Not Your) Stepping Stone Holidays in the Sun/Submission/Pretty Vacant/EMI Unlimited Edition/Anarchy in the UK/Problems
Released July 1996
Highest Chart Position No. 26
Personnel: Johnny Rotten (vocals)/Steve Jones (guitar)/Glen Matlock (bass)/Paul Cook (drums)

Jubilee (Virgin Records CDV2961)
God Save The Queen/Anarchy In The UK/Pretty Vacant/Holidays In The Sun/No One Is Innocent/My Way/Something Else/Friggin' In The Riggin'/Silly Thing/The Great Rock 'n' Roll Swindle/(I'm Not Your) Stepping Stone/Pretty Vacant (live)/EMI Unlimited Edition/ (Bonus videos) God Save The Queen/Anarchy In The UK/Pretty Vacant
Released June 2002
Highest Chart Position No. 29
Personnel: Johnny Rotten (vocals)/Sid Vicious (vocals)/Ronnie Biggs (vocals)/Tenpole Tudor (vocals)/Steve Jones (guitar & bass & vocals)/Paul Cook (drums)/Andy Allen (bass)

DVD Releases

Rock Case Studies (Edgehill RMS2477)
Book & DVD set – Disc runs 60 mins with no extras

The Filth & The Fury (New Line Home Video N5086)
USA edition – includes original documentary 'Un-Defining Punk'

John Lydon's Megabugs (Green Umbrella GUVD5479)
3D cover, 2 x DVD – 234 mins running time, every episode

Sid & Nancy (Momentum Pictures MP738D)
Includes 'Love Kills' making-of documentary
Featuring Glen Matlock & Steve Connolly

Live At The Longhorn (Castle Music Pictures CMP 1004)
Includes promo videos for *Anarchy in the UK* and *God Save the Queen*

Sid & Nancy (MGM 0792847970)
USA edition – double sided disc, features widescreen and 4.3

Sid & Nancy (Best Selection TBD 1041)
Japanese DVD

The Great Rock 'n' Roll Swindle (Sony/BMG 2028859)
Includes interview and commentary from Julien Temple

No Future (Klock Work KWDV-10)
Japanese DVD of 'The Filth & The Fury' includes excellent new interview with John

Chaos! (Universal Music 06025172343-8)
The secret history and Dave Goodman story – lots of extra interviews

Never Mind The Bollocks: Classic Albums (Eagle Vision EREDV282)
Includes extra interviews and songs

D.O.A (King Records KIBF 146)
Japanese DVD (best print of DOA you'll find anywhere!) Includes a gallery, tribute to Sid from Johnny Thunders

The Ultimate Review (Music Reviews Ltd CRP1990)
Basically 'Rock Case Studies' under another name, with more talking heads!!

Never Mind The Sex Pistols (Demon Vision DVDM014)
Includes; Glen Matlock, Malcolm McLaren, Steve Diggle, Steve Connolly, Alan Jones, John Tiberi etc

The Filth & The Fury (Film Four VCD0067)
UK version – including commentary and trailer

The Great Rock 'n' Roll Swindle (Rock of Wonder VABS-0004)
Japanese DVD – with more censored scenes!

In Japan (Masterplan MP 42095)
Live in Tokyo 16th November 1996 – plus DVD extras from Phoenix Festival UK 21st July 1996

The Best of British £1's (EMI 094633798793)
Although a PiL 'best of' DVD this disc includes some fantastic Sex Pistols extras, most notably the original EMI 'Anarchy' promo film

There'll always be an England (Fremantle Media FHED2464)
Full Brixton Academy gig from November 2007 shot by Julien Temple. Plus a Pistols tour of London hosted by the lads themselves.

Who Killed Nancy (Soda Pictures SODA089)
Alan G. Parker's long awaited documentary film which aims to get Vicious off the hook for murder. Extras include; Don Letts footage of Sid at The Roxy. Out-takes. Gag Reel. Interview with Parker. Sid Vicious gallery opening night in London.

Who Killed Nancy (King Records KIBF620)
Japanese DVD - Same as above but also includes Japanese TV interview with Parker from his rented apartment in LA. A Japanese box set including a T-shirt and booklet was also made available for a short time, but these are now deleted.

Previous Books by Alan G. Parker:

Sid's Way – The Life & Times of Sid Vicious (Omnibus Press)
With Anne Beverley & Keith Bateson

Satellite: Sex Pistols (Abstract Sounds Publishing)
With Paul Burgess

The Great Train Robbery Files (Abstract Sounds Publishing)
With Bruce & Nick Reynolds

Hardcore Superstar – The Traci Lords Story (Private Books) USA only

Rat Patrol from Fort Bragg: The Clash (Abstract Sounds Publishing)

Stiff Little Fingers – Song by Song (Sanctuary Books)
With Jake Burns

John Lennon & the FBI Files (Sanctuary Books)
With Phil Strongman

Too Fast To Live: Sid Vicious (Creation Books)

And Now For Something Completely Digital: Monty Python (Disinformation Books) With Mick O'Shea

Cum On Feel the Noize – The Story of Slade (Carlton Books)
Foreword by Suzi Quatro With Steve Grantley

The Who by Numbers (Helter Skelter)
With Steve Grantley

No One Is Innocent: Sid Vicious (Orion Books)
Foreword by Malcolm McLaren

Previous Books by Mick O'Shea:

The Zootopia Tree (Abstract Sounds Publishing)

Only Anarchists Are Pretty: Sex Pistols (Helter Skelter)
Foreword by Alan G. Parker

Guns & Roses A to Z Encyclopaedia (Chrome Dreams)

The Wonderland Gang (Publisher TBC)

Selected Bibliography:

These are the titles mentioned in the book. Most have run to several reprints, so we are deliberately not quoting the year of publication. Some titles are now out of print, but you may be able to get secondhand copies.

El Sid: Saint Vicious
David Dalton (Saint Martin's Press)

England's Dreaming
Jon Savage (Faber and Faber)

I Swear I Was There
David Nolan (Independent Music Press)

I Was A Teenage Sex Pistol
Glen Matlock & Pete Silverton (Reynolds and Hearn)

Memoirs of a Geezer: Music, Mayhem, Life
Jah Wobble (Serpent's Tail)

Rotten: No Irish, No Blacks, No Dogs
John Lydon (Hodder & Stoughton)

Please Kill Me: The Uncensored Oral History of Punk
Eddie 'Legs' McNeil & Gillian McCain (Abacus)

Rebel Rock: A Photographic History of The Sex Pistols
Dennis Morris (Epoch Productions)

Sex Pistols: Day By Day
Lee Wood (Omnibus Press)

Sex Pistols File
Ray Stevenson (Omnibus Press)

The Sex Pistols: The Inside Story
Fred & Judy Vermorel (Omnibus Press)

The Sex Pistols: 90 Days at EMI
Brian Southall (Omnibus Press)

The Wicked Ways Of Malcolm McLaren
Craig Bromberg (Harper Collins)

The Whispering Years
Bob Harris (BBC Books)

12 Days On The Road: The Sex Pistols and America
Noel E. Monk (Quill)

Vivienne Westwood: An Unfashionable Life
Jane Mulvagh (Harper Collins)

Films by Alan G. Parker:

Love Kills: The Making of 'Sid & Nancy'
(Momentum Pictures)

At The Edge: Stiff Little Fingers
Live at the Ocean – London
(Secret Films)

Never Mind The Sex Pistols
(Demon/2 Entertain)

Rebel Truce: The Clash
(Eagle Vision/Eagle Rock)
Time Out Magazine (London) best documentary winner – 2007

Still Burning: Stiff Little Fingers movie
(Fremantle Media)
With Don Letts

All Mod Cons: The Jam
(Universal Records)
With Don Letts

All Proud, All Live, All Mighty: The Almighty
Live at Astoria – London
(Landmark Productions)

Who Killed Nancy
(Moxie Makers/Soda Pictures)
BBC Radio 6 – Best New Director 2009
'For my money one of the best rock 'n' roll documentaries that's ever been made!'
(Andrew Loog Oldman – Original Manager of the Rolling Stones)

'Funny, surprising, intelligent and very well made'(Brit Flicks)

'Only one man was or is capable of making enough sense out of this to call it a movie, I'm proud to say that he was the one enlisted with the job, Alan G. Parker, the closest thing Sid ever got to a real biographer, and the Northern kid who understood us Southern kids, possibly better than we ever did!'
(Malcolm McLaren - Original Manager of the Sex Pistols)

Almost The Truth – The Lawyers Cut!
Monty Python 40th Anniversary Documentary
(Eagle Vision/IFC)
100 minute cinema version (worldwide)
6 one hour episodes (USA TV)
One hour edited edition (BBC 2 Monty Python night)
Nominated for an Emmy Award - 2010

'The Pythons have been compared to the Beatles. Comedy does not have the same cultural influence as music, but it's safe to say they were worthy contemporaries. A fact obviously not lost on either IFC or director Alan G. Parker' (The New Yorker – USA)

Respectable: The Mary Millington Story
(G2 Pictures/AG & AB Productions)
* *Currently in production* *

Alan G. Parker also appears in a number of documentaries including;

Punk's Not Dead (A film by Susan Dyner)
Sid Vicious: The Final 24 (Cineflix/Sky 1)
The Punk Years (BBC 3)
Understanding The Beatles (MTV)
The 100 Greatest Albums Ever Made! (VH1)
A History of Page 3 (ITV)
The Day They Shot John Lennon (Japanese TV)

Alan G. Parker and Mick O'Shea

Acknowledgements From Alan To The World

My wonderful, one and only business partner Alexa Morris, Phil and Sue @ Soundcheck Books (for taking up where the great man left off), Frank Lea for everything, Steve Grantley my brother from another mother, Steve Diggle, Ashley Reading @ Fortress Commercial Wealth, Darrell Milnes, Jon 'The 5th Beatle' McCaughey, Miah Vu, Duly (what can I tell you, thank you), Nick Reynolds, Dave Meehan and all @ Nyquest, Glen Matlock, Steve 'Roadent' Connolly, Andrew, Keith, Lucy and all @ Baker Street MM Productions, Ricky Warwick, Adam Parsons, Foxy Roxy G, Melissa 'Wee Me' Palmer, Carol 'Neve' McIntosh, Alan 'Leather & Bones' Jones, John 'Boogie' Tiberi, Steve Dior, Jake Burns, Ian McCallum, Ali McMordie, Mr Rav Singh (the go2 guy!), Pete Kodick, Steve 'Diamond Geezer' English, Chris Remington, Darryl Gates & Gino Angelov and all @ Diamond Jacks Tattoos (London), Keith Badman (this book took nearly as long as one of yours! Now there's a statement rarely made!!), Jerry White, Ian D Fleming, Terry Rawlings, Gary Crowley, Paolo Hewitt, Mick Jones, David 'Our Kid' Parker, Dano and all @ Vince Neil Ink (Las Vegas), Lord George X – The Cockney Don, Robert Kirby & Charlotte Knee @ United Agents (the best line in advice), David Ross @ The Vicious Files, Malcolm McLaren RIP, Anne J Beverley RIP, Nils Stevenson RIP, Steve New RIP, Rusty Egan, Steve Woof and all @ EMI Records, Don Letts, the one and only Johnny 'Brassneck' Osbourne, Kirk Brandon, Ginger/CJ and all The Wildhearts, Chris McCormack, Paul Roberts, Steve Gowans @ Channel 5, Mark Helfond, Lisa & all the Crew @ 430 Kings Rd, all the staff at HSBC Business Banking (especially Monika) and of course Sean Body for suggesting this idea, I hope it would have done you proud mate.

Many thanks to the 'Sixth Pistol' Brian Jackson for supplying most of the props for this book.

A special thank you to Phil Singleton who runs the *God Save the Sex Pistols* website for all his help and generosity. www.sexpistols.net

And of course all at The Sanctum, Home House, The Century Club, The Phoenix and The Arts Club – without whom etc ...

No Jah Wobbles were harmed or interviewed in the course of writing and researching this book!

www.myspace.com/aparker01
Alan G Parker at Facebook and Twitter

Mick's Acknowledgements

Professional thanks go to Alan G. Parker for bringing me in on a project initially started by the late Sean Body at Helter Skelter, and to Phil and Sue Godsell for picking up Sean's torch and finally bringing the book to fruition.

I'd also like to thank the following people: Tasha 'Bodacious Babe' Cowen, Shannon 'Mini-Hepburn' Stanley, Jackie and Richard at P-PR, Jade Overington, Paul Young (not the singer), Zoë Johnson-Meadows, Phil and Nic Williams, Martin and Angela Jones, Lisa 'T-bag' Bird.

Mick O'Shea at Facebook

This index covers Chapters 1 to 16 and the Afterword.
It does not include illustrations.